West Bengal Development Report

सत्यमेव जयते

Planning Commission
Government of India

West Bengal Development Report

सत्यमेव जयते

PLANNING COMMISSION
GOVERNMENT OF INDIA
NEW DELHI

Published by

ACADEMIC FOUNDATION
NEW DELHI

First Published in 2010 by
Academic Foundation
4772-73 / 23 Bharat Ram Road, (23 Ansari Road), Darya Ganj, New Delhi - 110 002 (India).
Phones : 23245001 / 02 / 03 / 04. Fax : +91-11-23245005. E-mail : books@academicfoundation.com
www.academicfoundation.com

Published under arrangement with :
Planning Commission,
Government of India,
New Delhi.

Cataloging in Publication Data--DK
Courtesy: D.K. Agencies (P) Ltd. <docinfo@dkagencies.com>

West Bengal development report / Planning Commission, Government of India.
p. cm.
Includes bibliographical references.
ISBN 13: 9788171887897
ISBN 10: 8171887899

1. Economic development--India--West Bengal. 2. Manpower policy--India--West Bengal. 3. Human services--India--West Bengal. 4. West Bengal (India)--Economic policy. 5. West Bengal (India)--Social policy. I. India. Planning Commission.

DDC 338.95414 22

Designed and typeset by Italics India, New Delhi
Printed and bound in India.

The Core Committee

The composition of the Core Committee for preparation of West Bengal State Development Report is as follows:

1	Shri Anwarul Hoda, *Member* Planning Commission, Government of India	Chairman
2	Smt. Jaya Das Gupta, *Principal Secretary,* Development & Planning Department, Government of West Bengal	Member
3	Dr. B.P. Syam Roy, *Special Officer and Ex-Officio Special Secretary,* Development and Planning Department, Government of West Bengal	Member
4	Shri Harish Chandra, *Adviser* Planning Commission, Government of India	Member-Secretary

एम. एस. आहलुवालिया
MONTEK SINGH AHLUWALIA

उपाध्यक्ष
योजना आयोग
भारत
DEPUTY CHAIRMAN
PLANNING COMMISSION
INDIA

FOREWORD

India has grown at a rate of over 9 per cent for the last three years. Yet, behind this single macro indicator of growth, lie huge inter-state variations in growth rates. This underscores the importance of the fact that economic circumstances and performance of the individual states, is varied, and thus it is necessary to examine development challenges of states in a framework of state specific constraints and resources.

One of the important Tenth Plan initiatives of the Planning Commission was to sponsor the preparation of the State Development Reports. To ensure quality, the work was given to National Level Institues of repute. These State Development Reports were to serve as well researched, analysed and credible documents to help chart out the developmental agenda for faster economic growth of states.

The West Bengal State Development Report reviews West Bengal's experience and highlights issues critical for the State's development in the years ahead. I hope its publication will stimulate debate on growth strategies appropriate for West Bengal. I am sure the road map indicated in the Report will provide useful information on the critical policy issues facing the State and policy options available to shift to a higher growth path and achieve all round human and economic development.

(Montek Singh Ahluwalia)

योजना भवन, संसद मार्ग, नई दिल्ली – 110001 दूरभाष : 23096677, 23096688 फैक्स : 23096699
Yojana Bhawan, Parliament Street, New Delhi : 110001 Phones: 23096677, 23096688 Fax : 23096699 E-mail : dch@yojana.nic.in

মুখ্যমন্ত্রী
পশ্চিমবঙ্গ
CHIEF MINISTER
WEST BENGAL

सत्यमेव जयते

Writers' Buildings, Kolkata-700 001
West Bengal, India
E-Mail : cm@writerscal.gov.in
: cm@wb.nic.in
Fax : 0091-033-22145480
Tel : 0091-033-22145533

MESSAGE

State Development Report is an expression and a description of the status of economic scenario of the State. It is also a benchmark of the sectoral development status on the given date. It gives us enough factual data and analysis of the transformation of the state economy—both inter-sectoral as well as intra-sectoral. It also enjoins us to reintrospect and revisit the priorities of the State economy and the way forward to improve delivery of services.

I am glad that Institute of Development Studies, Kolkata has prepared the West Bengal State Development Report 2008 objectively and professionally, based on validated data available in the public domain—both Central and the State and highlighted the strength and weakness of the State economy.

The State Government intends to internalise the findings of the State Development Report in its work programmes and address the relative deficit areas through appropriate interventions for ensuring faster and inclusive growth of our economy.

I thank the Planning Commission of India for commissioning this State Development Report through the Institute of Development Studies Kolkata, an Institution of excellence in the State of West Bengal.

(Buddhadeb Bhattacharjee)

ANWARUL HODA
Member
Planning Commission
Government of India

सत्यमेव जयते

YOJANA BHAVAN
PARLIAMENT STREET
New Delhi - 110 001
Tel. : 23096756(O)
23096774(Fax)
E-mail : anwarul.hoda@yojana.nic.in

MESSAGE

In keeping with the Central Plan Scheme of the "50 Year Initiative for Planning", the Planning Commission has been getting the State Development Report (SDR) prepared for each state. These SDRs aim to compile quality reference documents on the profile and strategy for accelerating the pace of development in the respective states. The Reports will be of immense help to both Central and State authorities and agencies engaged in steering the plan process of the State on a higher and equitable growth path.

The State Development Report (SDR), West Bengal presents a comprehensive and scholarly analysis of the major issues faced by the State's economy. It provides a road map for accelerated growth in the medium and long term. It offers a basis for West Bengal to strive to attain high levels of prosperity and human development.

I would like to place on record Planning Commission's appreciation to all those who have worked hard in preparing the report, especially the Institute of Development Studies, Kolkata. The effort made by the Institute in coordinating and preparing the final report deserves to be specially noted. In particular I would like to commend the contributions of Prof. Amiya Kumar Bagchi and Prof. Debdas Banerjee from the Institute in bringing out this valuable document.

I am thankful to the Government of West Bengal for rendering full cooperation and support to the partner agency involved in preparation of the report. The work done by the State Plan Adviser Shri Harish Chandra in liaising with State Government and partner agency is noteworthy. I would also like to place on record the active participation of the officers of the State Plan Division, particularly Dr. Sharad Pant, Deputy Adviser, Shri S. Talukdar, Economic Officer and Ms. Kuhumita Bhattacharya, Consultant.

(Anwarul Hoda)

Preface

The State Development Report has been prepared by the faculty of the Institute of Development Studies Kolkata (IDSK) with the assistance of some external collaborators and by utilising the background papers that were made available to the IDSK in 2007 for preparing the Report. The list of the background papers and their authors has been attached separately. The basic part of the work for this Report was carried out by Professor Debdas Banerjee, Dr. Subrata Mukherjee and Dr. Panchanan Das of the IDSK with separate chapters on employment, unorganised sector, environment, public finance and urbanisation contributed by our external collaborators, Professors Shankar Kumar Bhaumik, Ishita Mukhopadhyay, Ashis Ghosh, Jayanta Acharya and Smt. Nandita Sen Chakraborty. We are indebted particularly to the external collaborators for their help. Some portions of the Background Papers listed separately have been used for the report. We are also thankful to all the staff of the IDSK, especially to Smt. Sanchari Guha, for their unstinting help in preparing this report.

We acknowledge the initiatives taken by the Planning Commission, Government of India and by the Development and Planning Department, Government of West Bengal in entrusting us with the task of preparing the State Development Report. Comments made by participants in a workshop held in November 2007 on the first draft of the Report, especially those offered by Dr. Asim Dasgupta, Finance Minister, Government of West Bengal, Dr. Anwarul Hoda, member, Planning Commission, Government of India and Professor Nikhilesh Bhattacharya, member, State Planning Board, Government of West Bengal were particularly helpful in preparing the final report. I would also like to thank Professor Subimal Sen, Vice-Chairman, West Bengal State Council of Higher Education for critical help in obtaining data for the chapter on education.

We also acknowledge the constant help of Dr. B.P. Syam Roy, Special Officer and Ex-Officio Special Secretary, Department of Development and Planning, Government of West Bengal and Ms. Jaya Dasgupta, Principal Secretary, Department of Development and Planning, Government of West Bengal. None of the persons mentioned above are responsible for any errors remaining in the Report.

Amiya Kumar Bagchi
Director
Institute of Development Studies Kolkata

Contents

List of Tables, Figures and Appendices

Tables

Figures

Appendices

Introduction

Demographic Features

West Bengal has now emerged as the most densely populated state in India (Table 3). As Tables 1 and 2 indicate, the population of West Bengal practically doubled between 1971 and 2001, in spite of the fact that the fertility rate in West Bengal has declined fast. Urban population has been growing at a faster rate than the rural population.

Figure 1 indicates that there are great differences in the density of population as between the different districts, the districts of south-central West Bengal being generally more densely populated than those in the other regions. But the less densely populated districts are also worse served by infrastructural facilities than the others. One major contributory factor in this development has been immigration from the neighbouring Indian states and also from Bangladesh and Nepal. This imposes severe burdens on the infrastructure and land availability of the state.

TABLE 1

West Bengal: Population at a Glance

	1971	*1981*	*1991*	*2001*
Total population (in lakh)	443.12	545.81	680.78	801.76
Percentage of male population to total population	52.89	52.33	52.16	51.72
Percentage of female population to total population	47.11	47.67	47.84	48.28
Percentage of urban population to total population	24.75	26.47	27.48	27.97
Percentage of rural population to total population	75.25	73.53	72.52	72.03
Percentage of population of Kolkata urban agglomeration to total urban population	64.11	63.64	58.92	58.88
Percentage of main workers to total population	27.91	28.26	30.23	28.72

Source: Government of West Bengal. *Economic Review, 2007-08.*

TABLE 2

Population Density: India and West Bengal

	India	*West Bengal*
1981	216	615
1991	273	767
2001	324	904

Source: Government of West Bengal. *Economic Review, 2007-08.*

TABLE 3

Population Share and Population Density by Major States: 2001

States/UT	*Percentage to Total National Population*	*Density of Population (Per Sq. Km.)*
Andhra Pradesh	7.37	275
Assam	2.59	340
Bihar	8.07	880
Chhattisgarh	2.02	154
Gujarat	4.93	258
Haryana	2.05	477
Himachal Pradesh	0.59	109
Jammu & Kashmir	0.98	99
Jharkhand	2.62	338
Karnataka	5.13	275
Kerala	3.1	819
Madhya Pradesh	5.88	196
Maharashtra	9.42	314
Orissa	3.57	236
Punjab	2.37	482
Rajasthan	5.5	165
Tamil Nadu	6.05	478
Uttar Pradesh	16.17	689
Uttarakhand	0.83	159
West Bengal	7.81	904
INDIA	100	324

Source: Census of India, 2001.

Author, Dr. Panchanan Das, is a Senior Lecturer in Economics in West Bengal Education Service, and is gratefully indebted to Prof. Amiya Kumar Bagchi, Director, Institute of Development Studies, Kolkata, for helpful comments. Dr. Saswata Ghosh, faculty member, Institute of Development Studies, has calculated the HPI.

FIGURE 1

Population Density (Per Sq. Km.) by District in West Bengal: 2001

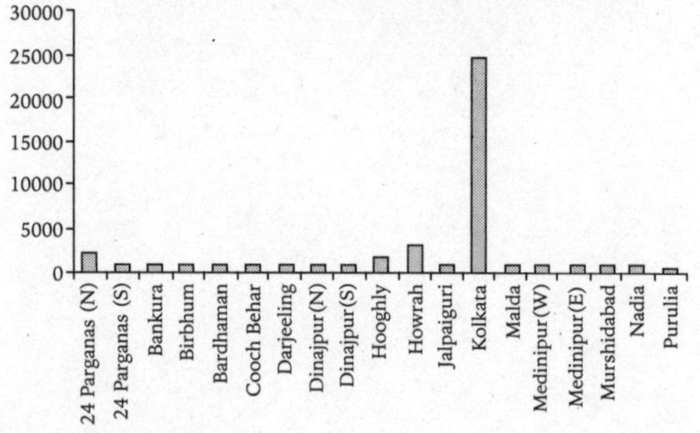

Source: Census of India 2001.

Table 4 displays the changing pattern of age distribution of total population in West Bengal over the past four census decades. The share of child population (age group below 15 years) to total population in West Bengal decreased gradually. The proportion of young population (within age group 15-29) in the state increased in the 1970s but declined in the next decade and kept at the same level thereafter. The percentage of population within working age group (30-59) also increased during this period.

TABLE 4

Age Distribution of Population in West Bengal

Age Structure	*Percentage to Total Population*			
	1971	*1981*	*1991*	*2001*
Below 15	43	39	37	33
15-29	25	29	27	27
30-59	27	26	29	33
60 and above	5	6	7	7

Source: Census of India.

Demographic Pressure on Land

In West Bengal, more than 60 per cent of total land area has been used in agriculture and the share of land use in non-agricultural sector accounts to 20 per cent; the other 20 per cent is either fallow or barren or forested (Table 5). In many districts, more than 70 per cent of land area is used in agriculture. The share is the highest in North Dinajpur and lowest in South 24 Parganas.

TABLE 5

District-wise Land Use Statistics of West Bengal: 2006-07

(in hectares)

	Total Area	*Percentage of Area under Non-Agl. Use*	*Percentage of Area under Agl. Land*
Bardhaman	698762	28.7	65.6
Birbhum	451118	21.0	70.4
Bankura	687998	21.3	50.1
Medinipur (East)	396594	24.6	73.4
Medinipur (West)	928581	16.9	59.8
Howrah	138676	35.8	59.3
Hooghly	313379	28.3	70.4
24 Parganas (North)	386524	31.0	67.3
24 Parganas (South)	948710	14.4	39.3
Nadia	390655	22.1	74.2
Murshidabad	532499	23.5	75.5
Dinajpur (N)	312466	9.9	88.8
Dinajpur (S)	221909	13.9	78.9
Malda	370862	22.8	57.0
Jalpaiguri	622700	13.4	53.9
Darjeeling	325469	10.6	43.7
Cooch Behar	331565	20.0	74.9
Purulia	625646	16.0	49.6
West Bengal	8684113	20.0	61.0

Source: Government of West Bengal. *Economic Review, 2007-08.*

Excessive demographic pressure on land and the historically given institutional structure have generated numerous types of land rights in India. Regions with the background of permanent settlement account for the largest concentration of landless or land-poor households. This legacy of colonialism is found mostly in the eastern region states and it eventually led to debt and dispossession among the peasantry and the high incidence of agricultural labour in those regions. In West Bengal, the share of agricultural labourers, particularly of male labourers, to the total rural workforce increased during the 1990s (Table 6). The census data also reveal that the percentage of cultivators decreased significantly (Bagchi and Das, 2005[1]). The incidence of land-poor households was higher in most of the districts in which agriculture provided the major means of livelihood. Petty producers have little access to institutional credit. With the rise in costs of cultivation they are forced to surrender their land rights and swell the rank of agricultural labourers who have little bargaining

1. Bagchi A.K. and P. Das (2005). "Changing Pattern of Employment under Neo-liberal Reforms: A Comparative Study of West Bengal and Gujarat", *The Indian Journal of Labour Economics* 48(4): 945–58.

TABLE 6

Percentage of Agricultural Labourers to Total Number of Workers in Rural Areas

	Male Worker				*Female Worker*			
	1971	*1981*	*1991*	*2001*	*1971*	*1981*	*1991*	*2001*
Bankura	35.61	31.47	28.49	29.76	80.06	62.70	58.19	50.27
Birbhum	42.14	38.65	36.33	36.16	67.41	68.93	59.15	49.75
Bardhaman	34.46	36.22	36.92	38.13	72.37	72.09	69.72	53.58
Cooch Behar	16.21	28.18	25.42	26.36	31.46	41.63	45.41	45.51
Darjeeling	11.50	13.13	16.38	13.36	9.62	9.59	15.25	16.35
Dinajpur (N)	28.27	34.87	37.00	38.87	63.42	64.60	66.57	54.31
Dinajpur (S)	28.27	34.87	29.32	33.69	63.42	64.60	64.73	54.29
Hooghly	36.61	33.08	31.38	30.63	80.95	72.19	67.42	45.28
Howrah	37.65	28.85	27.79	20.79	21.87	13.55	26.76	12.93
Jalpaiguri	11.91	19.08	18.80	16.92	5.17	16.00	21.72	27.96
Malda	33.67	34.82	34.69	32.78	58.72	51.62	43.18	31.90
Medinipur	32.21	29.28	22.88	30.90	73.60	54.35	35.88	41.10
Murshidabad	38.83	37.89	34.62	38.06	27.83	20.38	13.45	10.53
Nadia	31.94	34.77	33.41	32.39	41.33	33.99	29.39	13.96
Purulia	29.12	22.74	22.48	27.71	71.09	46.40	42.76	53.61
24 Parganas (N)	41.81	35.70	32.11	29.44	40.71	34.55	35.43	23.86
24 parganas (S)	41.81	35.70	33.71	30.72	40.71	34.55	27.35	28.87
West Bengal	33.26	32.19	30.03	31.04	54.51	48.25	41.76	38.56

Source: Government of West Bengal. *District Statistical Hand Book, 2006*. Bureau of Applied Economics & Statistics.

power. The share of non-agricultural labourers to the workforce also increased over the past four census decades; the rate of increase was particularly high during the 1990s. The non-farm activities grew at a faster rate in some districts namely, Howrah, Darjeeling, Jalpaiguri and 24 Parganas (both North and South) (Table 7).

TABLE 7

Percentage of Non-Agricultural Labourers to the Total Number of Workers in Rural Areas

	Male Worker				*Female Worker*			
	1971	*1981*	*1991*	*2001*	*1971*	*1981*	*1991*	*2001*
Bankura	15.10	20.36	22.91	31.74	6.86	12.91	13.07	27.68
Birbhum	16.30	18.21	23.04	33.89	18.27	17.82	21.78	40.00
Bardhaman	32.42	29.16	28.78	36.70	20.03	19.43	21.35	40.44
Cooch Behar	10.21	14.51	19.78	30.09	32.36	38.68	21.92	21.92
Darjeeling	49.55	52.69	49.47	65.89	56.81	56.69	52.56	63.35
Dinajpur (N)	8.66	10.79	12.70	23.17	15.07	18.43	16.93	24.69
Dinajpur (S)	8.66	10.79	16.12	24.06	15.07	18.43	15.35	29.25
Hooghly	26.17	30.01	35.65	45.28	12.50	20.92	26.07	43.86
Howrah	39.56	50.39	50.54	68.31	61.12	74.87	52.64	83.10
Jalpaiguri	38.40	38.43	42.53	56.72	88.45	73.80	61.99	54.36
Malda	16.62	20.45	23.36	37.61	30.86	37.30	42.17	60.73
Medinipur	15.16	20.71	28.18	34.90	13.92	20.08	21.51	37.67
Murshidabad	17.44	21.13	26.64	35.83	55.85	71.78	80.74	86.04
Nadia	21.74	24.97	28.21	39.90	43.27	58.63	62.88	74.79
Purulia	17.93	21.73	23.66	34.75	9.07	7.98	7.45	19.18
24 Parganas (N)	20.03	27.80	32.08	46.72	39.37	48.28	46.83	69.39
24 Parganas (S)	20.03	27.80	33.54	50.23	39.37	48.28	36.75	53.48
West Bengal	21.17	25.06	29.08	40.24	30.56	30.90	30.42	45.37

Source: As in Table 6.

Standard of Living

The high degree of occupational dependence on agriculture, especially in terms of agricultural labour, and its rapidly declining income share is an indication of a higher incidence of poverty in the countryside. However, the incidence of poverty measured by the head count ratio (HCR) declined both in rural and urban West Bengal following the national trend during the past two decades (Table 8). The poverty ratio on a head count basis estimated by the Planning Commission, Government of India, was higher in rural West Bengal than the all India average up to the early 1990s. But the monthly per capita cereal consumption in real terms was significantly higher in the former decade compared to the latter during the same period. In urban areas of the state, the poverty ratio was lower than the national average and was reflected in the higher monthly per capita cereal consumption expenditure compared to the national level (Table 8). Consumption inequality in terms of Gini coefficient, although increasing during 1993-2004, was lower in West Bengal compared to the all India level. The lower incidence of inequality of household consumption expenditure in rural areas in West Bengal was partly due to pro-peasant land reforms and state initiatives favouring the poor implemented through Panchayati Raj Institutions.

TABLE 8

Poverty and Inequality

	Rural			*Urban*		
	1983	*1993-94*	*2004-05*	*1983*	*1993-94*	*2004-05*
HCR						
West Bengal	63.05	40.8	28.5	32.32	22.41	15.4
India	45.65	37.27	28.7	40.79	32.36	25.9
Monthly per capita cereal consumption (MPCE) in kg						
West Bengal	15	13.59	13.18	11.6	11.17	10.39
India	13.4	12.72	12.12	10.6	10.42	9.94
Gini coefficient of MPCE						
West Bengal	30	25.4	27.4	33.5	33.9	38.3
India	30.4	28.6	30.5	33.9	34.4	37.6

Source: Government of India, Planning Commission, National Sample Survey Organisation.

There are some inherent problems in determining the threshold income or poverty line in the conventional income-based poverty measure. We have, therefore, used some non-income parameters also for scrutinising the living standard of the people in West Bengal. Provision of residential houses and access to basic amenities are among the prime non-income dimensions in judging the standard of living. By comparing the Census figures, as presented in Table 9, it is found that the decadal growth of residential houses was high everywhere in West Bengal during the 1990s. The share of households using drinking water from either handpump, or tubewell or tap increased from 82 per cent in 1991 to nearly 90 per cent in 2001 (Table 10). The proportion of households with better conditions of residential houses in terms of materials used in roofs, floors and walls also increased during this decade (Table 11). The percentages of households using electricity and latrine both in rural and urban areas are shown in Table 12. Although the use of electricity increased during the 1990s, 80 per cent of the rural households were unable to use electricity in 2001. As per Census data, although the proportion of rural households with no latrine declined between 1991 and 2001, roughly three-fourths of the rural households still had no latrine in 2001.

TABLE 9

Decadal Growth Rates of Residential Houses: 1991-2001

	Total	*Rural*	*Urban*
Bankura	20.9	21.8	11.2
Birbhum	24.4	24.6	21.9
Bardhaman	19.2	19.0	19.6
Cooch Behar	21.9	20.3	41.8
Darjeeling	28.7	23.6	41.4
Dinajpur (North)	32.5	33.2	27.1
Dinajpur (South)	30.3	29.4	37.3
Howrah	24.1	24.8	23.5
Hooghly	27.0	24.3	32.3
Jalpaiguri	24.9	22.2	38.8
Kolkata	4.0	—	4.0
Malda	28.9	28.3	36.1
Medinipur	23.7	23.4	25.4
Murshidabad	31.8	29.7	49.7
Nadia	33.7	36.5	24.9
Purulia	17.1	16.5	22.1
24 Parganas (North)	33.5	24.1	42.3
24 Parganas (South)	30.0	26.3	50.2

Source: Directorate of Census Operations (2004). *Census of India*. West Bengal.

TABLE 10

Percentage of Households by Availability of Drinking Water

	1991	*2001*
Handpump, tubewell	60.8	67.1
Tap	21.1	21.4
Well	15.8	10.0
Any other source	1.6	1.2
River, canal	0.6	0.3

Source: As in Table 9.

TABLE 11

Percentage Distribution of Households by Types of Residential Houses in West Bengal

	1991	*2001*
Predominant materials of roof		
Grass, thatch, bamboo,	37.3	21.6
Tiles/Slate	26.8	34.9
Concrete	15.1	20.9
G.I., metal, asbestos sheets	12.8	20.0
Any other material	4.9	1.4
Brick/Stone	3.1	1.3
Predominant materials of floor		
Mud	69.0	65.2
Cement	26.9	29.5
Wood, bamboo	1.9	0.7
Brick/Stone	1.3	2.6
Mosaic, floor tiles	0.7	1.8
Any other material	0.3	0.1
Predominant materials of wall		
Mud, unburnt brick	48.0	40.0
Burnt brick	30.3	37.4
Grass, thatch, bamboo, etc.	16.4	17.6
Concrete	2.7	2.1
Wood	1.5	1.0
G.I., metal, asbestos sheets	0.5	0.7
Any other material	0.5	0.9
Stone	0.2	0.2

Source: As in Table 9.

TABLE 12

Percentage of Households by Availability of Electricity and Latrine

		1991	*2001*
Total	Electricity	32.9	37.5
	Latrine	31.5	43.7
Rural	Electricity	17.8	20.3
	Latrine	12.3	26.9
Urban	Electricity	70.2	79.6
	Latrine	78.8	84.8

Source: As in Table 9.

West Bengal ranked 9th among 15 major states in India in terms of Human Poverty Index (HPI),[2] measured by using National Family Health Survey-3 data for the year 2005-06. Deprivation of public provisioning has been very high compared to health deprivation and deprivation in knowledge in every state in India. As for the district level data health deprivation is not available, HPI for each district in West Bengal is constructed by taking the weighted average of the indices of knowledge deprivation and that of public provisioning. Kolkata experienced the lowest deprivation followed by Hooghly and North 24 Parganas. The incidence of deprivation was considerably higher in Dinajpur (North), Murshidabad and Malda (Table 13).

TABLE 13

Human Poverty Index (HPI) by Districts in West Bengal

Districts	*Knowledge Deprivation*	*Provisioning Deprivation*	*HPI*
Kolkata	10.8	22.2	17.4
Medinipur	13.2	54.3	39.5
Hooghly	13.1	31.2	23.9
Howrah	12.7	40.5	30.0
24 Parganas (N)	11.9	39.7	29.3
Bardhaman	15.6	41.0	31.0
Darjeeling	14.2	48.5	35.8
Bankura	18.4	44.9	34.3
Nadia	16.9	40.0	30.7
24 Parganas (S)	16.1	55.7	41.0
Jalpaiguri	18.6	47.9	36.3
Birbhum	19.8	53.7	40.5
Cooch Behar	16.9	57.4	42.3
Purulia	22.7	51.2	39.6
Dinajpur (S)	18.3	52.1	39.0
Murshidabad	23.4	62.9	47.4
Dinajpur (N)	26.6	67.4	51.2
Malda	25.5	60.0	46.1

Source: Calculated from Census of India, 2001 and District Level Household Survey (DLHS), 2002-2004.

Growth Performance

From the data on the net state domestic product and its components, it would appear that NSDP growth rates picked up in the 1980s, the main contributor to that acceleration being agriculture.[3] As many analysts have found, the land reforms carried out by the Government of West Bengal, combined with the operationalisation of the elected Panchayati Raj Institutions provided both resources and incentives to the small and marginal peasants and thereby helped raise the rates of agricultural growth to a historic high. But from 1991, the pacesetter of growth has been the services sector, followed by manufacturing, partly because the rate of agricultural

2. HPI comprises three aspects of human deprivation: (a) deprivation in knowledge, (b) deprivation in health, and (c) deprivation in provisioning, both from the public and private sources.

3. Chapter 1 of this report provides a detailed analysis of growth and structural changes in West Bengal.

growth decelerated after the mid-1990s. But West Bengal's growth rate has exceeded the rates of growth of most other states in the beginning of the 21st century.

West Bengal's domestic product from unregistered manufacturing grew at a faster rate compared to that from the registered sector and the share of NSDP from the unregistered sector has been higher than the share of the registered sector since the mid-1980s. In West Bengal, within the services sector, trade, hotels etc., has been the dominating sub-sector, followed by banking and insurance.

The economy of West Bengal has been undergoing a substantial structural change in favour of non-farm activities since the early 1990s. But this change has been accompanied by a mismatch between the change in income share and employment share, particularly in the commodity sector. (West Bengal shares this characteristic with the rest of India.) The fall of employment in the organised sector in the post-reform period has not been compensated fully by the growth of employment in the informal sector in the state.

In spite of high demographic pressure on land and the consequently higher incidence of marginalisation of farming, as we have already noted, the agricultural growth rate in West Bengal was higher during the 1980s compared to other states in India. But the growth rates of food and non-food crops decelerated in most of the agricultural states in India since the early 1990s. A significant fall in public sector capital formation in agriculture, declining trend in the supply of institutional credit along with some technological reasons have been the major responsible factors behind the recent deceleration in agricultural growth. The pattern of agricultural growth in West Bengal, as revealed in Chapter 2 of this report, has shifted away from food grains to high value-added crops during the past two decades.

The eastern region states lagged behind the western part of the country in terms of industrial growth in the factory sector due to some historical and policy-related reasons. In West Bengal, unorganised industries contributed the major share of output and employment of the total industrial sector. West Bengal did not perform well in respect of industrial growth during the period under the industrial licence regime. But the rate of growth of output even in the factory sector increased significantly since the mid-1990s.[4] The emolument per employee in almost every industry group in the factory sector has been higher in West Bengal than in today's industrially advanced states in India. Also, the incidence of wage inequality in registered manufacturing is lower in the state compared to the industrially faster growing regions of the country. But the factory sector fails to absorb the growing labour force of the state and the situation has deteriorated in this respect during the post-reform period. Although the growth rate of labour employment in the factory sector was higher in the western region states, particularly Gujarat, than in West Bengal during the past two decades, the proportion of casual worker in this sector is very high and most of them are absorbed in the private sector in Gujarat.

The contribution of the services sector to the West Bengal's GDP has been increasing rapidly during the post-reform period. Within this sector trade-related activities are growing faster in West Bengal. In the countryside of the state, transport-related activities under own account service enterprises accounted for the highest share. But in urban areas, 'education' accounts for the largest number of own account service enterprises.

4. See Chapter 3 for detailed analysis of industrial development in West Bengal.

Chapter 1

Growth and Structural Changes

1.1 Introduction

One of the most disconcerting developments of the 1990s and thereafter in India, and indeed the world over, has been that economic growth has been accompanied by a much lower rate of growth in employment, and by zero or negative growth of what the ILO has termed "decent work" (Bagchi, 2004). There has been a significant transformation of output and employment from one sector to other but that transformation is out of step with the change in incomes derived from different sectors. Although there has been a mismatch between output growth and employment growth everywhere in India, the mismatch is very strong in the faster growing states like Gujarat (Bagchi, Das and Chattopadhay, 2005).

West Bengal performed better in agriculture since the early 1980s. The state started to lose its prominence in manufacturing growth since the mid-1960s but the rate of manufacturing growth increased after the mid-1990s. This chapter lays out the pattern of growth and structural change of states' income as observed in West Bengal over the period 1960-2006. The major issues discussed in this chapter are on the changing pattern of output and employment across major sectors. Growth and structural changes have been analysed with the data on domestic product of states of India published by the Economic and Political Weekly Research Foundation (2003) and Government of West Bengal (2008).

In explaining the pattern of employment in West Bengal we do not follow the methodology used in the standard labour market. This is because a large portion of employment, particularly in the informal sector, in a labour surplus economy like ours is created by the process of distress sale of labour. Moreover, the level of employment is highly influenced by the outcomes of the product and financial markets as well. The decline in investment rates and aggregate demand in the reform period, for example, has depressed labour demand all over the country (Bagchi, 2004). The most recent step-up of saving and investment in India has been primarily caused by the rise of the share of the corporate sector in GDP and national saving. We have utilised different quinquennial rounds of NSS data on employment and unemployment situation in India.

The chapter starts with the analysis of structural break in growth behaviour of different sectors of the state economies in Section 2. Das (2007) had taken care of unit root behaviour and structural break of income series originated from agriculture, manufacturing and services in West Bengal over the period 1960 to 2003. We have reproduced the main findings of that study without analysing the time series behaviour of the series. Section 3 analyses sectoral growth in the state over different periods. Sectoral dimensions of output and employment are examined in Section 4. Section 5 treats the issues of informalisation and casualisation of labour in the context of labour market flexibility. Section 6 concludes by providing summary findings of the chapter.

1.2 Structural Break in Output Growth

There has been considerable discussion on the trend break in India's growth rate of GDP (DeLong, 2001; Wallack, 2003; Rodrick and Subramanian, 2004). According to Wallack (2003), the most significant date for the break of GDP growth was 1980, whereas for GNP growth the break point was 1987. The major breaks in the growth path of the annual series of net state domestic

Author, Dr. Panchanan Das, is a Senior Lecturer in Economics in West Bengal Education Service, and is gratefully indebted to Prof. Amiya Kumar Bagchi, Director, Institute of Development Studies Kolkata, for helpful comments.

product (NSDP) and its sectoral components as observed in West Bengal are shown in Table 1.1. The break points are estimated by following Andrews and Ploberger (1994) on the basis of estimated F-statistics corresponding to different years shown in Figure 1.1. The major break appears corresponding to the maximum value of the test statistic, called the supremum value, shown in Table 1.1.

FIGURE 1.1

Sequence of Test Statistics for Structural Break

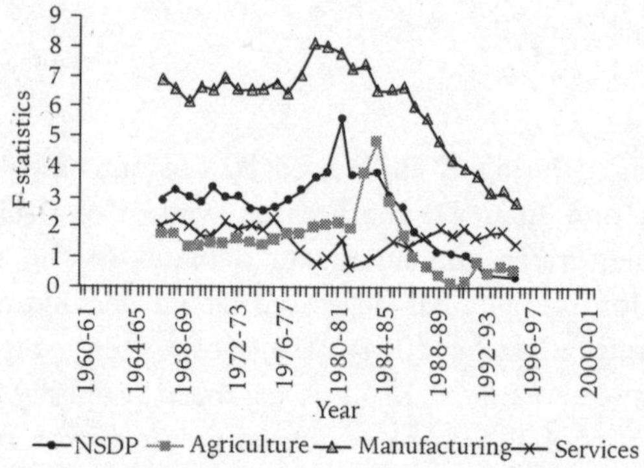

Source: Author's calculation.

TABLE 1.1

Test Statistics for Structural Break

	Year of Break	*Sup F-Statistic*
Agriculture	1983	4.824
Manufacturing	1978	8.077
Services	No break	
NSDP	1980	5.684

Source: The Economic and Political Weekly Research Foundation (EPWRF). *Domestic Product of States of India: 1960-61 to 2000-01;* Government of West Bengal. *Economic Review (2007-08).*

In West Bengal, the major structural break in growth of NSDP occurred in 1980, a long period before the initiation of liberalisation. West Bengal experienced a structural break in agricultural growth in 1983. In manufacturing growth, break appeared in 1978. Total services in West Bengal followed no such significant trend break. As there is no scope in performing time series analysis in detail to locate multiple breaks in the trend paths of different series of NSDP, we can utilise simple time series plots of the series as shown in Figure 1.2 to trace other break points, if any, at least visually. In agriculture, another break appeared in 1997 and growth of agricultural NSDP decelerated thereafter. In manufacturing also the secondary break point has been observed in the mid-1990s from where manufacturing growth accelerated significantly. Although the trend path of the services sector NSDP is smooth and thus no significant trend break appeared, the path has been steeper since the mid-1990s.

FIGURE 1.2

Components of NSDP (Rs. lakh) at 1993-94 Prices

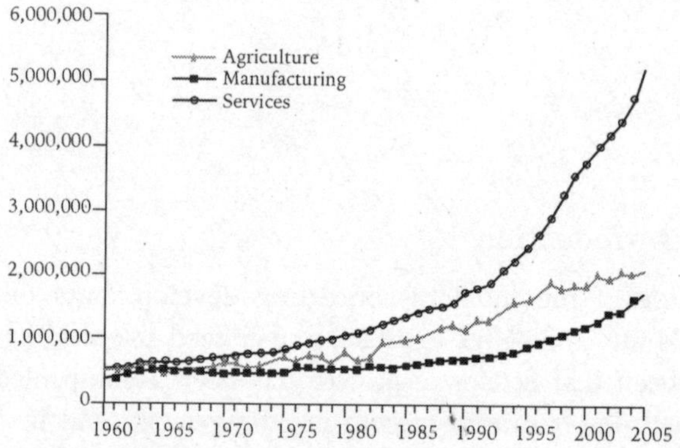

Source: The Economic and Political Weekly Research Foundation (EPWRF). *Domestic Product of States of India: 1960-61 to 2000-01;* Government of West Bengal, *Economic Review (2007-08).*

The growth acceleration in the manufacturing sector in West Bengal is largely attributed by the better performance of the unorganised sector. Although manufacturing industries, organised and unorganised, performed well in terms of output growth since the mid-1990s, the unorganised sector grew at a faster rate compared to the registered sector during the same period (Figure 1.3). Among services, trade-related activities have been dominating followed by banking and insurance in the state (Figure 1.4).

FIGURE 1.3

NSDP from Registered and Unregistered Industries (Rs. lakh) at 1993-94 Prices

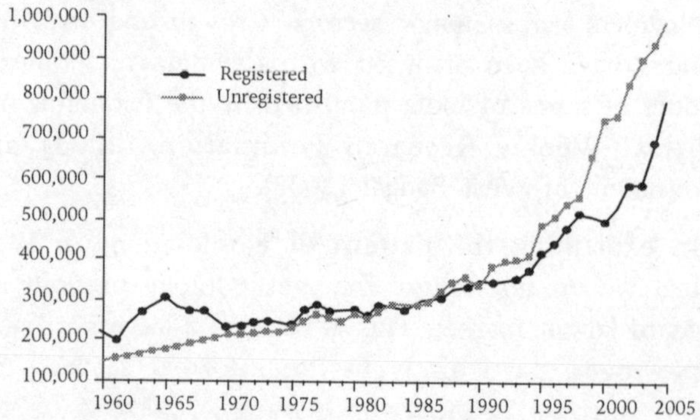

Source: As in Figure 1.2.

FIGURE 1.4

NSDP from Different Services (Rs. lakh) at 1993-94 Prices

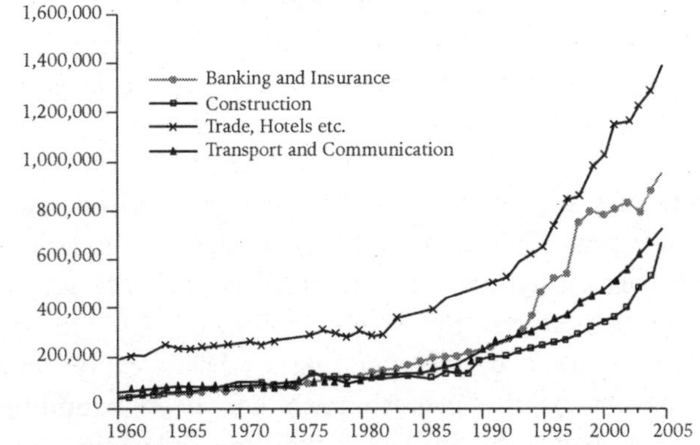

Source: As in Figure 1.2.

1.3 Growth Performance of West Bengal

The estimated growth rates of states' domestic product for different periods are shown in Table 1.2. In West Bengal, the overall economic growth rate improved in the 1980s, and accelerated further in the 1990s compared to the performance in the 1970s. The rate of growth of the state economy after the 1980s (1991-2006) had been nearly double the rate prevailed in the 1970s.

TABLE 1.2

Growth Rates of State's Income at Constant (1993-94) Prices

Periods	*Growth Rates of NSDP*
1971-2006	4.9
1971-1980	3.1
1981-1990	4.7
1991-2006	6.2

Source: As in Table 1.1.

Agriculture in West Bengal marked the end of 'impasse' in the 1980s (Table 1.3). The growth rate of state's income from agriculture in this decade increased by double the rate observed in the previous decade. The details about agricultural growth are analysed in the next chapter of the report.

Growth rates of states' income from total manufacturing (both registered and unregistered) over different periods are presented in Table 1.4. Manufacturing in West Bengal grew at around the rates of 2 per cent and 3 per cent, respectively during the 1970s and 1980s and the rate improved to 6.6 per cent during 1991-2006. The growth performance of this sector turned better after the mid-1980s compared to the period of state control.

TABLE 1.3

Growth Rates of Agricultural Income at Constant (1993-94) Prices

Periods	*Growth Rates*
1971 to 2006	4.3
1971 to 1980	3.0
1981 to 1990	6.1
1991 to 2006	3.4

Source: As in Table 1.1.

TABLE 1.4

Growth Rates of Manufacturing Income at Constant (1993-94) Prices

Periods	*Growth Rates*
1971 to 2006	3.7
1971 to 1980	2.1
1981 to 1990	3.1
1991 to 2006	6.6

Source: As in Table 1.1.

West Bengal started to lose its industrial primacy among the states in India since the mid-1960s and the recessionary effect on industry in the state was not only the most severe but long drawn out as well (Bagchi, 1998). Industrial growth in West Bengal, as in other constituent states in India, has largely been determined by the stance of economic policy adopted by the Central government, the allocation of central public investment in industry and infrastructure, the allocation of credit by banks and term lending institutions under the control of the Central government and the general attitude of large business houses and multinational corporations towards investment in that particular state.

From the middle of the 1960s, public sector investment in the eastern region slowed down very considerably. The massive decline in West Bengal's capital goods industries that occurred from 1966 could not be reversed in the subsequent years. While the total industrial investments in the state by the Central government accounted for nearly 13 per cent of the total investments sanctioned by the Government between 1947 and 1968, no significant new investments had been granted for West Bengal by the Central government in the 1970s and 1980s. The slow growth of manufacturing in the eastern part of the country, particularly in West Bengal, was a damaging consequence of the license permit raj (Bagchi, 1970; Chandrasekhar, 1988). The policy of equalising the prices of coal and steel led to the loss of comparative adavantage of resource-rich states such as West Bengal, Bihar, Orissa and Madhya Pradesh.

Strong trade unionism in West Bengal is often alleged as a major cause for industrial slowdown in the state. Labour militancy reached a peak in the late 1960s and continued for several years thereafter, particularly in West Bengal. But probably that militancy was an expression of the workers' anger against the massive labour displacement. The sharp fall of employment, especially in the late 1960s, led to acute labour agitations in West Bengal. Sometimes strikes were provoked or even engineered by the management of firms as an excuse for declaring lockouts (Bagchi, 1998). However, labour militancy declined very considerably in the 1980s and the decline continued in the 1990s. The *Indian Labour Yearbook* (1996) shows that West Bengal faced only 16 strikes affecting 27,000 workers, compared to 129 strikes in Gujarat affecting 1,20,000 workers. Although the incidence of strikes came down in the 1990s, on an average about two crore man-days were lost each year due to lockouts in the early 1990s. The handbook also reports that there were 80 lockouts in West Bengal showing the highest number of man-days lost due to lockouts in 1996.

The growth of the services sector has been the subject of much discussion in recent years. Table 1.5 shows the trend growth rates of income from services in West Bengal. Income from the services sector has been growing at a faster rate since the early 1990s. The higher growth of services income is largely due to the rapid growth income from trade-related activities followed by banking and financial services.

TABLE 1.5

Growth Rates of Income from Services at Constant (1993-94) Prices

Periods	*Growth Rates*
1971 to 2006	5.8
1971 to 1980	4.0
1981 to 1990	4.7
1991 to 2006	7.7

Source: As in Table 1.1.

The aggregate rates of growth (Tables 1.2 to 1.5) are not sufficient to understand properly the pattern of changes of growth performance of agriculture or any other sector in an economy.[1] The basic assumption behind growth estimation, either by fitting log linear trends or by averaging annual growth rates, is that the rate of growth remains at the same level during the estimation period. In this sense the conventional growth analysis ignores the effects of some external shocks owing to institutional or technological change, or unforeseen changes in weather conditions on agricultural output or productivity growth. As, in this study, the scope is limited for extended analysis of trend by incorporating stochastic components, the nature of the growth path has been examined, although grossly, by displaying the time series plot of the first differences of the logarithmic values of the relevant variable.[2]

Figure 1.5 shows the temporal change in annual growth rates of NSDP and its component from agriculture manufacturing and services in West Bengal over a long period from 1960 to 2006. This figure displays some dynamic characters of growth and structural changes in West Bengal. As discussed above, time series properties of long run growth of agricultural income in the state have been analysed in Das (2007)[3] and found that a structural break appeared in the growth path in 1983.

FIGURE 1.5

Annual Growth Rates of NSDP and its Major Components

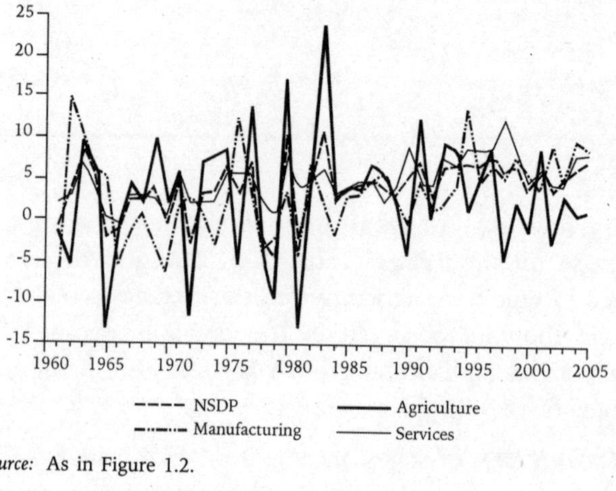

Source: As in Figure 1.2.

1. Over a reasonably long period of time annual growth rates of any economic variable are most likely to change in their mean and often in their variance so that their first two moments would be far from being constant over time, and consequently the trend might often be stochastic in nature.

2. The first difference of the logarithmic series, $\Delta Y_t = \ln Y_t - \ln Y_{t-1}$, gives annual growth rate of Y in period t. A rigorous analysis of data generating process, developed in the econometric literature since Nelson and Plosser (1982), is needed to capture the effects of randomness and of external shocks, if any, on the time series of area, production and yield.

3. Das (2007): Chapter 3 of the Ph.D. dissertation, "Output, Employment and Productivity Growth in Indian Manufacturing Industries: 1970-71 to 2002-03 – A Comparative Study of West Bengal and Gujarat", provides a detail comparison of long run growth and structural change of NSDP from agriculture, industry and services between West Bengal and Gujarat by considering unit root behaviour of the macroeconomic time series of these two states.

1.4 Changes in Sectoral Composition of Income and Employment

As an economy grows, the relative importance of agriculture declines and those of manufacturing and services increase, in terms of both output and employment share, over time. Thus, by exploring the changes in sectoral composition of income and employment over time in West Bengal we can analyse the pattern of structural change associated with economic growth.

Table 1.6 presents percentage shares of state's income by the major sectors in West Bengal over different periods. In West Bengal, there has been no systematic pattern of change in percentage share of state's income originating from agriculture. This sector contributed more than 29 per cent of NSDP in 1971 and the contribution declined by 3 per cent in 1981. The share of agriculture in the state grew up during the 1980s reaching at 30 per cent in 1991. In the next decade, however, the share declined and became roughly 20 per cent in 2006.

TABLE 1.6

Changes in Sectoral Composition of NSDP

Year	*Sectors*		
	Agriculture	*Manufacturing*	*Services*
1971	29.4	22.1	35.9
1981	25.9	19.9	42.3
1991	30.1	16.6	41.8
2006	20.0	17.2	50.2

Source: As in Table 1.1.

Manufacturing in West Bengal, on the other hand, generated 22 per cent of state's net domestic product in 1971 and its share declined consistently to 20 per cent in the early 1980s, 16.6 per cent in the early 1990s but increased merely by less than 1 per cent in 2006. Thus, the relative importance of manufacturing in state's total income has been declining over time. The income share from services in this state was more than 50 per cent in 2006 as against 36 per cent in 1971. In West Bengal, the relative contribution of services has been dominating over the years and at higher rates in the early 1980s and late 1990s.

One of the most stylised facts in the growth process, exhibited by cross section data among different countries as well as time series data of individual countries, is that the share of labour force engaged in agriculture falls with the rise in per capita GDP. In West Bengal, the percentage of labour engaged in agriculture declines at a slower rate following the national trend (Tables 1.7 and 1.8). The NSS data show that more than 60 per cent of rural male workers and more than 50 per cent of the rural female workers in West Bengal depended directly on agriculture for their livelihood in 2004.

In common with the experience of the other states of India, the percentage of workers employed in agriculture in West Bengal has declined much more slowly than the percentage of income generated by it. Thus, a mismatch between the movement of income share and employment share in agriculture has been observed in the state.

TABLE 1.7

Percentage of Labour Employed in Agriculture in Rural Areas

Periods	*Males*	*Females*
1977-78	77.7	68.7
1983	72.5	76.1
1987-88	72.2	70.8
1993-94	64.7	58.9
1999-2000	66.4	54.1
2004-05	64.0	54.0

Source: NSS Rounds 32, 38, 43, 50, 55 and 61 on *Employment and Unemployment Situation in India,* NSSO, Ministry of Statistics and Programme Implementation, Government of India, New Delhi.

TABLE 1.8

Percentage of Labour in Agriculture in Urban Areas

Periods	*Males*	*Females*
1977-78	5.9	13.4
1983	3.2	14.4
1987-88	4.7	15.4
1993-94	4.4	8.6
1999-2000	3.2	2.3
2004-05	2.7	1.2

Source: As in Table 1.7.

A considerably higher percentage of labour engaged in agriculture than the percentage contribution made by the agricultural sector to the domestic product implies that labour productivity is lower in agriculture compared to the non-agricultural sector. Given the low productivity and the income per capita of the workforce engaged in agriculture, the incidence of seasonal unemployment and overall underemployment in this sector is likely to be pretty high also. The larger gap of intersectoral productivity means transferring labour from agricultural to non-agricultural sectors. It entails larger gains in productive efficiency and overall labour productivity, propelling the process of overall growth through structural change.

Tables 1.9 and 1.10 present the percentage of usual status working force engaged in the manufacturing sector in rural and urban areas respectively. Manufacturing has been failing to absorb the growing labour force in the state, and indeed the share declined for urban male workers since the mid-1980s. In 2004, near about one-fourth of the urban male workers were absorbed in industrial activities in West Bengal. The female participation rate in manufacturing activities in the state is significantly high both in rural and urban areas.

TABLE 1.9

Percentage of Labour in Manufacturing in Rural Areas

Periods	*Males*	*Females*
1977-78	7.73	16.1
1983	8.53	15.3
1987-88	9.1	19.6
1993-94	11.7	30.0
1999-2000	10.9	36.1
2004-05	8.9	29.1

Source: As in Table 1.7.

Although rural households traditionally depend on agriculture for their livelihood, growth in the rural non-farm sector is likely to release agricultural workers for non-farm activities. In the rural economy, roughly 9 per cent of male labour and 29 per cent of female labour worked in different industries in the state in 2004. West Bengal registered a significant rise in the share of female workers engaged in industries during the 1990s but the share had fallen somehow in 2004.

TABLE 1.10

Percentage of Labour Employed in Manufacturing in Urban Areas

Periods	*Males*	*Females*
1977-78	34.6	22.4
1983	35.4	29.3
1987-88	32.1	26.9
1993-94	30.2	30.5
1999-2000	25.2	28.6
2004-05	26.0	28.0

Source: As in Table 1.7.

A larger proportion of the labour force in urban areas is employed in the services sector than in the manufacturing sector and this disparity is greater in the case of employment of female workers. (Tables 1.11 and 1.12). There has also been a considerable rise in the share of rural workers in the services sector between 1999 and 2004. In 2004, more than one-fifth of the male workers and 14 per cent of the female workers in the rural economy were engaged in this sector in West Bengal. In urban areas, 62 per cent of male workers and more than three-fourths of female workers in the state were engaged in different services in 2004. The relative share of employment in the services sector increased rapidly in the 1990s in the state.

TABLE 1.11

Percentage of Employment in Services in Rural Areas

Periods	*Males*	*Females*
1977-78	12.17	13.97
1983	16.48	8.17
1987-88	16.2	8.8
1993-94	20.5	9.3
1999-2000	19.4	9.4
2004-05	21.8	16.3

Source: As in Table 1.7.

TABLE 1.12

Percentage of Employment in Services in Urban Areas

Periods	*Males*	*Females*
1977-78	55.49	61.79
1983	56.64	54.85
1987-88	54.8	53.9
1993-94	55.7	58.5
1999-2000	62.1	66.7
2004-05	62.1	68.6

Source: As in Table 1.7.

Trade is the single largest component of the services sector in terms of its contribution to state's income. The explosion of trading services, particularly retail trading, is probably due to the failure of manufacturing as of agriculture to absorb the growing labour force. It becomes almost a natural decision for an individual to set up at least a small shop depending on his means and capital. A vast number of the job seekers face barriers to entry in other sectors and then flock to the informal sector, mostly in retail trading. In fact, all over India, a large segment of informal sector workers are employed in tertiary activities (Joshi, 2004). But one can term it as 'forced employment' (Guruswamy *et al.*, 2005). This may be an indication of the 'jobless growth' in the commodity sector mostly in the 1990s and beyond in the country.

Jobs in services are of heterogeneous types, and there are different types of jobs even within a particular service sector but the data of such type are not easily available in our country. And the degree of income inequality among workers in this sector is also likely to be very high: the world of the big stockbroker or provider of financial services would have no similarity at all from that of the hawkers or owners of shops in slum areas or peddlers in trains or bus stations. A very small share of the workforce, particularly women, with higher levels of education have found employment as professionals in banks, finance and insurance firms and other corporate service providers; data-entry work in several corporate services, both domestic as well as multinationals; in tourism and other services mainly as maids, attendants, and entertainers; and similar types of white collar jobs abroad. But a very large share of women workers is engaged in informal sector as casual workers. Many of them provide personal services such as domestic work, cleaning and cooking services and care of children and the aged in the urban areas at a very low rate of pay and their work remains irregular. Women constitute a significant part of the workforce in the state as in the country and the changes in sectoral composition of labour under usual status highlight the incidence of feminisation at least in a crude sense.

1.5 Informalisation and Casualisation of Labour

The NSS figures for unemployment rates, according to usual status, weekly status and daily status, for both male and female workers in rural and urban areas are indicative of higher incidence of underemployment in the labour market not only in West Bengal but in the industrial state of Gujarat as well (Bagchi and Das, 2005). Persons who have been reported unemployed for a relatively longer time during the reference period of one year are unemployed by usual status. However, it may be possible that some of them had some marginal employment for a short period of time. The unemployment rates obtained for the current weekly status would, in general, be less than those for the current daily status. The estimates based on the daily status measure the extent of unemployment in terms of person-days rather than the number of unemployed persons.

NSSO measures underemployment by comparing the usual status figures with the daily status and weekly status figures. But, as per definitions of the usual status, the daily status and the weekly status provided by NSSO, such a comparison actually highlights the degree of uncertainty in getting job throughout the period. If most of the people have regular wage employment, as observed in advanced industrial countries, the weekly status of employment does not normally diverge from their usual employment status. In our country, however, the divergence is substantial. Thus, to understand the actual employment situation, we need to know about the different categories of workers in employment and about the conditions of employment of each of the categories.

The proportion of regular employees, particularly for female workers, has been very low particularly in rural areas. In urban areas also the proportion is low in the state (Table 1.13). The work participation rate in rural and urban areas has registered a sharp decline between 1987 and 2004 (as indicated by the different rounds of NSS), except in the service sector, where there has been a rise in the share of workers' participation, particularly for women workers, during the 1990s.

TABLE 1.13

Percentage Distribution of Usually Employed Persons by Status of Employment

	Self-employed		*Regular Employed*		*Casual Labour*	
	Male	*Female*	*Male*	*Female*	*Male*	*Female*
Rural						
1987-88	54.2	62.3	9.5	6.1	36.3	31.6
1993-94	54.7	59.0	10.3	7.3	35	33.7
1999-2000	49.2	62.4	7.5	5.1	43.3	32.5
2004-05	53.1	46.9	7.4	13.7	39.5	39.4
Urban						
1987-88	36.9	44.8	50.5	42.4	12.6	12.8
1993-94	37.4	36.4	47.6	44.1	15	19.5
1999-2000	43.1	43.6	39.9	40.1	17	16.3
2004-05	44.6	39.4	37.6	50.2	17.9	10.4

Source: As in Table 1.7.

Thus one of the major debates today is centred on the casualisation of the workforce. Casualisation displaces the better-paid, more protected workers and increases insecure and low-paid employment. The NSS data on the principal status and subsidiary status of usually employed workers show that the proportion of the rural male workforce employed on a casual basis has increased over time, but at a very high rate in the 1990s, at the expense of self-employment and regular employment (Table 1.13). The type of employment for male workers in the countryside changed significantly from casual employment to self-employment during 1999-2004. The distribution of female work participation by status of employment indicates that there is a decline in the importance of the self-employed category in both rural and urban areas and an overall increase in the casual women workers from around 32 per cent in 1999 to nearly 40 per cent in 2004 in rural West Bengal. The incidence of casualisation of labour for both male and female workers in rural areas in West Bengal is fairly high in 2004-05. Lack of gainful employment coupled with colossal poverty has forced people to settle for distress sale of labour in the informal sector. The rise in the flexibility in the labour market and the high growth of informal sector during the reform period led to casualisation of work and increasing recruitment of female workers.

Also, the closure, downsizing or merger of several industries due to a variety of reasons, resulting in large scale unemployment in the organised manufacturing sector, has generated large scale casual employment, particularly for urban male workers. The casualisation of employment has increased for male workers in urban West Bengal since the late 1980s. The nature of employment for them shifted from permanent category towards self-employment during this period (Table 1.13). But the proportion of women workers in regular employment increased at a very high rate during 1999-2004 and most of them were absorbed in the services sector. More than 50 per cent of urban women workers were engaged in regular job.

The incidence of casual labour has been found to be relatively high in an economy where labour market has become more flexible due to its greater commitment to reforms and liberalisation compared to other states. In West Bengal, the percentage of casual worker, both male and female, has been significantly lower compared to Gujarat (Bagchi and Das, 2005).

1.6 Concluding Remarks

Structural break in overall economic growth occurred in West Bengal in a period before the initiation of economic liberalisation in the country. In West Bengal agriculture performed better in the 1980s but the growth rate declined thereafter. Manufacturing and services grew at higher rates during the post-reform period. There has been a mismatch in the movement of income share and employment share in the commodity sector. The incidence of casualisation of labour in West Bengal is notable but is lower compared to faster growing state like Gujarat.

Deceleration of output growth along with high unemployment in India is a recent cause of concern. In the neo-liberal regime, public expenditures on employment generating programmes have been curtailed in every state of the country and the process of liberalisation acts adversely to generate employment, particularly in the commodity sectors. The fall of employment in the organised sector in the post-reform period has not been compensated fully by the growth of employment in the informal sector.

References

Andrews, D. and W. Ploberger (1994). "Optimal Tests When a Nuisance Parameter is Present Only under the Alternative", *Econometrica* 62 (6): 1383-1414.

Bagchi, A.K. (2004). "Nanny States for Capital and Social Darwinism for the Workers", *The Indian Journal of Labour Economics* 47(1): 69-79.

———. (1998). "Studies on the Economy of West Bengal since Independence", *Economic and Political Weekly* 33(47, 48): 2973-78.

———. (1970). "Long-Term Constraints on India's Industrial Growth, 1951-1968", in E.A.G. Robinson and Kidron Michael (eds.), *Economic Development in South Asia*. London: Macmillan.

Bagchi A.K. and P. Das (2005). "Changing Pattern of Employment under Neo-liberal Reforms: A Comparative Study of West Bengal and Gujarat", *The Indian Journal of Labour Economics* 48(4): 945-58.

Bagchi A.K., P. Das and S. Chattopadhyay (2005). "Growth and Structural Change in the Economy of Gujarat (1970-71 to 2000-01)", *Economic and Political Weekly* 40(28): 3039-47.

Chandrasekhar, C.P. (1988). "Aspects of Growth and Structural Change in Indian Industry", *Economic and Political Weekly* 23(45-47): 2359-70.

Das, P. (2007). "Economic Growth and Structural Break in India: Testing Unit Root Hypothesis", *The Journal of Income and Wealth* 29(2): 29-43

DeLong, J.B. (2001). "India Since Independence: An Analytical Growth Narrative", July, *http://www.j-bradford-delong.net/*

Guruswamy, M., K. Sharma, J.P. Mohanty and T.J. Korah (2005). "FDI in India's Retail Sector: More Bad than Good?", *Economic and Political Weekly* 40(7): 619-23.

Joshi, S. (2004). "Tertiary Sector Driven Growth in India: Impact on Employment and Poverty", *Economic and Political Weekly* 39(37): 4175-78.

Nelson, C.R. and C.I. Plosser (1982). "Trends and Random Walks in Macroeconomic Time Series: Some Evidence and Implications", *Journal of Monetary Economics* 10: 139-62.

Rodrik, D. and A. Subramanian (2004). "From "Hindu Growth" to Productivity Surge: The Mystery of the Indian Growth Transition", *IMF Working Paper WP/04/77*, Washington DC, IMF, May.

Wallack, J. (2003). "Structural Breaks in Indian Macro Economic Data", *Economic and Political Weekly* 38(41): 4312-15.

Chapter 2

Agriculture

2.1 Introduction

In West Bengal, productivity growth in agriculture, particularly in food grain production, contributed significantly to overall economic growth of the state since the early 1980s. Agricultural growth has a significant impact on poverty reduction (Ravallion and Datt, 1996). After a long period of stagnation, agricultural growth in West Bengal was initiated in the early 1980s with the expansion of cultivation by using high yielding seeds (HYVs) and chemicals-based technology within the frame of more equitable distribution of land through agrarian reforms. The tenancy reforms in the shape of Operation Barga, as implemented in the state after the late 1970s, have granted the right to register tenancies and also the legal entitlement to higher crop shares in favour of the tenants through legislation.

There has been a growing concern in recent years about the deceleration of agricultural output in most of the agricultural states in India since the early 1990s. The positive impulse of the fast growing yield rate to output growth of the major crops as observed in the 1980s have been petered out in the phase of neo-liberal reforms in India. In the context of agricultural growth in India, Gulati and Bathla (2001) documented that a significant fall in public sector capital formation in agriculture was a major constraint on productivity growth in agriculture. Declining trend in the supply of institutional credit in the post-reform period in India has also been responsible for near stagnation in yield levels (Vyas, 2001). Adoption of HYVs technology without considering the soil and moisture conditions, inadequate rural infrastructure, weak network of agricultural marketing, sharply skewed land distribution and tenancy laws against the tenants in most part of the country are the major impediments to agricultural growth in India (GoI, 2000). The improper use of chemical fertiliser and pesticides in technology-intensive production of rice and wheat largely account for environmental degradation and erosion of soil fertility. The decline in public investment in irrigation induces over extraction of groundwater by the private operators and raises environmental costs (Sanyal, 2005).

Against this backdrop, this chapter attempts to take care of some recent issues of agricultural development in West Bengal. The state displays considerable heterogeneity in agro-climatic conditions.[1] The diversity in agro-climatic environment and resource endowment has resulted in interregional differences in cropping pattern and in productivity growth of major crops within the state. The extent of crop diversification facilitating growth rates of output and land productivity within the ambience of tenancy reforms and the expansion of new technology has been explored both at the state level and at the district level. Identification of region-specific strategies for agricultural development is one of the prime objectives of this study. The recent decline in institutional credit, particularly bank credit, to agriculture has been highly significant in the context of financial sector reforms in India. The analysis has been conducted for the major crops covering rice, wheat and total pulses in food grains, and oilseeds, jute and potato in non-food grains. The prospect of changing cropping pattern towards fruits, vegetables and floriculture as observed in West Bengal has also been examined in the context of openness of market for agricultural commodities.

Author, Dr. Panchanan Das, is a Senior Lecturer in Economics in West Bengal Education Service, and is gratefully indebted to Prof. Amiya Kumar Bagchi, Director, Institute of Development Studies Kolkata, for helpful comments.

1. West Bengal is divided into six agro-climatic zones: the Hill Region, the Terai Region, the Old Alluvial Region, the New Alluvial Region, the Coastal Region and the Western Laterite Region.

The discussion is focused mainly on the period covering 1980-81 to 2006-07. The information on area, production and yield for different crops has been compiled from *Economic Review 2007-08* published by the Government of West Bengal, *Statistical Abstracts of West Bengal* for different years published by the Bureau of Applied Economics and Statistics, Government of West Bengal and *Agricultural Statistics at a Glance 2005-06* published by the Directorate of Economics and Statistics, Ministry of Agriculture, Government of India. We have also used data from *State-wise Estimates of Value of Output from Agriculture and Allied Activities (2006 and 2008)* of the CSO. Data on landholdings are collected from National Sample Survey (NSS) 37th, 48th and 59th rounds on *Some Aspects of Operational Land Holdings in India*. The analysis is an indicative with a preference for verifying testable hypotheses that emerged in the recent experiences. The findings are presented in the form of tables and figures as the endeavour to provide simple illustrative representation of the key issues discussed in the text.

Section 2.2 discusses changes in cropping pattern in agriculture of the state. Section 2.3 compares growth rates of major crops in West Bengal with other major agricultural states in India. Growth performance of agriculture is analysed in terms of production, yield and area for important crops as produced in West Bengal during the past two and a half decades in Section 2.4. Input use pattern is discussed in Section 2.5. Land distribution in the context of tenancy reforms in the state is explored in Section 2.6. Section 2.7 focuses on the problem of indebtedness in agriculture in West Bengal.

2.2 Changes in Cropping Pattern

This section sets out a brief account on the recent changes in the cropping pattern in West Bengal. Cropped area changes through a change in net area sown and/or intensity of cropping. Changes in cropping intensity are brought about through multiple cropping supported by irrigation. The introduction of multiple cropping of non-traditional varieties of seeds with proper irrigation led to the increase in gross cropped area. Between 1980-81 and 2006-07, the index of cropping intensity, measured by the ratio of index of cropped area to index of net area sown, increased by more than 20 per cent (Table 2.1). As shown in Figure 2.1, cropping intensity in West Bengal increased substantially during the 1990s and thereafter, contributing to the increase in gross cropped area in the state. This rise in cropping intensity is associated mainly with an unprecedented increase in the cropped area of *Boro* rice. There has been a substantial diversification of crops under cultivation, as shown by the index of crop pattern,[2] in West Bengal during the past three decades. The index of cropping pattern in 2006-07 with 1980-81 as the base period is estimated at around 133.8 (Table 2.1).

The shifts in the cropping pattern have also been apparent from changes in area under different crops over time. In West Bengal, food grains accounted for 85 per cent of the gross cropped area in 1980 but their share declined to 78.6 per cent in 2006 (Table 2.2). The higher share of food grains in total cultivated area in the state is largely accounted for by the large share of marginal farmers in operational holdings. The marginal farmers normally allocate major part of their holdings for the production of food crops to meet their own consumption needs. Rice is the most dominating food crop covering more than 70 per cent of the cropped area of the state. Its share was rising in the 1980s, but it declined by 5 per cent in the 1990s. The share of cropped area under the traditional variety of *Aman* rice, the most widely cultivated variety in West Bengal, had fallen sharply from more than 58 per cent in 1980 to 47 per cent in 2000 but increased marginally thereafter. Acreage under *Aus*, another traditional variety of rice produced in the state, although less significant in volume, declined over time as well. The acreage shared by the *Boro*, the high yielding variety of rice, on the other hand, rose from less than 5 per cent to

---

2. Index of cropping pattern is measured by:

$$ICP_t = \frac{\sum_{i=1}^{n} C_{it} Y_{i0} P_{i0}}{\sum_{i=1}^{n} C_{i0} Y_{i0} P_{i0}} \times 100$$

where,

$C_{it} = \frac{A_{it}}{\sum_{i=1}^{n} A_{it}}$ is the proportion of area under the crop i in year t.

$C_{i0} = \frac{A_{i0}}{\sum_{i=1}^{n} A_{i0}}$ is the proportion of area under the crop i in the base period

Y_{i0} = Yield per hectare of the crop i in the base year and P_{i0} = Price per unit of the crop i in the base year.

around 18 per cent during the same period. However, the share of *Boro* in acreage cultivated declined after 2000-01. While the share of cropped area under wheat has roughly been stagnant at around 4 per cent, there was a perceptible decline in the share of area under pulses. The decline in the area under pulses in the state was more rapid than the rate of decline in area of rice under *Aman* variety. Pulses were largely replaced by *Boro*. The fall in area under food crops was largely due to a sharp decline in the area of cereals, particularly *Aman* rice, and pulses.

TABLE 2.1

Indices of Cropping Pattern and Cropping Intensity: West Bengal

Years	*Cropping Pattern*	*Cropping Intensity*
1980-81	100	100
1990-91	114.2	111.8
2000-01	128.8	113.4
2006-07	133.8	121.4

Source: Government of West Bengal. *Economic Review 2007-08*.

A marked diversification of cropping pattern away from food grains has occurred in West Bengal since the early 1990s. The share of cropped area under non-food grains increased substantially over the past two and a half decades. The percentage of acreage of oilseeds, particularly mustard, was nearly doubled during 1980-2006. The area under potato also increased magnificently during the same period (Table 2.2). But the share of cropped area under jute declined over this period, although increased marginally in the 1990s.

FIGURE 2.1

Cropping Intensity in West Bengal

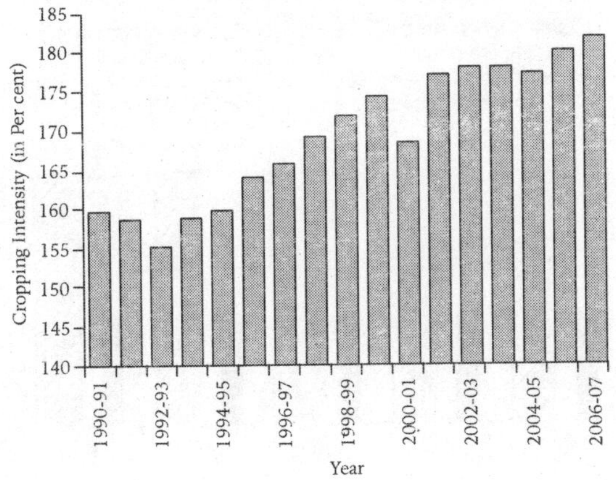

Source: As in Table 2.1.

TABLE 2.2

Area under Principal Crops in West Bengal

(Percentage to Total Cropped Area)

Year/Crops	*1980-81*	*1990-91*	*2000-01*	*2006-07*
Rice of which	**72.13**	**75.21**	**70.26**	**70.23**
(i) *Aus*	8.57	7.90	5.09	3.51
(ii) *Aman*	58.73	55.72	47.04	49.42
(iii) *Boro*	4.83	11.59	18.12	17.30
Wheat	3.94	3.48	5.51	4.33
Pulses	7.31	4.06	3.55	2.71
Total Food grains	**85.00**	**84.05**	**80.05**	**78.58**
Oilseeds	4.42	6.64	7.74	8.69
Jute	8.51	6.47	7.92	7.35
Potato	1.61	2.52	3.87	5.04
Non-Food grains	**15.00**	**15.95**	**19.95**	**21.42**

Source: As in Table 2.1.

Cropping pattern varies widely across districts in West Bengal. Table A-2.1 depicts the shares of acreage for major crops among different districts of the state in 2005-2006. Most of the districts in West Bengal are rice producing and *Aman* has been the leading variety. Howrah, Medinipur (East), Bardhaman, 24 Parganas (North) and Hooghly are the major *Boro* producing districts in the state. Murshidabad, Malda and Nadia lead in wheat and pulses production. Production of oilseeds is concentrated mainly in Nadia, 24 Parganas (North), Murshidabad and Malda. Jute, on the other hand, is cultivated intensely in Nadia, Cooch Behar, Murshidabad, Dinajpur (North) and 24 Parganas (North). Hooghly has led in potato production.

Price expectation and crop productivity play a crucial role in the determination of acreage under different crops in a region under the assumption of well-functioning agricultural markets and no constraints in supply of agricultural inputs (Vyas, 1996). The change in cropping pattern in favour of non-food crops took place in West Bengal in the wake of economic reforms of the 1990s in the shape of opening of the Indian market to global forces. Whether there has been a relationship between the changes in cropping pattern and the degree of openness of the Indian market for agricultural commodities is an empirical issue and we are not dealing in that issue as such.

The change in cropping pattern is also associated with the spread of new technology. The acreage growth of *Boro* rice in the state, for example, is highly associated with the expansion of irrigation and higher use of chemical fertiliser.[3] Cultivation of potato and mustard also became

3. *Boro* rice is grown in summer time and regular water supply is essential for its cultivation.

profitable, although the former is relatively more costly and risky than the latter, with their high yields due to the application of high yielding seeds, technical implements and development of irrigation.

Diversification towards Horticulture and Floriculture

Crop diversification, away from the traditional food and non-food crops assumes significance in the context of the market openness for agricultural commodities in India. Also, faster income growth and growing urbanisation have shifted the consumption pattern towards high value crops in the country (Ravi and Roy, 2006). Agriculture in West Bengal has been diversifying gradually towards high value crops of fruits, vegetables and flowers. West Bengal is one of the leading producers of fruits and vegetables contributing nearly 16 per cent to the country's total production in 2005-06, but the contribution of floriculture was less than 3 per cent to the national production of flower during this period (Government of India, 2008). Trends in total production of fruits and vegetables and flowers in West Bengal are shown in Figure 2.2. The state experienced a rising trend in the production of flowers since the late 1990s. The value of total fruits and vegetables produced in the state increased by more than double and that of flowers by nearly three times during 1990-91 to 2005-06.

Mango and banana are two important fruits produced in West Bengal. In 2006-07, nearly 42 per cent and 17 per cent of the area under fruits were used in production of mango and banana respectively. The respective output shares were 21 per cent and 30 per cent of total fruits production in the state. The recent trends in acreage and production of these two fruits are shown in Figure 2.3. Total production of fruits increased to 26.4 lakh tonnes in 2006-07 from 23 lakh tonnes in the previous year with the increase in acreage from 1.7 lakh hectares to 1.9 lakh hectares during this period. The production of both mango and banana increased over time but the latter at a faster rate. The leading varieties of vegetables produced in the state are cabbages, cauliflower, brinjal and cucurbits. Figure 2.4 presents acreage and output of these four vegetables in the state over the past five years.

FIGURE 2.2

Production of Fruits, Vegetables and Flowers

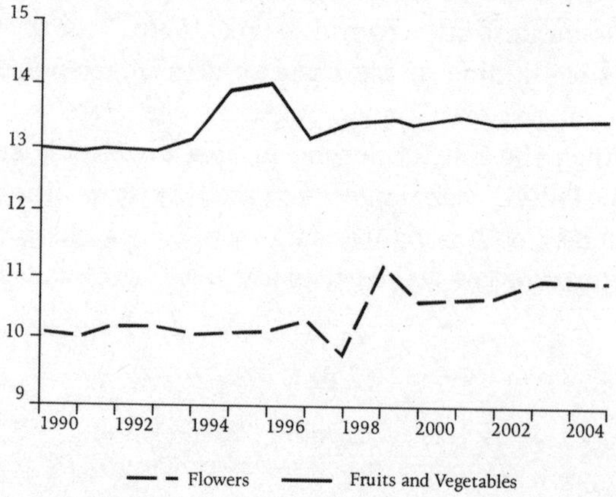

Note: Production figures shown in vertical axis are in logarithmic terms.

Source: CSO (2006, 2008), *State-wise Estimates of Value of Output from Agriculture and Allied Activities.*

FIGURE 2.3

Area and Production of Mango and Banana

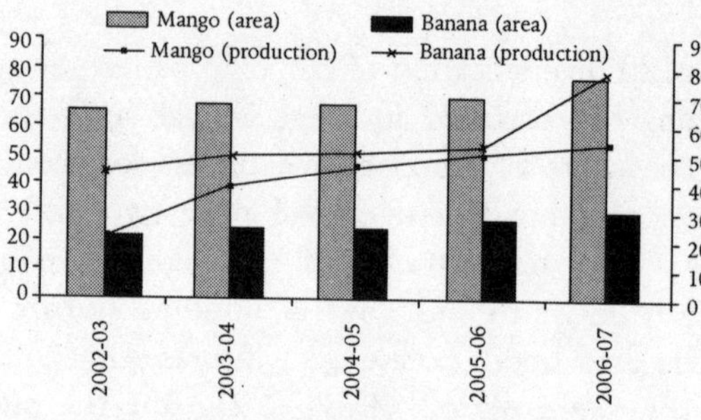

Note: Area in '000 hectares measured in left vertical axis and production in '000 tonnes measured in right vertical axis.

Source: Government of West Bengal, Directorate of Food Processing Industries and Horticulture.

FIGURE 2.4

Area and Production of Major Vegetables

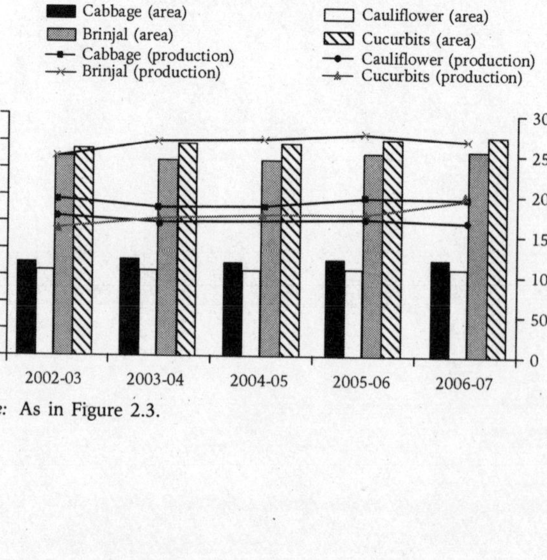

Source: As in Figure 2.3.

The horticultural crops in the state covered 1091 thousand hectares of land in 2006-07. The diverse soil and climatic conditions in the state make it possible to cultivate a wide variety of fruits and vegetables across the districts. There are substantial inter-district differences in crop diversification towards fruits and vegetables in West Bengal. Table A-2.2 presents acreage and output of fruits and vegetables across districts in the state in 2005-06. Malda registered the highest area under fruits followed by Murshidabad and North 24 Parganas. But in terms of total production of fruits, North 24 Parganas led in the state. Both in terms of acreage and output Murshidabad was the highest vegetable producing district in West Bengal.

Although the cultivation of fruits and vegetables and other high value perishable crops are subject to production and marketing risks, crop diversification in this direction in West Bengal is appealing. As discussed below, agriculture in West Bengal is predominated by the marginal holding class. The marginal farmers and also *bargadars* in West Bengal often have credit access from institutional sources to make necessary investments and purchase the necessary inputs.

2.3 Agricultural Growth in West Bengal Compared to Other States in India

West Bengal is one of the major agricultural states in India. Table 2.3 shows the contribution of West Bengal to the national economy in terms of its shares of output for major crops over different periods. Total food grain production in West Bengal was roughly 16 million tonnes contributing 7.4 per cent of the country's total food grain output and ranked 4th among the major states in India in 2006-07. With rice output of 14.51 million tonnes in 2006-07, the state led all the major states in production of rice and contributed nearly 16 per cent of the country's total rice output. The share of the state in food grains production has been increasing steadily during the past two and a half decades. In rice production, the share increased by 2 per cent in 2006 as compared with the figure in 1980, although it remained roughly at the same level during the 1990s. In the production of pulses, on the other hand, the share of West Bengal to the national economy declined considerably in the 1980s, it improved in the next decade, and then declined further sharply. In the non-food grains group, the production share improved remarkably for jute and potato. The production share of oilseeds improved during the 1980s and 1990s but declined thereafter.

TABLE 2.3

Share of West Bengal to All-India (In Percentage): Output of Major Crops

Crops	*1980-81*	*1990-91*	*2000-01*	*2006-07*
Rice	13.9	14.1	14.6	15.9
Wheat	1.3	1.0	1.5	1.1
Pulses	2.3	1.4	2.0	1.1
Total Food Grains	6.4	6.4	7.0	7.4
Oilseeds	5.3	7.1	10.8	6.9
Jute & Mesta	57.6	60.1	71.2	74.7
Potato	20.4	29.5	34.7	N.A.

Source: As in Table 2.1.

The most distressing development during the post-reform period in India has been the deceleration in agricultural growth. The rates of growth of output and yield per hectare for the major food and non-food crops declined during the 1990s compared to the 1980s in almost every state of the country. But the rate of deceleration is different across the major agricultural producing states. By utilising the data based on state-wise value of output for different crops published at regular intervals by the CSO,[4] the growth rates of output for the major food and non-food crops in West Bengal are compared with the respective rates in other states of the country during the period 1990-2005. The estimates obtained with this data base may be different from those with the data provided in *Agriculture at a Glance* because of their methodological differences in collecting data.

Table 2.4 presents the growth rates of rice production for the major rice producing states in India.[5] West Bengal performed better in rice production compared to other rice producing states in India. Andhra Pradesh, the second largest contributor to rice output in India, registered insignificant production growth and higher volatility during this period. The growth rate of rice was significantly low in Uttar Pradesh and negative in Tamil Nadu over the past 15 years. Punjab, on the other hand, registered a higher growth in rice production compared to West Bengal during the same period. Table 2.5 shows

4. CSO provides agricultural output data in value terms, both at current prices and at base year prices, by collecting physical quantities of different crops from the Directorate of Economics and Statistics under the Ministry of Agriculture, Government of India. Valuation of crop production is done by multiplying the quantities of production by the corresponding producers' prices. The data are currently available up to 2005.

5. Growth rates are estimated by considering exponential trend and applying generalised least square (GLS) method in the fixed effect pooled regression model.

comparative rates of growth of wheat output in West Bengal and the leading wheat producing states in India. The output of wheat grew at a faster rate in West Bengal than in the wheat-led states of Uttar Pradesh, Punjab and Haryana. The growth performance of pulses was very poor everywhere in the country during the post-reform period (Table 2.6). The growth rate of production of pulses was negative in Uttar Pradesh, the second largest pulse producing state in India. In Madhya Pradesh and Maharashtra also the rate was very low during 1990-2005. In West Bengal, the estimated growth rate of pulses was statistically insignificant during the same period.

TABLE 2.4

Trend Growth Rates of Production of Rice: 1990-2005

States	*Growth Rate*
Andhra Pradesh	0.17
Orissa	-0.19
Punjab	2.79*
Tamil Nadu	-2.56**
Uttar Pradesh	1.46*
West Bengal	2.03*

Note: * significant at less than 1 per cent level, ** significant at less than 5 per cent level, the rest are insignificant.

Source: CSO (2006, 2008). *State-wise Estimates of Value of Output from Agriculture and Allied Activities.*

TABLE 2.5

Trend Growth Rates of Production of Wheat: 1990-2005

States	*Growth Rate*
Haryana	2.61*
Punjab	1.46*
Uttar Pradesh	1.90*
West Bengal	3.46*

Note: * Significant at less than 1 per cent level.

Source: As in Table 2.4.

TABLE 2.6

Trend Growth Rates of Production of Pulses: 1990-2005

States	*Growth Rate*
Madhya Pradesh	2.1***
Maharashtra	1.3***
Uttar Pradesh	-1.0*
West Bengal	-0.1

Note: * Significant at less than 1 per cent level, *** significant at less than 10 per cent level, the rest is insignificant.

Source: As in Table 2.4.

Table 2.7 compares the growth rates of oilseeds produced in West Bengal with some major oilseeds producing states in India. The production of oilseeds, mainly mustard, grew at a higher rate in West Bengal than in Andhra Pradesh, Gujarat, Karnataka and Kerala during the period 1990-2005. Mustard is the major oilseed produced in West Bengal contributing roughly 5 per cent to its national production. While production in Rajasthan, the largest contributor of oilseeds in India, grew at the highest rate, the growth rate in Gujarat, the second largest supplier, was not statistically significant during the same period. West Bengal has been the leading jute producing state in India. Other jute producing states in the country are Assam and Bihar. Growth rate of this fibre crop was the highest in West Bengal during the study period (Table 2.8). While the production of jute declined at a significant rate in Assam, it increased at the rate of more than 3 per cent in West Bengal. In the production of potato, West Bengal ranked second in India, and its average growth rate in the state was 3.5 per cent per annum during the period 1990-2005 (Table 2.9).

TABLE 2.7

Trend Growth Rates of Production of Oilseeds: 1990-2005

States	*Growth Rate*
Andhra Pradesh	-2.7**
Gujarat	2.8
Karnataka	-1.4***
Kerala	1.6*
Madhya Pradesh	3.3*
Maharashtra	2.7*
Rajasthan	3.4**
West Bengal	2.1*

Note: * Significant at less than 1 per cent level, ** significant at less than 5 per cent level, *** significant at less than 10 per cent level, the rest is insignificant.

Source: As in Table 2.4.

TABLE 2.8

Trend Growth Rates of Production of Jute: 1990-2005

States	*Growth Rate*
Assam	-3.4*
Bihar	0.1
West Bengal	3.2*

Note: * Significant at less than 1 per cent level, the rest is insignificant.

Source: As in Table 2.4.

TABLE 2.9

Trend Growth Rates of Production of Potato: 1990-2005

States	*Growth Rate*
Bihar	2.4*
Gujarat	6.1*
Madhya Pradesh	3.5*
Punjab	6.2*
Uttar Pradesh	4.1*
West Bengal	3.5*

Note: * Significant at less than 1 per cent level.

Source: As in Table 2.4.

2.4 Growth of Production, Yield and Acreage of Major Crops in West Bengal

The growth rates of production, yield and area for the major food crops in West Bengal over different periods between 1981 and 2006 are shown in Table 2.10 and the temporal changes in their annual growth rates are shown in Figures A-2.1 to A-2.4 in the appendix. Production of food grains grew at the rate of around 3 per cent per annum during the period 1981-2006. The rate of growth of production of food grains in West Bengal was spectacular (nearly 7 per cent) in the 1980s but the rate declined to 2 per cent during the period 1991-2006 (Table 2.10). As shown in Table A-2.3, the output growth of food grains varied from more than 7 per cent in Nadia, Howrah and Bankura districts to less than 3 per cent in Hooghly during the 1980s. Birbhum and Bardhaman grew at around 6 per cent, but the districts in North Bengal did not perform well during this decade. Birbhum, Murshidabad and West Dinajpur[6] registered higher output growth of food grains compared to other districts during 1991 to 2005.[7]

West Bengal registered appreciable output growth of rice during the 1980s (Table 2.10). But the growth rate declined following the other rice producing states in the country during 1991-2006. Murshidabad, Nadia and West Dinajpur performed better in rice production compared to the other districts of West Bengal during the past two and a half decades (Table A-2.4). In the 1980s, Nadia district recorded the highest growth rate in rice production at nearly 10 per cent, followed by Murshidabad, Howrah and Bankura. Growth rates of rice output were higher in West Dinajpur, Murshidabad and Birbhum districts during 1991-2005.

Wheat is the second most important cereal produced in West Bengal. Although the growth rate of wheat production was insignificant in the 1980s, the rate increased significantly during 1991-2006 (Table 2.10). The production of wheat grew at higher rates in Malda, Cooch Behar and some parts in Jalpaiguri district (Table A-2.5). The growth of wheat output improved in almost every district in the state and at significantly higher rates in Birbhum and Medinipur[8] during 1991-2005.

The growth rate of pulses production as estimated with state level data was statistically insignificant both in the 1980s and in the next period (Table 2.10). Although the rate was negative in many districts, the growth rate was appreciably high in Purulia and Nadia during the 1980s, and in Birbhum and Hooghly districts in the next period (Table A-2.6).

Table 2.11 presents growth rates of the three major non-food crops, namely oilseeds, jute and potato, in West Bengal during the period 1981 to 2006. The time path of their annual growth rates are shown in Figures A-2.5 to A-2.7. In West Bengal, oilseeds, mainly mustard, is a fast growing non-food crop registering more than 4 per cent output growth during 1981-2006. Output growth of oilseeds in the state was spectacularly high (12.4 per cent per annum) in the 1980s. The growth rate of oilseeds production was the highest and recorded at more than 24 per cent per annum in Purulia district followed by 24 Parganas,[9] Birbhum and Medinipur during this decade. The rate had fallen during 1991-2005, but differently across the districts in West Bengal. Malda and Murshidabad registered better growth performance compared to other districts during this period (Table A-2.7). The production of jute in West Bengal grew at a faster rate during 1991-2005 than in the 1980s. West Dinajpur, Howrah, Murshidabad, Hooghly and 24 Parganas performed better during this period (Table A-2.8). The growth of production of potato was impressive as well during the period 1981-2006. The growth rate of state's total output of potato was spectacularly high in the 1980s but it declined thereafter. In some districts,

6. For meaningful comparison, the data for North and South Dinajpur districts are combined and represented by the name West Dinajpur.
7. District level data for production yield and area for different food and non-food crops are available up to 2005-06.
8. For meaningful comparison, the data for East and West Medinipur districts are combined.
9. North and South 24 Parganas combined.

particularly in 24 Parganas and West Dinajpur, potato production increased at higher rate during 1991-2005 (Table A-2.9).

Agricultural output growth directly depends on the growth rates of land productivity and cropped area not only in definitional sense but also in fundamental causal sense. One can infer from the estimated growth rates of output, yield and area under different food crops, as shown in Table 2.10, that the output growth of food grains and also of rice in West Bengal was primarily yield driven. The fall in output growth was accompanied by the fall in growth rate of yield during 1991-2006. This may be an indication of the falling impact of the new technology, particularly on *Boro* rice and, indeed, the impulse of output growth that originated from productivity growth seems to have petered out since the early 1990s. The growth acceleration in wheat production, on the other hand, during 1991-2006 was primarily because of the expansion of acreage under this crop. For pulses although the yield rate increased, acreage declined at a higher proportional rate during the study period.

TABLE 2.10

Trend Growth Rates of Production, Yield and Area: Food Grains

	Production	Yield	Area
Total Food Grains			
1981-2006	2.9*	3.0*	-0.1
1981-1990	6.9*	5.7*	1.2*
1991-2006	2.1**	1.6*	0.5
Rice			
1981-2006	3.5*	3.0*	0.5*
1981-1990	7.7*	6.2*	1.5*
1991-2006	1.8*	1.8*	0.0
Wheat			
1981-2006	1.8*	0.3	1.5*
1981-1990	0.1	-2.1	2.2
1991-2006	2.6*	0.1	2.5*
Pulses			
1981-2006	-1.4*	1.2*	-2.6*
1981-1990	-1.3	1.7**	-3.0*
1991-2006	0.5	1.1**	-0.6

Note: * significant at less than 1 per cent level, ** significant at less than 5 per cent level, *** significant at less than 10 per cent level, the rest are insignificant.

Source: Directorate of Economics and Statistics, *Agriculture at a Glance*. GoI; Directorate of Agriculture, Evaluation Wing, Government of West Bengal.

It is revealed from Table 2.11 that higher output growth of oilseeds in the 1980s was mostly caused by the higher yield rate as well as expansion of acreage. Output growth of jute in the 1980s in West Bengal was yield driven. Acreage under jute had actually fallen during this period and jute production grew at a lower rate in spite of high yield rate in this decade. But the increase in output growth of this fibre crop during 1991-2006 was primarily because of the expansion of its acreage. In the case of potato the increase in production at higher rate in the 1980s was mainly due to the increase in area under this crop.

TABLE 2.11

Trend Growth Rates of Production, Yield and Area: Non-Food Grains

	Production	Yield	Area
Oilseeds			
1981-2006	4.3*	2.1*	2.2*
1981-1990	12.4*	7.0*	5.4*
1991-2006	3.4*	1.5*	1.9*
Jute			
1981-2006	3.2*	2.1*	1.1*
1981-1990	1.8	3.7*	-1.9
1991-2006	2.9*	1.8*	1.1**
Potato			
1981-2006	4.7*	0.2	4.5*
1981-1990	9.0*	2.8*	6.2*
1991-2006	2.0**	-1.4	3.4*

Note: * significant at less than 1 per cent level, ** significant at less than 5 per cent level, the rest are insignificant.

Source: As in Table 2.10.

The pattern of co-movements of annual changes in production, yield and area also suggests that much of the production growth of rice and oilseeds is yield driven. The rise in yield rate of *Boro* rice and mustard was the major source of faster agricultural growth in West Bengal under the new seed-fertiliser technology-based cultivation. Increasing yields have become more important than the expansion of cultivated area as a source of growth of farm output in the decades of using new biochemical technology in farming. But the application of new seed-fertiliser technology leading to monoculture farming seems to have declined its yield raising potential because of soil degradation emanating mostly from the improper use of chemicals.

2.5 Input Use Pattern

Variations in the pattern of input use with variations in tenure and holding size may be significant influences on the efficiency and productivity of Indian agriculture. There is a debate on the nature of relationship between farm size and productivity and input use efficiency between different types of tenure. However, in all cases, the use of chemical fertilisers, organic manure, improved seeds, pesticides and irrigation has facilitated agricultural growth. According to NSS 59th Round data on SAS of farmers during 2003, the percentage of farmer households using modern inputs (such as chemical fertilisers, organic manure, improved seeds and pesticides) was considerably higher in West Bengal than the all India average (Table 2.12). Table A-2.10 gives an account of the consumption of chemical fertilisers (total of nitrogen, phosphorus and potassium) in the districts of West Bengal over different periods during the past two and a half decades. Fertiliser consumption increased more than four times during the period from 1980 to 2006. Within West Bengal, the use of fertilisers increased at the highest rate in the district of Medinipur followed by Bardhaman and Hooghly during this period.

TABLE 2.12

Percentage Distribution of Farmer Households using Different Inputs

Inputs	West Bengal		All India	
	Kharif	*Rabi*	*Kharif*	*Rabi*
Fertiliser	89	72	76	54
Organic manure	54	43	56	38
Improved seeds	63	58	46	34
Pesticides	80	65	46	31

Source: NSS Report No. 496, *Some Aspects of Farming*, 2003.

A higher yield rate needs more nutrients for the plants and chemical fertilisers are used for this purpose. But higher productivity can be sustained only with the application of balanced NPK ratios. The appropriate NPK ratio is crop-specific and also soil-specific, and to be adjudged on the basis of soil test. The ratio of nitrogen in fertilisers used in agriculture in West Bengal has been falling, while that of potassium shows a rising trend during 1980-81 to 2006-07 (Figure 2.5).

FIGURE 2.5

N:P:K in Fertiliser Use in West Bengal

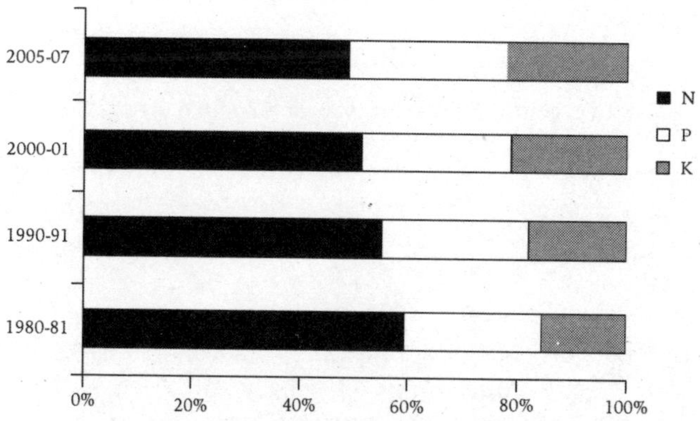

Source: *Statistical Abstracts* (various issues), Bureau of Applied Economics and Statistics, Government of West Bengal.

FIGURE 2.6

Area ('000 hectares) under HYVs in West Bengal

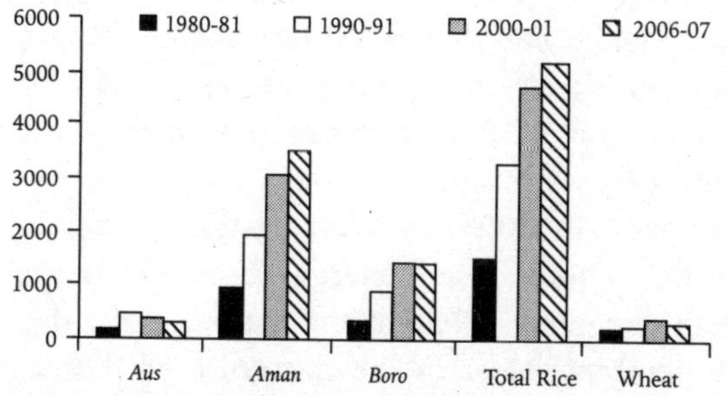

Source: Department of Agriculture, Government of West Bengal.

Although West Bengal receives high average annual rainfall (1400-2000 mm), the maximum of the rain falls occur during the southwest monsoon period (June to September). Its erratic temporal and spatial distribution with considerable year to year variation causes instability in agricultural production. Thus, adequate irrigation facilities are needed for sustainable agricultural development. Table 2.13 shows the percentage of cropped area irrigated by different sources in West Bengal and at the all India level. Figures reported in Table 2.13 are the gross irrigated area as a percentage of cropped area.[10] The percentages of cropped area under irrigation during both the *kharif* and the *rabi* seasons were much higher in West Bengal than the all India level in 2003. Tubewells were the major source of irrigation in the state, covering around one-third and more than 45 per cent of the cropped area during the *kharif* and *rabi* seasons

10. If a particular plot of land is irrigated more than once, the gross irrigated area will exceed total cropped area.

respectively. Canals were the next important source of irrigation both in the state and at the national level.

TABLE 2.13

Percentage Distribution of Cropped Area by Different Sources of Irrigation

	West Bengal		*All India*	
	Kharif	*Rabi*	*Kharif*	*Rabi*
River	3.53	5.28	2	2.2
Canal	10.39	10.54	7.75	7.68
Tubewell	32.44	45.38	21.01	33.82
Well	2.23	3.24	7.94	9.04
Tank	3.91	6.07	1.23	1.13
Others	5.24	5.16	2.27	2.46
Total	57.74	75.67	42.2	56.33

Source: As in Table 2.12.

The extent of farm mechanisation may be roughly indicated by the energy use pattern in ploughing and in irrigation across different holding classes. Table 2.14 gives the distribution of farmer households using energy of different types in ploughing and irrigation for each holding class. In 2003, in West Bengal 53 per cent of farmer households used energy (both electricity and diesel) in ploughing, while at the national level the share was 48 per cent. Most of the tractors used diesel rather than electricity. NSS 59th Round data on SAS of farmers revealed a wide inter-state variation in farm mechanisation: some higher-income states, such as Maharashtra and Karnataka, as well as some lower-income states such as Orissa and Jharkhand exhibited more dependence on animal power in ploughing. The use of mechanised implements differed significantly as between size clases of holdings in West Bengal and the rest of India on an average. In West Bengal, the use of diesel tractors was the highest in the size class 0.01-0.4 hectares, while at the national level the extent of farm mechanisation in terms of the use of diesel operated tractors was mainly concentrated among the holding class of more than 10 hectares.

In the case of irrigation, about 87 per cent of farmer households in the state used energy run by diesel, while the rest used electricity. At the all-India level, the share of farmers using electricity was much higher compared to West Bengal. The incidence of the use of pump sets propelled by diesel increased steadily with size class of landholding in West Bengal, whereas there was no such monotonic relationship between the use of electricity for irrigation and holding size. At the all India level, however, the use of electricity in irrigation was an increasing function of holding size.

TABLE 2.14

Percentage Distribution of Farmer Households in Different Size Classes using Energy

	West Bengal			*All India*		
	Electricity	*Diesel/ Petrol*	*Animal Power*	*Electricity*	*Diesel/ Petrol*	*Animal Power*
Ploughing						
< 0.01	0	79	21	0.4	54.3	45.3
0.01 – 0.4	0.7	56.2	43	0.6	52.9	46.4
0.41 – 1	0.3	48.9	50.8	0.4	44	55.6
1.01 – 2	0.5	50.1	49.1	0.4	43.2	56.4
2.01 – 4	2	43.9	54.1	0.4	46.6	53.1
4.01 – 10	0	37.9	62.1	0.4	55.3	44.3
>10	0	0	0	1.5	70.1	28.4
All sizes	0.5	52.6	46.8	0.4	47.5	52
Irrigation						
< 0.01	26.7	73.3	0	9.8	85.3	4.8
0.01 – 0.4	14.5	85.1	0.3	20.6	78.3	1.1
0.41 – 1	11.1	88.3	0.6	30.3	68.9	0.8
1.01 – 2	9.8	90.2	0	38.9	59.7	1.3
2.01 – 4	15.8	84.2	0	51.3	48	0.8
4.01 – 10	6.9	93.1	0	61.6	37.8	0.6
>10	0	0	0	73	26.6	0.4
All sizes	12.8	86.8	0.4	33.5	65.5	1

Source: As in Table 2.12.

2.6 Distribution of Landholdings

In dwelling on the issue of agricultural development, the size distribution of landholding and the nature of land right exercised by the cultivator should be given due consideration. We have utilised the NSS (37th, 48th and 59th Round) data on landholdings in India and the data from Agricultural Census of India, 2000-01, to bring out the pattern of land distribution and incidence of tenancy in West Bengal. The land productivity, although depends on farm size, is largely determined by the nature of land right. The productivity differential between owner-cultivator and tenant, even of a small plot of land, is likely to arise from differential access to institutional credit and technological inputs (Sanyal, 2005). Banerjee, Gertler and Ghatak (2002) studied the impact of Operation Barga on the yield rate of rice with a panel of rice producing districts in West Bengal and found that the tenancy reform as implemented in the state reduced productivity distortions in sharecropping by registering sharecropping contracts, protecting sharecroppers from eviction, and legislating minimum shares accruing to the tenant. As registered sharecroppers are legally entitled to apply for agricultural loans from formal credit institutions, security of tenure could reduce interest costs substantially and thereby provides investment incentives.

Progress of Tenancy Reforms

The progress of land reforms in West Bengal has occurred in the shapes of the redistribution of agricultural land, the regulation of sharecropping relationships and the distribution of homestead plots. According to the latest official data available (as on November 2007), *pattas* for 452,944 hectares of land have been redistributed among 2,967,629 persons engaged in agriculture.[11] Operation Barga is often referred to as a very successful programme of tenancy reforms in West Bengal and indeed as the first serious attempt to implement the legal provisions of tenure security protection for *bargadars* and control over the crop-share between landlords and tenants.[12] As of November 2007, 454,630 hectares of land had been recorded for 1,534,449 registered *bargadars* under this programme. Table A-2.11 presents the spatial distribution of total vested land and total area of land recorded in the state across districts in West Bengal. Medinipur (West) led in terms of land distribution among the beneficiaries, while Bardhaman displayed the highest share of land recording among the registered bargadars. The other better performing districts were Jalpaiguri, Malda, South 24 Parganas and Uttar Dinajpur in terms of the share of distributed land among the *patta* holders. The share of land recorded under Operation Barga was relatively high in Birbhum, Jalpaiguri, South 24 Parganas, Cooch Behar and Malda.

Land reforms in West Bengal have an appreciable effect on land distribution as well as on the nature of tenancy right in the state. The agrarian reforms also played a major role in creating the favourable conditions for private investment in agriculture by reducing class conflict and social unrest (Gazdar and Sengupta, 1997). Banerjee Gertler and Ghatak (2002) observed that the effect of tenancy reform component explained about 28 per cent of the subsequent growth of agricultural productivity in West Bengal. Land reform measures adopted by the Left Front government are well acclaimed in many other studies as a major factor attributing to the higher agricultural growth of the 1980s in West Bengal. The agrarian reforms seem to have had a noticeable effect on the distribution of operational holdings of land in West Bengal. In fact, land reform measures as implemented in the state confer greater freedom and security for smaller farmers and lessening of the power of landlords and big farmers (Bagchi, 1998). 'Operation Barga' was launched by the Left Front government in October 1978 granting legal rights to cultivate land was supposed a major incentive for the marginal and small peasants to raise agricultural production. This measure defined property rights in a more meaningful manner and narrowed the gap between ownership and actual operation, and widened the access of the small cultivators, the largest share of the total holdings, to technology and other inputs including institutional credit and subsidies (Sanyal *et al.*, 1998). There has, however, been a growing concern in the recent years about the deceleration of agricultural output since the early 1990s compared to the high growth phase of the 1980s.

Changes in Size Distribution of Operational Holdings

The NSS 61st Round data as displayed in Figure 2.7 indicate a wide variation in the average size of land possessed by rural households across the major states in India. The average holding size was considerably small in West Bengal in 2003-04 compared to other agricultural states in India. West Bengal accounts for the highest incidence of marginalisation of landholdings among the major agricultural producing states in India. In Rajasthan the average size of landholdings was the highest, while in Kerala it was the lowest during this period.

The smaller average in the size of landholdings in West Bengal, as shown in Figure 2.7, has been largely due to the higher concentration of households within the marginal size class in the land distribution. The higher incidence of landholdings in the marginal class is caused by the land reforms as implemented in the state and also by the mounting demographic pressures on land.

Tables 2.15(a) and 2.15(b) present the distribution of landholdings in terms of percentage of households and area owned, respectively, over different NSS rounds on land holdings in different size classes defined in the Agricultural Census of India.[13] Most of the landholders in West Bengal have been concentrated within the marginal group of landholdings and the share of this group

11. Agricultural population includes cultivators and agricultural labourers.

12. According to the West Bengal Land Reform Act (amended) the landlord-*bargadar* relationship changed in two fundamental ways. First, through anti-eviction measures, the landlords were largely prevented from forcibly throwing the *bargadars* off the land. In fact, the *bargadar* rights were made hereditary and thus, perpetual. Second, the state guaranteed that the *bargadars* would receive a fair share of the crop (75 per cent if the *bargadar* provides the non-labour inputs and 50 per cent if the landlord provides those inputs).

13. The Agricultural Census of India has defined 5 broad size classes of landholdings: marginal (1.000 hectare or less), small (1.001 and 2.000 ha.), semi-medium (2.001-4.000 ha.), medium (4.001-10.000 ha.) and large (more than 10.000 ha.)

increased dramatically from roughly 61 per cent in 1970-71 to nearly 89 per cent in 2002-03. The rate of increase of marginal landholders was very high during 1970-71 to 1980-81 mostly because of tenancy reforms in the form of Operation Barga introduced in the late 1970s. The percentage share of land area within the marginal size class has also been increasing but at different rates. The share of land area in this size class increased at a faster proportional rate during 1991-92 to 2002-03 compared to the previous periods.

FIGURE 2.7

Average Area of Land Possessed (in Hectare) by Rural Households in Major States in India in 2003-04

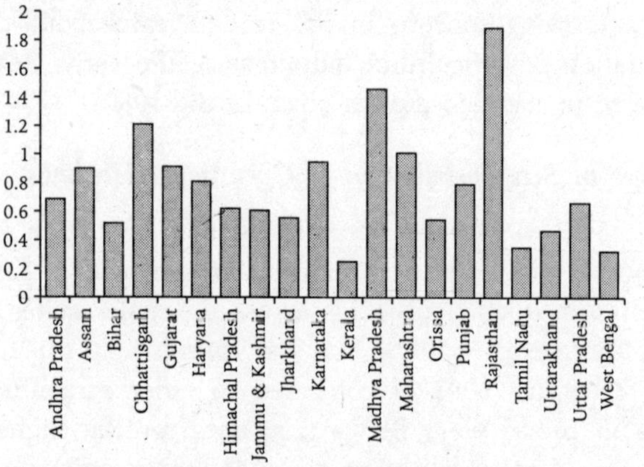

Source: *NSS Report No. 515 (61st Round): Employment and Unemployment Situation in India*. Ministry of Statistics and Programme Implementation, Government of India.

TABLE 2.15(a)

Percentage Distribution of Landholdings

Size Class	*1970-71*	*1981-82*	*1991-92*	*2002-03*
Marginal	61.2	74.3	80.7	88.8
Small	22.8	15.8	13.4	8.9
Semi-medium	12.9	8.1	5	2.1
Medium	3	1.7	0.9	0.2
Large	0.1	0.1	0	0

Source: GoI (2006). *NSS Report No. 492: Some Aspects of Operational Land Holdings in India, 2002-03.*

TABLE 2.15(b)

Percentage Distribution of Area of Landholdings

Size Class	*1970-71*	*1981-82*	*1991-92*	*2002-03*
Marginal	24.8	29.3	40	58.3
Small	28.9	28.8	30.7	26.7
Semi-medium	31.1	28.3	22.1	12.2
Medium	14.6	11.4	7.3	2.7
Large	0.6	2.3	0	0

Source: As in Table 2.15(a).

The pattern of distribution of operational area among different size classes obtained from data provided by the Agricultural Census of India, 2000-01, as displayed in Figure 2.8 is roughly the same as the type of the distribution estimated in NSS 59th Round for the period 2002-03. According to the information available in both of the data sources, the marginal landholding class occupies the major part of the net cropped area with ownership right in West Bengal. The incidence of marginalisation of operational holdings is not uniform across its districts. Table A-2.12 presents percentage of total landholdings and land owned by the marginal and small holding classes across different districts in West Bengal in 2000-01. In East Medinipur marginal farmers took up more than 85 per cent of the total operational land of the district in 2000-01. The concentration of marginalisation in the distribution of landholdings was relatively lower in Bankura, Birbhum and Purulia districts other than the hilly districts of Darjeeling and Jalpaiguri during this period. Small landholding class was dominating in the district of Bankura, while its incidence was the lowest in East Medinipur.

FIGURE 2.8

Percentage Distribution of Area of Operational Landholdings among Different Classes

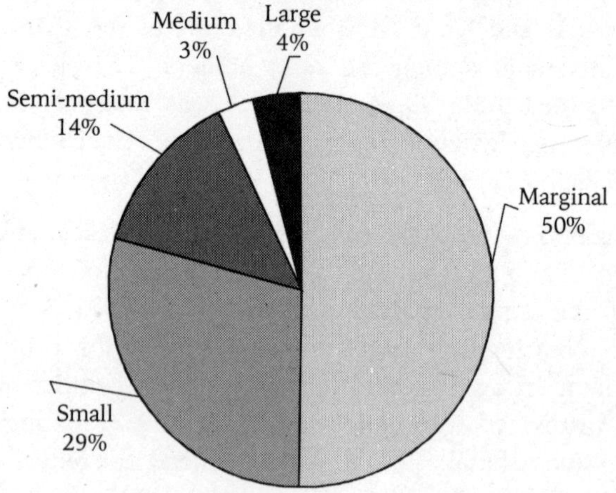

Source: *Agricultural Census of India, 2000-01.*

Table 2.16 presents Gini coefficient of concentration in the size distribution of landholdings estimated by the NSSO for 1970-71, 1980-81, 1991-92 and 2002-03 as observed in West Bengal and the country as a whole. West Bengal has maintained a lower rate of concentration of operational holdings compared to the all-India ratio. Progress in land reforms during the 1980s severely restricted the growth of the larger size groups of operational holdings and their concentration in the state.

Although inequality in land distribution increased marginally in the state following the national trend during the 1970s, it declined consistently at a faster rate compared to the national trend during the subsequent periods. The index of concentration fell sharply between 1991-92 and 2002-03.

TABLE 2.16

Trend in Gini Coefficient of Operational Holdings

	West Bengal	*All India*
1970-71	0.43	0.57
1981-82	0.49	0.60
1991-92	0.43	0.59
2002-03	0.31	0.56

Source: As in Table 2.15(a).

Incidence of Tenancy Farming

This section examines the extent and nature of tenancy and the terms of the tenancy contracts in West Bengal. The data on the number of tenants and the acreage under tenancy are available both in NSSO and Agricultural Census in India. However, the former is considered more reliable as it is based on independent household surveys while the agricultural census is based on a re-tabulation of the land records of owner-cultivators. Again, the share of operated area leased-in is normally a better measure of tenancy than the share of owned area leased-out as lessees have fewer incentives to under-report the extent of area leased-in than that of lessors to understate the leased-out area. For the reasons mentioned above, this report examines the incidence of tenancy by using NSS data on area leased-in.

Table 2.17 presents percentage of tenant holdings and leased-in area in West Bengal and the country as a whole over the three NSS Rounds (37th, 48th and 59th). Roughly 23 per cent of households leased-in land area of around 12 per cent of the operated land area in 1981-82. The respective shares declined to 14 per cent and just above 9 per cent in 2002-03. Despite the incidence of tenancy declined at a sharper rate in West Bengal than the national trend, particularly during the 1980s, the extent of tenancy both in terms of the percentage shares of tenant households and leased-in area in the state was higher than the national rate in 2002-03, and indeed West Bengal has been the second most tenant concentrated state in India.[14]

TABLE 2.17

Percentage of Tenant Holdings and Leased-in Area

	Tenant Holdings	*Leased-in Area*
West Bengal		
1981-82	23.1	12.3
1991-92	14.4	10.4
2002-03	14.1	9.3
India		
1981-82	15.2	7.2
1991-92	11	8.3
2002-03	9.9	6.5

Source: As in Table 2.15(a).

The incidence of produce sharing contracts has been traditionally high in West Bengal where the smaller holdings have a dominant role. In the 1980s and also in the 1990s, the incidence of sharecropping was higher in the state than at the all India level (Table 2.18). But tenancy cultivation in West Bengal has shifted rapidly towards the fixed rental contracts, both in terms of money and produce. As a result sharecropping tenancy declined at a higher proportional rate in the state compared to the national rate over time and in 2002-03, the percentage of sharecroppers in total tenancy in West Bengal had become much lower than the share as observed in the country as a whole (Table 2.18).

TABLE 2.18

Percentage Distribution of Area Leased-in by Terms of Lease

Forms of Contract/Years	*Fixed Money*	*Fixed Produce*	*Share of Produce*	*Others*
West Bengal				
1981-82	2.8	11.9	55.6	29.7
1991-92	8.6	11.7	46.5	33.2
2002-03	23.7	28.5	34.9	12.9
All India				
1981-82	10.9	6.3	41.9	40.9
1991-92	19	14.5	34.4	32.1
2002-03	29.5	20.3	40.3	9.9

Source: As in Table 2.15(a).

The shift of tenancy from produce sharing contracts to fixed rental contract in money terms at a significantly higher rate during the period 1991-92 to 2002-03 was largely due to the higher incidence of leased-in land area

14. In 2002-03, the percentage of tenant holdings was highest in Orissa (19 per cent), while the percentage of leased-in area was highest in Punjab (17 per cent).

within the large holding class who usually opt for fixed money contracts for leasing. Table 2.19 presents the distribution of operational area by types of tenancy among different size classes in West Bengal. While the small and marginal farmers constitute the dominant group of landholdings in the state, the large landholders with holding size more than 10 hectares captured three-fourth of the leased-in land area in 2000-01.

TABLE 2.19

Percentage Distribution of Operational Area among Different Size Classes

	Owned	*Leased-in*	*Other Holdings*	*Partly Owned*
Marginal	53.8	17.6	82.2	41.9
Small	28.7	6.6	11.9	34.7
Semi-medium	13.7	1.4	3.7	18.3
Medium	3.0	0.1	2.2	4.6
Large	0.9	74.3	0.0	0.5

Source: Agricultural Census of India, 2000-01.

2.7 Incidence of Indebtedness

Farmers' indebtedness and the associated agrarian crises have become a serious cause of concern not only in West Bengal but in other states of the country as well. The Situation Assessment Survey (SAS) of farmers carried out in NSS 59th Round reported that around 49 per cent of the farmer households[15] were indebted in India in 2003. The incidence of indebtedness varied widely across the major agricultural states in India: it was the highest in Andhra Pradesh (82.0 per cent), followed by Tamil Nadu (74.5 per cent) and Punjab (65.4 per cent). The average outstanding loan per farmer household was the highest in Punjab, followed by Kerala, Haryana, Andhra Pradesh and Tamil Nadu. In West Bengal, roughly 50 per cent of the farming households were reported to be indebted and 55 per cent of them were cultivators during the same period. Table 2.20 presents percentage distribution of indebted farmer households across different land-ownership classes in West Bengal. The incidence of indebtedness is the highest among marginal farmers.

Rural households are forced to take loans for different purposes. Table 2.21 shows percentage distribution of outstanding loans for different purposes in each size class of landholdings in West Bengal as in 2003. Farmer households of the state utilised roughly 46 per cent of the outstanding loans for farming activities, 44 per cent for consumption and other purposes and the rest for non-farming activities. The marginal landholding groups, however, used a major portion of their total borrowing in consumption and other non-productive purposes simply because their earnings are not sufficient even for basic consumption.

TABLE 2.20

Percentage Distribution of Indebted Farming Households in West Bengal in 2003

Size Class	*Percentage of Indebted Households*
< 0.01	0.7
0.01 - 0.40	58.2
0.40 - 1.00	29.8
1.01 - 2.00	8.5
2.01 - 4.00	2.4
4.01 -10.00	0.4
all sizes	100

Source: NSS 59th Round, *Situation Assessment Survey of Farmers—Indebtedness of Farmer Households*, Report No. 498(59/33/1)

TABLE 2.21

Percentage Distribution of Outstanding Loan by Purpose of Loan across Landholding Classes in 2003

Size Class	*Farming*	*Non-Farming*	*Consumption and Others*
< 0.01	20.7	19.2	60.1
0.01 - 0.40	30.9	15.1	54.0
0.40 - 1.00	50.7	4.7	44.6
1.01 - 2.00	67.7	8.8	23.5
2.01 - 4.00	53.3	12.9	33.8
4.01 -10.00	59.8	0	40.2
All sizes	45.7	10.3	44.0

Source: As in Table 2.20.

The RBI guidelines have set targets for agricultural finance at 18 per cent of net bank credit of which 13.5 per cent for direct finance and 4.5 per cent for indirect finance to agriculture. According to the guidelines, the direct finance to agriculture relates to short-term loans for agricultural inputs and medium and long-term loans for investments that could be provided directly to individual farmers. The indirect finance to agriculture, on the other hand, includes finance in favour of dealers engaged in providing agricultural inputs, electricity boards and food processing units. But most of the public and private sector banks have failed to fulfil the targets. Apart from commercial banks, cooperative banks and the regional rural banks provide financial services to the rural sector in

15. Farmer households include both cultivators and non-cultivators in farming activities.

India. Although the cooperative banking system[16] is a major purveyor of financial services to the rural sector, the Central government ostensibly stepped down from its responsibility for financial restructuring of the cooperative banks on the ground that the ownership of these institutions is vested with state governments (Satish, 2007).

The percentage changes in the contribution of institutional sources to total outstanding loan taken by farmer households in West Bengal as well as in the country as a whole over the past two and a half decades are shown in Table 2.22. While the contribution of institutional sources to total agricultural credit increased during the 1980s at a substantially higher rate in West Bengal compared to the national level, the share had fallen remarkably in the post-reform period. This may be an indication of financial exclusion in agriculture during the post-reform development in India. The incidence of financial exclusion has been fairly well-documented in the NSSO and other field surveys. The findings of NSS 59th Round (2003) reveal that only 27 per cent of the total number of cultivator households received credit from formal sources while 22 per cent received credit from informal sources at the national level. The remaining households, mainly small and marginal farmers, have virtually no access to credit.

TABLE 2.22

Percentage Share of Institutional Sources in Outstanding Cash Debt of Rural Households

Year	*West Bengal*	*India*
1981	65.5	61.2
1991	82.0	66.0
2003	58.0	56.0

Sources: NSS Report Nos. 322 (37th Round), 420 (48th Round) and 498 (59th Round).

When the share of credit access from institutional sources among different size class of farmer households is examined, it becomes apparent that the bulk of the institutional loans have been absorbed by the semi-medium and medium sized farmer. Table 2.23 shows percentage share of institutional and non-institutional sources in outstanding loan taken by farmer households in each size class of land possessed in West Bengal. Small farmers with landholding of over 2 hectares have been relatively favoured by banks in receiving direct agriculture lending. Marginal farmers, on the other hand, continue to depend on non-institutional finance.

Over the last decade and a half, the objectives of the public policy for extending agricultural credit to the vulnerable section of rural households to overcome the historical problems of imperfect and fragmented rural credit markets have been reversed mainly due to the commitment towards financial sector reforms. The financial sector liberalisation of the 1990s has led to a debilitation of the institutional framework for agricultural credit. At the national level the rural branches of commercial banks declined from 58.2 in 1989-90 to 51.7 in 1994-95 and further to 44.48 in 2005-06. Moreover, the RBI stopped its contribution to the national rural credit (long-term operations) fund of the NABARD in the beginning of the financial year 1992-93 (Satish, 2007). This severely constrained the growth of refinance resources available for long-term lending to agriculture.

TABLE 2.23

Percentage Distribution of Outstanding Loans by Source of Loans across Landholding Classes in 2003

Size Class	*Institutional Loan*	*Non-Institutional Loan*
< 0.01	23.4	76.6
0.01 - 0.40	42.7	57.3
0.40 - 1.00	63.1	36.9
1.01 - 2.00	80.1	19.9
2.01 - 4.00	75.4	24.6
4.01 -10.00	21.3	78.7
All sizes	58	42

Source: As in Table 2.20.

2.8 Concluding Remarks

This study reveals that West Bengal, after seriously implementing land reforms, experienced remarkable progress in agriculture. But the deceleration in agricultural growth since the early 1990s, as observed in the state as well as in the country, may be due to several reasons. Some of them are listed below:

- The fall in investment in agriculture, particularly public investment, is one of the most important issues of agricultural development in recent times. But the inadequacy of statistical information on investments in agriculture is a major limitation to capture the issue properly. Investments in canal irrigation constitute the major portion of total

16. This system consists of state cooperative banks, district central cooperative banks, primary agricultural cooperative credit societies, state cooperative agriculture and rural development banks and primary cooperative agriculture and rural development banks.

investments in agriculture on public accounts. Declining public investments and increasing exposure to the markets during the neo-liberal reform period have added to the sufferings of the millions of cultivators, mainly marginal and small farmers in the country. Although the complementarity between public investments and private investments in agriculture has been a debated issue, the Commission for Agricultural Costs and Prices (CACP) has pointed out that the decline in public investment has adversely affected private investment in the eastern region of the country.

- Several documents prepared for the Eleventh Plan focusing on agriculture pointed out that technological exhaustion was the major cause for the severe agrarian crisis and poor agricultural growth during the 1990s (Planning Commission, 2007). Moreover, the intensive cultivation of mono-crop (paddy-wheat sequence) along with a wide imbalance in NPK ratio in the use of chemical fertilisers affected soil fertility adversely (Narayanamoorthy, 1995).
- Farm Management Studies of different years, particularly from the mid-1990s, revealed that the cost of cultivation of most of the crops increased at a higher proportional rate than the rate of increase of value of output of them mainly because of disproportional rise in input and output prices.[17]

Marginalisation of farming may be one of the major causes for lower productivity. NSS 59th Round Report on Consumption Expenditure of Farmer Households noted that monthly receipt from farming with operational area less than 1 hectare was lower than their monthly consumption expenditure. To sustain the achievements of tenancy reforms, the Government of West Bengal should intervene in favour of cooperative farming. It would capture the scale effect in crop output and also generate additional employment opportunities in the rural economy. *Panchayats* are to be involved in a decisive manner in the process to protect the interests of the poor and marginal farmers. Diversification of crops towards horticulture and floriculture may be linked to food processing and allied activities creating employment opportunities in the rural areas. Animal husbandry and fisheries also provide scope for further value addition and multiplier effect on output and employment.

References

Bagchi, A.K. (1998). "Studies on the Economy of West Bengal since Independence", *Economic and Political Weekly* 33(47&48): 2973-78.

Banerjee A., P. Gertler, and M. Ghatak (2002). "Empowerment and Efficiency: Tenancy Reform in West Bengal", *Journal of Political Economy* 110(2): 239-280.

Bhalla, G.S. and G. Singh (1997). "Recent Developments in Indian Agriculture: A State Level Analysis", *Economic and Political Weekly* 32(13): A2-A18.

Bhaumik, S.K. (1993). *Tenancy Relations and Agrarian Development: A Study of West Bengal*. New Delhi: Sage Publications.

Chattopadhyay, M., C. Neogi and S.K. Maity (1993). "Growth and Instability in Crop Production in Eastern India", *Asian Economic Review* 35: 61-94.

Gazdar, Haris. and Sengupta, Sunil (1997). "Agrarian Politics and Rural Development in West Bengal" in Jean Dreze and Amartya Sen(ed.) *Indian Development: Selected Regional Perspectives*. pp 129-204. New Delhi: Oxford University Press.

Government of India (2008). *State-wise Estimates of Value of Output from Agriculture and Allied Activities with New Base Year 1999-2000 (1999-2000 to 2005-06)*. Central Statistical Organisation, Ministry of Statistics and Programme Implementation,

———. (2000). *Mid-term Appraisal on Ninth Five Year Plan (1997-2002)*, Planning Commission, New Delhi.

Gulati, A. and S. Bathla (2001). "Capital Formation in Indian Agriculture: Revisiting the Debate", *Economic and Political Weekly*, May

Narayanamoorthy, A. (1995). "Fertiliser Consumption after Decontrol: Myths and Realities", *Artha Vijnana* 37(4): 359-79.

Nelson, C.R. and C.I. Plosser (1982). "Trends and Random Walks in Macroeconomic Time Series: Some Evidences and Implications", *Journal of Monetary Economics* 10: 139-162.

Planning Commission (2007). *Agricultural Strategy for Eleventh Plan: Some Critical Issues*. Planning Commission, Government of India, New Delhi. May.

Ravallion, M., and G. Datt (1996). "How Important to India's Poor is the Sectoral Composition of Growth in India", *World Bank Economic Review* 10: 1-25.

Ravi, C., and D. Roy (2006). *Consumption Patterns and Food Demand Projections: A Regional Analysis*. Draft Report submitted to IFPRI. New Delhi.

Rawal, V. and M. Swaminathan (1998). "Changing Trajectories: Agricultural Growth in West Bengal, 1950 to 1996", *Economic and Political Weekly* 33

Saha, A. and M. Swaminathan (1994). "Agricultural Growth in West Bengal in the 1980s: A Disaggregation by Districts and Crops", *Economic and Political Weekly* 29

Sanyal, M.K. (2005). "Policy Environment and Agricultural Trends Post Independence India", in Binay Bhusan Chaudhuri (ed.) *Economic History of India from Eighteenth to Twentieth Century* VIII(3), under the project of History of Science, Philosophy and Culture in Indian Civilisation, New Delhi.

Sanyal M.K., P.K. Biswas and S. Bardhan (1998). "Institutional Change and Output Growth in West Bengal Agriculture End of Impasse", *Economic and Political Weekly* 33(47&48): 2979-86.

Satish, P. (2007). "Agricultural Credit in the Post-Reform Era—A Target of Systematic Policy Coarctation", *Economic and Political Weekly* 44(26): 2567-2575, June 30.

Vyas, V.S. (2001). "Agriculture: Second Round of Economic Reforms", *Economic and Political Weekly*, March 10.

———. (1996). "Diversification in Agriculture: Concept, Rationale and Approaches", *Indian Journal of Agricultural Economics* 51(4): 636-643. October-December.

17. During 2000-01 to 2004-05 the value of per hectare *Aman* paddy increased by 21.6 per cent, while cost of cultivation per hectare increased by 30.13 per cent.

Appendix

TABLE A-2.1

Area under Principal Crops by District: 2005-06

(Percentage to total cropped area)

Districts	*Rice*	*Aus*	*Aman*	*Boro*	*Wheat*	*Total Pulses*	*Total Foodgrains*	*Total Oilseeds*	*Jute*	*Potato*
Bankura	85.6	3.5	69.9	12.2	1.5	0.2	87.5	5.9	-	6.2
Birbhum	78.3	1.1	66.8	10.4	6.4	3.9	88.7	7.8	0.0	2.9
Bardhaman	85.6	2.0	55.9	27.7	0.3	0.2	86.1	5.6	2.1	5.8
Cooch Behar	63.0	2.7	52.9	7.5	3.1	2.1	69.1	5.1	15.7	5.4
Darjeeling	30.7	3.9	25.6	1.2	2.0	1.9	58.0	0.4	2.2	5.9
Dinajpur (N)	62.7	0.3	42.4	20.0	8.6	1.2	75.1	9.0	12.1	1.9
Dinajpur (S)	78.1	4.1	58.8	15.3	3.4	0.3	81.9	8.7	6.0	1.1
Hooghly	66.2	2.0	41.2	23.0	0.1	0.5	66.8	6.7	6.6	19.7
Howrah	87.9	1.0	51.3	35.6	0.1	0.3	88.3	3.9	2.3	5.1
Jalpaiguri	55.6	10.3	41.0	4.3	4.1	0.9	63.4	3.0	9.0	5.7
Malda	58.8	1.9	38.8	18.2	12.3	6.8	81.4	10.5	6.0	0.7
Murshidabad	48.5	4.4	27.6	16.5	15.0	6.6	71.0	11.1	15.3	1.2
Medinipur (W)	77.4	4.8	58.2	14.4	1.4	0.8	79.8	10.0	0.6	8.4
Medinipur (E)	91.3	3.3	57.1	30.9	0.0	2.3	93.7	4.2	0.3	0.7
Nadia	44.5	7.7	18.7	18.0	7.9	7.8	60.4	17.2	20.1	0.9
Purulia	87.8	0.5	86.9	0.4	1.1	4.3	97.2	1.8	-	0.4
24 Parganas (N)	69.3	4.5	40.6	24.2	1.9	2.9	74.0	11.2	12.1	1.4
24 Parganas (S)	92.5	0.5	79.2	12.8	0.8	2.1	95.4	3.1	0.3	0.5

Source: B.A.E.S, *Statistical Handbook, West Bengal, 2006.*

TABLE A-2.2

Area and Production of Fruits and Vegetables: 2005-06

Districts	*Fruits*		*Vegetables*	
	Area	*Production*	*Area*	*Production*
Bankura	3.74	43.1	51.63	808.81
Birbhum	3.58	44.36	46.15	566.23
Bardhaman	7.634	75.174	56.926	639.124
Cooch Behar	5.13	73.51	51.68	938.37
Dinajpur (N)	8.023	130.839	33.529	360.602
Dinajpur (S)	3.915	42.678	45.232	553.667
Darjeeling	11.055	186.503	22.363	240.627
Hooghly	12.16	145.16	52.57	585.38
Howrah	2.88	52.09	13.6	168.24
Jalpaiguri	10.26	210.03	51.83	732.82
Malda	28.59	196.51	50.52	635.46
Murshidabad	21.71	233.96	77.78	1152.76
Nadia	12.5	184.81	79.1	1077.12
Medinipur (E)	8.42	142.47	51.12	395.41
Medinipur (W)	4.07	71.13	43.852	575.18
Purulia	2.9	39.44	33.22	471.43
24 Parganas(N)	17.99	297.26	64.39	765.74
24 Parganas(S)	8.13	141.7	64.33	811.95

Note: Area in '000 hectares and production in '000 tonnes.

Source: As in Table A-2.1.

TABLE A-2.3

Growth Rates of Production: Food Grains

Periods/Districts	*1981-2005*	*1981-1990*	*1991-2005*
Bankura	3.1*	7.2*	0.2
Birbhum	3.6*	6.0*	3.4*
Bardhaman	3.6*	5.8*	1.8*
Cooch Behar	2.4*	4.8*	2.4*
Dinajpur (N+S)	3.9*	4.4*	3.6*
Hooghly	2.8*	3.8*	1.6**
Howrah	2.8*	7.2*	1.3
Jalpaiguri	2.1*	1.6	2.5*
Malda	3.1*	5.4*	1.9*
Murshidabad	3.7*	5.2*	3.2*
Nadia	3.5*	7.6*	1.9*
Medinipur (E+W)	3.8*	6.3*	1.7*
Purulia	3.3*	6.1**	2.6***
24 Parganas (N+S)	3.2*	5.7*	1.3*

Note: * significant at less than 1 per cent level, ** significant at less than 5 per cent level, *** significant at less than 10 per cent level, the rest are insignificant.

Source: B.A.E.S, *Statistical Abstract (1978 to 1989, 1993-94, 2001-02, 2002-03), Statistical Handbook, 2006.*

TABLE A-2.4

Growth Rates of Production: Rice

Periods/Districts	*1980-2005*	*1980-1990*	*1991-2005*
Bankura	3.4*	7.4*	0.2*
Birbhum	3.5*	6.5*	3.0*
Bardhaman	3.6*	6.2*	1.9*
Cooch Behar	2.4*	4.6*	2.4*
Dinajpur (N+S)	4.3*	5.7*	3.2*
Hooghly	3.0*	4.1*	1.6**
Howrah	3.0*	7.6*	1.3*
Jalpaiguri	2.0*	1.2	2.0*
Malda	3.3*	6.1*	1.8*
Murshidabad	4.4*	7.6*	3.0*
Nadia	4.4*	9.9*	1.4**
Medinipur (E+W)	3.8*	6.5*	1.6*
Purulia	3.4*	5.8**	2.6*
24 Parganas (N+S)	3.3*	5.9*	1.0**

Note: * significant at less than 1 per cent level, ** significant at less than 5 per cent level, the rest are insignificant.

Source: As in Table A-2.3.

TABLE A-2.5

Growth Rates of Production: Wheat

Periods/Districts	*1980-2005*	*1980-1990*	*1991-2005*
Bankura	-1.4***	-2.0	-0.5
Birbhum	3.7*	0.5	9.4*
Bardhaman	-4.0*	-11.0*	4.4**
Cooch Behar	1.7*	6.5*	2.1
Dinajpur (N+S)	1.5*	-2.3	4.6*
Hooghly	-11.9*	-18.1*	-9.5*
Howrah	-1.5	-17.5*	6.9***
Jalpaiguri	4.5*	6.3*	4.6*
Malda	4.5*	8.6*	1.9*
Murshidabad	2.8*	2.3	2.8*
Nadia	0.6	-0.4	1.6*
Medinipur (E+W)	2.9*	-2.6	5.1*
Purulia	4.2*	5.0	4.3**
24 Parganas (N+S)	0.5	4.2	3.5**

Note: * significant at less than 1 per cent level, ** significant at less than 5 per cent level, *** significant at less than 10 per cent level, the rest are insignificant.

Source: As in Table A-2.3.

TABLE A-2.6

Growth Rates of Production: Pulses

Periods/Districts	*1980-2005*	*1980-1990*	*1991-2005*
Bankura	-9.0*	-7.6*	-10.6*
Birbhum	1.9**	-8.2*	6.9*
Bardhaman	-4.6*	-10.5*	4.6
Cooch Behar	1.1**	3.9*	-0.2
Dinajpur (N+S)	-4.8*	-7.2*	-9.5*
Hooghly	-7.7*	-16.4*	7.5**
Howrah	-17.0*	-8.9*	-12.2*
Jalpaiguri	-1.7*	-8.1*	2.5
Malda	-3.1*	1.0	-1.9
Murshidabad	-1.1	-6.7*	2.9**
Nadia	-1.0	3.6*	2.1
Medinipur (E+W)	-0.9	1.5	0.6*
Purulia	-1.3	7.5*	-3.7**
24 Parganas (N+S)	-2.2*	-5.6	0.8

Note: * significant at less than 1 per cent level, ** significant at less than 5 per cent level, the rest are insignificant.

Source: As in Table A-2.3.

TABLE A-2.7

Growth Rates of Production: Oilseeds

Periods/Districts	*1980-2005*	*1980-1990*	*1991-2005*
Bankura	1.9*	9.8*	-0.8
Birbhum	2.9*	17.3*	4.6*
Bardhaman	0.7	6.6*	1.9
Cooch Behar	5.0*	6.2*	4.5*
Dinajpur (N+S)	3.4*	13.6*	1.6
Hooghly	2.8*	11.8*	-0.5
Howrah	1.8*	0.5	2.2
Jalpaiguri	2.5*	7.4*	1.5
Malda	5.7*	14.0*	9.4*
Murshidabad	5.0*	10.6*	5.3*
Nadia	6.6*	13.4*	2.9*
Medinipur (E+W)	9.6*	17.0*	4.5*
Purulia	1.7	24.5*	-5.1*
24 Parganas (N+S)	6.3*	18.7*	1.3

Note: * significant at less than 1 per cent level, the rest are insignificant.

Source: As in Table A-2.3.

TABLE A-2.8

Growth Rates of Production: Jute

Periods/Districts	*1980-2005*	*1980-1990*	*1991-2005*
Bankura	-11.0*	0.1	-21.5*
Birbhum	0.5	-8.9	-0.3
Bardhaman	2.4*	-2.6	3.8*
Cooch Behar	3.4*	3.8*	3.6*
Dinajpur (N+S)	4.1*	-5.0	5.4*
Hooghly	4.5*	1.0	2.9**
Howrah	5.1*	-5.4	8.5
Jalpaiguri	0.1	3.3*	0.9
Malda	-0.7	-0.5	2.4***
Murshidabad	4.6*	5.5	3.7*
Nadia	2.5*	3.8	1.1**
Medinipur (E+W)	-1.0***	-0.6	-3.7*
Purulia	Nil	Nil	Nil
24 Parganas (N+S)	3.5*	-2.6	5.4*

Note: * significant at less than 1 per cent level, ** significant at less than 5 per cent level, *** significant at less than 10 per cent level, the rest are insignificant.

Source: As in Table A-2.3.

TABLE A-2.9

Growth Rates of Production: Potato

Periods/Districts	*1980-2005*	*1980-1990*	*1991-2005*
Bankura	6.8*	15.4*	2.1**
Birbhum	4.8*	12.8*	3.8*
Bardhaman	2.9*	6.8*	2.5*
Cooch Behar	15.3*	18.1*	9.7*
Dinajpur (N+S)	8.9*	2.7*	13.7*
Hooghly	3.6*	7.4*	0.4
Howrah	6.2*	11.0*	7.9*
Jalpaiguri	18.3*	19.1*	13.8*
Malda	8.5*	9.2*	7.0*
Murshidabad	4.3*	2.5*	4.2*
Nadia	5.7*	1.0*	6.5*
Medinipur (E+W)	7.7*	14.2*	1.8**
Purulia	4.4*	13.6*	4.1**
24 Parganas (N+S)	5.1*	2.5*	7.2*

Note: * significant at less than 1 per cent level, ** significant at less than 5 per cent level, the rest are insignificant.

Source: As in Table A-2.3.

TABLE A-2.10

Consumption of Chemical Fertilisers ('000 Metric Tonnes)

Periods/Districts	*1980-81*	*1990-91*	*2000-01*	*2006-07*
Bankura	13.2	34.5	54.6	75.7
Birbhum	19.5	54.4	64.6	81.2
Bardhaman	41.8	85.8	118.1	175.1
Cooch Behar	6.8	33.0	58.0	35.2
Darjeeling	3.3	15.1	32.2	42.4
Dinajpur (N+S)	14.6	39.3	60.9	95.5
Hooghly	36.6	76.6	102.3	145.6
Howrah	13.9	41.6	57.9	20.2
Jalpaiguri	4.8	23.7	53.8	43.9
Malda	13.4	44.2	43.3	94.1
Medinipur (E+W)	32.3	87.7	162.9	213.2
Murshidabad	24.0	55.1	51.6	137.5
Nadia	24.2	52.5	51.1	90.9
Purulia	6.1	27.6	46.9	13.6
24 Parganas (N+S)	28.2	73.6	126.8	100.9
West Bengal	282.8	753.0	1085.1	1365.1

Source: As in Table A-2.3.

TABLE A-2.11

Land Distribution and Land Recording by Districts (As on 2007): Percentage of State's Total

Districts	*Land Distributed*		*Land Recorded*	
Bankura	5.7	(5.9)	6.0	(7.6)
Birbhum	4.3	(5.4)	10.2	(7.4)
Bardhaman	5.5	(7.3)	10.4	(8.7)
Cooch Behar	5.7	(4.4)	7.4	(5.5)
Darjeeling	2.8	(1.8)	1.5	(0.8)
Dinajpur (N)	6.5	(5.1)	2.0	(2.1)
Dinajpur (S)	4.6	(4.4)	4.8	(4.7)
Howrah	0.4	(0.9)	2.2	(2.8)
Hooghly	1.2	(2.4)	5.6	(7.5)
Jalpaiguri	9.0	(4.4)	8.6	(4.0)
Malda	6.9	(5.3)	7.0	(5.3)
Medinipur (E)	4.4	(7.7)	4.7	(10.9)
Medinipur (W)	20.8	(22.5)	6.9	(9.9)
Murshidabad	4.1	(5.4)	6.0	(5.6)
Nadia	2.0	(3.4)	4.2	(4.2)
Purulia	6.6	(3.1)	0.8	(0.6)
24 Parganas (N)	2.7	(4.9)	4.3	(4.8)
24 Parganas (S)	6.8	(5.7)	7.6	(7.5)

Note: Figures in parentheses give percentage of beneficiaries.

Source: Government of West Bengal, *Economic Review*, 2007-08.

TABLE A-2.12

Percentage Distribution of Area of Landholdings by Districts: 2000-01

	Total Landholdings		*Landholdings Owned*	
	Marginal	*Small*	*Marginal*	*Small*
Bankura	42.93	46.39	45.34	44.03
Birbhum	49.02	44.55	53.00	40.82
Bardhaman	50.49	39.50	56.11	34.81
Cooch Behar	59.04	36.79	59.34	36.83
Darjeeling	26.77	14.34	50.97	28.34
Dinajpur (N)	57.61	36.26	57.66	37.01
Dinajpur (S)	55.23	41.09	57.51	38.91
Hooghly	64.99	32.06	65.66	31.55
Howrah	80.35	18.63	79.46	19.58
Jalpaiguri	38.20	21.56	57.23	31.44
Malda	61.66	34.84	63.99	32.65
Medinipur (W)	67.97	30.34	71.48	27.13
Medinipur (E)	85.74	13.72	86.95	12.67
Murshidabad	57.03	38.74	60.73	35.88
Nadia	56.81	41.08	56.20	41.59
Purulia	49.73	44.39	49.65	44.32
24 Parganas (N)	66.50	31.97	68.97	29.86
24 Parganas (S)	67.44	31.11	68.86	30.11

Source: Agricultural Census of India, 2000-01.

FIGURE A-2.1

Temporal Changes in Annual Incremental Rates of Area, Production and Yield

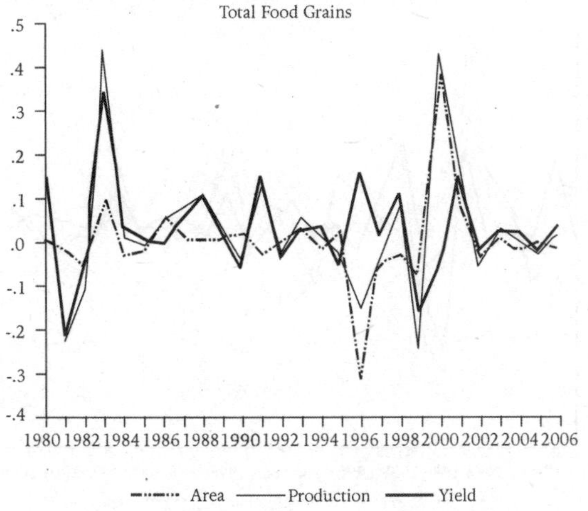

Source: *Agriculture at a Glance*. Director of Economics and Statistics, GoI; Directorate of Agriculture, Evaluation Wing, Government of West Bengal.

FIGURE A-2.2

Temporal Changes in Annual Incremental Rates of Area, Production and Yield

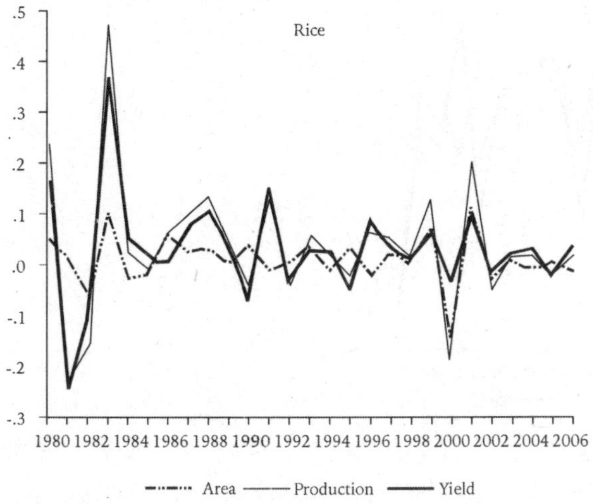

Source: As in Figure A-2.1.

FIGURE A-2.3

Temporal Changes in Annual Incremental Rates of Area, Production and Yield

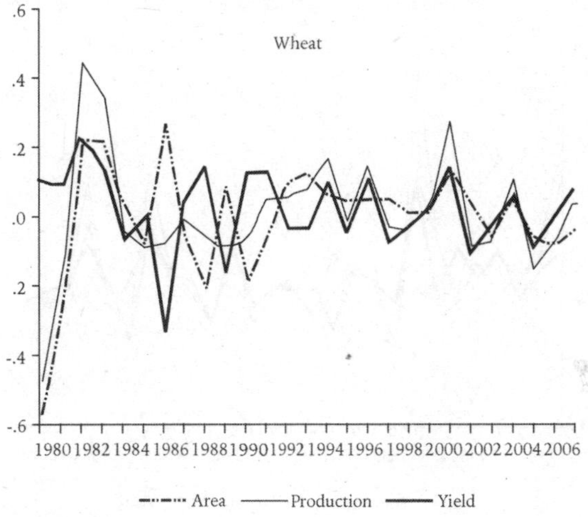

Source: As in Figure A-2.1.

FIGURE A-2.4

Temporal Changes in Annual Incremental Rates of Area, Production and Yield

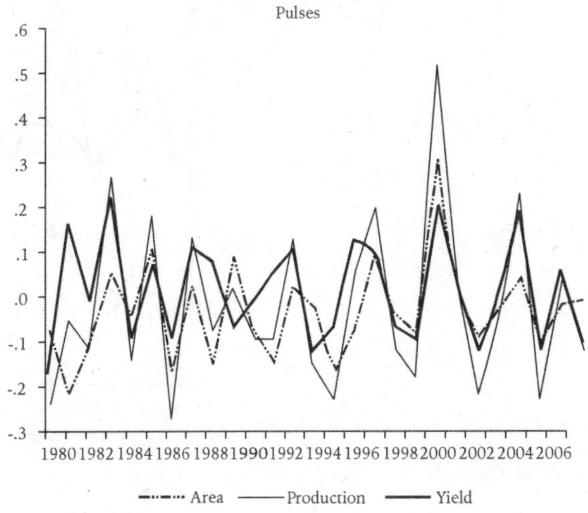

Source: As in Figure A-2.1.

FIGURE A-2.5

Temporal Changes in Annual Incremental Rates of Area, Production and Yield

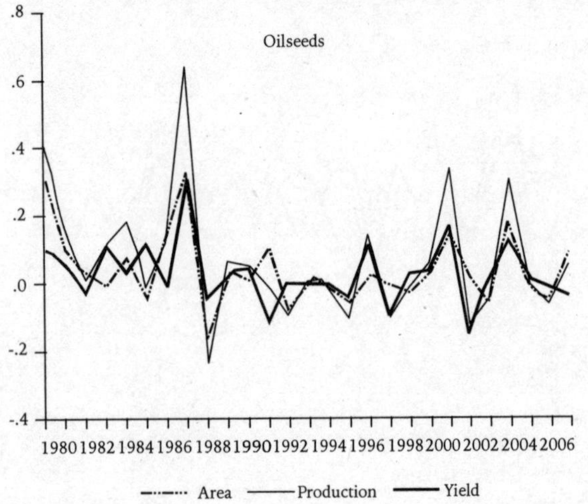

Source: As in Figure A-2.1.

FIGURE A-2.6

Temporal Changes in Annual Incremental Rates of Area, Production and Yield

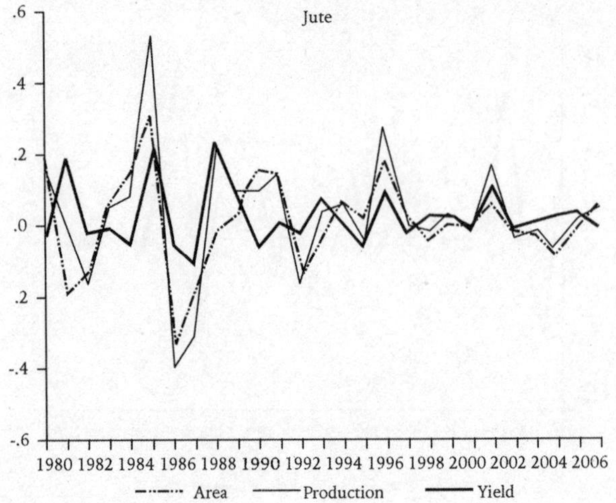

Source: As in Figure A-2.1.

FIGURE A-2.7

Temporal Changes in Annual Incremental Rates of Area, Production and Yield

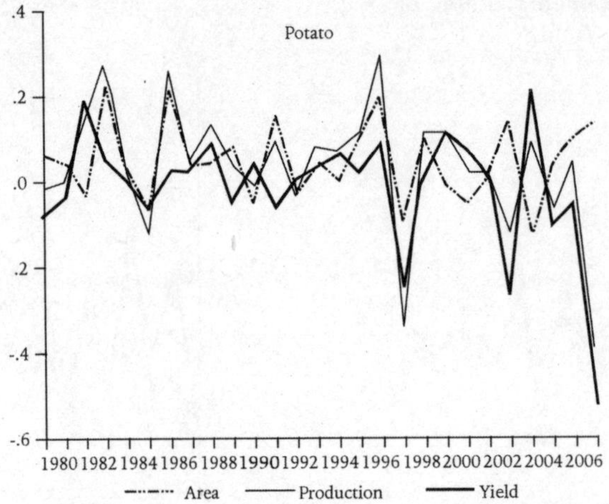

Source: As in Figure A-2.1.

Chapter 3

Industry

3.1 Introduction

This chapter is an exploration of industrial development, particularly in the registered manufacturing sector, in West Bengal over the past three decades. In India, different regions have been growing at uneven rates. The regional disparities in growth have been highly associated with unequal incidence of industrial development (Kaldor, 1975). In terms of new industrial investment, the western and southern states have gained, and the eastern states are in decline. Gujarat, in the western part, for example, shared 16 per cent of the industrial investment in medium and large scale industries in the country between 1991 and 2003, and ranked second (next to Maharashtra) in terms of such investment among the major states in India (Hirway, 1998). In West Bengal, an eastern region state, on the other hand, the share of new investment in industries was less than 4 per cent during this period.[1] The western region states have continued to dominate the eastern region states in terms of their shares of value added and employment in the factory sector of the country.

One of the major factors influencing manufacturing growth in any country and in any region within a country is the nature of government policies at the national level as well as at the regional level. During the regulated-policy regime the Central government directly and indirectly influenced the pace of industrialisation of every state in the country. West Bengal got not only a disproportionately smaller share of industrial licences but the number of industrial licences received by the state declined rapidly as well during the period of state control. While public investment, particularly in steel and engineering, in the eastern region, from the end of the First Five Year Plan period,[2] stimulated some growth in West Bengal, that stimulus was not enough to compensate for the relative sluggishness of private investment (Bagchi, 1998).

3.2 Industrial Policies of the Government of West Bengal

Before the end of the 1980s, the pattern of industrialisation within a particular state was mainly determined by the industrial policies of the Union Government. Thereafter, states in the country got some flexibility in implementing their own economic policies under the guideline of national policies. The government of West Bengal had its own proposals for an alternative economic policy on the vital issues of industrial development, rehabilitation of sick units, generation of employment opportunities and protection of the legitimate interest of the labour. The state industrial policy of 1993, and also of the latter years, of the government of West Bengal provides a package of assistance for establishment of new units, expansion of existing units and rehabilitation of sick units. Since the other states were competing for attracting industrial investment, in emulation of other states, many tax concessions were also announced in the different state budgets of the government of West Bengal.

Author, Dr. Panchanan Das, is a Senior Lecturer in Economics in West Bengal Education Service, and is gratefully indebted to Prof. Amiya Kumar Bagchi, Director, Institute of Development Studies, Kolkata, for helpful comments.

1. As per the data on industrial entrepreneurs memorandums (IEMs) provided by the CMIE: Gujarat (2003), June, total investment in Gujarat is about Rs. 168,186 crore and in West Bengal total investment comes to about Rs. 40243 crore over the period 1991 and 2003. Maharashtra is at the top in attracting new industrial investment amounting to Rs. 230,043 crore, 22 per cent share of investment under IEMs in India during the same period.

2. A number of public sector establishments like the Durgapur Steel Plant, Alloy Steel Plant, Mining & Allied Machinery Corporation, Chittaranjan Locomotive Works, Hindustan Fertiliser Corporation, etc., were established in West Bengal during the 1950s.

The government of West Bengal announced the Incentive Scheme, 2000, (notification no. 91-CI/H/4F-54/2000 dated 13.02.2001) for setting up large, medium and small scale industrial units in the state. Under this scheme an eligible industrial unit, defined in the notification, is entitled to enjoy investment subsidy as well as interest subsidy along with some other incentives at the rates specified in the notification. The rate and type of incentive depend on the location of the industrial unit. The West Bengal Industrial Development Corporation (WBIDC) has been working as a single window to assist large-scale industrial units in the state. Similarly, Small Industry Development Agency (SIDA) has been set-up to provide assistance to small scale industries.

3.3 Value Added, Employment and Number of Factories: Share of West Bengal to All-India Level

West Bengal was the second most industrialised state of the major states in terms of value-added and was at the top in terms of number of factories and employment even in the mid-1960s in spite of its rapid slow down from the very beginning of Independence of the country.[3] Thereafter, the state started to lose its industrial primacy. Public investment in West Bengal fell down and the rate of industrial growth declined further through the process of deindustrialisation. The industrial recession in the state was the most severe and long lasting. Accordingly, the state experienced a fall in its relative share of number of factories, net value-added and employment over the past four decades. Its share of net value-added in the factory sector had fallen from more than 14 per cent in 1971 to 4 per cent in 2002. The employment share in this sector dropped from 16 per cent to 7 per cent during the same period. But West Bengal dominated today's industrial Gujarat, both in terms of output and employment shares in the 1970s and also in the early 1980s in spite of its recessionary phase in industrial growth (Das, 2007).

TABLE 3.1

Percentage Shares of West Bengal to All-India: Number of Factories, Net Value-Added and Employment in Manufacturing Industries

Year	*Number of Factories*	*Net Value-Added*	*Employment*
1971	9.87	14.38	16.19
1981	6.60	10.41	12.01
1991	5.01	6.29	9.04
2002	4.74	4.16	6.99

Source: Das, 2007.

TABLE 3.2

Percentage Shares of Factories, Net Value-Added and Employment by Two-Digit Industries in West Bengal

Industry Groups (NIC Codes)	*Number of Factories*			*Net Value-Added*			*Employment*		
	1981	*1991*	*2002*	*1981*	*1991*	*2002*	*1981*	*1991*	*2002*
Food products (20-21)	16.63	15.99	17.48	2.94	5.12	2.32	7.80	7.43	9.28
Beverages, tobacco (22)	0.65	1.20	8.02	0.66	0.95	4.25	0.57	0.83	3.39
Textiles (23-25)	5.95	4.16	3.50	18.94	14.02	13.32	30.69	27.48	34.92
Textile products (26)	2.40	2.03	1.59	0.58	0.69	0.56	0.73	0.67	0.77
Wood, furniture (27)	4.66	4.39	3.94	0.44	0.45	0.26	0.61	0.73	1.19
Paper, printing (28)	6.40	6.62	5.22	4.60	2.69	2.85	3.70	3.02	2.75
Leather (29)	1.93	2.22	4.00	1.45	0.72	1.23	1.58	1.43	2.15
Chemicals (30)	5.81	6.26	6.19	4.61	7.68	11.64	4.45	4.55	5.49
Rubber, petroleum (31)	5.30	5.84	6.13	4.68	7.38	2.26	2.75	3.33	2.96
Non-metallic products (32)	3.23	3.83	3.29	2.34	1.85	2.23	2.55	2.43	2.58
Basic metals (33)	12.56	11.84	9.30	18.72	14.08	10.55	13.02	14.89	15.31
Metal products (34)	9.98	9.25	7.18	3.51	2.74	2.39	2.84	2.84	2.88
Machinery (35-36)	14.22	15.00	13.77	14.93	12.69	6.57	10.04	9.71	7.31
Transport equipment (37)	4.47	3.59	2.94	11.99	9.06	2.53	11.81	8.98	5.29
Other manufacturing (38)	1.46	1.41	1.60	0.92	1.03	1.14	0.96	1.15	0.94

Source: As in Table 3.1.

3. In the late 1940s more than 600,000 workers were engaged in various industries in the organised sector in West Bengal—a figure equalling the total employment in the factories of the present Maharashtra and Gujarat put together.

3.4 Industrial Structure

In terms of value-added, the leading industries in West Bengal manufacture basic metals, chemicals and textiles. Table 3.2 shows the shares of factory units, net value-added and employment in the registered sector over different time periods in West Bengal. While the relative importance of chemicals grew over the last two decades, the share of basic metals and textiles declined considerably during the same period. The relative weight of transport equipment in the manufactures of the state also went down at a rapid rate after the early 1980s. In West Bengal, textiles contributed more than 13 per cent of net value-added absorbing more than one-third employees to the state's factory sector in 2002. While the share of net value-added of textiles declined throughout (by 6 per cent between 1981 and 2002), its employment share increased in the 1990s. The share of factory units in this sector declined from 6 per cent in 1981 to 3.5 per cent in 2002. Basic metals industry is the second most dominating industry in the state contributing 10 per cent of net value-added and 15 per cent of employment to the state's registered sector in 2002. The shares of net value-added and number of factories of this industry declined but its employment share increased over time. While both the net value-added and employment shares declined in transport equipments industries, they were increasing in chemical industries in the state during 1981-2002.

In British India, while cotton textiles were dominated by the domestic capitalists, jute textiles were controlled by the British businessmen. At that time, a major portion of both the jute and cotton goods was sold abroad. Today, a large portion of output of these two industries has been catered in the domestic market and they are facing crises partly owing to the economic policy of the Union Government. While the packaging policy of the Government of India is an impediment to the survival of the jute industry, the growth of cotton textile has been limited by sluggish per capita consumption of its product.[4] The domestic sector accounts for 85 per cent of the total demand for jute products and a major part of it goes to packaging. But the jute industry is facing a problem of low demand largely because of the increase in use of synthetic material for packaging.

3.5 Characteristics of Manufacturing Industries in the Registered Sector

Table 3.3 presents figures of capital intensity (fixed capital stock per employee), labour productivity (gross value-added per employee) and emoluments per employee in the registered manufacturing sector in West Bengal. Capital intensity in registered manufacturing increased during 1981-2002, but it is much lower in the factory sector in West Bengal than, for example, in the western region, state of Gujarat (Das, 2007). Labour productivity measured by value-added per employee in this sector in the state also increased, but emolument per employee remained at the same level during this period. Table 3.4 gives a comparative statement of the major structural ratios of the two-digit manufacturing industries in the factory sector in West Bengal in 2002. Capital intensity varies widely across two-digit industries in the state. Capital-labour ratio varied between 1.3 in textiles and 26 in machineries among two-digit manufacturing industries in 2002. Relatively higher capital-intensive industries in the state were chemicals, petroleum products and basic metals. The remaining industries were considerably less capital-intensive.

Labour productivity increased but unevenly across the two-digit industry group, during 1981-2002. Labour productivity was higher, and growing at a higher rate in chemical industries. It was the minimum in food products industry group. Wood, furniture, transport equipments and textiles were the relatively slow growing industries in the state over the period 1981-2002.

TABLE 3.3

Characteristics of Manufacturing Industries

	1981	*1991*	*2002*
Capital intensity	1.38	3.3	5.44
Value-added per employee	0.41	0.67	1.47
Emolument per employee	0.11	0.14	0.15

Note: Capital intensity is measured by the value (Rs. lakh) of fixed capital at 1993-94 prices per employee; value-added per employee is expressed in lakh rupees; emolument per employee is expressed in lakh rupees per annum.

Source: As in Table 3.1.

Employees are not paid similarly for similar kinds of job in manufacturing industry (Table 3.4). Employees in petroleum, basic metals, transport equipments and machinery were paid relatively better than in other industries at the beginning of the present century. Emoluments were lower in food products, beverages, non-metallic products and textile industries. But, in most of the industries, emolument per employee was higher in West Bengal compared to that prevailed in the western

4. *Economic Review* (2005-06), Government of West Bengal.

region states, particularly Gujarat, despite higher labour productivity in Gujarat (Das, 2007).

TABLE 3.4

Characteristics of Two-Digit Industries (2002)

Industry Groups (NIC Code)	*Capital Intensity*	*Value-Added Per Employee*	*Emolument Per Employee*
Food products (20-21)	2.68	0.42	0.06
Beverages, tobacco (22)	2.76	1.58	0.08
Textiles (23-25)	1.26	0.49	0.13
Textile products (26)	1.91	0.97	0.11
Wood, furniture (27)	1.72	0.33	0.06
Paper, printing (28)	6.40	1.42	0.18
Leather (29)	2.47	0.80	0.14
Chemicals (30)	20.48	3.25	0.19
Rubber, petroleum (31)	17.63	1.51	0.23
Non-metallic products (32)	4.90	1.16	0.12
Basic metals (33)	10.05	1.21	0.22
Metal products (34)	2.59	1.07	0.15
Machinery (35-36)	25.92	1.20	0.18
Transport equipment (37)	3.04	0.64	0.19
Other manufacturing (38)	2.04	1.70	0.17

Note: Capital intensity is measured by the value (Rs. lakh) of fixed capital at 1993-94 prices per employee; value-added per employee is expressed in lakh rupees; emolument per employee is expressed in lakh rupees per annum.

Source: As in Table 3.1

3.6 Output and Employment Growth in Registered Manufacturing

Many studies have documented a mismatch between output growth and employment growth in Indian manufacturing in the 1980s, leading to virtually jobless growth. The situation has been no different in West Bengal. Figure 3.1 displays the time paths of values of gross output, measured in left vertical axis and number of employees, measured in right vertical axis, in the factory sector in West Bengal. Industrial output grew up consistently with some fluctuations, but the level of employment in registered industries declined in the 1980s followed by a stagnating or rising phase in the earlier decade.

Output and employment growth estimated from the ASI data for all industries taken together located in West Bengal are shown in Table 3.5. West Bengal has been lagging behind the western region states in terms of the growth rates of output and employment in the factory sector. While output growth in total manufacturing (both registered and unregistered) of West Bengal improved considerably in the 1980s and further in the 1990s compared to the rate in the 1970s (this has been discussed in Chapter 1), the rate of growth of industrial output in the registered sector declined during these periods. Thus, the increase in the rate of growth of output in the manufacturing sector of the state in the 1990s or after the mid-1980s, was mainly due to the better performance of the unregistered sector. Employment in registered industries in West Bengal declined throughout the period and job losses in this sector took place at a higher rate, both in the 1980s and 1990s.

FIGURE 3.1

Output and Employment in Registered Manufacturing

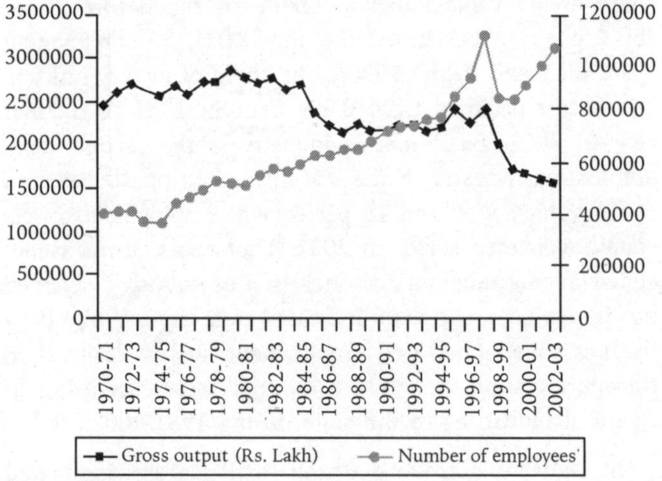

Source: Das, 2007.

TABLE 3.5

Output and Employment Growth in the Factory Sector

Periods	*Output Growth*	*Employment Growth*
1970-2002	3.07	-1.37
1970-1980	3.83	0.88
1981-1990	2.79	-3.18
1991-2002	2.80	-3.60
1970-1985	3.29	0.13
1986-2002	3.02	-1.88

Note: Growth rates are estimated by using semi-logarithmic trend equation and are statistically significant at 1 per cent level.

Source: As in Table 3.1.

The analysis of output and employment growth across industry groups in the state can be carried out by utilising the ASI two-digit disaggregated data at the state level. Table 3.6 displays the growth rates of output and employment across two-digit industry groups in West Bengal for the period 1979-2002. Growth rates varied widely across two-digit industries within the state over the years. In West Bengal, beverages followed by chemicals and non-metal products grew more rapidly all through and they performed better in the 1990s compared to their growth performance in the 1980s. The rate of growth of output in textiles, paper including printing industries and basic metals in the state also increased in the 1990s. Growth of machineries and transport equipments, on the other hand, was affected adversely experiencing negative and statistically insignificant growth in the post-reform period. There had also been no significant growth improvement for the remaining industries in the state in this period.

Employment growth in almost all industries in West Bengal was negative during 1979 to 2002. In textiles, the absorber of more than one-third of the factory workers, in the state, employment had fallen at the rate of 4 per cent in the 1980s and although employment growth improved in the next decade, it still remained negative during the period 1991-2002. Basic metals, another important industry group absorbing more than 15 per cent of total factory sector workers in this state, displayed job losses throughout the period and at a higher rate in the 1990s. The rate of loss of employment was highest in transport equipment industry group. Beverage industries in West Bengal alone experienced positive employment growth and the rate improved significantly in the 1990s compared to the previous decade. But the relative importance of this industry group in providing employment is very low. Job losses widened across industries and became more severe during the period 1991 to 2002.

The data relating to ASI sectoral division of workers highlight some contrasting features of labour absorption in the registered manufacturing sector in West Bengal and Gujarat (Table 3.7). Around one-fourth of the industrial workforce in West Bengal has been absorbed in the public sector, whereas in Gujarat the share of public sector employment in registered manufacturing is less than 2 per cent in 2001. Only 8 per cent factory workers in West Bengal are in contractual jobs, while in Gujarat this share is as high as around 30 per cent. Thus, the faster output growth of the organised sector did not generate employment on a permanent basis in industrial state of Gujarat.

TABLE 3.6

Output and Employment Growth in Registered Manufacturing: Two-Digit Industries

Industry Groups (NIC Codes)	*Output Growth*			*Employment Growth*		
	1979-2002	*1979-1990*	*1991-2002*	*1979-2002*	*1979-1990*	*1991-2002*
Food products (20-21)	2.91	3.70	4.25	-0.63***	-3.15	-0.50***
Beverages, tobacco (22)	9.01	3.81*	10.49	6.85	-2.73	8.99
Textiles (23-25)	0.99	-1.45*	3.41	-1.95	-4.05	-0.71***
Textile products (26)	4.64	2.81***	5.32*	-2.03	-4.44	-3.56*
Wood, furniture (27)	2.16*	3.83**	4.64***	0.60**	-1.79*	1.48***
Paper, printing (28)	1.57	-1.81***	5.07	-3.11	-5.77	-4.78
Leather (29)	4.31	3.03	5.33*	-1.15	-3.08	1.78**
Chemicals (30)	6.05	4.22	7.86	-1.28	-1.86	-1.36*
Rubber, petroleum (31)	3.77	5.49	5.74	-1.78	-0.48***	-4.39
Non-metallic products (32)	4.74	1.73	7.67	-2.11	-3.17	-3.28
Basic metals (33)	2.87	0.43***	4.63	-1.71	-1.88*	-2.94
Metal products (34)	3.11	1.90***	3.23	-2.02	-3.09	-3.10
Machinery (35-36)	1.10*	0.98	-1.04***	-3.04	-3.07	-5.53
Transport equipment (37)	-0.63***	0.28***	-3.29***	-5.70	-5.67	-11.46
Other manufacturing (38)	7.11	7.84	6.26***	-1.61*	-0.94***	-4.43**

Note: In estimating output and employment growth across two-digit industries, fixed effect panel regression model in log linear form is used. In y = a + bt +u; y gives gross output/number of workers and t denotes time variable, industry groups are cross section units.

* significant at 5 per cent level, ** significant at 10 per cent level, *** insignificant; the rest are significant at 1 per cent level.

Source: As in Table 3.1.

TABLE 3.7

Percentage of the Number of Workers to the Total Number of Workers in Registered Manufacturing, 2000-2001, according to the Type of Sector and Employment

	West Bengal	*Gujarat*
Public sector	25.67	1.82
Joint sector	1.28	4.65
Private sector	73.05	93.53
Directly employed	92.06	69.97
Contact workers	7.95	30.03

Source: As in Table 1.

As a significant portion of the workers in registered manufacturing industries are engaged in the public sector in West Bengal, much of the job losses are in public sector enterprises in the state, but we cannot verify this owing to the lack of ownership-wise data at the state level. Job losses in Gujarat manufacturing industries, on the other hand, are mostly in the private sector. Workers in both of the states were affected adversely in the past decades due to the closure of a large number of jute mills in West Bengal and cotton mills in Gujarat. During the period 1987-1990, for example, over 45,000 workers in jute mills lost their jobs as a result of lockouts in 15 mills (Bagchi, 1998). The sickness and ultimate mortality of such industries are likely to increase further in the post-reform phase causing a sharp rise in frictional unemployment.

3.7 Sources of Employment Growth

Decompositions of employment growth into growth rates of labour-capital ratio, capital-output ratio, output per factory and number of factories[5] in the registered manufacturing sector in West Bengal for different periods are presented in Table 3.8. Employment growth in manufacturing is largely determined by the technology used in production. Job destroying technology reflected by the negative growth of labour-capital ratio is highly attributable to zero or negative employment growth in manufacturing activities. Labour-capital ratio decreased in the state over different period. Labour intensity in manufacturing production in the registered sector declined round the years in almost every industry group in the state. Basic chemicals, leather, wood and non-metallic mineral products in West Bengal registered relatively larger fall of this ratio in the post-reform period. Beverages in West Bengal alone showed a rise in labour intensity during this period. Negative employment growth in West Bengal manufacturing was not only due to the labour displacing technology but also because of the closure of many factories in the state.

TABLE 3.8

Sources of Employment Growth in Registered Manufacturing

Period	*Employment*	*Labour-Capital Ratio*	*Capital-Output Ratio*	*Output Per Firm*	*Number of Firm*
1970-71 to 2002-03	-1.5	-3.7	-0.7	3.1	-0.2
1970-71 to 1985-86	-0.6	-1.8	-1.6	3.7	-0.9
1985-86 to 2002-03	-2.3	-5.5	0.1	2.5	0.5

Note: Growth rates are calculated by taking average of annual growth rates in percentage.

Source: As in Table 3.1.

3.8 Growth Rates of Productivity and Wage in the Factory Sector

The way of fixing wages even in registered industries hardly reconciles the positive relation between productivity

5. In order to understand why the productivity growth does not pass on to employment growth sufficiently, employment growth needs to be decomposed into different components by utilising a simple algebra. We may think labour employment in registered manufacturing, as in other sectors, depends on the nature of technology adopted by a firm (A), level of output produced by a firm (Y) and the number of firm (F) in that sector:

$$L = f(A, Y, F) \qquad (3.1)$$

Technology can be represented as the product of labour intensity and capital-output ratio:

$$A = \frac{L}{K} \times \frac{K}{Y} \qquad (3.2)$$

Use of labour-intensive technology obviously raises employment of labour at a faster rate than capital employment. Similarly, larger the size of a firm, in terms of output, larger will be the employment of labour as for increasing the number of factory units, higher would be the level of total employment. Thus, total employment growth rate can be approximated as the sum of growth rates of labour-capital ratio, capital-output ratio, output per firm and number of firms:

$$L = \left(\frac{L}{K}\right) + \left(\frac{K}{Y}\right) + \left(\frac{Y}{F}\right) + F \qquad (3.3)$$

The first term in the right hand side is the growth of labour intensity, the second term is the growth of capital-output ratio, the third term is the growth of average size of a firm in terms of output and the last term is the growth of number of firms in organised manufacturing industry. The mathematical decomposition shown in equation (3.3) helps to identify the main sources for employment growth in the manufacturing sector.

TABLE 3.9

Wage and Productivity Growth by Two-Digit Industries

Industry Groups (NIC Codes)	*Real Wage*			*Productivity*		
	1979-2002	*1979-1990*	*1991-2002*	*1979-2002*	*1979-1990*	*1991-2002*
Food products (20-21)	0.1***	6.4	-1.9**	2.6*	18.4	-0.4***
Beverages, tobacco (22)	-2.7	0.4***	-4.2	3.5***	-26.7***	-2.2***
Textiles (23-25)	1.9	0.7***	1.2	3.0	-4.6	3.0
Textile products (26)	1.7	4.5	0.1***	3.3*	16.8***	2.7***
Wood, furniture (27)	0.8*	0.9	0.0***	-1.5	-0.4***	-4.2
Paper, printing (28)	1.1	-1.8	0.9	4.5	-1.1***	6.7
Leather (29)	0.2***	-0.8***	0.5***	5.0	7.2*	8.9
Chemicals (30)	1.5	2.2	0.5***	8.6	1.6***	10.5
Rubber, petroleum (31)	2.9	1.4	2.2	1.1***	0.7***	-4.9***
Non-metallic products (32)	1.2	2.0*	0.5	5.3	1.5	7.6
Basic metals (33)	1.6	1.3***	1.9	3.3	2.6***	7.2
Metal products (34)	0.8	-0.1***	1.3	3.6	1.0***	3.8
Machinery (35-36)	1.1	1.0***	0.5	3.5	3.7***	2.8
Transport equipment (37)	1.6	3.2	0.4***	2.1	4.4	1.0***
Other manufacturing (38)	-0.6***	0.5***	-2.5*	4.9	31.4*	5.2**
Adjusted R-squared	0.9995	0.9999	0.9998	0.9976	0.9997	0.9981
Durbin-Watson stat	1.5457	2.2219	1.9959	1.8131	2.4052	2.1231

Note: Growth rates are estimated by applying fixed effect pooled regression model. * significant at 5 per cent level, ** significant at 10 per cent level, *** insignificant; the rest are significant at 1 per cent level.

Source: As in Table 3.1.

and wage in organised manufacturing industries in a developing country like India. Table 3.9 presents the estimated growth rates of wage per worker and labour productivity across two-digit industry groups over different periods in West Bengal. In most of the industries, labour productivity grows at a faster proportional rate than growth rate of wage per labour.

The growth rates of wage and productivity varied widely across major industries in the state. Growth rate of real wage ranges between -2.7 per cent in beverages and tobacco industries to 2.9 per cent in petroleum products, but productivity growth varies from -1.5 per cent in wood and furniture industry group to 8.6 per cent in chemicals over the period 1979-2002.

Rate of growth of real wage per labour declined in almost every industry group in the state during the period 1991-2002 compared to the previous period, and indeed in many industries there had been actual fall of wage rate in real terms in this period. Maximum fall in wage rate took place in food products industries followed by textile products in the deregulation phase compared to the earlier period. Labour productivity in a large number of industries in West Bengal also declined during the post-reform period, but at a disproportional rate. Disproportional growth of productivity and wage rate as observed may be the cause of added vulnerabilities and insecurities among the working class.

3.9 Concluding Remarks

In West Bengal, the manufacturing sector has not performed as an engine of growth over the past three decades in a causal sense. The rate of growth of labour demand is given by the excess of the rate of growth of output over the rate of growth of labour productivity. Output growth in the manufacturing sector has played an insignificant role in promoting employment growth in the state.

The slower manufacturing growth in the eastern region of the country between the mid-1960s and late 1970s was the focus of a serious academic debate (Ahluwalia, 1985; Nayyar (ed.), 1994). Also there were several criticisms of the country's industrial policy framework, mostly on the regime of licensing, for regional diversities in growth. In many cases, the intended purpose of controls was undermined by the might of oligopoly business houses (Bagchi, 1970 and Chandrasekhar, 1988).

The economic reforms in the line of de-licensing of most industries accompanied by disinvestment and withdrawal of subsidies have provided scope for new opportunities for the growth of giant enterprises, particularly transnational enterprises, and also have created new threats to domestic small industrial units in the form of increasing vulnerability of such enterprises (Bhaduri, 2005). Faster productivity growth in the registered manufacturing sector in the post-reform period is not related with the increase in employment and indeed, higher productive efficiency in this sector in a high growth region like Gujarat is associated with macro-inefficiency in terms of unemployment.

References

Ahluwalia, I.J. (1985). *Industrial Growth in India, Stagnation Since the Mid-Sixties*. Delhi: Oxford University Press.

Bagchi, A.K. (1970). "Long-Term Constraints on India's Industrial Growth, 1951-1968", in E.A.G. Robinson and Kidron Michael (eds.) *Economic Development in South Asia*. London: Macmillan.

———. (1998). "Studies on the Economy of West Bengal since Independence", *Economic and Political Weekly* 33(47, 48): 2973-78.

Bhaduri, A. (2005). "Joblessness", *Brazilian Journal of Political Economy* 25(2): 45-59.

Chandrasekhar, C.P. (1988). "Aspects of Growth and Structural Change in Indian Industry", *Economic and Political Weekly* 23(45-47): 2359-70.

Das, P. (2007). "Output, Employment and Productivity Growth in Indian Manufacturing Industries: 1970-71 to 2002-03: A Comparative Study of West Bengal and Gujarat", *Ph.D. Dissertation* submitted to Calcutta University.

Hirway, I. (1998). "Paradigms of Development: Issues in Industrial Policy in India", *Queen Elizabeth House Working Paper Series, Working Paper* Number 22.

Kaldor, N. (1975). "Economic Growth and the Verdoorn Law - A Comment on Mr. Rowthorn's Article", *Economic Journal* 85: 891-96.

Nayyar, D. (ed.) (1994). *Industrial Growth and Stagnation: The Debate in India*. Oxford.

APPENDIX

TABLE A-3.1

Sources of Employment Growth: Two-Digit Industries in West Bengal

Industry Group (NIC Code)	*Labour-Capital Ratio*		*Capital-Output Ratio*		*Output Per Firm*		*Number of Firm*	
	1979-1990	*1991-2002*	*1979-1990*	*1991-2002*	*1979-1990*	*1991-2002*	*1979-1990*	*1991-2002*
Food products (20-21)	-4.9	-7.7	0.3	4.4	4.7	1.1	-2.1	1.0
Beverages and tobacco (22)	-37.2	4.6	27.1	-5.7	7.0	-5.3	-1.7	15.6
Textiles (23+24+25)	-9.8	-5.2	3.5	2.8	5.6	3.0	-4.5	-1.8
Textile products (26)	-6.1	-8.7	-2.2	1.0	5.8	6.0	-2.0	-0.5
Wood and wood products (27)	-2.6	-10.3	5.4	4.9	-4.6	7.9	-1.2	-1.0
Paper and paper products (28)	-7.7	-6.9	6.2	1.5	-0.5	2.7	-3.1	-0.6
Leather and fur products (29)	-6.3	-10.7	4.0	3.9	2.2	1.7	-1.9	3.0
Basic chemicals and chemical products (30)	-12.1	-12.1	7.0	2.1	3.5	8.1	0.7	0.2
Rubber, plastic and petroleum products (31)	-6.7	-9.4	-0.9	2.4	3.0	4.2	-1.2	1.8
Non-metallic mineral products (32)	-5.3	-10.2	1.0	2.4	1.4	6.6	0.1	-0.6
Basic metals and alloys (33)	-7.0	-6.6	5.7	-0.4	4.3	6.0	-1.5	-1.6
Metal products (34)	-6.3	-8.0	5.3	1.6	-1.2	4.9	-3.4	-1.4
Machinery and equipment (35+36)	-6.7	-8.0	2.9	3.4	2.0	0.2	-1.0	0.1
Transport equipment (37)	-6.9	-7.3	3.7	0.8	1.9	1.0	-3.7	-1.5
Other manufacturing industries (38)	-5.2	-10.9	-21.6	4.9	24.8	2.1	-1.9	1.5

Source: As in Table 3.1.

FIGURE A-3.1

Annual Growth Rates: Manufacturing in West Bengal

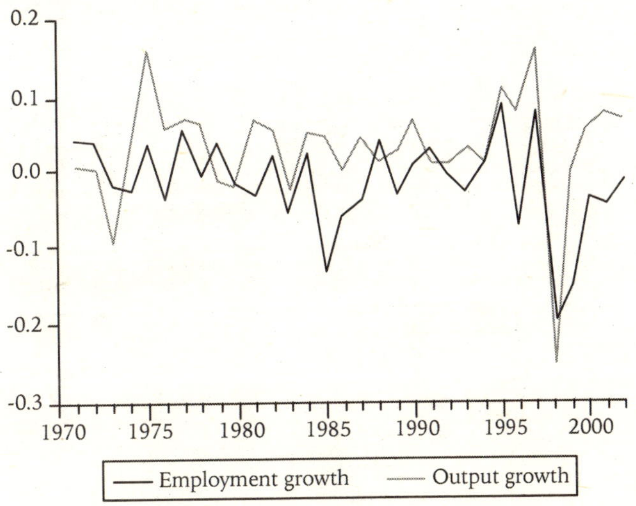

Source: As in Figure 3.1.

Chapter 4

The Services Sector

The size of the tertiary sector—comprising transport and communication, trade, hotels and restaurant, banking and insurance, real estate and ownership of dwelling and business services, public administration, other services—in terms of share of NSDP at constant prices, has been larger than either the primary or the secondary sector in the state (Figure 4.1).

FIGURE 4.1

Share of the Services Sector in NSDP

Percentage of Services in NSDP

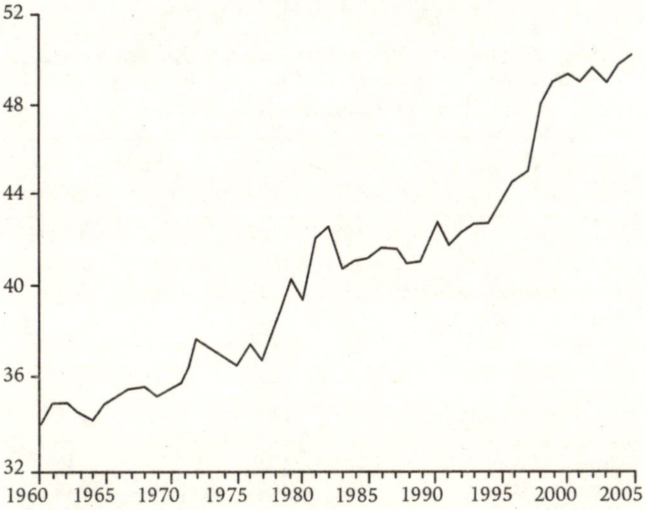

Source: The Economic and Political Weekly Research Foundation (EPWRF). *Domestic Product of States of India: 1960-61 to 2000-01*; Government of West Bengal. *Economic Review (2007-08)*.

As per capita income rises, demand shifts away first from the agricultural commodities and, then, even from industrial goods; more and more demand is created for services such as education, health, tourism, etc. Thus, an increasing share of national/state income originates in the services. If the labour productivity remained unchanged, the services sector also generates relatively more employment.

The alternative hypothesis suggests that as economic specialisation and automation amplify with economic growth, the services once provided within the firm or household are contracted out of the organisation to specialised agencies, i.e., the same product now shift the place, from the sector of production to the sector of distribution (i.e., services). This may mean that the same volume of services is being provided as before but these services are now measured as a separate market activity. However, it is possible that increased specialisation leads to higher service quality and/or lower costs, which would increase the demand for, and production of such services.

The third hypothesis explains the growing relative importance of service in national/state employment by the slower growth of labour productivity in services than in the industry. The slower average growth in labour productivity in services will mean higher average cost in services. If the demand for services is relatively inelastic, then as the economy expands, the share of services in total employment as well as income would increase.

In West Bengal, the responsiveness of the growth of the services activities to the growth of the commodity sector (agriculture and allied activities and manufacturing) and to the growth of real income of the rest of the economy is found to be more than proportional in such sub-sectors as trade, banking and transport (Tables 4.1 and 4.2). Growth in sectors like real estate and public administration was less than proportional to the growth in the rest of the state's economy.

TABLE 4.1

Relationship between Real Income from Services and Commodity Sector (Aggregate of Agriculture and Allied Plus Manufacturing), 1980-81 to 1998-99

Service Activity	*Elasticity*	*t-Ratio*	*R2*	*DW-Statistic*
Trade, hotel and restaurant	1.2454	55.5926	0.9945	2.5884
Banking and insurance	1.5072	22.3954	0.9671	2.0187
Transport, storage and communication	1.7456	14.6269	0.926	1.2031
Real estate, ownership and business service	1.0195	11.9412	0.8928	0.5695
Public administration	1.0734	9.253	0.8327	1.7472
Others services	0.7327	27.9262	0.9786	1.6542

Note: Elasticities are computed from the following function, log Sj = α + β log Yc, where Si is the real income from sector i and y is real SDP.

Source: NSSO. "Unorganised Service Sector in India, 2001-02", *Characteristics of Enterprises*, NSS 57th Round (July 2001-June 2002), Report No. 483.

TABLE 4.2

Relationship between Real Income from Services and the Rest of the WB Economy, 1980-81 to 1998-99

Service Activity	*Elasticity*	*t-Ratio*	*R2*	*DW-Statistic*
Trade, hotel and restaurant	1.1177	31.023	0.9826	1.5525
Banking and insurance	1.847	28.5148	0.9795	1.856
Transport, storage and communication	1.6235	19.0187	0.9549	1.1351
Real estate, ownership and business service	0.9117	13.6365	0.9158	0.3387
Public administration	0.9651	10.0612	0.8549	1.5382
Others services	0.6426	47.0439	0.9923	1.802

Note: Elasticities are computed from the following function, log Sj = α + β log Yc, where Si is the real income from sector i and y is real SDP.

Source: NSSO. "Unorganised Service Sector in India, 2001-02", *Characteristics of Enterprises*, NSS 57th Round (July 2001-June 2002), Report No. 483.

The tertiary sector, rural and urban taken together, employment in the state was 51.4 lakh in 1983. Thereafter, it increased steadily and in 2004-05, total employment in the sector was 90.4 lakh. Of course, the services economy in the urban is larger than the rural in terms of employment. Notwithstanding, during 1983 to 2004-05, the sector in rural West Bengal grew at a rate (3.56 per cent) which was higher than that in the urban. Moreover, between 1999 and 2005, urban tertiary sector had displaced about 3 lakh workers, while the rural sector created additional 9.5 lakh jobs.

4.1 Unorganised Services Economy

In rural West Bengal, own account service enterprises in 'other transport and related activities' accounted for the

TABLE 4.3

West Bengal: Usual Status/Workers in the Tertiary Sector, 1983 to 2004-05

(Nos. in lakh)

Year	*Aggregate (Rural + Urban)*	*Rural*	*Urban*
1983	51.4	21	30.4
1993-94	74.7	34.7	40
1999-2000	83.4	34.3	49.1
2004-05	90.4	43.8	46.6

Source: NSSO. "Unorganised Service Sector in India, 2001-02", *Characteristics of Enterprises*, NSS 57th Round (July 2001-June 2002), Report No. 483.

highest share, followed by the 'real estate, renting and business activities'[1], 'Mechanised road transport', shared the highest number of service establishments in the rural. To note, the survey did not cover the service sector enterprises pursuing the activities of wholesale and retail trade, repair of motor vehicles, motorcycles and personal and household goods (G); financial intermediation (J); public administration and defence (L); private households with employed persons (P) and extra-territorial organisations and bodies (Q).

In the urban, 'education' accounts for the largest number of own account service enterprises. This was followed by 'other transport and related activities'. Of the urban services establishments, the largest is 'restaurants', in numbers (Table 4.4), In terms of employment, however, 'education' is the leading sub-sector within the rural 'own

TABLE 4.4

Estimated Number of Unorganised Service Enterprises, by Tabulation Category/Activity and by Sector and Type of Enterprise, 2001-02

Tabulation Category & NIC Code	*Rural*		*Urban*	
	OAE	*Establishment*	*OAE*	*Establishment*
Hotels(H1)	137	358	836	1152
Restaurants (H2)	84831	13853	46539	22184
Storage & warehouse (I1)	395	221	2188	198
Mechanised road transport (I2)	14215	26862	25113	9289
Other transport and related activities(I3)	396405	3505	139145	2805
Communication (I4)	6141	1444	7957	8859
Real estate, renting & business activities (K)	51783	15302	49909	16486
Education (M)	152932	3825	141594	9383
Health & social work(N)	84140	4072	42755	10175
Other community social & personal services(O)	106992	6776	37650	12725
All	897971	76218	493686	93256

Source: NSSO. "Unorganised Service Sector in India, 2001-02", *Characteristics of Enterprises*, NSS 57th Round (July 2001-June 2002), Report No. 483.

1. NSSO, *Unorganised Service Sector in India, 2001-2002, Characteristics of Enterprises*, NSS 57th Round (July 2001-June 2002), Report No. 483.

account service enterprises', this was followed by 'other community social and personal services'. The highest share of employment in rural service establishments was that of 'mechanised road transport' (Table 4.5).

TABLE 4.5

Estimated Numbers of Workers in Unorganised Service Enterprises, by Tabulation Category/Activity and by Sector and Type of Enterprise, 2001-02

Tabulation Category & NIC Code	*Rural*		*Urban*	
	OAE	*Establishment*	*OAE*	*Establishment*
Hotels(H1)	287	2443	2054	10842
Restaurants (H2)	115965	38969	73051	90013
Storage & warehouse (I1)	786	1446	2315	1086
Mechanised road transport (I2)	15457	74871	26076	34796
Other transport and related activities(I3)	40062	11100	142610	17356
Communication (I4)	10246	3222	12308	24549
Real estate, renting & business activities (K)	68510	50968	59082	105737
Education (M)	156287	24920	143830	68749
Health & social work(N)	97361	19663	46054	53654
Other community social & personal services(O)	144424	30780	81645	60493
All	1009948	258383	589024	467276

Source: NSSO. "Unorganised Service Sector in India, 2001-02", *Characteristics of Enterprises*, NSS 57th Round (July 2001-June 2002), Report No. 483.

TABLE 4.6

Number Per Thousand Enterprises, by Problems Faced, 2001-02

Type of Problem	*Rural*	*Urban*
No specific problem	217	248
Non-availability of electric connection	18	8
Power cut	26	23
Shortage of capital	218	252
Marketing of products/services	163	135
Lack of other infrastructure facility	119	51
Local problems	40	53
Harassment	11	36
Competition from others	426	443
Non-availability of labour	1	2
Labour problem	8	4
Fuel not available or costly	4	6
Non-recovery of service charges/fees/credits	100	54
Others	35	26

Source: NSSO. "Unorganised Service Sector in India, 2001-02", *Characteristics of Enterprises*, NSS 57th Round (July 2001-June 2002), Report No. 483.

In the urban, like in the rural, the largest number of the workforce remained engaged in own account enterprises of 'education', followed by 'other transport and related activities'. In urban service establishments, 'real estate, renting and business activities' provided most of the employment. In the rural as well as urban areas, the major problems faced by the services enterprises are competition from others, shortage of capital and marketing of products/services (Table 4.6).

4.2 Comparative Growth Status

TABLE 4.7

Rural: Distribution of Enterprises (per Thousand) by Growth Status (Over a Period of Last 3 Years)

States	*Expanding*	*Stagnant*	*Contracting*	*Not Applicable*	*N.R.*
West Bengal	260	528	112	100	1
Gujarat	219	572	102	107	0
Tamil Nadu	218	526	45	211	0
Madhya Pradesh	192	603	75	129	0
Bihar	182	742	46	30	0
Uttar Pradesh	132	509	182	176	1
Andhra Pradesh	111	592	111	185	0
Karnataka	108	438	173	281	0
Maharashtra	108	438	173	281	0
Orissa	90	621	177	112	0
India	165	557	124	154	0

Source: NSSO. "Unorganised Service Sector in India, 2001-02", *Characteristics of Enterprises*, NSS 57th Round (July 2001-June 2002), Report No. 483.

TABLE 4.8

Urban: Distribution of Enterprises (per Thousand) by Growth Status (Over a Period of Last 3 Years)

States	*Expanding*	*Stagnant*	*Contracting*	*Not Applicable*	*N.R.*
West Bengal	322	457	93	126	2
Bihar	234	626	43	97	0
Tamil Nadu	211	553	81	155	0
Uttar Pradesh	188	454	147	211	0
Madhya Pradesh	182	483	179	156	0
Karnataka	157	551	79	214	0
Maharashtra	150	475	167	208	0
Orissa	138	583	144	135	0
Gujarat	102	622	85	191	0
Andhra Pradesh	78	587	147	188	0
India	176	507	131	185	0

Source: NSSO. "Unorganised Service Sector in India, 2001-02", *Characteristics of Enterprises*, NSS 57th Round (July 2001-June 2002), Report No. 483.

An inter-state comparison of the growth status (over a period of the last three years of the NSS Survey) reveals that in terms of the percentage of services enterprises those are expanding, in the rural as well as urban, West Bengal stands above all other major states in India (Tables 4.7 and 4.8).

TABLE 4.9

Districts in West Bengal: Share (%) of Primary, Secondary and Tertiary Sectors in Respective District Domestic Product at Constant Prices

District	*Sector*	*1990-91*	*1991-92*	*1992-93*	*1993-94*	*1994-95*	*1995-96*	*1996-97*	*1997-98*	*1998-99*	*1999-2000*
24 Parganas (South)	Primary	35.1	38.4	39.2	31.7	34.1	30.2	31.6	28.2	27.9	27.7
	Secondary	18.5	12.5	17.2	27.9	26.7	29.9	24	29.6	29.3	29.5
	Tertiary	46.4	44.1	43.6	40.4	39.2	39.9	44.4	42.2	42.8	42.8
Kolkata	Primary	0.7	0.8	1.3	1.5	1	0.8	0.9	0.8	0.7	1
	Secondary	32.4	32.5	31.6	24.3	23.8	24	20.6	18.7	18.6	18.6
	Tertiary	66.9	66.7	67.1	74.2	75.2	75.2	78.5	80.5	80.7	80.4
Nadia	Primary	44.2	45.4	44.6	48.8	48.7	47.5	43.8	43.9	42.5	40.9
	Secondary	16.2	16.5	16.5	14.6	14	14.5	17.6	17.3	17.5	18.3
	Tertiary	39.6	38.1	38.8	36.6	37.3	38	38.6	38.8	40	40.8
Murshidabad	Primary	47.2	41.1	41.1	45.5	45.9	44	43.2	42.7	41	38.2
	Secondary	25.1	25.7	25.9	18.7	18.1	19.5	20.1	19.9	35.5	21.4
	Tertiary	33.7	33.2	33	35.8	36	36.5	36.7	37.4	23.4	40.4
Uttar Dinajpur	Primary	48.5	44.5	49.2	53	54.3	51.4	50.5	50.5	49.7	48.2
	Secondary	15	9.8	14.1	8.9	8.3	9.1	9.3	8.9	8.8	9.4
	Tertiary	36.5	45.7	36.7	38.1	37.4	39.5	40.2	40.6	41.5	42.4
Dakshin Dinajpur	Primary	_	43.7	46.3	50.5	51.8	49.1	48.4	48.4	48	46.3
	Secondary	_	20.7	16.9	9.4	9.2	9.7	9.9	9.9	9.8	10.4
	Tertiary	_	35.6	15.6	40.1	39	41.2	41.7	41.7	42.2	43.3
Malda	Primary	44.8	43.4	41.5	52.7	52.8	52.3	50	52.1	48.4	47.2
	Secondary	18	18.1	19.3	10.8	10.4	10.7	11.9	11.1	12.1	13.5
	Tertiary	37.2	37.8	39.2	36.5	36.8	37	38.1	36.8	39.5	39.3
Bardhaman	Primary	33.9	33.9	34.1	41.8	41	38.3	37.6	38.1	37.5	35
	Secondary	31	30.6	30.2	22.9	23.3	24.4	29.5	24.3	24.2	25.5
	Tertiary	35.1	35.5	35.7	35.3	35.7	37.3	33.5	37.6	38.3	39.5
Bankura	Primary	48.1	48	46.5	50.1	51.4	50	49.3	50.3	45.6	45.6
	Secondary	19.6	20	20.6	13.4	12.6	13.4	13	12.4	13.9	14.1
	Tertiary	32.3	42	32.9	36.5	36	36.6	37.7	37.3	40.5	40.4
Medinipur	Primary	36.3	41.5	38.6	43.3	43.9	41.7	42.1	41.7	39.2	39.1
	Secondary	25.4	23.1	24.7	18.3	17.8	18.9	17.8	17.7	18.3	18.5
	Tertiary	38.3	35.4	36.7	38.4	38.3	39.4	40.1	40.6	42.5	42.4
Howrah	Primary	9.9	11.6	11.6	15.8	15.8	14	13.8	14.1	13	13
	Secondary	50.7	49.2	48.7	31	30.7	32.4	33.9	32.3	32.1	32.4
	Tertiary	39.4	39.2	39.7	53.2	53.5	53.6	52.3	53.6	54.9	54.6
Hooghly	Primary	31.4	34.7	32.4	34.8	35	33.9	33.7	31.9	38.5	21.5
	Secondary	36.5	34.2	35.3	25	24.7	25.6	24.1	23.3	29.8	30.4
	Tertiary	32.1	31.1	32.3	40.2	40.3	40.5	40.2	44.8	31.7	48.1
24 Parganas (North)	Primary	23.2	24.5	22.8	25.2	24.3	23.5	22.9	23	23.5	29.3
	Secondary	36.2	35.2	35.7	29.4	29.8	30.9	30.9	30	29.3	41.4
	Tertiary	40.6	40.3	41.5	45.4	45.9	45.6	46.2	47	47.2	29.3
Jalpaiguri	Primary	43.9	44.1	45.4	44.4	43.3	42.2	40.9	41.9	40.4	40
	Secondary	19.5	18.7	20.4	22.8	20.5	21	20.1	19.4	19.5	19.8
	Tertiary	36.6	37.2	34.2	32.8	36.2	36.8	39	38.7	40.1	40.2
Darjeeling	Primary	37.4	42.3	38	31.5	32.4	11.6	26.2	46.7	34.8	33.1
	Secondary	18.9	18.4	17	28.2	27.6	11.4	30.2	25.5	25.5	26.2
	Tertiary	43.7	39.3	45	40.3	40	77	43.6	27.8	39.7	40.7
Cooch Behar	Primary	46.9	48	46.1	57.4	56.2	54.9	53.7	53.9	52.9	50.7
	Secondary	11.1	9.8	11.4	7.8	7.9	8.3	8.6	8.5	11.8	9.5
	Tertiary	42	42.2	42.5	34.8	35.9	36.8	37.7	37.6	35.3	39.8
Purulia	Primary	38.5	38.5	4.8	44.6	46.8	44.4	42.1	46.7	40.6	42.7
	Secondary	17.8	18.1	17.4	14.8	14	14.8	15.8	13.9	15.8	15.4
	Tertiary	43.7	43.4	41.8	40.6	39.2	40.8	42.1	39.4	43.6	41.9
West Bengal	Primary	31.3	32.8	32	35.9	36.2	34.3	33.9	33.9	32.5	29.5
	Secondary	27.3	27.1	26.8	21.3	21	21.9	21.5	20.9	21.2	20.5
	Tertiary	41.4	40.1	41.2	42.8	42.8	43.8	44.6	45.2	46.3	50

Source: Government of West Bengal. *District Statistical Hand Book*. Bureau of Applied Economics & Statistics.

TABLE 4.10

Growth of the IT Industry in West Bengal

Year-wise No. of Units Issued Registration by STPK (No.)	*Total No. of Units Issued Registration by STPK (Cumulative) (No.)*	*No. of Operating Units under STPK during the Year (No.)*	*No. of Exporting Units under STPK during the Year (No.)*	*Value of Software Exports by STPK Units Rs. million*	*Estimated Value of Total Software Exports (Including Non-STPK) Rs. million*
6	6	3	3	0	60
2	8	8	3	30	120
3	11	11	4	60	150
9	20	20	6	90	200
4	24	24	14	180	600
7	31	27	17	390	1000
8	39	30	27	940	2000
138	177	55	47	1790	3500
59	236	81	66	3720	5000
13	249	105	76	6110	8000
23	272	114	90	8320	12000
21	293	122	102	12520	16000
26	319	144	112	17410	22000
39	358	166	142	22040	27000

Source: STP Kolkata.

Excepting Bardhaman, Howrah, Cooch Behar and Purulia, in all other districts in the state, the primary sector lost its significance in terms of its share in DDP. The share of the secondary sector also declined in most of the districts, except in 24 Parganas (North and South), Darjeeling and Nadia. The share of the sector in Howrah-erstwhile, major location of industries in the state, declined substantially from 50.7 per cent in 1990-91 to 32.4 per cent in 1999-2000. The share of the secondary sector in the state, as a whole, declined from 27.3 per cent in 1990-91 to 20.5 per cent in 1999-2000. On the other hand, the share of the tertiary sector in WB increased from 41.4 to 50.0 per cent, between 1990 and 2000. Almost all the districts shared the growth of the tertiary sector (Table 4.9). The growth of the services sector has been relatively faster in Kolkata, Howrah and 24 Parganas (North and South).

Table 4.9 shows the variation of sectoral composition of domestic product by districts in West Bengal during the 1990s. Of the different sub-sectors of the services, 'trade, hotel and restaurant' is the largest in size. Particular, the districts such as Bardhaman, Howrah, 24 Parganas (South) and Murshidabad, are noteworthy in this respect. In the case of 'banking and insurance', some of the districts such as Bardhaman, Birbhum, Bankura, Medinipur, Kolkata, Uttar Dinajpur and Purulia recorded growth, during 1990-2000, while there was relative shrinkage in other districts.

4.3 Information Technology

The IT industry in West Bengal is nearly 15-year old. The financial year 1992-93 marks the birth of the IT industry in West Bengal, when six units got themselves registered with Software Technology Park (STP), Kolkata. Till 1998-99, the industry grew at a modest rate. The service offerings included software application and product development.

The industry got a major fillip in 1999-2000 with the entry of large number of firms, 138 to be exact (Table 4.10). In addition to software application and product development, the service offerings included embedded software, business process outsourcing, medical transcription, call centres and other ITES like CAD, CAM. In other words, the basket of offerings gave a variety of choice to the clients. Further, the exports increased significantly from 940 millions in 1998-99 to 1,790 millions in the following year. Since then, the industry has maintained a healthy growth not only in terms of exports but in terms of number of operating firms as well.

Two points deserve special mention: (a) The industry is dominated by firms rendering software application; and

(b) the industry is highly concentrated with top 10 firms accounting for over 80 per cent of total export earnings (Table 4.11).

According to the West Bengal Electronics Industry Development Corporation Limited (WEBEL, a GoWB undertaking), the state is on a fast track IT highway and is poised to become one of the top three states in India by 2010 to contribute 15 to 20 per cent of the country's total IT revenue. The CAGR of the software industry in the state has been around 119 per cent. In the year 2003-04, while the country's average growth in the knowledge sector was about 28 per cent, West Bengal recorded a growth exceeding 50 per cent.

TABLE 4.11

Year-wise Performance of Top 20 STP-Kolkata Units (Functioning in 2005-06)

STPK Units	*2005-06 (Base Year)*	*Previous Four Years*			
		2004-05	*2003-04*	*2002-03*	*2001-02*
TATA Consultancy Services	1032.34	907.77	573.8	356.23	220.12
IBM India Pvt. Ltd.	351.81	234.25	125.44	42.65	70.88
Cognizant Technology Solution India Pvt Ltd	214.63	150.4	103.41	70.23	61.74
Computech International Ltd	76.68	69.82	112.88	79.22	27.62
Siemens Information Systems Ltd	40.57	19.81	8.61	4.29	1.22
Skytech Solutions Pvt Ltd	26.22	23.72	21.82	12.55	18.24
Usha Comm India Pvt Ltd	24.67	30.77	49.25	47.74	57.07
NIIT Technologies Ltd	24.54	20.14	16.25	25.9	29.35
Lexmark International (India) Pvt. Ltd.	21.3	16.2	10.58	5.45	
Ontrack Systems Ltd	20.89	21.22	17.28	12.39	4.71
BNKe Solutions Pvt. Ltd.	20.06	16.12	8.99	3.82	0.72
Vishnu Solutions Pvt. Ltd.	15.57	19.34	11.34	10.26	1.1
Vision Comptech Ltd.	14.62	12.07	9.49	5.25	1.16
Eforce India Pvt. Ltd.	12.7	13.17	7.4	5.17	3.53
Connectiva Systems India Pvt. Ltd.	11.22			Started STP operation In 2005-06	
HCL Technologies Ltd.	10.94	6.69	16.37	5.72	3.2
IXIA Technologies Pvt Ltd.	10.91			Started STP operation in 2005-06	
Xplore-tech Services Pvt. Ltd.	10.28	4.08		Started STP operation in 2004-05	
TATA Interactive Systems	10.12			Started Stp operation in 2005-06	
Xponse IT Services Pvt. Ltd.	10.07	1.41		Started STP operation in 2004-05	

Source: As in Table 4.10.

Chapter 5

Employment

The fluctuation in employment or unemployment has to come to terms with the periodic instability of the growth process. The trend in employment, in fact, is the 'outcome' of the changing combinations of capital, technology and the labour market institutions. The estimated aggregate employment in the state increased gradually from 17.8 million in 1983 to 27.6 million in 2004-05 (see 'Employed-AV' in Table 5.1).[1] The compound annual rate of growth (CAGR) of employment (i.e., Employment-AV) that was 3.01 per cent during 1983 to 1993-94 declined significantly to 0.67 per cent during the period 1993-94 to 1999-2000 (Table 5.2). Thereafter, employment tended again to grow at a higher rate, i.e., 1.77 per cent, during 1999-2000 to 2004-05.

It is important to recognise that between 1983 and 1993-94, i.e., during the period when small and marginal peasant-based agriculture in West Bengal was surging ahead the employment growth rate in the state exceeded the all-India average, which was hovering around 2.43 per cent. During 1993-94 to 1999-2000, while the all-India rate was 1.12 per cent, West Bengal was lagging behind with the CAGR of 0.67 per cent. Thereafter, once again

TABLE 5.1

West Bengal: Number of Employed (Numbers in Lakh), 1983 to 2004-05

Concept of Employed	*Year*	*Rural*			*Urban*			*Rural + Urban*		
		Male	*Female*	*Persons*	*Male*	*Female*	*Persons*	*Male*	*Female*	*Persons*
Employed (US) (ps+ss)	1983	111.91	39.5	151.41	45.46	9.1	54.56	157.37	48.6	205.97
	1993-94	147.93	46.34	194.27	58.04	13.09	71.13	205.97	59.44	265.4
	1999-2000	155.33	44.16	199.49	66.08	12.11	78.19	221.41	56.28	277.68
	2004-05	172.4	51.94	224.42	61.73	14.72	75.3	234.13	66.66	299.73
Employed (CWS)	1983	103.01	18.57	121.58	44.05	7.24	51.29	147.06	25.81	172.87
	1993-94	138.26	35.28	173.54	57.44	12.39	69.83	195.71	47.67	143.37
	1999-2000	143.68	34.8	178.48	65.26	11.64	76.9	208.94	46.44	255.38
	2004-05	164.89	43.19	207.84	60.69	13.86	74.51	225.59	57.05	282.35
Employed (CDS)	1983	92	15.34	107.34	42.06	6.7	48.76	134.06	22.04	156.1
	1993-94	131.91	24.02	155.93	55.05	10.3	65.35	186.96	34.32	221.28
	1999-2000	129.74	23.78	153.52	63.14	9.98	73.13	192.89	33.76	226.65
	2004-05	148.37	30.64	178.83	57.48	11.11	68.55	205.85	41.75	247.38
Employed-AV	1983	102.3	24.47	126.77	43.86	7.68	51.54	146.16	32.15	178.31
	1993-94	139.37	35.22	174.58	56.85	11.93	68.77	196.21	47.14	243.35
	1999-2000	142.91	34.25	177.16	64.83	11.25	76.07	207.74	45.49	253.23
	2004-05	161.89	41.92	203.7	59.97	13.23	72.79	221.86	55.15	276.49

Source: NSS Rounds 38, 50, 55 and 61 on *Employment and Unemployment Situation in India*. New Delhi: NSSO, Ministry of Statistics and Programme Implementation, Government of India.

1. 'Employed-AV' i.e., average numbers of employed is obtained using estimates of usual status (ps+ss), current weekly status and current daily status.

TABLE 5.2

CAGR of Employment: West Bengal and All-India Compared

Concept of Employed	Period	West Bengal									All-India								
		Rural			Urban			Rural+Urban			Rural			Urban			Rural+Urban		
		Male	*Femal*	*Person*	*Male*	*Femal*	*Person*	*Male*	*Femal*	*Person*	*Male*	*Femal*	*Person*	*Male*	*Femal*	*Person*	*Male*	*Femal*	*Person*
Employed (US)	1983 to 1993-94	2.69	1.53	2.4	2.35	3.53	2.56	2.6	1.94	2.44	1.71	1.41	1.6	3.15	3.38	3.2	2.06	1.66	1.93
(ps+ss)	1993-94 to 1999-2000	0.82	–0.8	0.44*	2.19	–1.29	1.59	1.21	–0.91	0.76	0.94	0.15	0.66	2.61	0.94	2.27	1.38	0.26	1.02
	1983 to 1999-2000	2.01	0.68	1.69	2.29	1.75	2.21	2.09	0.89	1.83	1.43	0.95	1.26	2.96	2.49	2.86	1.81	1.15	1.6
	1983 to 2004-05	2.03	1.28	1.85	1.43	2.26	1.51	1.86	1.48	1.76	1.17	1.17	1.17	1.94	2.28	2.02	1.35	1.31	1.35
	1993-94 to 2004-05	1.40	1.04	1.32	0.56	1.07	0.52	1.17	1.05	1.11	0.65	0.94	0.76	0.79	1.23	0.91	0.68	0.98	0.80
	1999-2000 to 2004-05	2.11	3.30	2.38	–1.35	3.98	-0.75	1.12	3.44	1.54	0.30	1.90	0.88	–1.35	1.58	–0.70	–0.15	1.86	0.52
Employed (CWS)	1983 to 1993-94	2.34	6.3	3.45	2.56	5.25	2.98	2.76	6.02	3.31	2.19	3.36	2.55	3.32	4.78	3.59	2.47	3.57	2.78
	1993-94 to 1999-2000	0.64	-0.23	0.47	2.15	1.04	1.62	1.1	–0.43	0.81	0.97	0.77	0.91	2.67	1.26	2.4	1.42	0.85	1.26
	1983 to 1999-2000	2.04	3.88	2.35	2.41	2.92	2.49	2.15	3.62	2.39	1.75	2.41	1.95	3.08	3.49	3.16	2.09	2.57	2.22
	1983 to 2004-05	2.21	4.00	2.53	1.50	3.07	1.75	2.01	3.76	2.31	1.40	2.26	1.67	2.04	3.02	2.23	1.56	1.18	1.80
	1993-94 to 2004-05	1.61	1.86	1.65	0.50	1.02	0.59	1.30	1.65	1.36	0.65	1.22	0.84	0.83	1.36	0.95	0.70	1.24	0.86
	1999-2000 to 2004-05	2.79	4.41	3.09	-1.44	3.55	-0.63	1.55	4.20	2.03	0.27	1.76	0.76	–1.33	1.48	–0.76	–0.17	1.71	0.39
Employed (CDS)	1983 to 1993-94	3.49	4.36	3.62	2.6	4.18	2.83	3.72	4.31	3.38	2.28	2.74	2.41	3.46	4.17	3.58	2.57	2.95	2.67
	1993-94 to 1999-2000	-0.28	-0.17	-0.26	2.31	-0.51	1.89	0.52	-0.27	0.4	0.73	0.56	0.68	2.47	1.77	2.35	1.2	0.76	1.09
	1983 to 1999-2000	2.11	2.69	2.19	2.49	2.45	2.49	2.23	2.62	2.29	1.71	1.94	1.78	3.1	3.29	3.13	2.07	2.15	2.09
	1983 to 2004-05	2.25	3.27	2.40	1.46	2.38	1.60	2.01	3.02	2.16	1.35	1.77	1.47	2.07	2.89	2.22	1.53	1.94	1.64
	1993-94 to 2004-05	1.07	2.24	1.25	0.39	0.69	0.44	0.88	1.80	1.02	0.47	0.84	0.59	0.77	1.68	0.93	0.55	0.98	0.67
	1999-2000 to 2004-05	2.72	5.20	3.10	–1.86	2.17	-1.29	1.31	4.34	1.77	0.16	1.19	0.48	-1.24	1.57	–0.74	–0.23	1.25	0.17
Employed-AV	1983 to 1993-94	2.99	3.53	3.09	2.5	4.28	2.79	2.84	3.71	3.01	2.05	2.37	2.15	3.31	4.06	3.45	2.36	2.6	2.43
	1993-94 to 1999-2000	0.42	–0.46	0.24	2.21	–0.97	1.7	0.96	–0.59	0.67	0.88	0.47	0.75	2.59	1.29	2.34	1.34	0.59	1.12
	1983 to 1999-2000	2.05	2.06	2.05	2.4	2.34	2.39	2.15	2.13	2.15	1.62	1.67	1.64	3.04	3.04	3.04	1.99	1.87	1.95
	1983 to 2004-05	2.16	2.54	2.23	1.47	2.56	1.62	1.96	2.54	2.06	1.30	1.67	1.42	2.02	2.69	2.15	1.48	1.81	1.58
	1993-94 to 2004-05	1.37	1.60	1.41	0.49	0.94	0.52	1.12	1.44	1.17	0.59	1.01	0.74	0.80	1.40	0.93	0.65	1.07	0.78
	1999-2000 to 2004-05	2.53	4.12	2.83	–1.55	3.30	–0.88	1.32	3.93	1.77	0.24	1.66	0.72	-1.31	1.54	-0.73	-0.18	1.64	0.37

Source: NSS Rounds 38, 50, 55 and 61 on *Employment and Unemployment Situation in India*. New Delhi: NSSO, Ministry of Statistics and Programme Implementation, Government of India.

employment grew at a much faster rate (1.77 per cent) in West Bengal than the average state in India (0.37 per cent). Incidentally, the latter period also coincides with the period of revival of agricultural sector from its previous sluggishness, in the state.

Despite urbanisation in the state, urban employment (Employment-AV) (male plus female) declined from 76 to 73 lakh between 1999-2000 and 2004-05. More affected was the male employment, while female labour force found increased job opportunities; the latter increased from 11.25 lakh in 1999-2000 to 13.23 lakh in 2004-05 (Table 5.1).

We will later see that actually the growth in female employment in the urban sector is largely explained by the opening up of opportunities for them in the manufacturing sector, in the era of globalisation, while male manufacturing workers increasingly constituting the 'reserve army'. One could gauge the phenomenon from the Tiljala-Topsia area in the eastern part of Kolkata.

While about 5 lakh male urban workers lose their 'usual status' (relatively stable jobs) of work, more than 2.5 lakh female workers gained 'usual status' in the urban, between 1999-2000 and 2004-05 (Table 5.1). However, to note, 'usual status' does not necessarily mean better conditions of work than either CWS or CDS. It is the labour market conditions that determine the conditions of work in the current era when state has been minimising its interventionist role.[2]

By any measure of employment—be it US, CWS or CDS—urban male employment declined at a significant rate while urban female employment had a significant rise since the mid-1990s in West Bengal (Table 5.4). The share of urban West Bengal in state's aggregate employment, however, is found to be higher than that in the all-India, indicating a structural change in the state *vis-a-vis* all-India.

Urbanisation in West Bengal has become slower and at the same time lagging behind the all-India rate, during the last three decades, notwithstanding the higher share of urban employment in the state as compared to that in the all-India draws particular attention. Proportionately more jobs are created in the urban areas in the state than it is the case for all-India.

However, the male-female distribution of employment in West Bengal is asymmetrical. For instance, in 2004-05, of the total employed (rural+urban) in West Bengal, less than 20 per cent were females, whereas the same was more than 30 per cent in all-India (Table 5.4). The same pattern of distribution of male-female employment emerges as one compares separately the rural and urban areas in the state.

In aggregate, the share of West Bengal in total employment in India has increased, except for a marginal drop in 1999-2000 (Table 5.5). The growth in rural employment in the state, in fact is the contributing factor.

TABLE 5.3

Percentage of Employed, West Bengal and All-India Compared, 1983 to 2004-05

Concept of Employed	*Year*	*West Bengal*		*All-India*	
		Rural	*Urban*	*Rural*	*Urban*
Employed (US) (ps+ss)	1983	73.51	26.49	80.82	19.18
	1993-94	73.2	26.8	78.15	21.85
	1999-2000	71.84	28.16	76.48	23.52
	2004-05	74.88	25.12	77.87	22.13
Employed (CWS)	1983	70.33	29.67	78.94	21.06
	1993-94	71.31	28.69	77.13	22.87
	1999-2000	69.89	30.11	75.54	24.46
	2004-05	73.61	26.39	76.92	23.08
Employed (CDS)	1983	68.76	31.24	78.44	21.56
	1993-94	70.47	29.53	76.35	23.65
	1999-2000	67.73	32.27	74.53	25.47
	2004-05	72.29	27.71	75.67	24.33
Employed-AV	1983	71.1	28.9	79.51	20.49
	1993-94	71.74	28.26	77.26	22.74
	1999-2000	69.96	30.04	75.57	24.43
	2004-05	73.67	26.33	76.89	23.11

Source: NSS Rounds 38, 50, 55 and 61 on *Employment and Unemployment Situation in India*. New Delhi: NSSO, Ministry of Statistics and Programme Implementation, Government of India.

5.1 Marginalisation

The proportion of subsidiary status (us, ss) workers to total workers (us, ps+ss) gives a rough indication about marginalisation of employed. By the indicator, marginalisation has been taking place more rapidly in the state than in all-India (Table 5.6). Moreover, the phenomenon is stronger in rural West Bengal than in the urban, primarily because of large scale marginalisation of rural female employed. Altogether, in both West Bengal and all-India, with varying degree of course, it is the marginalisation of females in rural as well as urban that dominates the phenomenon, and the rate of which has increased with the turn of the century.

2. For instance, domestic workers are quite often 'usual status' workers, yet their conditions of work in terms of wage, working hours or social security is found to be worse.

TABLE 5.4

Male-Female Distribution (%) of Employment: West Bengal and All-India, 1983 to 2004-05

Concept of Employed	Year	West Bengal						All-India					
		Rural		Urban		Rural + Urban		Rural		Urban		Rural + Urban	
		Male	Female	Male	Female	Male	Female	Male	Female	Male	Female	Male	Female
Employed	1983	73.91	26.09	83.33	16.67	76.41	23.59	63.47	36.53	79.34	20.66	66.51	33.49
(US) (ps+ss)	1993-94	76.15	23.85	81.59	18.41	77.61	22.39	64.19	35.81	78.96	21.04	67.42	32.58
	1999-2000	77.86	22.14	84.51	15.49	79.73	20.27	65.27	34.73	80.55	19.45	68.86	31.14
	2004-05	76.82	23.14	81.98	19.54	78.11	22.24	63.39	36.52	77.93	21.79	66.61	33.26
Employed	1983	84.73	15.27	85.89	14.11	85.07	14.93	70.37	29.63	82.5	17.5	72.92	27.08
(CWS)	1993-94	79.67	20.33	82.26	17.74	80.41	19.59	67.82	32.18	80.27	19.73	70.66	29.34
	1999-2000	80.5	19.5	84.87	15.13	81.81	18.19	68.07	31.93	81.55	18.45	71.37	28.63
	2004-05	79.33	20.78	81.46	18.6	79.89	20.2	66.44	33.54	79.25	20.63	69.39	30.56
Employed	1983	85.71	14.29	86.26	13.74	85.88	14.12	71.96	28.04	83.43	16.57	74.43	25.57
(CDS)	1993-94	84.59	15.41	84.24	15.76	84.49	15.51	70.99	29.01	82.41	17.59	73.69	26.31
	1999-2000	84.51	15.49	86.35	13.65	85.1	14.9	71.2	28.8	83	17	74.2	25.8
	2004-05	82.97	17.13	83.85	16.2	83.21	16.88	70.06	29.83	80.95	19.08	72.71	27.22
Employed-AV	1983	80.7	19.3	85.1	14.9	81.97	18.03	68.16	31.84	81.67	18.33	70.93	29.07
	1993-94	79.83	20.17	82.66	17.34	80.63	19.37	67.45	32.55	80.49	19.51	70.41	29.59
	1999-2000	80.67	19.33	85.22	14.78	82.04	17.96	67.99	32.01	81.66	18.34	71.33	28.67
	2004-05	79.47	20.58	82.39	18.17	80.24	19.95	66.4	33.53	79.33	20.54	69.39	30.53

Source: NSS Rounds 38, 50, 55 and 61 on *Employment and Unemployment Situation in India*. New Delhi: NSSO, Ministry of Statistics and Programme Implementation, Government of India.

TABLE 5.5

Share (%) of West Bengal in Aggregate Employment in India, 1983 to 2004-05

Concept of Employed	Year	Rural			Urban			Rural + Urban		
		Male	Female	Person	Male	Female	Person	Male	Female	Person
Employed	1983	7.12	4.37	6.12	9.75	7.49	9.29	7.72	4.74	6.72
(US) (ps+ss)	1993-94	7.88	4.42	6.64	8.99	7.61	8.7	8.16	4.87	7.09
	1999-2000	7.82	4.18	6.56	8.77	6.66	8.36	8.08	4.54	6.98
	2004-05	8.55	4.47	7.06	8.77	7.48	8.33	8.61	4.91	7.34
	1983	7.18	3.07	5.96	9.82	7.61	9.43	7.81	3.69	6.69
Employed	1993-94	7.68	4.13	6.53	9.09	7.97	8.87	8.04	4.72	7.07
(CWS)	1999-2000	7.53	3.89	6.37	8.81	6.95	8.47	7.89	4.37	6.88
	2004-05	8.52	4.42	7.14	8.76	7.69	8.53	8.59	4.93	7.46
	1983	6.81	2.91	5.72	9.77	7.83	9.45	7.52	3.6	6.52
Employed	1993-94	7.71	3.44	6.47	8.95	7.84	8.75	8.04	4.13	7.01
(CDS)	1999-2000	7.26	3.29	6.11	8.86	6.84	8.52	7.72	3.88	6.73
	2004-05	8.24	3.99	6.95	8.59	7.04	8.29	8.33	4.51	7.28
	1983	7.04	3.61	5.95	9.78	7.63	9.38	7.69	4.13	6.65
	1993-94	7.76	4.06	6.55	9.01	7.8	8.77	8.08	4.62	7.06
Employed-AV	1999-2000	7.55	3.84	6.66	8.81	6.81	8.45	7.9	4.3	6.87
	2004-05	8.44	4.33	7.05	8.71	7.42	8.38	8.51	4.81	7.36

Source: NSS Rounds 38, 50, 55 and 61 on *Employment and Unemployment Situation in India*. New Delhi: NSSO, Ministry of Statistics and Programme Implementation, Government of India.

5.2 Status Distribution of Employed

More than half of the total are self-employed, be it in West Bengal or all-India (Table 5.7). The ratio of self-employed to the total has been rising in the state ever since the mid-1980s, while it gradually decreased in all-India during 1983 to 2004-05.

The rural-urban dichotomy once more is strongly visible so far as the growth of self-employed sector in the state *vis-a-vis* all-India is concerned. In the urban West Bengal, the spacer for regular employment continuously getting eroded and steadily taken over by the self-employed, while casual labour maintained an almost steady share of 14-16 per cent during 1983 to 2004-05 (Table 5.7). The phenomenon in West Bengal assumes particular significance when placed in the perspective of all-India: the share of 'regular employed' in the all-India has in fact increased during the last 20 years.

TABLE 5.6

Marginalisation of Employment in West Bengal and All-India

Region	Sex	Percentage of Subsidiary Status Workers to Total Workers: West Bengal 1983	West Bengal 1993-94	West Bengal 1999-2000	West Bengal 2004-05	All-India 1983	All-India 1993-94	All-India 1999-2000	All-India 2004-05
Rural	Male	4.45	3.41	1.87	1.92	3.39	2.71	1.69	2.01
	Female	52.85	54.59	27.5	42.7	27.06	28.66	22.74	25.99
	Person	17.08	15.62	7.55	11.35	12.04	12	9.01	10.93
Urban	Male	2.57	2.18	1.06	2.02	2.36	1.54	0.97	1.47
	Female	25.44	27.27	12.82	33.55	20.26	21.94	15.83	18.67
	Person	6.38	6.8	2.88	7.92	6.06	5.83	3.86	5.21
Rural + Urban	Male	3.91	3.06	1.63	1.94	3.16	2.41	1.49	1.87
	Female	47.72	48.58	24.34	40.68	26.26	27.71	21.73	24.93
	Person	14.25	13.26	6.23	10.48	10.89	10.65	7.79	9.67

Source: NSS Rounds 38, 50, 55 and 61 on *Employment and Unemployment Situation in India*. New Delhi: NSSO, Ministry of Statistics and Programme Implementation, Government of India.

TABLE 5.7

Percentage of US (FS+SS) Workers as Self-Employed, Regular Employee and Casual Labour in West Bengal and All-India

Region	Sex	Year	West Bengal: Self-Employed	West Bengal: Regular Employee	West Bengal: Casual Labour	All-India: Self-Employed	All-India: Regular Employee	All-India: Casual Labour
Rural	Male	1983	49.69	11.43	38.88	60.5	10.3	29.2
		1993-94	54.7	10.3	35	57.7	8.5	33.8
		1999-2000	49.2	7.5	43.3	55	8.8	36.2
		2004-05	53.4	7.3	39.3	58.1	9	32.9
	Female	1983	60.6	5.3	34.1	61.9	2.8	35.3
		1993-94	59	7.3	33.7	58.6	2.7	38.7
		1999-2000	62.4	5.1	32.5	57.3	3.1	39.6
		2004-05	61	8.3	30.7	63.7	3.7	32.6
	Person	1983	52.54	9.83	37.64	61.01	7.56	31.43
		1993-94	55.73	9.58	34.69	58.02	6.42	35.55
		1999-2000	52.12	6.97	40.91	55.8	6.82	37.38
		2004-05	55.2	7.5	37.3	60.2	7.1	32.8
Urban	Male	1983	35.74	50.6	13.66	40.9	43.7	15.4
		1993-94	37.4	47.6	15	41.7	42	16.3
		1999-2000	43.1	39.9	17	41.5	41.7	16.8
		2004-05	44.7	37.3	17.9	44.8	40.6	14.6
	Female	1983	35.15	45.93	18.92	45.8	25.8	28.4
		1993-94	36.4	44.1	19.5	45.8	28.4	25.8
		1999-2000	43.6	40.1	16.3	45.3	33.3	21.4
		2004-05	52.4	36.7	10.9	47.7	35.6	16.7
	Person	1983	35.64	49.82	14.54	41.91	40	18.09
		1993-94	37.22	49.96	15.83	42.56	39.14	18.3
		1999-2000	43.18	39.93	16.89	42.24	40.07	17.69
		2004-05	46.2	37.2	16.6	45.4	39.5	15
Rural + Urban	Male	1983	45.66	22.74	31.6	56.02	17.94	26.04
		1993-94	49.83	20.81	29.36	53.6	17.07	29.32
		1999-2000	47.38	17.17	35.45	51.29	17.85	30.86
		2004-05	51.11	15.21	33.66	54.66	17.18	28.16
	Female	1983	55.84	12.9	31.26	60	5.52	34.48
		1993-94	54.02	15.41	30.57	56.79	6.33	36.88
		1999-2000	58.35	12.63	29.01	55.54	7.54	36.93
		2004-05	59.1	14.57	26.33	61.38	8.32	30.3
	Person	1983	48.06	20.42	31.52	57.35	13.78	28.87
		1993-94	50.77	19.6	29.63	54.64	13.57	31.78
		1999-2000	49.6	16.25	34.15	52.61	14.64	32.75
		2004-05	52.94	14.96	32.1	56.93	14.27	28.86

Source: NSS Rounds 38, 50, 55 and 61 on *Employment and Unemployment Situation in India*. New Delhi: NSSO, Ministry of Statistics and Programme Implementation, Government of India.

TABLE 5.8

CAGR of US (PS+SS) Workers as Self-Employed, Regular and Casual Labour, West Bengal and All-India

Region	Sex	Year	West Bengal				All-India			
			Self-Employed	*Regular Employee*	*Casual Labour*	*Total*	*Self-Employed*	*Regular Employee*	*Casual Labour*	*Total*
Rural	Male	1983 to 1993-94	3.64	1.68	1.67	2.69	1.25	-0.13	3.14	1.71
		1993-94 to 1999-2000	-0.95	-4.38	4.46	0.82	0.14	1.53	2.1	0.94
		1983 to 1999-2000	1.95	-0.56	2.67	2.01	0.85	0.47	2.76	1.43
		1983 to 2004-05	2.37	-0.08	2.08	2.03	0.97	0.53	1.73	1.17
		1993-94 to 2004-05	1.18	-1.72	2.48	1.4	0.71	1.17	0.4	0.65
		1999-2000 to 2004-05	3.79	1.56	0.15	2.11	1.4	0.75	-1.6	0.3
	Female	1983 to 1993-94	1.27	4.68	1.42	1.53	0.88	1.06	2.3	1.41
		1993-94 to 1999-2000	0.13	-6.56	-1.4	-0.8	-0.22	2.48	0.53	0.15
		1983 to 1999-2000	0.86	0.44	0.39	0.68	0.48	1.57	1.65	0.95
		1983 to 2004-05	1.31	3.42	0.79	1.28	1.3	2.49	0.8	1.17
		1993-94 to 2004-05	1.35	2.23	0.19	1.04	1.71	3.88	-0.62	0.94
		1999-2000 to 2004-05	2.83	13.87	2.13	3.3	4.08	5.57	-1.98	1.9
	Person	1983 to 1993-94	2.98	2.15	1.61	2.4	1.11	0.03	2.8	1.6
		1993-94 to 1999-2000	-0.67	-4.74	3.24	0.44	0.01	1.68	1.51	0.66
		1983 to 1999-2000	1.64	-0.41	2.2	1.69	0.71	0.63	2.33	1.26
		1983 to 2004-05	2.08	0.57	1.8	1.85	1.11	0.88	1.37	1.17
		1993-94 to 2004-05	1.23	-0.91	1.99	1.32	1.1	1.69	0.03	0.76
		1999-2000 to 2004-05	3.57	3.89	0.51	2.38	2.43	1.7	-1.72	0.88
Urban	Male	1983 to 1993-94	2.8	1.76	3.27	2.35	3.34	2.76	3.71	3.15
		1993-94 to 1999-2000	4.63	-0.78	4.34	2.19	2.53	2.49	3.13	2.61
		1983 to 1999-2000	3.46	0.83	3.66	2.29	3.05	2.66	3.5	2.96
		1983 to 2004-05	2.49	0	2.72	1.43	2.37	1.59	1.68	1.94
		1993-94 to 2004-05	2.21	-1.64	2.19	0.56	1.45	0.48	-0.22	0.79
		1999-2000 to 2004-05	-0.63	-2.67	-0.33	-1.35	0.17	-1.88	-4.09	-1.35
	Female	1983 to 1993-94	3.87	3.12	3.82	3.53	3.38	4.33	2.44	3.38
		1993-94 to 1999-2000	1.73	-2.84	-4.19	-1.29	0.75	3.65	-2.16	0.94
		1983 to 1999-2000	3.08	0.91	0.83	1.75	2.42	4.08	0.74	2.49
		1983 to 2004-05	4.18	1.2	-0.33	2.26	2.47	3.82	-0.22	2.28
		1993-94 to 2004-05	4.48	-0.6	-4.13	1.07	1.6	3.33	-2.69	1.23
		1999-2000 to 2004-05	7.88	2.15	-4.06	3.98	2.63	2.95	-3.34	1.58
	Person	1983 to 1993-94	2.98	2.59	3.39	2.56	3.35	2.99	3.31	3.2
		1993-94 to 1999-2000	4.14	-2.13	2.69	1.59	2.14	2.67	1.69	2.27
		1983 to 1999-00	3.4	0.84	3.14	2.21	2.91	2.87	2.72	2.86
		1983 to 2004-05	2.74	0.14	2.14	1.51	2.4	1.96	1.14	2.02
		1993-94 to 2004-05	2.51	-2.14	0.95	0.52	1.5	0.99	-0.9	0.91
		1999-2000 to 2004-05	0.6	-2.15	-1.09	-0.75	0.74	-0.98	-3.92	-0.7
Rural + Urban	Male	1983 to 1993-94	3.45	1.73	1.88	2.6	1.63	1.57	3.22	2.06
		1993-94 to 1999-2000	0.37	-1.98	4.44	1.21	0.64	2.14	2.25	1.38
		1983 to 1999-2000	2.32	0.37	2.8	2.09	1.27	1.78	2.86	1.81
		1983 to 2004-05	2.4	-0.02	2.16	1.86	1.24	1.15	1.72	1.35
		1993-94 to 2004-05	1.4	-1.67	2.44	1.17	0.86	0.74	0.32	0.68
		1999-2000 to 2004-05	2.67	-1.3	0.08	1.12	1.13	-0.91	-1.96	-0.15
	Female	1983 to 1993-94	1.61	3.67	1.72	1.94	1.13	2.99	2.31	1.66
		1993-94 to 1999-2000	0.38	-4.13	-1.77	-0.91	-0.11	3.23	0.29	0.26
		1983 to 1999-2000	1.16	0.76	0.44	0.89	0.68	3.08	1.57	1.15
		1983 to 2004-05	1.75	2.05	0.67	1.48	1.42	3.27	0.71	1.31
		1993-94 to 2004-05	1.88	0.54	-0.31	1.05	1.7	3.53	-0.81	0.98
		1999-2000 to 2004-05	3.71	6.44	1.46	3.44	3.91	3.89	-2.1	1.86
	Person	1983 to 1993-94	2.98	2.43	1.84	2.44	1.46	1.78	2.86	1.93
		1993-94 to 1999-2000	0.37	-2.99	3.16	0.76	0.39	2.31	1.53	1.02
		1983 to 1999-2000	2.02	0.43	2.32	1.83	1.07	1.97	2.38	1.6
		1983 to 2004-05	2.22	0.3	1.85	1.76	1.31	1.51	1.34	1.35
		1993-94 to 2004-05	1.5	-1.7	1.85	1.11	1.17	1.26	-0.08	0.8
		1999-2000 to 2004-05	2.87	-0.13	0.29	1.54	2.12	0.01	-1.99	0.52

Source: NSS Rounds 38, 50, 55 and 61 on *Employment and Unemployment Situation in India*. New Delhi: NSSO, Ministry of Statistics and Programme Implementation, Government of India.

The volume of regular employment in West Bengal has declined at the CAGR of 1.7 per cent during 1993-94 to 2004-05, while self-employment grew at the CAGR of 1.5 per cent (Table 5.8). In the rest of the India, on the other hand, 'regular employment' never ceased to increase. It is also important to recognise that West Bengal is way ahead of others in terms of growth of casual employment. Between 1993-94 and 2004-05, while casual employment declined in all-India at the rate of nearly 1 per cent, the same increased in West Bengal at the rate of nearly 2 per cent. The casualisation of rural workforce occurred at a rate (i.e., nearly 2 per cent) higher than the urban (i.e., 1 per cent), in the state. By contrast, in all-India, the rate of casualisation in the rural, though positive was much less (0.03 per cent), while in the urban it, in fact, declined at the rate of 0.9 per cent during the period 1993-94 to 2004-05 (Table 5.8). The casualisation of rural workforce accompanied the growth of rural non-farm employment in West Bengal, and especially of female non-farm employment (Table 5.9). Incidentally, the share of rural female non-farm employment in the state is much higher than that in all-India. Further, the relative size of the rural non-farm sector in terms of employment is much larger in West Bengal than at all-India.

TABLE 5.9

Percentage of Non-Farm Employment to Total in West Bengal and India

Category	*West Bengal*				*India*			
	1983	*1993-94*	*1999-2000*	*2004-05*	*1983*	*1993-94*	*1999-2000*	*2004-05*
Rural Male	26.8	35.24	33.53	36.1	22.27	25.9	28.67	33.5
Female	24.8	41.16	45.95	41.2	12.24	13.89	14.77	16.7
Person	26.28	36.65	36.28	37.3	18.6	21.6	23.84	27.3
Urban Male	96.72	95.6	96.8	97.3	89.68	90.99	93.41	93.9
Female	87.6	91.4	97.7	96.9	68.75	75.32	82.3	81.9
Person	95.2	94.83	96.94	97.2	85.36	87.69	91.25	91.2
Total Male	47	52.25	52.42	52.24	37.69	42.56	46.48	49.14
Female	36.55	52.23	57.09	53.5	18.92	22.56	24.69	26.15
Person	44.53	52.24	53.36	52.35	31.41	36.04	39.7	41.44

Source: NSS Rounds 38, 50, 55 and 61 on *Employment and Unemployment Situation in India*. New Delhi: NSSO, Ministry of Statistics and Programme Implementation, Government of India.

TABLE 5.10

Employment Elasticity: West Bengal and India

Concepts of Employed Used	*Employment Elasticity During*					
	1983 to 1993-94	*1993-94 to 1999-2000*	*1983 to 1999-2000*	*1993-94 to 1999-2000*	*1993-94 to 2004-05*	*1999-2000 to 2004-05*
US, PS+SS	0.42	0.11	0.3	0.11	0.16	0.22
CWS	0.57	0.12	0.39	0.12	0.2	0.29
CDS	0.58	0.06	0.37	0.06	0.15	0.26
Average of three concepts	0.52	0.1	0.35	0.1	0.17	0.26
Base Year	1980-81			1993-94		

Source: NSS Rounds 38, 50, 55 and 61 on *Employment and Unemployment Situation in India*. New Delhi: NSSO, Ministry of Statistics and Programme Implementation, Government of India.

Chapter 6

Unorganised Sector

The unorganised sector refers to enterprise whose activities or collection of data is not regulated under any legal provision and/or which do not maintain any regular accounts. In particular, units not registered under the Factories Act, 1948, constitute unorganised component of manufacturing.

In 1991-92, the share of unregistered manufacturing exceeded that of the registered sector in NSDP originating in the manufacturing sector, as a whole, and, the upwardly trend continued, thereafter. Nearly 60 per cent of NSDP in manufacturing comes from the unregistered units (Figure 6.1) in spite of the fact that these units have steadily lost state patronage ever since the economic reforms programme was launched in India. It is not that these units had many distinct state-sponsored advantages in the pre-1991 period, but still many of the products of these units were given coverage under the 'reserved category' that had acted as 'hedge' against competition from large manufacturers. One has to further probe how these unorganised units survive against the onslaught of liberalised markets and still contributes heavily to the state's income as well as employment. But one thing that is clear from their large-scale existence and 'continuity' is their competitive edge over the large-scale organised sector enterprises who have 'scale economies' as well as various 'state patronage', like easy institutional credit, on their side even in the era of deregulation. If the public institution of R&D extends knowledge and facilities to the unorganised manufacturing units, the survival rate as well as exportability of the latter would enhance further.

FIGURE 6.1

West Bengal: Share of Unregistered Manufacturing in NSDP Originating in the Manufacturing Sector, 1980 to 2005

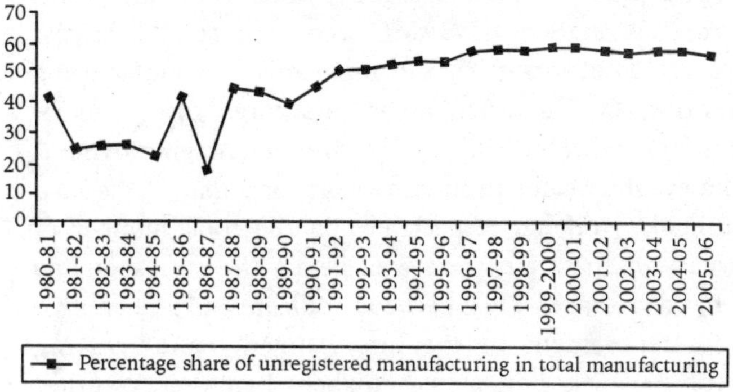

Source: The Economic and Political Weekly Research Foundation (EPWRF). *Domestic Product of States of India: 1960-61 to 2000-01*; Government of West Bengal. *Economic Review (2007-08)*.

6.1 Number of Enterprises

The rank of West Bengal was second, next to Uttar Pradesh, and accounted for 13.2 per cent share in the total number of enterprises in India as a whole, in 1994-1995. The state also ranked second in the country, in terms of employment in the unorganised manufacturing enterprises.[1] Total number of unorganised manufacturing units increased in rural West Bengal, during 1980-1990.[2] However, following NSS 45th Round (July 1989-June 1990) and 51st Round (July 1994-June 1995), total number of enterprises—own account manufacturing enterprises (OAMEs) and both types of establishments, i.e., non-directory (NDMEs) and directory (DMEs)[3] declined in

1. NSSO, Report No. 433.
2. *Economic Census*
3. OAME is defined as an enterprise which is run without any hired worker, NDME is defined as an enterprise employing less than six workers and DME is an enterprise which employs six or more workers (NSSO, 1998).

rural West Bengal. During 1994-95 to 1999-2000 (NSS, 55th Round), there had been a reverse trend in rural West Bengal—the number of informal sector manufacturing units[4] (a sub-set of the unorganised sector that was covered by the earlier rounds of NSS) increased. In urban areas, the trend was almost the same, excepting for the fact that though the total number of enterprises decreased between 1989-90 and 1994-95, there had been marginal increase in DMEs. During 1994-95 to 1999-2000, the number of informal manufacturing units increased.

6.2 Employment

According to *Economic Census* (1980 and 1990), aggregate employment increased in the rural areas while it decreased in urban West Bengal. Between 1989 and 1995 (NSS, 45th and 51st Rounds), employment in both, rural and urban areas decreased. The scale of decrease was relatively more in rural West Bengal. The general decline in aggregate employment notwithstanding, there was marginal increase in per unit employment in urban DMEs. In rural West Bengal, OAME accounted for the largest share of employment in the unorganised manufacturing activities. In the urban areas, the three categories of units—OAME, NDME and DME—shared employment more evenly. Shares of hired workers and that of the paid household workers, respectively, in the total number of workers in the state were well below the corresponding all-India average. This perhaps indicates the degree of underemployment in the unorganised manufacturing sector in West Bengal was higher than that in other developed states in the country. Between 1994-95 and 1999-2000, the level of employment in informal manufacturing (NSS, 55th Round) in urban WB increased, while that in the rural remained stagnant.

6.3 Gross Value-Added

The GVA per worker as well as per enterprise in both rural and urban OAMEs, NDMEs and DMEs increased in 1994-95 as compared to that in 1989-90. In particular, the relative growth in urban OAMEs as well as NDMEs and rural DMEs had been significantly higher. The rank of West Bengal was at the bottom in cases of rural as well as urban OAMEs and urban NDMEs. In other categories of enterprises, the rank of West Bengal was also much lower than the other states. Considering all categories of enterprises, the average value-added in the units in the state is lower than any of the major states in India. The fact implies that the small unorganised manufacturing enterprises in the state are mostly involved in the production of low value-added goods.

The labour-productivity is lower in the unorganised manufacturing units in the state as compared to the average of 10 major states in cases of both OAMEs and NDMEs and slightly above the average for DMEs. The small enterprises have large export potential. Exports of leather and leather products accounted for highest share in total exports from the state followed by metal products. In terms of share of exports to state production in the industry group, leather and leather products accounted for the maximum, followed by non-metallic mineral products.[5] The United Nations Industrial Development Organisation (UNIDO) identified about 350 SME clusters in India. Of these, 138 clusters in 16 states covering 18 types of industries are categorised according to their growth potentials.[6] Nineteen clusters that are there in the shortlist are located in West Bengal, and nine of them were targeted for restructuring and modernisation.

6.4 Unorganised Manufacturing

The number of working rural unorganised manufacturing (UM) units declined 38 per cent in 1994-1995 from that in 1989-90. The overall decline in UM was particularly owing to about 40 per cent decline in OAMEs. However, there was a reverse trend during 1994-95 to 1999-2000; an increase of about 9 per cent took place mainly due to 12.2 per cent increase in OAMEs (Table 6.1).[7] In the urban, there had been a decline in the number of working UM units by 3.03 per cent, during 1990-1995. Thereafter, there was a growth of 6.51 per cent, between 1995 and 2000. NSS 55th Round (1999-2000), in fact, covers informal sector which is only a sub-set of the UM, as mentioned earlier. However, OAMEs are certainly comparable, if not the NDM'Es and DMEs, over the different NSS rounds. Thus, the observed aggregate growth in 1999-2000 compared to 1994-95, seems to be an underestimate.

4. The National Sample Survey Organisation conducted the first ever nationwide survey on informal sector, non-agricultural enterprises, during 55th round (July 1999- June 2000). In this survey, all unincorporated proprietary and partnership enterprises have been defined as informal sector enterprises. This definition differs from the concept of unorganised sector used in National Accounts Statistics. In the unorganised sector, in addition to the unincorporated proprietary or partnership enterprises, enterprises run by cooperative societies, trusts, private and public limited companies (non-AS) are also covered. The informal sector can therefore, be considered as a subset of title unorganised sector. It is to be noted that the number of units of OAMEs, and the NDMEs to a great extent, in the 55th round are certainly comparable, if not the DMEs, to the earlier NSS rounds.

5. *Second All-India Census of SSI Units*, 1988.

6. UNIDO (2000)

7. NSS, 45th (July 1989-June 1990), 51st (July 1994-June 1995) and 55th (July 1999-June 2000) Rounds.

TABLE 6.1

Number of Unorganised Manufacturing Enterprises and Employment: NSS Rounds Compared, 1989 to 2000

	Urban				Rural			
	OAME	NDME	DME	All	OAME	NDME	DME	All
Number of enterprises (in '000)								
45th (1998-1990)	2359	101	23	2483	258	105	26	390
51st (1994-95)	1425	84	22	1531	239	107	31	378
	(-39.62)	(-16.30)	(-2.18)	(-38.33)	(-7.39)	(-2)	(-19.85)	(-3.03)
55th (1999-2000)	1598	-	-	1664	280	-	-	402
	(-12.16)			(8.67)	(16.93)			(6.5)
Employment (in '000)								
45th (1998-1990)	–	–	265	5106	–	–	217	1032
51st (1994-95)	2893	250	226 (-14.78)	3370 (-34.00)	417	338	254 (-16.79)	1010 (-2.19)
55th (1999-2000)	–	–	–	2925 (-13.19)	–	–	–	1028 (-1.81)

Note: (1) Figures within parantheses denote percentage change.
(2) Discrepancy in aggregation arises due to rounding-off the NSS figures.

So far as UM employment is concerned, there had been an overall (taking OAMEs, NDMEs and DMEs together) decline, by 34 per cent, in 1994-95, compared to 1989-90, in the rural. There was further decline by 13.2 per cent, during 1995-2000. In the urban, there was an overall decline, during 1990-1995, but at a much lower rate (2.2 per cent) than that in the rural. The following period, however, witnessed a positive growth rate of 1.8 per cent (Table 6.1).

6.5 Performance

The decline in employment notwithstanding, (real) gross value added (GVA) per worker, labour productivity, increased in UM units, in West Bengal, during 1990-2000 (Table 6.2). The urban units were almost double the size of the rural units in terms of per unit GVA. The average size of the urban DME declined, during 1990-1995. Otherwise, there had been a general increase in the size of the units in the unorganised sector.

6.6 A Comparative Study of UM in 10 Major States

By the aggregate number of workers in informal manufacturing in 1999-2000, West Bengal was next to Uttar Pradesh in the rank arranged in descending order (Table 6.3). In the informal manufacturing sector, female-

TABLE 6.2

Gross Value Added (Real) Per Worker and Per Enterprise in UM, in West Bengal: NSS Rounds Compared, 1990-2000

	Rural			Urban		
	OAME	NDME	DME	OAME	NDME	DME
Gross value added (real) per worker						
1989-90 (45th)	16.42	35.78	30.54	29.06	46.79	80.84
1994-95 (51st)	16.08	37.01	39.01	33.45	53.37	64
1999-2000 (55th)	26.05	50.03a		38.81	74.85a	
Gross value added (real) per enterprise						
1989-90 (45th)	31.55	108.78	354.38	52.53	154.74	671.49
1994-95 (51st)	32.65	110.04	394.16	58.37	168.46	517
1999-2000 (55th)	–	–	–	–	–	–

Note: 'a' NDME and DME combined.

male ratio was higher in rural West Bengal and Tamil Nadu, among 10 major states. Thus, any assistance to the growth of UM in WB rural areas would likely to induce female employment at a relatively higher scale.

In terms of value added per worker in the informal manufacturing, West Bengal's position was not as good as other states (Table 6.4). One of the basic reasons for the poor performance of the state's informal manufacturing is the low-level of technology in use. The latter perhaps is explained by credit constraint. But more important factor is the entrepreneurship gap. The unorganised manufacturing in West Bengal is largely dominated by trading capital. How the nature of capital assumes a critical role is evident in the century-old cast iron foundry industry concentrated in Howrah. While the industry in the district has been languishing, during the last two decades, the same has flourished based on improved technology and entrepreneurship in Coimbatore (Tamil Nadu).

TABLE 6.3

Informal Manufacturing Sector: State-wise Distribution of Estimated Number of Workers and Male-Female Ratio, 1999-2000

State	*No. of Workers (Lakh) (Rural +Urban)*	*Rural*		*Urban*	
		Male	*Female*	*Male*	*Female*
Tamil Nadu	31.47	0.44	0.56	0.65	0.35
West Bengal	39.53	0.46	0.54	0.78	0.22
Orissa	16.75	0.51	0.49	0.66	0.34
Madhya Pradesh	16.06	0.64	0.36	0.76	0.24
Assam	2.86	0.66	0.34	0.86	0.14
Bihar	16.62	0.66	0.34	0.85	0.15
Punjab	5.16	0.69	0.31	0.91	0.09
Rajasthan	10.58	0.69	0.31	0.73	0.27
Maharashtra	26.82	0.72	0.28	0.84	0.16
Uttar Pradesh	46.19	0.73	0.27	0.77	0.23

Source: NSS 55th Round on *Employment and Unemployment Situation in India*, NSSO, Ministry of Statistics and Programme Implementation, Government of India.

TABLE 6.4

Ranks of 10 Major States: Annual Value Added Per Worker in Informal Manufacturing, Rural and Urban, 1999-2000

State	*Rural*	*Urban*
Punjab	1	2
Maharashtra	2	1
Rajasthan	3	6
Assam	4	3
Tamil Nadu	5	5
Uttar Pradesh	6	10
West Bengal	7	10
Bihar	8	9
Madhya Pradesh	9	7
Orissa	10	4

Source: NSS 55th Round on *Employment and Unemployment Situation in India*, NSSO, Ministry of Statistics and Programme Implementation, Government of India.

TABLE 6.5

Unorganised Manufacturing Enterprises: Estimated Numbers of Enterprises, in the Rural, by Enterprise Categories in 10 Major States

State	*OAME (in lakh)*		*NDME (in '000)*		*DME (in '000)*	
	1994-95	*2000-01*	*1994-95*	*2000-01*	*1994-95*	*2000-01*
Andhra Pradesh	8.26	11.15	94	63	44.9	24.9
Bihar	11.04	6.6	39.4	20	6.3	3.2
Gujarat	2.09	2.22	12.6	10.6	16.4	13.5
Karnataka	4.99	6.13	34.6	40.9	70.8	32.2
Madhya Pradesh	4.27	5.13	20.2	10.5	4.1	5.8
Maharashtra	3.9	6.17	29.8	32.8	17.7	18
Orissa	12.92	8.98	24.9	17.2	4.8	4.4
Tamil Nadu	5.45	7.54	65	64	33.1	28.1
Uttar Pradesh	16.52	14.86	132.8	98.5	51.2	46.9
West Bengal	14.24	20	84.2	90.9	22.4	32.5
India	95.35	110.58	667.9	629.5	294.2	246.9

Source: NSS 51st and 56th Rounds on *Unorganised Manufacturing Sector in India*, NSSO, Ministry of Statistics and Programme Implementation, Government of India.

The number of rural NDMEs increased only in three of the 10 major states, *viz.*, Karnataka, Maharashtra and West Bengal. The number of rural DMEs increased in Madhya Pradesh, Maharashtra and West Bengal (Table 6.5).

The percentage share of different size categories of rural enterprises changed slightly in the state during the reference period. The share of NDMEs declined and that of either OAMEs or DMEs increased. In case of urban enterprises, the share of OAMEs increased and the share of both NDMEs and DMEs declined (Table 6.6).

So far as employment is concerned, during the period 1994-95 to 2000-01 in the rural OAMEs it increased in Andhra Pradesh, Gujarat, Karnataka, Madhya Pradesh, Maharashtra, Tamil Nadu and West Bengal. The number declined in Bihar, Orissa and Uttar Pradesh (Table 6.7).

Employment in rural NDMEs increased in Andhra Pradesh, Karnataka, Maharashtra and West Bengal, while in rural DMEs employment increased in Andhra Pradesh, Madhya Pradesh, Maharashtra, Uttar Pradesh and West Bengal. In the urban OAMEs, employment increased in Andhra Pradesh, Karnataka, Madhya Pradesh, Maharashtra, Tamil Nadu and West Bengal. The number declined in Bihar, Gujarat, Orissa and Uttar Pradesh (Table 6.8). Employment in urban NDMEs increased in Andhra Pradesh, Gujarat, Karnataka, Tamil Nadu, Maharashtra and West Bengal, whereas employment in urban DMEs increased in Andhra Pradesh, Karnataka, Maharashtra, Orissa, Tamil Nadu and West Bengal.

TABLE 6.6

Estimated Numbers of Urban Enterprises by Enterprise Categories in 10 Major States

State	OAME (in lakh)		NDME (in '000)		DME (in '000)	
	1994-95	2000-01	1994-95	2000-01	1994-95	2000-01
Andhra Pradesh	2.1	3.22	54.9	63.4	12.7	18.4
Bihar	1.48	1.03	38.5	19.6	6.1	2.8
Gujarat	2.64	1.81	70.1	78.4	55.2	37.1
Karnataka	1.74	2.82	46.8	48.1	14.1	18.0
Madhya Pradesh	1.46	1.73	44.4	31.1	9.7	8.7
Maharashtra	2.25	3.56	124.7	137.7	77.5	77.6
Orissa	0.55	0.51	10.9	10.1	2.3	2.5
Tamil Nadu	3.7	4.86	98.5	142.3	45.0	54.3
Uttar Pradesh	4.91	4.89	148	131.7	39.3	38.4
West Bengal	2.39	4.85	107.2	122.7	31.4	39.8
India	27.15	36.07	932	1082.2	360.2	400.2

Source: NSS 51st and 56th Rounds on *Unorganised Manufacturing Sector in India*, NSSO, Ministry of Statistics and Programme Implementation, Government of India.

TABLE 6.7

Estimated Numbers of Employment in Rural Enterprises by Enterprise Categories in 10 Major States

State	OAME (in lakh)		NDME (in '000)		DME (in '000)	
	1994-95	2000-01	1994-95	2000-01	1994-95	2000-01
Andhra Pradesh	15.64	19.48	139.3	197	178.7	239.7
Bihar	19.11	11.27	111.6	63.3	103.6	45.7
Gujarat	3.39	3.58	37.8	32.4	186.2	172
Karnataka	8.15	8.53	90.1	131.7	397.7	289.1
Madhya Pradesh	7.61	8.71	48.9	32.2	31.9	70.3
Maharashtra	6.8	9.34	85.4	101.6	180.1	205.1
Orissa	28.4	19.75	67.2	46.4	43.3	40.6
Tamil Nadu	9.12	11.68	214.6	211.5	332	292.2
Uttar Pradesh	32.43	26.4	412.4	296.8	496.2	745.2
West Bengal	28.93	37.68	250.4	285.8	226.1	362.6
India	178.45	191.47	1828.9	1932.9	2452.5	2905.7

Source: NSS 51st and 56th Rounds on *Unorganised Manufacturing Sector in India*, NSSO, Ministry of Statistics and Programme Implementation, Government of India.

Total employment in the unorganised sector is estimated as 119.57 lakhs in the farm sector and 151.32 in the non-farm sector, in 2007 (Table 6.9).[8] In the farm sector it is estimated that unorganised employment in the year 2007 would be 97.3 per cent of the sector-total, and that in the non-farm sector would be 90.2 per cent.

TABLE 6.8

Estimated Numbers of Employment (in lakh) in Urban Enterprises by Enterprise Categories in 10 Major States

State	OAME		NDME		DME	
	1994-95	2000-01	1994-95	2000-01	1994-95	2000-01
Andhra Pradesh	3.97	5.5	1.76	2.05	1	1.6
Bihar	2.53	1.81	1.14	0.63	0.44	0.2
Gujarat	4.6	2.88	2.5	2.81	5.41	3.56
Karnataka	2.84	4.32	1.47	1.58	1.14	1.67
Madhya Pradesh	2.69	2.94	1.48	1.05	0.73	0.71
Maharashtra	4.08	5.88	4.32	4.71	6.43	6.72
Orissa	0.9	0.85	0.34	0.31	0.2	0.21
Tamil Nadu	6.26	7.5	3.41	4.9	4.58	5.33
Uttar Pradesh	9.82	9.56	4.64	4.31	3.35	3.34
West Bengal	4.17	6.95	3.38	4	2.54	3.57
India	48.17	59.14	30.57	36.2	32.02	35.52

Source: NSS 51st and 56th Rounds on *Unorganised Manufacturing Sector in India*, NSSO, Ministry of Statistics and Programme Implementation, Government of India.

6.7 Estimating the Size of Unorganised Sector in 2007

TABLE 6.9

Estimated Numbers (in lakhs) of Organised and Unorganised Workers in West Bengal in the Year 2007

Sector	Total Employment	Organised Sector Employment	Unorganised Sector Employment
Farm	122.93	3.36	119.57 (97.26%)
Non-farm	167.75	16.33	151.32 (90.25%)
Total	290.58	19.69	270.89

Source: Author's calculation

6.8 Welfare and Social Security Schemes for Unorganised Workers

The cumulative total number of beneficiaries of different welfare and social security schemes in West Bengal, up to March 2006, is shown in (Table 6.10).

However, none of these schemes provide a comprehensive coverage of social security with all the necessary constituent elements of health benefits, life insurance and old age security. These schemes may be implemented in addition to the proposed national minimum social security system.

8. Using the residual method, i.e., deducting the number of organised employment from total employment in the state we get the number of unorganised employment.

TABLE 6.10

Number of Unorganised Sector Workers Covered under Different Schemes of Social Security, West Bengal

Scheme	*No. of Workers Covered*
Scheme for Financial Assistance to the Workers in Locked-out Industrial Units (FAWLOI)	287,711
State Assisted Scheme of Provident Fund for Unorganised Workers (SASPFUW)	683,525
Total no. Identity card issued to Beedi Workers (up to December 2005)	901,739
Total no. enrolled in Building and other construction Workers Act	11,815
Provident Fund for Landless Agricultural Labourers (PROFLAL)	903,715
Total enrolled in Fishermen's Group Personal Accident Insurance Scheme	162,000

Source: GoWB, *Labour in West Bengal*, various years; and Budget speech of related Departments.

6.9 Estimated Number of Workers in West Bengal Eligible for the Proposed National Social Security Network

A. Farm Sector:

- Nearly 29.9 per cent of total unorganised labours in the farm sector, i.e., 35.75 lakh are unpaid labourers.[9]
- Estimated number of cultivators possessing land above 2.00 hectares: According to Census 2001, 43.43 per cent of those employed in agriculture are cultivators and 56.57 per cent are agricultural labourers. Thus estimated number of cultivators in 2007 would be 53.39 lakh. According to Employment-Unemployment Survey I NSSO 1999-2000, 2.2 per cent cultivators possess land above 2.00 hectares. Thus, estimated number of cultivators possessing medium and large holdings in 2007 would be 1.17 lakh.

B. Non-Farm Sector:

- Unpaid family labour: 10.91 per cent of total unorganised labour in the non-farm sector, i.e., 16.51 lakh.
- Estimated employment through contractors in the ASI sector: 10.9 per cent of total employed in 2002-03, respectively. Contractual employment has increased over the years. The estimated total employment in the factory sector in 2007 would be 4.56 lakh. Therefore, contract employment would be around 0.5 lakh.
- Estimated number of construction workers in 2007 would be 0.45 lakh.
- Estimated number of workers in the organised private 'transport, storage and communication', in the year 2007 would be 0.05 lakh.[10]

Farm Sector:

- Total no. of unorganised workers = 119.57 lakh.
- Minus, the estimated no. of unpaid family labour = 35.75 lakh
- Minus, the estimated no. of persons possessing land above 2.00 hectares = 1.17 lakh
- Therefore, the number of workers eligible for the proposed national social security scheme = 82.65 lakh

Non-Farm Sector:

- Total no. of unorganised workers = 151.32 lakh
- Minus, tile estimated no. of unpaid family labour = 16.51 lakh
- Plus, tile estimated no. of workers employed through contract in the ASI sector = 0.5 lakh
- Plus, tile number of construction workers = 0.45 lakh
- Plus, tile estimated number of workers in private 'transport, storage, communication' in the organised sector = 0.05 lakh
- Therefore, tile number of workers eligible for the proposed national social security scheme = 135.31 lakh

9. According to NSSO, *Informal Sector in India 1999-2000*.
10. Computed from GoWB, *Labour in West Bengal*, various issues.

Chapter 7

Rural Development

Rural development broadly has economic as well as social dimensions. These can again be classified into two parts: one that is induced by economic growth within the region; and, the other one depends on the devolution of funds and schemes from above, say, from the Central government, state government and other agencies at home and abroad.

When 'endogenous'[1] growth of the rural economy is considered, certainly, what comes first is the growth and subsequent retardation in the agrarian economy in West Bengal. In measuring the overall rural development, the distributive aspect of agricultural growth plays the crucial role. Growth in agriculture generates demand for improved rural infrastructure—like, roads, power, education, health, etc.—yet, the supply side also has specific roles to play; it induces growth. For instance, better health provision in the rural areas ultimately increases human capacity for improved productivity.

Look at the spread of private investments in converting the dwelling units from *kachcha* to *semi-pucca* or even to *pucca*. In this way, people in the rural areas have themselves improved their own material conditions of life. During the 1990s, there had been very significant negative growth in *kachcha* dwelling unit construction in all of the districts, and massive construction of semi-*pucca* and *pucca* houses (Table 7.1). This huge asset formation would not have been possible had the economy not been moving forward.

7.1 Migration

Migration of people from rural West Bengal to other states has been substantial during the last two decades, despite there being a high rate of agricultural growth (Table 7.2). A large section of these rural migrants go to the rural areas in states such as Haryana, Assam, Orissa and Bihar (undivided). On the other hand, there has been a growing phenomenon of rural labour force from West Bengal joining the urban labour market perhaps informal unorganised, especially in Delhi and Maharashtra and generally in Orissa, Assam, Haryana and Punjab.

TABLE 7.1

Trend in Rural Housing, by Type, 1981-2001 (% Change)

District	*Kachcha*		*Semi-Pucca*		*Pucca*	
	1981-1991	*1991-2001*	*1981-1991*	*1991-2001*	*1981-1991*	*1991-2001*
Cooch Behar	37.7	-56.7	141.5	129.1	133.4	90.2
Jalpaiguri	50.5	-57.6	107.4	119.5	50.5	27.9
Darjeeling	21.6	-54.7	44	58.2	111.5	28.1
Dinajpur	59	-54.8	150.9	121.2	196.9	83.4
Malda	16.8	-44.8	64.4	22.2	155	96.2
Murshidabad	42.3	-50.5	67	28.3	161.4	53.3
Nadia	46.1	-75.1	367.2	57.3	103.6	44.3
24 Parganas	40.8	-37.9	54.3	25.9	184.4	42.2
Howrah	4	-66.1	18.1	7.1	173.3	41.2
Hooghly	25.6	-54.9	58.5	23.2	157.5	18.3
Medinipur	55.8	-47.1	149.5	41.7	338.4	37.7
Bankura	63.3	-42.2	109.2	67.5	200.8	5.4
Purulia	34.1	-49.4	103.2	18.1	150.7	2.2
Bardhaman	39.1	-23.1	63.3	44.3	98.3	-0.4
Birbhum	47.5	-19.4	87	72.9	230.3	21.8
West Bengal	44.9	-45.1	87.1	45.2	153.5	34.7

Source: Census of India, 1981, 1991, 2001.

1. Planning Commission.

TABLE 7.2

Out-Migration from West Bengal Rural (Last Residence) to Other States in India, 1981-2001

Year	*Rural-Rural*			*Rural-Urban*		
	Total	*Male*	*Female*	*Total*	*Male*	*Female*
1981	491,469	110,153	381,316	244,762	120,146	124,616
1991	361,768	79,460	282,308	198,545	98,111	100,434
2001	455,477	114,914	340,563	317,586	198,061	119,525

Source: As in Table 7.1.

The distinctive features of out-migration are, first, in the case of rural to rural, it is more the female migrants that far outweigh the male migrants. Second, as it appears the 'family' is not moving out. However, in the case of rural-urban migration perhaps it is more of family migration that shows a relatively balanced male-female migration in terms of numbers (Table 7.2).

7.2 Employment

Rural employment as a ratio of state aggregate had been declining during the last two decades of the twentieth century. But it was still about 72 per cent (Table 7.3). Almost all the sectors in rural West Bengal suffered employment setback during the period 1993-94 to 1999-2000. Except for the two minor sectors, *viz.*, mining and quarrying, and electricity, gas and water, for the rest of the rural economy annual increase in number of employed had been much lower during 1993-94 to 1999-2000 than it was during the period 1983 to 1993-94. More disturbing phenomenon is that in services sector, employment declined by 68,000 and in construction by 5,000 each year during 1993-2000 in the rural.

Annual compound growth rate of NSDP (at constant prices) originating in 'agriculture and allied activities' was 6.88 per cent during the period 1983 to 1993-94, while that of employment (usual status, both principal and subsidiary) was 0.99 per cent. Between 1993-94 and 1999-2000, the former declined to 4.02 per cent, while the latter declined by a greater proportion, to 0.36 per cent. Thus, employment elasticity that was 0.14 during 1983-1993, declined to 0.09 during 1993-2000 in agriculture and allied activities.

During 1993-94 to 1999-2000, employment in agriculture and allied activities increased by 124,000 on an average per year for the rural males, while it declined by 57,000 per year for the rural females. The loss of employment by the rural females, during the period, is also evident in transport, storage and mining and quarrying. On the whole, although both rural males and females faced shrinking job opportunities, the rural labour market had been particularly adverse to female labour force. The pattern of female migration from the state thus, seems to be more due to 'push' factors than anything else.

The trend, however, halted and got reversed by the turn of the century. In other words, relatively fewer jobs are created in the urban as compared to rural West Bengal (Table 7.3). However, relatively more jobs were created in the rural non-farm sector.

Rural non-farm employment in West Bengal has been growing in size, especially rural industries are occupying greater share in employment. There has been substantial increase in employment in rural manufacturing during the last two decades. During 2000-2004, number of rural 'own account manufacturing enterprises' increased in the state from 14.24 lakh to 20 lakh, while that of NDMEs from 84 thousand to more than 90 thousand and DMEs from 22 thousand to more than 32 thousand. No other state in India is comparable to West Bengal as regards the growth of rural enterprises at such a scale. In fact, in most of the other major states, rural enterprises showed distinct trend of decline during the period.

TABLE 7.3

Employment in Rural West Bengal

Category of Employment	*Year*	*Ratio(%) of Rural to State Aggregate*	*Share in Rural Employment (%)*	
			Male	*Female*
Usual principal status plus usual subsidiary status	1983	73.5	73.9	26.1
	1993-94	73.2	76.1	23.9
	1999-2000	71.8	77.9	22.1
	2004-05	74.9	76.8	23.1
Current weekly status	1983	70.3	84.7	15.3
	1993-94	71.3	79.7	20.3
	1999-2000	69.9	80.5	19.5
	2004-05	73.6	79.3	20.8
Current daily status	1983	68.8	85.7	14.3
	1993-94	70.5	84.6	15.4
	1999-2000	67.7	84.5	15.5
	2004-05	72.3	83	17.1
Average employment	1983	71.1	80.7	19.3
	1993-94	71.7	79.8	20.2
	1999-2000	70	80.7	19.3
	2004-05	73.7	79.5	20.6

Source: NSS rounds 38, 50, 55 and 61 on *Employment and Unemployment Situation in India*, NSSO, Ministry of Statistics and Programme Implementation, Government of India, New Delhi.

An inter-state comparison would tell us the magnitude of the growth of 'alternative' employment opportunities in rural West Bengal (Table 7.4). The number of employment increased in rural OAMEs from 28.9 lakh to 37.7 lakh, in rural NDMEs from 2.5 to 2.9 lakh and in DMEs from 2.3 to 3.6 lakh, during the period from 2000 to 2004.

TABLE 7.4

Estimated Number of Rural Workers Per 10,000 Population in Different States in 2001

States	*OAME*	*NDME*	*DME*	*ALL*
West Bengal	653	50	63	766
Orissa	635	15	13	663
Tamil Nadu	336	61	84	481
Andhra Pradesh	353	36	43	432
Karnataka	246	38	83	367
Uttar Pradesh	201	23	57	281
Maharashtra	168	18	37	223
Madhya Pradesh	197	7	16	220
Gujarat	119	11	57	187
Bihar	152	9	6	167
India	260	26	39	325

Source: NSSO, *Unorganised Manufacturing Sector in India*, 2000-2001, Employment, Assets and Borrowings, NSS 56th Round.

TABLE 7.5

Percentage of Population Below the Poverty Line: All-India and 15 Major States

States	*Rural*		*Urban*	
	1993-94	*1999-2000*	*1993-94*	*1999-2000*
All-India	39.36	36.35	30.37	28.76
Andhra Pradesh	27.97	25.48	35.44	32.28
Assam	58.25	61.78	10.13	12.45
Bihar	64.41	58.85	45.03	45.1
Gujarat	28.62	26.22	28.86	21.7
Haryana	30.52	14.86	13.4	13.79
Karnataka	37.73	38.5	32.41	24.55
Kerala	33.95	26.5	28.2	31.89
Madhya Pradesh	36.93	39.35	46.02	46.29
Maharashtra	50.21	50	33.52	32.16
Orissa	59.12	62.67	36.99	34.27
Punjab	17.61	14.24	6.79	6.74
Rajasthan	25.92	15.01	30.6	24.36
Tamil Nadu	37.27	39.37	37.83	29.82
Uttar Pradesh	39.08	29.87	34.23	36.39
West Bengal	**54.15**	**56.16**	**20.97**	**16.74**

Note: State-specific poverty lines for 1993-94 have been adjusted for inflation by reference to the consumer price index for agricultural labourers (for rural population) and the consumer price index for industrial workers for the urban population.

Source: Sundaram (EPW, 2001).

7.3 Trend in Rural Poverty

There has been secular decline in rural poverty in the state during the last two decades. The Headcount Ratio (HCR) of rural poverty shows a declining trend from 73.16 per cent in 1973-74 to 40.8 per cent in 1993-94, 31.85 per cent in 1999-2000, and further to 28.6 per cent in 2004-05.[2] GoI, *Economic Survey* (2002) observes:

> ...while some states such as Punjab and Haryana have succeeded in reducing poverty by following the path of high agricultural growth, others have focussed on particular areas of development e.g. Kerala has focussed on human resource development, West Bengal on vigorous implementation of land reform measures and empowerment of *Panchayats*, and Andhra Pradesh on direct public intervention in the form of public distribution of food grains.

Since 1999-2000, the decline in poverty in the state has been faster than all-India. Still, there are (as in 2004-2005) 173.2 lakh BPL population in rural West Bengal, constituting 7.8 per cent of the rural BPL population in the country. However, it is comforting to note that the rural BPL population in the state as a proportion of all-India (rural) has declined from 9.3 per cent in 1999-2000. Estimates of poverty prevalence ratios show that in the rural areas, the ratios in 1999-2000 were higher than in 1993-94 in Assam, Karnataka, Madhya Pradesh, Orissa, Tamil Nadu and West Bengal. However, in Maharashtra (the industrially developed state), the poverty ratio remained virtually unchanged between 1993-94 and 1999-2000 (Table 7.5).[3]

The Jawahar Rozgar Yojana (JRY) was launched as a centrally sponsored scheme in 1989 by merging the National Rural Employment Programme (NREP) and Rural Landless Employment Guarantee Programme (RLEGP). The main objective of the programme was the generation of additional gainful employment for unemployed and underemployed men and women in rural areas through creation of rural economic infrastructure, community and social assets. The resources under the scheme were allocated to the states/UTs on the basis of proportion of rural poor in the state/UTs to the total rural poor in the country. JRY was restructured and streamlined with effect from April 1999 and named as Jawahar Gram Samridhi Yojana (JGSY). Works under the scheme could be taken up during any part of the year as per the felt need for employment generation, preferably during the lean agricultural season but could be continued thereafter as per the necessity.

In West Bengal, during the period 1991-92 to 1995-96, there was a steady growth in expenditure under JRY. In the following years, expenditure under the scheme as such declined (Table 7.6). What is striking is that since

2. Planning Commission.

3. Based on the size distribution available from the NSS 55th Round, *Employment-Unemployment Survey*.

1993-94, when agricultural growth rate in the state showed declining trend, employment generation under JRY also declined substantially. Perhaps the increase in the cost per person-day of employment generated was one of the reasons behind.

TABLE 7.6

JRY Scheme: Year-wise Expenditure and Person-Days of Employment Generation in West Bengal

Year	*Expenditure (Rs. Million)*	*Person-Days of Employment Generated (in lakh)*	*Cost Per Person-Day of Employment Generated (Rs.)*
1989-90	1997.5	558.81	35.75
1990-91	1701.9	516.85	32.93
1991-92	1934.2	491.99	39.31
1992-93	2141.3	525.55	40.74
1993-94	2415.1	497.32	48.56
1994-95	2509.4	489.37	51.28
1995-96	2616.6	366.69	71.35
1996-97	1283.8	178.53	71.91
1997-98	1240.5	154.62	80.23
1998-99	1260.4	137.41	91.73

Source: GoWB, Panchayat and Rural Development.

7.4 Rural Infrastructure

For studying the impact of the JRY programme the Ministry of Rural Development, GoI sponsored a quick evaluation study and the report was published in November 2000. This evaluation study was done by International Institute for Sustainable Development and Management (IISDM), Ahmedabad.

The evaluation study presented composition on wages and materials at different levels of implementation, namely district, block and *gram panchayat*. The desirable ratio between wages and materials is 60:40. However, the figures for West Bengal show a comparatively higher weight of the 'wage' component than the 'material' (meant for asset creation), especially at *gram panchayat* (GP) level (Table 7.7). In the short-run, more funds for 'wages' means more employment generation. However, in the long-run, the employment effect of the latter policy is likely to be adverse once the JRY scheme is discontinued.

Works/assets created under JRY can broadly be classified into five categories: (a) rural roads, (b) water supply and irrigation, (c) land development, (d) construction of social and other buildings, and (e) social and farm forestry. Table 3.8 shows that rural road construction under the JRY programme was not on the top of the list of priorities in West Bengal, unlike many other states which are much less densely populated such as Gujarat (258 per sq. km.), Madhya Pradesh (196), Tamil Nadu (480), Assam (340).

TABLE 7.7

Composition of Wages and Materials in JRY Funds Utilised

Level of Implementation	*West Bengal*	*All-India*
District	71.4 : 28.6	58.1 : 41.9
Block	57.1 : 42.9	52.8 : 47.2
Gram Panchayat	70.9 : 29.1	51.2 : 48.8

Source: IISDM Study.

TABLE 7.8

State-wise Expenditure Incurred on Rural Roads under JRY in India, 1990-91 to 1998-99 (Rs. million)

	1990-91	*1994-95*	*1995-96*	*1996-97*	*1997-98*	*1998-99*
Andhra Pradesh	453.7	32.1	0	0	0	NR
Assam	198.5	293.3	76.1	40.9	218.2	477.8
Bihar	906.9	268.3	NR	206.2	948	NR
Gujarat	234.2	264	103.9	62.7	338.2	248.7
Haryana	72.8	51.9	0	0	0	NR
Himachal Pradesh	35.8	6.5	0	43.6	23.5	25.1
Karnataka	210.6	119.6	309.8	0	0	306.5
Kerala	327.4	181	78.4	206.9	158.8	177.9
Madhya Pradesh	119.7	197.3	6.9	137.8	668.3	646.6
Maharashtra	40	235.5	70.5	471.7	419.5	422.9
Orissa	449.4	470.4	469.5	240.6	0.5	503
Punjab	0.7	0	0	0	6.1	NR
Rajasthan	145.3	30.4	0	0	0	195.1
Tamil Nadu	405.5	308.2	90	653.4	933.7	NR
Tripura	8.2	18.9	10.5	19.1	12.5	41.7
Uttar Pradesh	806.5	933.6	681.5	799.9	0	NR
West Bengal	180.1	339.4	94.2	522.4	507.9	157.2
India	4713.3	3821.7	2002.3	3419.6	4262.51	3261.2

Source: GoI, Ministry of Transport and Highways, *Basic Road Transport Statistics of India, 1998-99.*

The village producers, those who are generating 'surplus' for the rest-of-the world, are naturally dependent on a battery of intermediaries in-between the market place and the village, and thus are denied of 'fair' price for their outputs. The condition of health, sanitation and education are also difficult to improve and thus, leave adverse mark on the state-aggregate of Human Development Index.

In the absence of data of similar kinds in the following years and depending on the data (year-wise) on road lengths in the districts and the state as a whole, the situation since then seems to have improved, especially under the Pradhan Mantri Gram Sadak Yojana (PMGSY).

Notwithstanding, comparatively greater lengths (about 64 per cent) of the roads maintained by *Zilla Parishad, Panchayat Samiti* and *Gram Panchayats* are still unsurfaced, i.e., earthen roads without any layer of road materials.

An effort has been made to develop District Performance Index (DPI) for each district of the state. The utilisation ratio of funds available in 1998-99, in five main poverty alleviation programmes is taken. The programmes considered are: (i) Integrated Rural Development Programme, (ii) Training of Rural Youth for Self-Employment, (iii) Development of Women and Children in the Rural Areas, (iv) Jawahar Rozgar Yojana, and (v) Employment Assurance Scheme. The year 1998-99 has been chosen because IRDP, DWCRA and TRYSEM programmes ceased to exist afterwards. The index has been calculated using UNDP methodology of constructing Dimension Index (see Table 7.9). The formula used is given below:

$$\text{Dimension Index} = \frac{\text{Actual value} - \text{Minimum value}}{\text{Maximum value} - \text{Minimum value}}$$

District Performance Index (DPI) is calculated by taking simple average of the index value of each programme. On the basis of DPI, the districts are ranked accordingly. The rank correlation of weighted and unweighted district performance index is highly correlated and found to be 0.93. Thus, for the purpose of ranking the use of weighted or unweighted DPI makes no difference.

The ranks of the districts in terms of performance (DPI) implementation of the five poverty alleviation programmes when compared with the ranks of the districts in per capita income (PCI) gives the impression that the DPI was higher in better endowed districts. For instance, in the high-PCI district of Jalpaiguri (ranking 3rd in PCI index), Bardhaman (2nd), or Darjeeling (1st), in particular, the implementation of the poverty alleviation schemes also has been quite meticulous. On the other hand, the districts such as South 24 Parganas, North 24 Parganas and Malda marked for low PCI did not experience better implementation of the schemes.

Admittedly, per capita DPI is not strongly correlated with per capita consumption; some of the richer districts like Darjeeling and Jalpaiguri show relatively lower average consumption expenditure. Even then, districts with low per capita consumption expenditure were also the districts with poor DPI. Similar is the picture when DPI is compared with district rural poverty ratio. Purulia having the largest concentration of BPL population in the rural, ranked 7th in DPI, or Bankura, the second largest in terms of rural BPL population ranked 11th in DPI. Either the policy as such was not clear at the apex level, or it

TABLE 7.9

District Performance Index (in 5 Poverty Alleviation Programmes) in 1998-99, Compared with District Per Capita Income, Rural Monthly Per Capita Consumption and Rural Poverty Ratio

District	*IRDP Index*	*TRYSEM Index*	*DWCRA Index*	*JRY Index*	*EAS Index*	*DPI*	*Rank of DPI*	*Rank of PCI*	*Rank of Rural Monthly Per Capita Consumption*	*Rank of Rural Poverty Rate*
Howrah	0.127	0.182	0.128	0.349	0.733	0.304	15	7	1	17
North 24 Paragnas	0.215	0.177	0.151	0.413	0.194	0.23	17	10	2	16
Bardhaman	0	1	0.133	0.885	1	0.604	2	2	3	15
Darjeeling	0.211	0.358	0.148	0.835	0.857	0.482	5	1	9	14
Medinipur	0.481	0.036	0.592	0.828	0.712	0.53	4	8	4	13
Hooghly	0.117	0.321	0.129	0.816	0.57	0.42	9	4	5	12
Cooch Behar	0.785	0	0.201	1	0.411	0.479	6	12	8	11
South 24 Paragnas	0.04	0.175	1	0	0.092	0.261	16	13	11	10
Uttar Dinajpur	0.507	0.001	0.172	0.658	0.793	0.426	8	17	7	9
Dakshin Dinajpur	0.288	0.318	0.126	0.686	0.392	0.362	13	11	6	8
Nadia	0.747	0.565	0	0.119	0.371	0.361	14	5	10	7
Malda	0.08	0.314	0.194	0.858	0.476	0.384	12	9	12	6
Jalpaiguri	1	0.525	0.284	0.742	0.754	0.661	1	3	13	5
Murshidabad	0.541	0.194	0.533	0.973	0.644	0.577	3	14	14	4
Birbhum	0.286	0.36	0.131	0.826	0.479	0.417	10	16	15	3
Bankura	0.407	0.267	0.119	0.859	0.406	0.412	11	6	16	2
Purulia	0.761	0.407	0.21	0.813	0	0.438	7	15	17	1

was the divergence in the efficiency of the district administration of the programmes that explains the 'mismatch' between the district performance indices and the various district development indices.

7.5 Use of Energy

About 80 per cent of the rural households in the state remained deprived of grid power (see Figure 7.1). This is quite unusual for the state that is one of the pioneers in the field of power generation in the country in the early twentieth century. States like Madhya Pradesh that used to be considered as one of the backward states in India until a decade ago, has also been able to expand power connectivity to more than 62 per cent of the rural households, while only about one-fifth of the rural households in West Bengal had privilege.

The essential linkages between energy and socio-economic development need to be emphasised. It is important to recognise that people living in poverty and destitution have benefited very little from conventional energy policies and their implementation. In West Bengal (rural), in 1999-2000, households possessing land of size up to 0.4 hectares (or, less than 3 *bighas)* and constituting 72.8 per cent of all classes of households used to spend 8.4 per cent of monthly per capita total consumption expenditure on 'fuel and light'.[4]

Households owning much less than one *bigha* (actually, less than 0.01 hectare, or 1 per cent *cottha)* spend 8.6 per cent of the total per capita monthly consumption expenditure on 'fuel and light'. On the other hand, in the size class of land possessed 0.41-1.00 hectare, expenditure oh 'fuel and light' is 7.4 per cent of the total monthly per capita consumption expenditure. In the size-class 1.00-2.00 hectares, it is 7.0 per cent; in the size-class 2.01-4.00, it is 6.6 per cent; and in the size class of more than 4.01 hectares (or, above *30 bighas)* the ratio is 6.9 per cent. So, richer the household less is the relative expenditure on energy—a disturbing phenomenon so far as the distributive justice is concerned (see Figure 7.2).

In absolute terms, while per capita monthly expenditure on 'fuel and light' of a household possessing more than 4.01 hectares was Rs. 38.98, in 1999-2000. The households possessing less than 0.1 hectare used to spend Rs. 40.12 per capita, or the household possessing less than 0.40 hectares used to spend Rs. 35.69. West Bengal is not an exception. In all-India (rural), the inverse relation between land possessed and per capita spending on 'fuel and light' is even robust: Poorer household pays a higher price per unit of energy services than the household in the upper income groups.

FIGURE 7.1

Number of Rural Households Per '000 Households who used Electricity for Lighting, 1999-2000

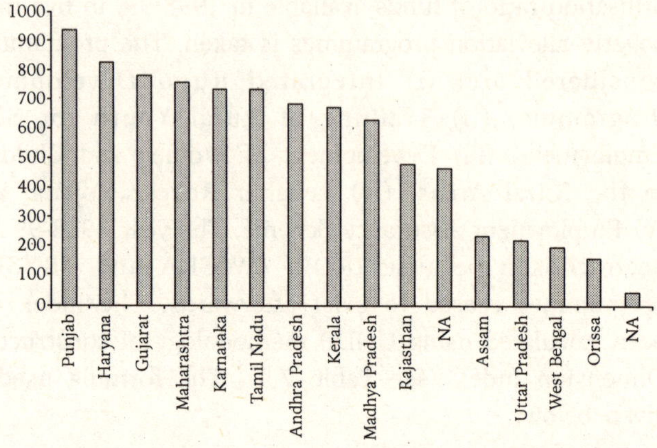

Source: Based on NSS Report No. 472, *Energy Used by Indian Households, 1999-2000.*

It is important to recognise that the problem to provide 'access to all households' is not of effective demand for power. In fact, the poorer households would prefer to have paid connection of grid power for the improvement of their own well-being: electricity connection would bring down their current expenditure on 'fuel and light' and thereby increase household savings. In 1999-2000, a rural family of 4 members, in the lower income group, used to spend more than Rs. 160 per month on 'fuel and light'. Considering a 5 per cent rate of inflation, the latter amount in 2005-06 would not be less than Rs. 225. This amount is considerably higher than the average monthly expenditure of the urban electricity consumers in the consumption group of 'up to 25 units' or 'up to 60 units', in the CESC/WBSEB area.

Thus, so far as the power distribution is concerned, apart from the disparity between the lower and upper income groups, the disparity between rural and urban also appears to be significant. This virtually acts as transfers of 'economic surplus' from the rural to the urban via the sale of kerosene, etc., as fuel. In fact, connecting the rural households to the power grid would enhance state, is aggregate savings.

7.6 Telecommunication

In general, tele-density is low in rural India. However, there are states such as Kerala and Punjab where tele-density is relatively high (Table 7.10). West Bengal is

4. NSS Report No.472, *Differences in Level Consumption among Socio-Economic Groups, 1999-2000.*

among the states with lowest tele-density. In other words, West Bengal is one of the most neglected states in India in the central telecommunication network. The rapid expansion of the mobile connections in rural West Bengal amply suggests that there is effective demand for the tele-services.

FIGURE 7.2

West Bengal, Rural: Distribution of Monthly Expenditure on 'Fuel and Light', 1999-2000

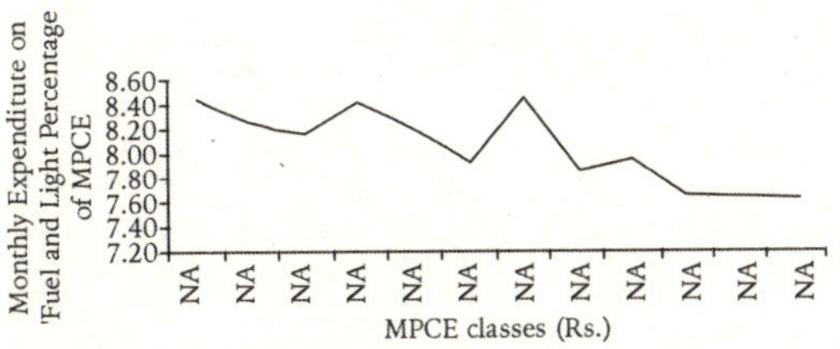

Source: NSS round 55 on *Employment and Unemployment Situation in India*, NSSO, Ministry of Statistics and Programme Implementation, Government of India, New Delhi.

TABLE 7.10

Tele-Density across Major States

State	*Tele-Density*
Andaman & Nicobar Islands	8.8
Andhra Pradesh	2.34
Assam	0.73
Bihar	0.66
Chhattisgarh	0.51
Gujarat	2.69
Haryana	3.1
Himachal Pradesh	7.25
Jammu & Kashmir	0.85
Jharkhand	0.58
Karnataka	2.63
Kerala	10.65
Madhya Pradesh	0.79
Maharashtra (-) Mumbai	2.8
Eastern-I	1.29
Eastern-II	1.26
Orissa	1.16
Punjab	5.29
Rajasthan	1.67
Tamil Nadu (-) Chennai	2.99
Uttarakhand	1.84
Uttar Pradesh	0.55
West Bengal (-) Kolkata	1.13
India	**1.86**

Source: Rajya Sabha Unstarred Question No. 2736, dated 11.05.2006.

7.7 Cold Storage

Next to jute, potato is the major cash crop in West Bengal. About one-third of potatoes in India are grown in West Bengal. Incidentally, the hindrance to the spread of the cultivation is not so much the inputs as it is the cold storage facilities, without which the cultivators simply face price failure immediately after harvest and fail to recover the costs of production. This has been a perennial problem. However, as in 2005, nearly 28 per cent of potato production in the state as a whole could not be preserved in cold storage. Except the districts of Bardhaman and Bankura, the potato growers in rest of the districts experience serious shortage of cold storage facilities (Table 7.11). The otherwise backward districts like Dakshin Dinajpur and Purulia do not have a single cold storage though potato cultivation is not insignificant there.

TABLE 7.11

Potatoes: Gaps between Production and Cold Storage Capacity, 2005

District	*Production (Tonnes)*	*Cold Storage Capacity (Tonnes)*	*Col.2 - Col.1 (%) / Col.1*
	1	2	3
Bardhaman	1132500	1230805	8.7
Birbhum	214300	136066	-36.5
Bankura	539000	580269	7.7
Medinipur(E)	56700	9900	-82.5
Medinipur(W)	1268700	959974	-24.3
Howrah	150100	45819	-69.5
Hooghly	1807900	1594821	-11.8
24 Parganas (N)	126000	24800	-80.3
24 Parganas (S)	74500	0	-100
Nadia	108300	13661	-87.4
Murshidabad	245600	45333	-81.5
Uttar Dinajpur	150700	50360	-66.6
Dakshin Dinajpur	56000	0	-100
Malda	48800	4000	-91.8
Jalpaiguri	577200	284300	-50.7
Darjeeling	98100	0	-100
Cooch Behar	427900	161126	-62.3
Purulia	24300	0	-100
West Bengal	7106600	5141234	-27.7

Source: Bureau of Applied Economics and Statistics. *Statistical Handbook, West Bengal, 2006*. Government of West Bengal.

Chapter 8

Urban Development

8.1 Introduction

Growth of towns and cities and the process of the people living in the idyllic villages turning into an urban community or moving into a town that is already there is the outcome of historical and social change and economic development of a country. Urbanisation has generally been linked to the advances in agricultural productivity and consequent growth of artisanal activities and to the emergence of manufacture and advent of industrialisation. In pre-colonial times, in India towns developed around large trading centres, army camps or places of pilgrimage. In Bengal, where textile production—both silk and cotton—was of very high standard during pre-colonial times, there were a number of large towns, such as Tamralipta, Dhaka (now in Bangladesh), Murshidabad, Malda etc., which grew out of the thriving and dynamic commercial and manufacturing activities in their respective hinterlands. Some of these towns were even larger than contemporary cities of Europe.

As the economic control and administrative powers were captured by the British mercantile capitalist rulers, the economic basis of old towns of Bengal weakened the rich handicraft industry of Bengal and other provinces of India were systematically decimated by the colonial rulers. The construction of railways, the setting up jute mills along the river Ganga, coal mining in south—western territories of the state and tea plantations in northern districts of the state during the colonial rule initiated a process of growth of some new urban centres, particularly in and around Calcutta which was a port town as well as the administrative headquarters of foreign rulers till 1911. Calcutta eventually came to be reckoned as the second city of the empire. It has been claimed by some economic historians that there was de-urbanisation under British rule in many regions of India when handicrafts and the courts of Indian rulers declined (see, for example, Irfan Habib's famous critique of vol.1 of the *Cambridge Economic History of India*)

TABLE 8.1

Population of the City of Calcutta and the Calcutta Urban Agglomeration

Year	*Calcutta City*	*Calcutta Urban Agglomeration*
1872	428000	
1901	933754	14,90000
1941	2167485	35,80000
1951	2698494	45,90000

Source: Census of India.

Table 8.1 shows how the city of Calcutta had grown with massive upsurge in population from the later part of the 19th century to the end of colonial rule. Apart from commercial, trading and manufacturing linkages with other parts of the country, the periodic famines caused by the imperial policy, the systematic neglect of agriculture and impoverishment of the peasantry, contributed to migration of people towards the city of Calcutta and such massive concentration of population in and around Calcutta UA.

Urbanisation during colonial rule took place in the backdrop of decay of old towns, stagnation of agriculture, destruction of age old handicrafts, loss of jobs of artisans, impoverishment of peasantry and small pockets of industrial activities catering to external markets.

Such a pattern of urban growth left a mark on the post-colonial trajectory of urban development in the State.

Authors, Jayanta Acharya and Nandita Sen Chakraborty, are former Principal and Lecturer (Selection Grade) in Economics, respectively, of S.A. Jaipuria College, Kolkata.

The policies pursued by the Government, both of the Centre and the states, during the initial decades after Independence had missed the essential links between urban development and improvement in living conditions in villages and small towns and growth in productivity in agriculture. As a result, the lopsided growth of big cities on the one hand and decline and the decay of old small towns, on the other, had characterised the process of urbanisation for some time till the early 80s, when some changes in the concept of urban governance and adoption of holistic planning for urban development began to take shape.

According to the United Nations (2001), the year 2007 will mark a watershed in the history of human settlement when for the first time the number of urban people will equal those of the rural people (Hust, 2005). The Census 2001 has, however, put the proportion of people living in urban areas in India at 27.78 per cent, that is, less than one-third of this country and her population is urban. West Bengal, in 2001, had an urban population of 2.1 million, that is 28.03 per cent to its total population. Though a little higher than all-India level, the percentage of urban population in West Bengal is much lower than it is in many states, such as Punjab, Maharashtra, Gujarat, Tamil Nadu etc.

8.2 Concepts and Definitions

Before we begin the analysis of pace and pattern of urbanisation, some important clarifications have to be made in regard to the concepts and definitions that one comes across in the literature on urban development. The urban area in India is comprised of statutory towns, census towns, urban agglomeration (UA) and its outgrowths (OGs). Statutory towns mean all places with a municipality, corporation, cantonment board or notified town area committee. Then some places are identified as census towns (CT) on the basis of demographic features (population > 5000), employment pattern (male population engaged in non-agricultural activities > 75 per cent) and settlement patterns (density of population > 400 persons per sq. km). Urban agglomeration (UA) is a continuous spread of towns and contiguous urban areas with at least one statutory town in the core and several non-statutory settlements with pronounced urban features as outgrowths of the core town fanning out in the periphery. The emergence of UAs with OGs is a major phenomenon in India's urban scenario.

Towns have also been placed in the census operations into six categories on the basis of demographic criteria i.e, the size of the population. It is evident that more than half of the towns in West Bengal belong to Class IV, V and VI categories having a population size below 20,000 (Table 8.2). Out of 375 towns of all categories, 128 towns have a population between 5000 and 10,000 and 58 towns belong to Class I category with more than 1 lakh population.

TABLE 8.2

Classification of Towns by Population Size

Category of Towns	*Size of Population*	*Number of Towns*
Class I	1,00,000 and more	58
Class II	From 50,000 to 99,999	29
Class III	From 20,000 to 49,999	56
Class IV	From 10,000 to 19,999	76
Class V	From 5000 to 9,999	128
Class VI	Below 5000	28

Source: Census of India, 2001, Provisional Population Totals, Paper 2, WB Series–20.

The definitions and concepts used in the Census Operations and literature on urban development having now been clarified, we can have a look at some fundamental facts relating to urbanisation in West Bengal, the referral time being Census 2001, West Bengal had an urban population of 21.9 million in 2001 which is 28.03 per cent to total population of the state. Following the Census definitions, there are 375 urban centres in the state of which altogether 125 are urban local bodies (ULB). Of 125 ULBs, there are 6 municipal corporations, 116 municipalities, 3 notified area authorities. The remaining 250 urban centres are Census Towns which satisfy the criteria employed by the Census authorities. The excessive concentration of urban population in and around Calcutta and the massive sprawling area of urban agglomeration of Calcutta are reflected in the fact that 41 ULBs fall within the Calcutta Metropolitan Area (CMA) and the remaining 84 outside CMA. Total population of the ULBs within the CMA is around 106 lakhs. Nearly one-half of urban people of West Bengal live within Calcutta UA. The density of urban population in West Bengal can be well perceived when we consider the fact that the urban population stands at 28.03 per cent of the state's total population, while the urban area is only 2.93 per cent.

8.3 Trends of Urbanisation

8.3.1 Growth in Number of Towns, UAs, OGs across All Size Classes

The growth in the level of urbanisation can be measured in terms of changes in the number of towns,

TABLE 8.3

Number of Towns of Different Size-Classes of Towns

Census Year	*Class I*		*Class II*		*Class III*		*Class IV*		*Class V*		*Class VI*		*Total*	
	UA	*Towns*	*UA*	*Towns*	*UA*	*Towns*	*UA*	*Towns*	*UA*	*Towns*	*UA*	*Towns*	*UA*	*Towns*
A 1951	-	7	-	14	-	29	-	41	-	18	-	11	-	120
1961	2	12	5	18	7	48	1	45	-	49	-	12	15	184
1971	2	15	7	31	4	49	-	60	-	59	-	9	13	223
1981	9	24	10	40	6	52	7	52	-	63	-	20	32	251
1991	13	44	7	35	10	64	7	96	1	121	-	22	38	382
2001	16	58	3	29	2	56	-	76	-	128	-	28	21	375

Note: A - In 1951 there is no concept of UAs while UAs of 1961 were known as "Town Groups".

Source: As in Table 8.2.

UAs, metropolitan cities and of increase in the share of urban population in total population. The data on these indicators of level of urbanisation in West Bengal for the period 1951-2001 are provided in Table 8.3 and Table 8.4. During the 50-year period after Independence, the number of towns of all size classes has increased from 120 to 375.

But as we dissect the growth pattern further, we find that the change has been more remarkable in case of class I towns (with more than one lakh population). The number of UAs, a new phenomenon in the urban scenarios has also increased from 15 to 21 during the period. But these figures do not capture the true profile of urbanisation in the state as the smaller towns in categories IV to VI (with a population of 20,000 to 5000 or less) have not shown comparable growth in number. The graduation from lower category towns to higher ones has not occurred on any appreciable scale.

8.3.2 Uneven Pattern of Urbanisation

The asymmetric and lopsided nature of distribution of urban population across different sizes of cities/towns would be evident from Table 8.4. As Table 8.4 shows, the proportion of people of the state living in Class I town has shot up from 76.84 per cent in 1971-1981 to 83.54 per cent in 1991-2001, whereas the proportion of people living in all other class of towns has declined. The magnitude of decline is from 10.78 per cent in 1981 to 4.34 per cent in 2001 in case of Class II towns; from 7.71 per cent to 5.96 per cent in case of Class III towns and so on. Urban decay in some parts of the state is the other side of the coin of robust growth.

The disparity of growth of urban centres is not only spatial but temporal as well. Between 1951 and 1971, the share of urban population in West Bengal was stable as the percentage of urban population increased from 23.88 in 1951 to 24.75 in 1971 i.e., an increase of less than 1 percentage point in two decades. The period after 1971 witnessed a steady growth of urban population. In 1981 the percentage of urban population to total population increased from 24.75 to 26.47, in 1991 from 26.47 to 27.48 and in 2001 from 27.48 to 28.03. The increase in the urban population in subsequent two decades between 1981-2001 is 3.28 percentage points (Table 8.5).

TABLE 8.4

Percentage of Population Living in Different Size Categories of Towns to Total Urban Population

Census Period	*Class I*	*Class II*	*Class III*	*Class IV*	*Class V*	*Class VI*
1971-1981	76.84	10.78	7.71	4.67 (Class IV to VI)		
1981-1991	81.71	6.58	7.66	4.05 (Class IV to VI)		
1991-2001	83.54	4.34	5.96	3.14	2.59	0.43

Source: Tables 4.3a and 4.3b in Sivaramakrishnan *et al.* (2005).

TABLE 8.5

Growth in Number of Towns and Urban Population

Census Year	*Total No. of UAs/Towns*	*Percentage of Urban Population to Total Population*	*Decennial Growth Rate (%)*	*Decadal Percentage Point Increase/ Decrease*
1951	120	23.88	32.52	+3.47
1961	184	24.45	35.97	0.57
1971	223	24.75	28.41	+0.3
1981	291	26.47	31.73	+1.72
1991	382	27.48	29.49	+1.01
2001	375	28.03	20.20	0.55

Source: As in Table 8.2.

Variations in the growth of urban population across the districts in West Bengal are also remarkable indicating a high degree of spatio-temporal diversity. Three districts, *viz.*, Kolkata, North 24 Parganas and Howrah have a share of urban population of more than 50 per cent while three other districts—Bardhaman, Hooghly and Darjeeling have a share of urban population of 25 to 50 per cent to total population. There are nine districts which have less than 15 per cent of urban population far below the state average (Tables 8.5a, 8.5b, 8.5c and 8.5d). It is evident that the urban growth decelerated in all the districts over time, particularly from 1971 onwards. The deceleration is more prominent in less urbanised districts. It is evident from the pattern of growth of urban population in the districts in the state that the distribution of urban population as between the districts is highly skewed in favour of Kolkata and neighbouring districts.

TABLE 8.5a

Decadal Rate of Growth for Urban Areas in Districts With More Than 50 Per cent Living in Urban Areas

Name of the Districts	*Percentage of Urban Population to Total Population*	*Decadal Growth Rate for Urban Areas 1951-2001 (in %)*				
		1951-1961	*1961-1971*	*1971-1981*	*1981-1991*	*1991-2001*
Kolkata	100	13.35	11.21	10.73	6.61	4.11
North 24 Parganas	54.30	57.16	46.03	35.49	32.22	30.00
Howrah	50.39	57.97	22.84	32.09	38.12	16.47

Source: As in Table 8.2.

TABLE 8.5b

Decadal Rate of Growth for Urban Areas in Districts with between 25 to Less than 50 Per cent Living in Urban Areas

Name of the Districts	*Percentage of Urban Population to Total Population 2001*	*Decadal Growth Rate (in %)*				
		1951-1961	*1961-1971*	*1971-1981*	*1981-1991*	*1991-2001*
Bardhaman	37.18	73.20	58.98	59.33	49.38	21.17
Hooghly	33.48	46.71	31.24	38.18	29.29	24.23
Darjeeling	32.44	53.09	24.60	56.57	40.37	31.51

Source: As in Table 8.2.

TABLE 8.5c

Decadal Rate of Growth for Urban Areas in Districts with Urban Population between 15 to Less than 25 Per cent

Name of the Districts	*Percentage of Urban Population to Total Population*	*Decadal Growth Rate (in %)*				
		1951-1961	*1961-1971*	*1971-1981*	*1981-1991*	*1991-2001*
Nadia	21.27	51.53	32.57	53.06	36.25	12.30
Jalpaiguri	17.74	87.19	35.75	85.16	47.24	31.77
South 24 Parganas	15.77	54.85	109.17	69.92	44.48	43.31

Source: As in Table 8.2.

TABLE 8.5d

Decadal Rate of Growth for Urban Areas in Districts having Urban Population Less than 15 Per cent to Total Population

Name of the District	*Percentage of Urban Population to Total Population 2001*	*Decadal Growth Rate (in %)*				
		1951-1961	*1961-1971*	*1971-1981*	*1981-1991*	*1991-2001*
D. Dinajpur	13.09	61.34	106.06	60.75	16.10	19.74
Murshidabad	12.49	44.87	27.10	39.28	42.87	48.14
U. Dinajpur	12.06	263.65	52.30	48.52	98.76	16.40
Medinipur	10.49	32.19	25.69	36.32	43.34	23.14
Purulia	10.07	17.85	43.13	25.98	25.93	21.54
Cooch Behar	9.10	42.38	35.28	26.50	38.64	33.04
Birbhum	8.58	46.06	23.82	39.08	32.29	12.60
Bankura	7.37	29.11	24.21	19.45	28.27	1.20
Malda	7.32	44.44	33.95	42.88	91.92	29.15

Source: As in Table 8.2.

8.4 Urbanisation, Employment, Unemployment Situation in Rural and Urban Areas

Urban growth can generally be attributed to many factors. The more important among them are a natural increase of the urban population of the base year, addition of population of newly emerging towns, extension of jurisdictional area of the existing towns and their agglomerations and net rural-urban (RU) migration that takes place between two periods. It has been estimated (Sivaramakrishnan *et al.*, 2005) that during 1991-2001, the natural increase derived on the basis of SRS data on birth rate and death rate for the urban population accounted for about 59.4 per cent of the increase in urban population during 1991-2001, at the national level. The same estimates show that RU migration has contributed between 21.00 to 27.40 per cent of growth in urban population during 1991-2001. It is obvious that RU migration has not occurred on a quite a large scale during the last decade. On the contrary, the estimated annual rate of RU migration between 2.1 to 2.7 per cent has not been very wide off the overall rate of annual growth rate of population of 2.1 per cent. As a result, in India the growth of urban population and the size of the urban sector has not been much vibrant.

In West Bengal, the same pattern repeats itself and in sharper terms. Between 1971 and 2001, the decadal variation in urban population in the state has shown a steeply declining trend from 31.73 per cent during 1971-1981 to 29.49 per cent during 1981-1991 and finally to 20.20 per cent at the last census. The share of urban population in total population in the state has also varied between 26.47 per cent in 1981, 27.48 per cent in 1991 and 28.03 per cent in 2001—the range of variation being very modest at 1 per cent or thereabout.

8.4.1 Employment, Unemployment Scenario in Urban Areas

The low rate and small extent of urbanisation in West Bengal can be explained in terms of low rate of growth in number of towns across all class sizes over the census decade, low rate of emergence of new towns and hence, low accretion of urban population and very moderate level of RU migration, as witnessed during the 1990s. This important socio-economic phenomenon can best be explained in terms of changing scenario of employment, rural-urban wage differential and gap in rural-urban poverty ratio.

NSS studies on employment and unemployment situation in different rounds provide the changing pattern regarding how work forces in rural and urban areas participate in various economic activities. We can delineate the important changes taking place in employment situation from the study by Bagchi and Das (2005) in respect of West Bengal. While the contribution of agriculture and manufacturing to NSDP in West Bengal has been declining from 28.35 per cent to 23.82 per cent and from 22.79 per cent to 14.36 per cent respectively over the period 1971-2001, the share of service sector has gone up from 34.81 per cent to 51.68 per cent during the same period. But the share of employment of labour in the three sectors has not witnessed commensurate changes. Tables 8.6 and 8.7 show the trend of employment in agriculture, manufacturing and service sector in both rural and urban areas.

TABLE 8.6

Percentage of Labour Engaged in Different Sectors in Rural Areas, West Bengal

Period	*Agriculture*		*Manufacturing*		*Service*	
	Male	*Female*	*Male*	*Female*	*Male*	*Female*
1987-88	72.2	70.8	9.1	19.6	16.2	8.8
1993-94	64.7	58.9	11.7	30.0	20.5	9.3
1999-2000	66.4	54.1	10.9	36.1	19.4	9.4
2004-05	64.0	54.0	8.9	29.1	21.8	16.3

Source: NSS on *Employment and Unemployment Situation in India* (43rd, 50th, 55th, 61st Round).

Though the share of agricultural output in NSDP has declined, the share of labour engaged in agriculture has not fallen correspondingly, indicating prevalence of low productivity. But what is important to take note of is that the proportion of rural workforce engaged in manufacturing and service sectors has registered a steady upward trend. The upward trend is most remarkable in case of female labour engaged in manufacturing in rural economy. This phenomenon is very important in the context of urbanisation in West Bengal as it signifies the emergence of non-farm sector of economic activities in rural economy of the state which has no doubt weakened the process of RU migration and thus, caused a low pace and level of urbanisation in the state. We can now look at the situation of employment in the urban sector in the state (Table 8.7).

TABLE 8.7

Percentage of Labour Engaged in Different Sectors in Urban Areas

Period	*Agriculture*		*Manufacturing*		*Service*	
	Male	*Female*	*Male*	*Female*	*Male*	*Female*
1987-88	4.7	15.4	32.1	26.9	54.8	53.9
1993-94	4.4	8.6	30.2	30.5	55.7	58.5
1999-2000	3.2	2.3	25.2	28.6	62.1	66.7
2004-05	2.7	1.2	26.0	28.0	62.1	68.6

Source: As in Table 8.6.

As would be evident from Table 8.7, the employment in agriculture in the urban areas is expectedly very low and insignificant. The proportion of labour engaged in manufacturing has been declining though moderately and stayed at around 25 per cent for male and around 28 per cent for female workers during the period 1987-88 to 2004-05. The service sector has surely shown a robust growth engaging more than 60 per cent of labour. The service sector emerging in the urban economy attracts labour with specialised skill that is not in abundant supply in the rural areas. With a declining manufacturing sector and the setting up of highly capital-intensive industrial units, the employment scenario in the urban sector is not very much encouraging as would appear from the Table 8.8.

TABLE 8.8

Percentage Distribution of Usually Employed Persons by Status of Employment

	Self-Employed		*Regular Employed*		*Casual Labour*	
	Male	*Female*	*Male*	*Female*	*Male*	*Female*
RURAL						
1987-88	54.2	62.3	9.5	6.1	36.3	31.6
1993-94	54.7	59.0	10.3	7.3	35.0	33.7
1999-2000	49.2	62.4	7.5	5.1	43.3	32.5
2004-05	53.1	46.9	7.4	13.7	39.5	39.4
URBAN						
1987-88	36.9	44.8	50.5	42.4	12.6	12.8
1993-94	37.4	36.4	47.6	44.1	15.0	19.5
1999-2000	43.1	43.6	39.9	40.1	17.0	16.3
2004-05	44.6	39.4	37.6	50.2	17.9	10.4

Source: As in Table 8.6.

The process of casualisation of employment is obvious as the proportion of casual labour employed has gone up between 1987-88 and 2004-05, both for male and female labour in rural as well as urban areas. Regular employment for male in urban areas has fallen from 50.5 per cent to 37.6 per cent. The economic reforms launched in the 1990s have witnessed gradual withdrawal of the state initiative in infrastructural investment, in capital formation in agriculture and encouraged inflow of foreign direct investment in setting up production units that cannot create jobs in keeping with the massive quantum of capital invested. All these developments in the post-reform period have combined to bring forth a highly skewed pattern of urbanisation which is eminently large city-centred. The urban sector has lost its strong gravitational pull of attracting people from the rural sector as work participation rate (WPR) in the urban sector has tended to decline through the 90s.

The data on employment situation for all classes of towns and cities in West Bengal (Table 8.9) would drive the point home in more precise terms. Class I towns in the state enjoy an advantage as percentage of regularly employed persons has shown a rising trend over the period 1993-94 to 2004-05 while that of casual labour has shown a declining trend during the same period. On the other hand, the opposite trend, i.e, declining regular employees and rising casual labour is observed in case of Class III and other lower category towns. This would explain the ever increasing concentration of population in Class I towns and decay of small and moderate towns in the state.

TABLE 8.9

Types of Employed by Usual Status (PS+SS) in Different Classes of Towns and Cities

	Self-Employed	*Regular Employees*	*Casual Labour*	*Total*
Class-I city				
1993-94	21.6	18.7	11.0	51.3
1999-2000	20.5	21.7	6.7	48.8
2004-05	19.4	21.6	8.2	49.2
Class-II city				
1993-94	17.1	22.1	7.4	46.6
1999-2000	18.6	17.8	7.5	43.8
2004-05	21.5	18.0	7.6	47.1
Class-III city				
1993-94	18.3	23.5	7.0	48.9
1999-2000	23.9	16.6	9.6	50.1
2003-04	30.7	13.1	9.1	52.8
All towns and cities				
1993-94	18.5	23.3	7.9	49.7
1999-2000	20.1	18.6	7.7	46.4
2003-04	22.4	18.1	8.0	48.5

Source: As in Table 8.6.

8.5 Quality of Urban Life

The highly asymmetric nature of urban growth brings to the fore the issue of quality of urban life in the state. We now examine the quality of urban life in West Bengal in terms of access to safe drinking water, sources of drinking water to urban households, lighting, fuel for cooking and the type of kitchen available. The hygienic aspect of urban life can be assessed in terms of type of latrine, connectivity of waste water outlet, type of drainage and so on.

8.5.1 Sources of Drinking Water

In West Bengal, as the census 2001 puts it, about 57 per cent of urban population has access to tap as source for drinking water while the all-India coverage is much higher at 68.7 per cent (Table 8.10). But even so, the quality of water available to the people is the more important issue as some areas of the state are reported to have subsoil water contaminated by arsenic.

TABLE 8.10

Percentage Distribution of Urban Households According to Sources of Drinking Water

	West Bengal			India		
	1981	*1991*	*2001*	*1981*	*1991*	*2001*
Tap	48.3	52.2	56.7	63.2	65.1	68.7
Handpump & tubewell	31.5	34.0	35.6	11.8	16.3	21.4
Well	14.7	12.0	6.5	20.4	15.9	7.7
Tank, pond, lake		0.2			0.3	
River, canal		Neg			0.2	
Spring		0.5			0.2	
Any other		0.5			1.5	

Source: Census of India, 1981, 1991, 2001.

The data on access to tap as the source of drinking water for the urban people in West Bengal are available from other surveys also, such as, NSS 55th Round (1999), NFHS-2 (1998) and MICS 2000, UNICEF while Census 2001 puts it at 57 per cent, the NFHS-2 shows it to be 25.3 per cent, NSS at 56.0 per cent. Multiple Indicator Survey India (MICS 2000) indicate that 96.3 per cent of urban households are under the coverage of improved source of drinking water which include tap exclusive to households, public tap, sanitary well, tubewell with motor, handpump and rainwater harvesting.

Census and these other surveys provide information on distribution of urban households by types of various amenities such as source of energy, fuel used, toilet, drainage and the like. These facilities if and when enjoyed by urban dwellers determine to a large extent the hygiene and quality of urban life.

8.5.2 Fuel used for Cooking and Source of Energy

As in the case of sources of drinking water, various studies show some variations in respect of use of fuel and sources of energy accessed by urban people in the state. In respect of LPG used as fuel for cooking in urban West Bengal, Census 2001 puts the figure at 37.4 per cent, NSS (55th Round) at 34.7 per cent, NFHS-2 at 10.6 per cent (Table 8.11). In spite of differences in the findings of the various surveys, the fact is undeniable that at the beginning of the 21st century, a little more than one-third of urban population in West Bengal was using LPG as fuel for cooking, the rest depending on firewood, cowdung cake, coal, etc. No wonder that the urban environment gets polluted through the use of such fuels for cooking.

In the matter of source of energy used for lighting, all the various surveys are of the view that about 71 to 80 per cent of urban population use electricity for lighting in the urban areas (Table 8.12), while the remaining 19 to 28 per cent fall back on kerosene for the purpose.

TABLE 8.11

Percentage Distribution of Urban Households by Type of Fuel used for Cooking

	1999-2000 (55th Round)	*Census 2001*	*1998-99 (NFHS-2)*
Fire wood	12.1	12.7	30.8
Crop residue	-	2.1	-
Cowdung cake	1.6	1.8	-
Coal, lignite, charcoal	24.2	27.4	15.3
Kerosene	19.2	15.6	6.6
LPG	34.7	37.4	10.6
Electricity	0.3	0.3	-
Biogas	Negligible	0.2	-
Others	4.0	0.8	-
No cooking	3.9	1.7	-

Source: Census 2001, NSS 55th Round, NFHS-2, 1998-99.

TABLE 8.12

Percentage Distribution of Urban Households with Different Sources of Energy used for Lighting

Sources of Energy	*Census 1981*	*Census 1991*	*Census 2001*	*NSS 50th 1993-94*	*NSS 55th 1999-2000*	*2006-07 June**
Electricity	57.9	70.2	79.6	71.4	80.5	83.62
Kerosene	-	-	19.5	27.9	19.2	-
Solar energy	-	-	0.3	-	-	-
Other oil	-	-	0.1	-	-	-
Any other	-	-	0.2	-	-	-
No lighting	-	-	0.3	-	-	-

Note: * Urban Household Survey, Dept. of Municipal Affair, WB.

Source: Census 1981, 1991, 2001, NSS 50th, 55th Round.

8.5.3 Toilet and Drainage Facilities

How good and decent the urban life is depends very much on type of kitchen available within dwelling premises, whether the kitchen is open belching smoke all around, type of latrine-pit, water closet or septic tank, type of drainage—closed or open, and such other things.

The quality of hygiene enjoyed by the urban population is evident from the fact that 15 per cent households live without any latrine facilities (Table 8.13b). Both NSS and Census data show that about one-half of urban households in the state enjoy more hygienic and modern water closet facilities. Another important indicator of good quality urban life is closed drainage connectivity which is accessible to only 22 per cent households in the state (Table 8.13c).

8.6 Slums

The existence of slums in urban areas is all too evident and slums seem to grow concomitantly with the growth and extent of urbanisation. Slums sprout on the degenerated periphery and in some cases within the fold of urban centres. Poor people from different directions flock to major urban centres in search of livelihood and settle in congested, unhygienic tenements. The growth of slums is thus pronounced in the neighbourhood of industrial towns. In West Bengal, slum population is found to be concentrated in and around towns on both sides of the river Hooghly which have been the nerve centres of industrial enterprises—like jute, chemical and engineering industries since early 20th century.

Before the Census 2001, no efforts were made to segregate the slum population data relating to the major urban centres of the country. We can now have a look at the data on slum population obtained through the Census 2001.

Out of 65 towns in the state having a population of 50,000 or more as per 1991 Census, 59 towns were identified by the Census authorities for the purpose of collection of slum data. Five towns in West Bengal, e.g., Titagarh, Champdani, Garulia, Bhadreswar and Uluberia are found to have more than 50 per cent of total population living in slums. Titagarh with a total population of 1,24,198 (2001) has the highest number of slum dwellers of 98,062 i.e., 78.96 per cent (Table 8.13).

All these towns though small in size, have developed over the last century around traditional industries such as jute or textile. There are 22 towns having slum population between 1.0 to 20.0 per cent of total population. Out of six corporations in the state, Kolkata, Asansol and Durgapur have slum population between 30 to 33 per cent. Howrah Municipal Corporation though having second largest population size in the state next to Kolkata is only the 5th by the size of the slum population (11.72 per cent).

TABLE 8.13a

Percentage Distribution of Households by Availability/Non-Availability of Kitchen, 2001

	Kitchen Available		*Kitchen Not Available*		*Cooking in Open*		*No Cooking*	
	Rural	*Urban*	*Rural*	*Urban*	*Rural*	*Urban*	*Rural*	*Urban*
West Bengal	67.3	68.2	14.9	21.8	17.1	8.3	0.7	1.7

Source: Analytical Report on Housing Amenities, Census of India 2001, Series-1.

TABLE 8.13b

Percentage Distribution of Urban Households by Type of Latrine within the House

	Pit Latrine		*Water Closet*		*Other Latrine*		*No Latrine*	
	WB	*AI*	*WB*	*AI*	*WB*	*AI*	*WB*	*AI*
Census 1981							22.3	41.9
Census 1991							21.2	36.1
Census 2001	22.9	14.6	55.2	46.1	6.8	13.0	15.2	26.3
NSS 54th 1998	7.2	8.4	55.8	35.2	21.8	30.9	15.2	25.5

Note: WB for West Bengal, AI for All-India.

Source: As in Table 8.13a.

TABLE 8.13c

Percentage Distribution of Urban Households by Drainage and Toilet Facilities

	Closed Drainage	*Open Drainage*	*No Drainage*	*Bathroom*
Census, 2001	21.8	45.3	32.9	58.6

Source: As in Table 8.13a.

TABLE 8.14

Percentage of Slum Population to Total Population of Some Towns

Name of the Town	*Civic Status*	*Total Slum Population*	*Per cent of Slum Population to Total Population*
Titagarh	M	98062	78.96
Champdani	M	75583	73.22
Garulia	M	47178	61.82
Uluberia	M	119468	59.11
Bhadreswar	M	56589	53.41

Source: Analysis of Slum Data, Census of India, 2001.

8.7 Development Programmes for Urban Areas

Since the early 1980s, the strategy of development of urban areas in West Bengal has been focused on following aspects:

1. Democratic and participatory governance of ULBs. Election to ULBs on the basis of universal suffrage to all the ULBs including municipal corporations has been held. As a result, the felt needs of the people of urban areas have been reflected in the programmes adopted by ULBs.
2. Emphasis has been laid on improvement of the quality of life of the people living below the poverty line, particularly of the children and women. Preparation and implementation of such programmes are done through the three-tier community development societies consisting of members of the poor families.
3. Development of slum areas with a view to improving infrastructure for basic civic amenities, social development and renovation, building dwelling houses.
4. Provision of basic minimum services like water supply, universal education, building roads and sanitation amenities.
5. Integrated development of small and medium towns outside Kolkata metropolitan area to arrest the flow of people to the city and to ensure that these towns become centres of growth, creating more job opportunities.
6. Improvement of environment of urban slums.
7. Development of cities and towns with financial assistance and technical help from foreign countries.

The objectives of this strategy of urban development are being implemented through implementation of various central sector schemes (CSS) with assistance of both the Central and state governments, state schemes with funds allocated under the state budget. The ULBs are also supported with transfer of resources from the state government as per recommendations of the SFC, 11th Finance Commission Award and enhanced power to raise tax and non-tax resources through suitable amendment of relevant Acts. Efforts are also made to implement development schemes under public-private partnership.

The important central sector, centrally sponsored and state funded schemes for development of urban areas in the state are as follows:

8.7.1 National Slum Development Programme (NSDP) and Finance Commission Award

These two centrally sponsored programmes had been in operation since 1996-97. The Finance Commission Award had begun with 10th Finance Commission and continued afterwards under 11th Finance Commission since 2000-01. The total amounts released under these two programmes are Rs. 182.08 crore and Rs. 116.22 crore respectively. On recommendation of the 11th FC, Rs. 78.0 crores were awarded to the ULBs for construction of roads, drains, toilets and provision of drinking water and street light.

8.7.2 Integrated Development of Small and Medium Towns (IDSMT)

The thrust of this programme is on development of ULBs outside the Kolkata metropolitan area with the purpose of narrowing down the level of development between the ULBs within the KMA and ULBs outside the KMA situated in the far-flung areas of the state. The number of towns brought under this programme is 82 for which the Central government sanctioned a fund of Rs.23.95 crore till end of March 2002.

8.7.3 Swarna Jayanti Sahari Rojgar Yojana (SJSRY)

This programme is directed towards improvement of the quality of life of the families living below poverty line. As on March-end 2002 the Central government released Rs.36.72 crore and the state government released Rs.25.23 crore under this programme.

8.7.4 Jawaharlal Nehru National Urban Renewal Mission (JNNURM)

This programme launched in late 2005 includes KMA and Asansol urban area as Mission cities. Like other CSS, this programme also envisages fund release by the Centre as well as the states for improvement of water supply and sewerage, drainage and slum area development. Under this programme Rs. 1073.30 crore and Rs. 850.62 crore have been sanctioned for urban infrastructure improvement and for provision of basic services for the poor, respectively, in urban areas in Mission cities. All infrastructural development schemes under megecity programmes have been subsumed under JNNURM.

8.7.5 Externally Aided Programmes

Some of the programmes for infrastructural development in big cities are in need of massive investment of funds and technology-intensive. Efforts have been made by the state government to attract external aids for such projects. DFID, the UK Government aided agency, World Bank, ADB and some of the other western countries are extending funds for investment in these projects. The state government is also providing funds to the projects aided by external agencies and foreign governments.

8.8 Expenditure for Urban Development by State and Central Governments

To sum up, the strategy of urban development in the state has the following components:

- emphasis on development of small and medium towns to arrest the increasing concentration of population in large cities;
- creation of employment opportunities in both rural and urban areas;
- improvement of quality of urban life:
- development of urban infrastructure in all classes of towns;
- improvement of quality of life of people living below poverty line, specially of women and children;
- participatory governance of ULBs;

TABLE 8.15

Expenditure for Rural and Urban Development (in Rs. Crore)

Department	*Year*	*Plan Sector*				*Non-Plan Sector*	*Total (Plan+ Non-Plan)*
		SP	*CS*	*CN*	*Total*		
Panchayats & RD (PN)	Actuals 2000-01	413.31	0.15		413.46	310.56	724.02
	Actuals 2001-02	582.20			582.20	312.44	894.64
	Actuals 2002-03	232.32	1.88		234.20	373.14	607.34
	Actuals 2003-04	327.75	1.53		329.28	409.71	738.99
	Actuals 2004-05	392.05	2.43		394.48	445.14	839.62
	Actuals 2005-06	711.03		0.14	711.17	492.96	1204.13
	Actuals 2006-07	774.08		4.59	778.67	651.55	1430.22
	R.E 2007-08	1535.43	0.83	1.00	1537.2	700.22	2237.48
	B.E 2008-09	1632.07	0.83	1.00	1633.9	709.24	2343.14
Municipal Affairs (MA)	Actuals 2000-01	271.49	1.82		273.31	527.13	800.44
	Actuals 2001-02	326.82	2.52		329.34	702.95	1032.29
	Actuals 2002-03	130.50	3.99		134.49	532.89	667.38
	Actuals 2003-04	82.54	4.42		86.96	800.82	887.78
	Actuals 2004-05	171.45	14.28		185.73	611.62	797.35
	Actuals 2005-06	320.70	12.10		332.80	748.60	1081.40
	Actuals 2006-07	459.17	29.73		488.90	853.32	1342.22
	R.E 2007-08	777.75			777.75	921.02	1698.77
	B.E 2008-09	915.52			915.52	990.98	1906.50
Urban Development (UD)	Actuals 2000-01	129.32	4.00		133.32	122.60	255.92
	Actuals 2001-02	114.27			114.27	170.61	284.88
	Actuals 2002-03	56.48			56.48	115.67	172.15
	Actuals 2003-04	39.35	15.00		54.35	90.16	144.51
	Actuals 2004-05	58.57			58.57	124.89	183.46
	Actuals 2005-06	124.59			124.59	117.85	242.44
	Actuals 2006-07	255.64			255.64	190.99	446.63
	R.E 2007-08	528.47	0.05		528.52	204.86	733.38
	B.E 2008-09	1102.31	0.05		1102.3	213.12	1315.48

Source: Department of Finance, Government of West Bengal.

- improvement in environment, hygiene and basic services to the poor living in slums and rural periphery of big cities and towns.

Provision of adequate funds is an essential prerequisite for implementation of this strategy. The state government releases and spends funds for development of urban areas through two of its departments *viz.*, Municipal Affairs Department and Urban Development Department having well-defined jurisdiction over municipal bodies, corporations and ULBs within various UAs. Table 8.15 shows how the expenditure for both rural and urban development has been stepped up over the period between 2000-01 and 2007-08. Rural development indeed provides the stimulus and dynamics for urban development. The Table 8.15 shows the investment of funds under Central sector and centrally sponsored schemes.

References

Bagchi, A.K. and P. Das (2005). "Changing Pattern of Employment under Neo-liberal Reforms: A Comparative Study of West Bengal and Gujarat", *The Indian Journal of Labour Economics* 48(4): 945-58.

Chatterjee, M. and P. Giri (2001). *Functional Classification of Urban Areas in India.* Centre for Urban Economic Studies, University of Calcutta.

Dasgupta, B. (1988). *Urbanization, Migration and Rural Change—A Study of West Bengal.* Calcutta: A Mukherjee & Co.

GoI (2001). *Analytical Report on Housing Amenities.* Series I. Office of Registrar General and Census Commissioner, New Delhi.

Hust, E. and M. Mann (ed.) (2005). *Urbanization and Urban Governance in India.* Manohar, Centre De Sciences Humanes, South Asia Institute.

Kundu, A. (2003). "Urbanisation and Urban Governance", *Economic and Political Weekly*, July 19.

Sivaramakrishnan, K.C., A. Kundu, B.N. Singh (2005). *Handbook of Urbanization in India.* OUP.

Chapter 9

The Power Sector

9.1 Introduction

The power sector is the integrated network of generation, transmission and distribution. As electricity cannot be stored in the grid, demand and supply of this commodity have to be maintained in balance. In India, the demand for power has been outstripping the supply of it. Substantial peak and energy shortages prevail in the country due to inadequacies in generation, transmission & distribution as well as inefficient use of electricity (GoI, 2005).

To sustain the higher economic growth as achieved in India since the 1980s, development of the basic infrastructure facilities is essential. Electrical power is one of the key inputs for overall growth and development of the country, especially in commerce and industry sectors, and has strong linkages to other infrastructure elements, such as transport and telecommunications.

Electricity is in the concurrent list of the constitution of India. The Central Electricity Authority (CEA) under the ministry of power, Government of India, provides overall guidance to the power sector. Both the union and the state governments formulate policies and laws on the subject but the responsibility of implementation rests with the states. Distribution of electricity in particular comes in the domain of the states. As the actual implementation of state policies on the power sector varies from state to state, the performance of this sector dispersed unevenly across different regions of the country. This chapter sets out to provide some issues relating to the performance of the electricity industry in West Bengal during the post-reform period.

9.2 Power Sector Reforms

Power sector reforms were initiated in India in generation, transmission and distribution segments in 1991. Since then West Bengal, as other states of the country, has experienced some major changes in the operation of the power sector. West Bengal Electricity Regulatory Commission (WBERC) was set up to consider mainly the tariff issues. The Electricity Act of 1991 permitted private entities to establish, operate and maintain power plants of any size and to enter into long-term power purchase agreements with the State Electricity Boards (SEBs).[1] In order to attract foreign private capital into the power sector, the Government of India offered generous incentives to the independent power producers (IPPs). The Electricity Laws (Amendment) Act was enacted in 1998 to promote further private sector participation. But the reforms towards the private sector participation slowed down capacity addition in this industry in India (Purkayastha, 2001).

The power sector reforms became comprehensive through the initiation of the Electricity Act of 2003.[2] Section 3(1) of the Act empowers the Central government to formulate the National Electricity Policy in consultation with CEA and state governments. The power sector reforms in India brought in significant changes in the direction of open access in transmission, phased open

Author, Dr. Panchanan Das, is a Senior Lecturer in Economics in West Bengal Education Service. Author is gratefully indebted to Prof. Amiya Kumar Bagchi, Director, Institute of Development Studies, Kolkata, for helpful comments and also to Dr. Anirban Guha, Director (Engineering) WBERC, for proving data on power sector in West Bengal.

1. Foreign investment can now take place either in the form of a joint venture with an Indian partner or as a fully-owned operation with 100 per cent foreign equity. Foreign equity up to 74 per cent in the field of electric generation and transmission can be approved by the RBI through automatic approval route.
2. Electricity Act 2003 was enacted and came into force in a comprehensive manner from 15.06.2003. The Act was amended twice: the Electricity (Amendment) Act, 2003 and the Electricity (Amendment) Act, 2007.

access in distribution, license free generation and distribution, power trading, mandatory metering and stringent penalties for theft of electricity. It was claimed that the Act could protect consumers and provide power for all through a competitive structure. But the Act pays no attention to the consequences of phasing out cross subsidies[3] by the regulators. As cross subsidies cannot be sustained in the presence of open access, the Act will hurt the poorer people using electricity. The Act allows distribution companies including private sector companies to own generation capacity. An Accelerated Power Development & Reform Programme (APDRP) has also been taken in the distribution sector.

West Bengal State Electricity Board (WBSEB) controlled both the generation and supply of power in the state outside the Kolkata metropolitan area during the pre-reform period. In that area, the load factor was low and subsidy element for supply of electricity to rural areas was high. The WBSEB suffered from high transmission and distribution (T&D) losses and inefficiency in billing and tariff collection.[4] The weaker financial health of WBSEB due to various reasons might have been one of the main reasons for the shortfall in capacity addition.

The Electricity Act (2003) laid out the vision for a deregulation in the power sector and states have the charge of implementing the process of restructuring. After introducing the power sector reforms, the Central and state government companies turn into Central and state sector utilities respectively. The WBSEB has the major controlling power of supplying electricity within the state boundary. The Indian Electricity Act, 2003, separated out the T&D networks of the board into West Bengal Electricity Transmission Company (WBSETC) and West Bengal State Electricity Distribution Company (WBSEDC). The Act brought together structural and regulatory reforms designed to encourage private participation and transform the state's role from service provider to regulator.

9.3 Supply of Power

As electricity cannot be stored, the analysis of demand-supply gap in the power sector in any region is very much crucial. The northern and southern regions of the country faced maximum excess demand for power.[5] West Bengal has increasingly faced a serious power shortfall because of the excess industrial and residential demand for power. Also the generation and demand for power are highly affected by the seasonality factor. During the winter season the demand for electricity, mainly for domestic and commercial purposes, goes down and in the summer load shedding becomes a common feature in West Bengal. Even the day peak of the system cannot be maintained in that season. The seasonal pattern of power generation in West Bengal is shown in Figure 9.1.

BOX 9.1

Policy Changes as a Part of the Power Sector Reforms in West Bengal

- WBERC has been functional effectively from 10.3.1999.
- Re-organisation Committee set up to study the State Power Sector has submitted its recommendations to State government.
- The State government has set up the West Bengal Rural Energy Development Corporation (WBREDC) as an independent company under the Companies Act to manage distribution for rural and agricultural consumer segments with the assistance of Rural Energy Cooperatives.
- Four Task Forces have been formed to initiate the implementation of reform programme.

Source: Annexure III.1 *Status of Power Reform in Different States,* Infrastructure Development Action Plan for Chhattisgarh—Final Report.

FIGURE 9.1

Seasonal Pattern of Power Generation (Excluding Central Sector Power Stations) in West Bengal

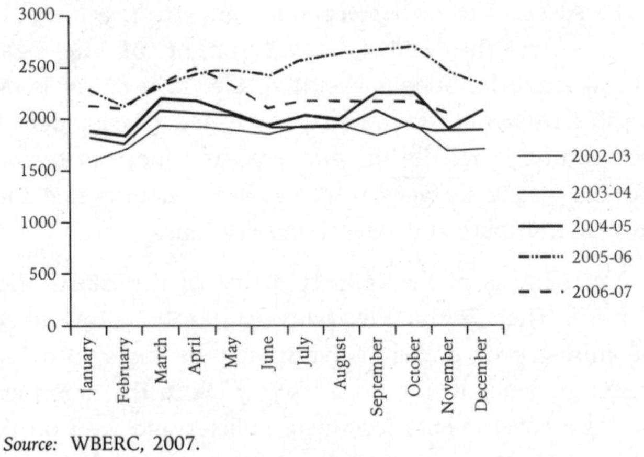

Source: WBERC, 2007.

9.3.1 Generation of Power

In 2003-04, the installed generating capacity in India was nearly 112 GW. Before 2003, the Central or state governments regulated the power entities. The Electricity Act, 2003, has put in place a highly liberal framework for generation. There is no requirement of licensing for generation or techno-economic clearance of CEA for thermal generation projects. The current policy is that for

3. Cross subsidy is defined as the difference between the cost to serve and the tariff charged.
4. Total commercial losses of the State Electricity Boards (SEB) in India are estimated at INR 225 bn in 2004 (GoI, 2005).
5. Peak Demand Shortfall—Northern region: 38.5 per cent, Southern region: 25.3 per cent, Western region: 23 per cent, Eastern region: 20.8 per cent.

hydroelectric generation also, the limit of capital expenditure, above which concurrence of CEA is required, would be raised suitably. Captive generation has been freed from all controls. The installed generation capacity in West Bengal has increased by 1000 MW during 2000-2001 to 2007-08 (Figure 9.2). Capacity addition of 418 MW was realised in 2007-08 and the cumulative capacity became 8034 MW in this period.

FIGURE 9.2

Total Installed Capacity of Power Stations in West Bengal

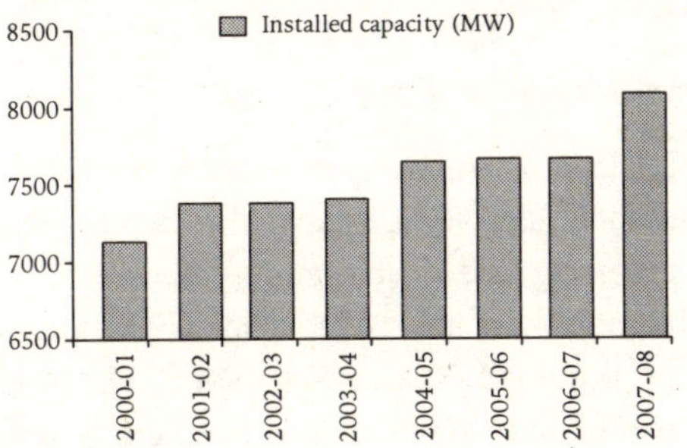

Source: WBERC, 2007.

A higher load factor of the system indicates the efficiency of the power system. The performance in terms of plant load factor of the power sector in West Bengal was not satisfactory (Figure 9.3), because of bad quality of coal.

FIGURE 9.3

Plant Load Factor (in Percentage)

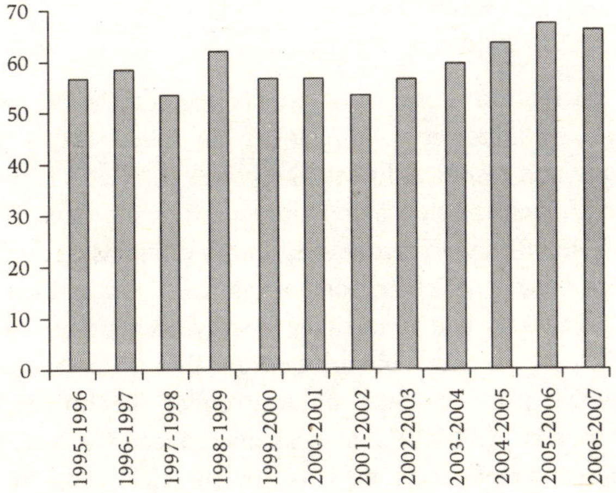

Source: WBERC, 2007.

The major portion of the total installed capacity in the country is controlled by the public sector. West Bengal Power Development Corporation Limited (WBPDCL)[6] generates roughly one-third of electricity in West Bengal (Figure 9.4). The main thermal power plants under WBPDCL are in Kolaghat, Bakreswar, Santaldih, Bandel and Sagardighi. Bandel Thermal Power Station and Santaldih Thermal Power Station have been undertaken by WBPDCL as per re-organisation measures of power sector in West Bengal. Tables 9.2a to 9.2c provide figures for capacity in MW and generation in GWh of the state sector, Central sector and private sector thermal power plants during 2005-06.

The Central Electricity Regulatory Commission is empowered to regulate the central power utilities in accordance with the Electricity Regulatory Commission Act, 1998. The central power utilities include the National Thermal Power Corporation (NTPC), the National Hydroelectric Power Corporation (NHPC) and the Nuclear Power Corporation (NPC) in the generation sector, and the Power Grid Corporation, in the interstate transmission sector. The central power utilities own and operate 30 per cent of the country's total generation capacity, while SEBs and EDs have 59 per cent of the total. In addition, five privately owned utilities, operating in certain urban centres and responsible for power distribution within their franchised areas, and some independent power producers have a share of 11 per cent of the generation.

FIGURE 9.4

Generation of Electricity in 2005-06

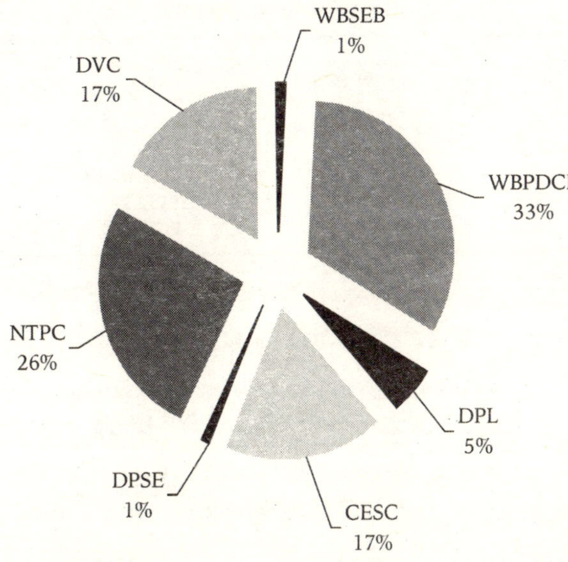

Source: WBERC, 2007.

Generation of electricity mainly from thermal power in the state increased from 12765 MU in 1992-93 to 35218 MU in 2007-08. Table 9.1 provides yearly generation of power in MU since the early 1990s by utilities. In West Bengal, WBPDCL generates the highest production of

6. WBPDCL is fully owned by the Government of West Bengal established in July 1985.

power, followed by DVC and CESC. Within the state sector, Kolaghat thermal power station generates the largest portion of electricity of the state.

TABLE 9.1

Generation of Power in West Bengal (in MU)

	State Sector			Central Sector		Private Sector	
Year	WBSEB	WBPDCL	DPL	DVC	NTPC	CESC Ltd.	DPSCL
1992-93	2865	4289	978	946	N.A.	3439	248
1993-94	3700	5366	902	1704	N.A.	3505	238
1994-95	3745	5805	907	2013	N.A.	3724	219
1995-96	3200	6232	905	1989	6508	3833	229
1996-97	3753	6235	1012	1880	6391	3663	227
1997-98	3839	5814	861	2414	6038	3982	160
1998-99	3630	6687	593	3037	5476	4715	N.A.
1999-2000	3944	6237	848	3882	6792	5378	N.A.
2000-01	N.A.	N.A.	N.A.	N.A.	N.A.	N.A.	N.A.
2001-02	N.A.	N.A.	N.A.	N.A.	N.A.	N.A.	N.A.
2002-03	511	13935	1359	4013.2	8223	6330	244
2003-04	500	14150	1921	5184	8714.1	6687	250
2004-05	508	15052	2028	6218.3	9700.6	7054	260
2005-06	482	15109	2176	7769	11463.9	7630	270.5
2006-07	371.3	10354	1292	5349	6984.2	5385	166
2007-08	516.6	14811.3	961	5609.1	7682.7	5485	152.3

Source: WBERC, 2007.

TABLE 9.2a

Installed Capacity and Power Generation by Plants in 2005-06: State Sector

	Capacity (MW)	Generation (GWh)
DPL	395	2175.9
Bandel	540	2158.55
Santaldih	480	1223.38
Kolaghat	1260	7352.7
Bakreswar	630	4374.32

Source: WBERC, 2007.

TABLE 9.2b

Installed Capacity and Power Generation by Plants in 2005-06: Central Sector

	Capacity (MW)	Generation (GWh)
D.V.C.		
Durgapur	350	1799.93
Maithan GT	90	85
Mejia TPS	840	5884.07
NTPC		
Farakka STPS	1600	11464

Source: WBERC, 2007.

TABLE 9.2c

Installed Capacity and Power Generation by Plants in 2005-06: Private Sector

	Capacity (MW)	Generation (GWh)
CESC		
Mulajore	120	0
New Cossipore	160	447.35
Titagarh	240	1830.73
Southern Repl	135	989.8
Budge Budge	500	4362.72

Source: WBERC, 2007.

9.3.2 Transmission of Power

The Central Transmission Utility (CTU) and State Transmission Utility (STU) have the key responsibility of network planning and development based on the National Electricity Plan in coordination with all concerned agencies as provided in the Act. The CTU is responsible for the national and regional transmission system by using High Voltage Direct Current (HVDC) technology. The STU is responsible for planning and development of the intrastate transmission system by applying Alternating Current (AC) technology. Open access in transmission allows the generating companies to sale electricity to different distribution licensees across the country. The Electricity Act prohibits the STUs from engaging in trading in electricity, by recognising power trading as a distinct activity.

9.3.3 Distribution of Power

Distribution is the most critical segment in the power sector. A large part of the losses in the phase of T&D include non-technical losses like power theft and improper billing.[7] Transmission loss is measured at 230 kv, 110 kv, 66 kv and 33 kv voltage levels, and is called assessment of energy balance. Distribution loss is measured at 22/11 kv and LT levels, and it is called energy accounting. As the T&D loss was not able to capture all the losses in the network, the concept of Aggregate Technical and Commercial (AT&C) loss was introduced.[8] AT&C loss captures technical as well as commercial losses in the network and is a true indicator of total losses in the system. High technical losses in the system are primarily due to inadequate investments over the years for system improvement works, which has resulted in unplanned extensions of the distribution lines, overloading of the

7. T&D loss is the ratio of the difference between the input kilowatt hours and the sold kilowatt hours to the input kilowatt hours: (Input units–billed units)/Input units.
8. AT&C loss is defined as the difference between units input and inputs realised. The units realised are equal to the product of the units billed and the collection efficiency. Collection efficiency is the ratio of actual amount collected and amount billed. AT&C loss = (units input–units realised)/units inputs = 1 – (billing in units/input in units)* (collection in rupees/billing in rupees).

system elements like transformers and conductors and lack of adequate reactive power support. The commercial losses are mainly due to low metering efficiency, theft and pilferages. High Voltage Distribution System is also an effective method for reduction of technical losses, prevention of theft, improved voltage profile and better consumer service.

The Accelerated Power Development & Reform Programme (APDRP) was launched in 2001 to reduce AT&C losses. Table 9.3 presents AT&C losses by utilities in West Bengal during 2000-2006. The losses declined from more than 32 per cent in 2000-01 to 23 per cent in 2006-07 for all utilities taken together. Such losses were higher in the WBSEB and CESC compared to the other utilities in the state.

TABLE 9.3

AT&C Losses (in Per cent) by Utilities in West Bengal

	WBSEB	*CESC*	*DVC*	*DPL*	*DPSC*	*SHRESCL*	*TOTAL*
2000-01	41.07	23.37	9.92	29.2	8.74	25.69	32.15
2001-02	39.54	22.65	8	16.09	8.48	28.58	31.11
2002-03	37.45	19.21	5.06	9.32	5.85	21.16	28.06
2003-04	34.48	17.8	16	6.25	4.35	29.13	26.16
2004-05	33.2	17.07	16.53	4.55	6.55	27.77	25.05
2005-06	32.73	15.74	15.88	6.19	5.9	29.37	24.43
2006-07	30.75	15.02	11.64	6.04	6.5		22.77

Source: WBERC, 2007.

9.4 Consumption of Electricity

Per capita power consumption is one of the major indicators of development in any region. In West Bengal, per capita consumption of electricity increased from 106 kWh in the mid-1970s to more than 204 kWh in 1999-2000 but it was lower than the national average (Table 9.4). The demand for power grows with economic growth as well as with the changes in demographic structure and rising urbanisation.

TABLE 9.4

Per Capita Consumption of Electricity (in kWh)

	West Bengal	*All-India*
1974-75	106.1	174.9
1980-81	117	120.5
1989-90	136.2	236
1996-97	194	334
1999-2000	204.4	354.75

Source: Planning Commission, *10th Plan Document.*

Table 9.5 displays the changes in consumption pattern of electricity in different uses in West Bengal since the early 1990s. Electricity consumption in every sector increased substantially in almost all sectors displayed in Table 9.5, during the period 1990-2006. In agriculture, however, the rate of increase of power consumption was relatively lower compared to the other sectors. Roughly one-fourth of the total consumption of electricity was used in the domestic sector, around 11 per cent in the commercial sector and 42 per cent in industries in the state during 2006-07.

TABLE 9.5

West Bengal: Consumption of Power in MU

	1990-91	*2000-01*	*2006-07*
Domestic	1960.97	4374.25	6547.607 (24.7)
Commercial	1096.12	1910.51	2828.514 (10.7)
Industries	4263.95	6870.8	11109.15 (41.8)
Agriculture	454.01	997.2	940.0116 (3.5)
Others	1046.44	1319.98	5132.871 (19.3)
TOTAL	8821.47	15472.74	26558.15 (100.0)

Note: Figures in parentheses indicate percentage to total consumption

Source: Bureau of Applied Economics and Statistics, WBERC, Government of West Bengal.

TABLE 9.6

Percentage Distribution of Power Consumption by Utilities and Sectors: 2007

	Domestic	*Commercial*	*Industries*	*Agriculture*	*Others*	*TOTAL*
WBSEB	57.9	51.6	40.5	100.0	44.6	48.9
CESC	40.9	47.3	16.7	0.0	20.0	26.0
DPL	0.7	0.5	14.7	0.0	3.6	7.1
DPSC	0.0	0.6	5.7	0.0	4.8	3.4
WBPDCL	0.1	0.0	0.0	0.0	0.1	0.0
WEBREDA	0.0	0.0	0.0	0.0	0.0	0.0
DVC	0.0	0.0	22.4	0.0	26.9	14.6
NTPC	0.3	0.0	0.0	0.0	0.0	0.1

Source: As in Table 9.1.

Table 9.6 provides the relative contributions of different utilities to power consumption in different sectors in West Bengal, in 2007. The major part of electricity consumption in every sector has been provided through WBSEB in the non-metropolitan areas in the state. In agriculture, the entire consumption of electricity, mainly for irrigation purposes, is supported by WBSEB. CESC, the private sector utility in the state, on the other hand, supplies one-fourth of total electricity consumption of the state, and its major parts passes to the commercial and domestic sectors.

9.5 Tariff Structure

Much of the commercial losses in West Bengal, as also in other states of the country, result from the underlying tariff structure and low revenue collection rates. In India, the tariff structure is defined by consumer class and a cross subsidy structure is used to subsidise domestic and agricultural users. In West Bengal, the tariff for different classes of consumers has reached within ±20 per cent of average cost of supply except irrigation, lifeline consumer and certain one or two type of classes of consumers. For lifeline consumer, the price is gradually reducing as per National Tariff Policy. For irrigation tariff has been kept low for non-peak hours only. The tariff for few certain classes of consumer are slightly higher than the average cost of supply. The rate of tariff charged by the WBSEB is significantly lower than the rate charged by the CESC (Table 9.7).

For industrial segment tariff is reduced significantly (Table 9.8). In WBSEDCL and CESC area, the tariff of industrial segment is reducing significantly and for large consuming industries in WBSEDCL area, it can be as low as Rs. 2.67 paisa per unit. Table 9.8 reflect the decreasing trend of industrial tariff in the state. In fact, the average tariff of HT industry in CESC area has been reduced from 493 paisa/kWh in 2003-04 to 352 paisa/kWh in 2007-08, i.e., a drop of Rs. 1.41 per kWh in four years only. Similarly, the average rate of industrial tariff of WBSEDCL (erstwhile WBSEB) has reduced over the same period significantly as shown in Table 9.8.

TABLE 9.7

Tariff (in Paisa/kWh) as Approved by WBERC

	WBSEB	*CESC*	*DPL*	*DPSC*	*SHRESCL*	*TOTAL*
2000-01	265.89	381.61	251.66	286.11	138.36	306.06
2001-02	269.86	389.72	190.88	298.81	228.49	300.56
2002-03	327.52	399.91	215.27	307.43	226.01	341.84
2003-04	341.8	417.44	204.27	312.82	323.59	353.42
2004-05	315.31	391.3	192.89	313.46	334.15	330.57
2005-06	326.75	380.61	221.24	327.63	341.01	335.14
2006-07	319.07	374.4	247.79	330.27		331.51
2007-08	320.86	375.73	248.12	434.47		334.69

Note: Tariff has not been determined for DVC by the commission due to court cases still in process.

Source: As in Table 9.1.

TABLE 9.8

Tariff for Industrial Use

Name of the Licensee	*Supply Voltage*	*Consumer Category*	*Average Tariff for Industrial Consumers in Paisa/kWh*		
			2005-06	*2006-07*	*2007-08*
WBSEDCL	11 KV	Industrial	421.15	411.68	408.2
	33 KV	Industrial	382.72	360.63	357.47
	132 KV	Industrial	340.19	303.76	301.55
CESC	HT	Industrial	387	362	352

Source: As in Table 9.1.

9.6 Rural Electrification

The Ministry of Power, Government of India, had introduced the scheme Rajiv Gandhi Grameen Vidyutikaran Yojana (RGGVY) in April 2005 to provide access to electricity to the rural households. Under this scheme 32 project proposals were submitted for 18 districts out of which 13 projects covering 13 districts were sanctioned during the Tenth Plan period at the estimated cost of Rs. 385 crore. To promote social and rural development by providing electricity through conventional and non-conventional sources of energy in the rural areas, West Bengal Rural Energy Development Corporation Limited (WBREDCL) has been set up. The position of district-wise rural electrification is shown in Table 9.10.

TABLE 9.9

District-wise Position of Mouzas Electrified as on November 2006

Districts	*2001*	*2006*
Bardhaman	2380	2474
Birbhum	2217	2226
Bankura	2470	3279
East Medinipur	5572*	2297
West Medinipur	5572*	5276
Howrah	734	734
Hooghly	1897	1897
24 Parganas (North)	1506	1583
24 Parganas (South)	1808	2030
Nadia	1248	1248
Murshidabad	1794	1871
Uttar Dinajpur	1250	1466
Dakshin Dinajpur	1154	1425
Malda	1597	1620
Jalpaiguri	732	732
Darjeeling	539	604
Cooch Behar	1121	1139
Purulia	1577	2177
West Bengal	29596	34078

Note: * includes East and West Medinipur combined.

Source: Bureau of Applied Economics and Statistics and State Planning Board, Government of West Bengal.

The farmers of West Bengal, as in other states in India, depend extensively on groundwater irrigation in farming. Access to groundwater irrigation is either through ownership or through purchase of pump irrigation services. As per the 59th Round of NSS data (NSSO, 2003), more than 50 per cent of farming households hired irrigation services from other farmers. The state also registered the lowest number of electrified water extracting machines: only 12.2 per cent are electrified as against a national average of 50 per cent (GoI, 2001).

In West Bengal, the tariff rate of electricity used in irrigation is higher as compared to other states in India. Farmers in West Bengal pay an annual fixed electricity tariff of Rs. 6800 for standard 5HP pumps, while in Punjab, Haryana, Tamil Nadu and Andhra Pradesh farmers enjoy free electricity (Mukherji, 2006).

9.7 Renewable Sources of Power

Although thermal power has been the major source of energy, the threat of global warming has brought into focus the need for alternative sources of energy.[9] There has been increasing environmental concern about the contribution of coal-fired power generation to air emissions. Coal burned in power plants on an average has an ash content of 40 per cent and more. Low-quality fuels generate large amounts of ash and particulates along with emissions of sulphur dioxide, nitrogen oxides, carbon dioxide and heavy metals. Power sector contributes about 40 per cent of the total carbon emissions (SAR, 1996).

Wind mills, solar photo voltaic cells, biomass, etc., are the renewable sources of energy. In West Bengal, solar power has a number of advantages over the other alternatives. A solar power unit with capacity of 2 MW is being installed in West Bengal to support the thermal power system in mining operations. Another unit with capacity 15 MW is being planned for supporting the thermal power system in Purulia district (Bose, 2008).

TABLE 9.10

Change in Flat Rate Electricity Tariff in West Bengal, 1995 to 2003

	Electricity Tariff for Shallow Tubewells (Rs./year/tubewell)		*Electricity Tariff for Submersible Tubewells (Rs./year/tubewell)*	
	North Bengal	*Other districts*	*North Bengal*	*Other districts*
1991	1100	1100	1100	1100
1995	1380	1700	1380	1700
1996	1660	2040	2500	3060
1999	2676	3284	4028	4932
2001	4064	5008	5080	6252
2003	4434	5460	5540	6810

Source: Mukherji, 2006.

References

Bose, D.K. (2008). "Prospects of Solar Power in India under Global Warming", *Economic and Political Weekly* 43(47): 14-17.

Government of India (2005). *Economic Survey, 2005-06*

———. (2005). *The Gazette of India,* No. 23/40/2004-R&R (Vol.II). New Delhi: Ministry of Power.

———. (2001), *All India Report on Agricultural Census, 2001-02.* New Delhi: Ministry of Agriculture, Government of India.

Mukherji, A. (2006). Political ecology of groundwater: The contrasting case of water abundant West Bengal and water scarce Gujarat, India, *Hydrogeology Journal* 14(3): 392-406.

Purkayastha, P. (2001). Power Sector Policies and New Electricity Bill, *Economic and Political Weekly:* 2257-62, June 23.

SAR (1996). Second Assessment report of IPCC, *Climate Change 1995: The Science of Climate Change.* Cambridge.

9. The major source of emission of green house gases, particularly CO_2, has been the thermal power stations.

APPENDIX A-9.1[10]

Policy of Government of West Bengal on Mini/Micro Hydro Electric Power Station up to 3 MW

- The high and extra high voltage industrial consumers will be allowed to set up captive power plant through no-conventional energy sources including Mini/Micro Hydel Power Station upto 3 MW
- Transmission and wheeling of power generated.
- The facility for wheeling of power will be provided by the utility at a wheeling charge of 30 paise/kWh that will be revised from time to time. The wheeling of power will be allowed to not more than one unit of the same industrial undertaking. However, a captive power plant may be set up through a joint venture company constituted by a maximum of 2 (two) industrial undertakings who would be eligible to exclusively consume the power from the captive power plant in one unit each of the participating industrial undertaking in the joint venture company. For this purpose the industrial undertaking will be required to make its own transmission lines upto nearest grid sub-station of the utility along with the associated protective system as per specification of the utility, and the said transmission line shall be maintained by the generator.

Policy in Respect of Captive Power Plants Utilising Conventional Fuel:

- New industries may be allowed to set up captive power plant for continuous running provided the same is not connected to the power utility's grid and there is no third party sale. If such captive generation is through installation of diesel generator, control of noise pollution must be as per stipulations of the Pollution Control Board.
- Already operating industries wishing to switch over to captive generation—partly or fully—may be allowed to set up captive generation plant provided such plant is not connected to the power utility's grid and there is no third party sale.
- Environment clearance should be obtained from the West Bengal Pollution Control Board and Environment Department of the State Government.
- Consumers drawing backup power or partial power from power utility shall pay monthly demand charge on contract demand at double the normal demand charge rate provided the actual drawal is less than the contract demand. In the event, actual demand in a month exceeds the contract demand and the excess demand shall be charged at three times the normal charge rate.
- Electricity duty will be payable under the Bengal Electricity Duty Rules as amended from time to time. Metering arrangement should be made for recording consumption of power generated in the captive plants.
- Industrial units may apply to the West Bengal State Electricity Board for clearance u/s-44 of the Electricity (Supply) Act, 1948, after obtaining clearance from West Bengal Pollution Control Board and the Environment Department, Government of West Bengal. Before given consent u/s-44 (1) of the Act, the WBSEB shall consult Central Electricity Authority in cases where the capacity of the captive plant exceeds 25 MW.

---

10. Source: *http://wbpower.nic.in/initiatives.htm*

Chapter 10

Public Health

10.1 Introduction

The health status of a population depends on nutrition, access to safe drinking water and sanitation facilities, environment, type of shelter, awareness about health and health care. This chapter provides an assessment on the health and health care situation in West Bengal. The major focus is on providing exhaustive and comprehensive accounts of different aspects of health status and health care scenario than providing analytical insights on select issues. This study is primarily based on the data from National Sample Surveys, National Family Health Surveys, World Health Survey (for West Bengal), Sample Registration System, Census, State Bureau of Health Intelligence (Government of West Bengal), Central Bureau of Health Intelligence and Reserve Bank of India.

10.2 Health Status in West Bengal

The health status of a population is usually measured in terms of indicators of mortality and morbidity. The commonly used mortality indicators are crude death rate, infant mortality rate, child mortality rate and maternal mortality rate. The last three indicators are important as they reflect crucial aspects of health of a society, that is, the health status of mothers and children. Also life expectancy at birth depends largely on infant mortality rate (IMR). The recent Sample Registration System estimates of IMR show that West Bengal is in the fourth position (38), after Kerala (14), Maharashtra (36) and Tamil Nadu (37). Figure 10.1 displays the movement of IMR for Kerala, Tamil Nadu and West Bengal in last 16 years (1990-2005). The figure shows that West Bengal has been able to reduce IMR substantially over the years.

The temporal changes in IMR in rural and urban areas of the state during the period 1981-2005 are shown in Figure 10.2. In the rural areas, the IMR decreased significantly from 98 in 1981 to 44 in 2005, while in urban areas, it declined slowly during the same period. It is important to notice that the rural-urban gap in IMR in West Bengal has not drastically reduced since 1994.

FIGURE 10.1

Changes in Infant Mortality Rate (IMR)

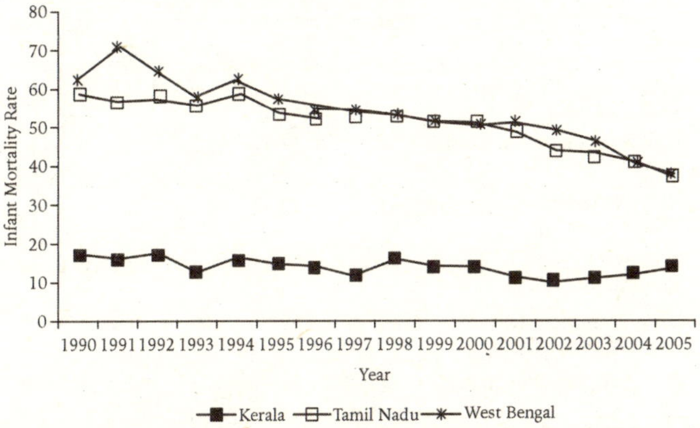

Source: Sample Registration System, Registrar General of India.

FIGURE 10.2

West Bengal: Infant Mortality Rate

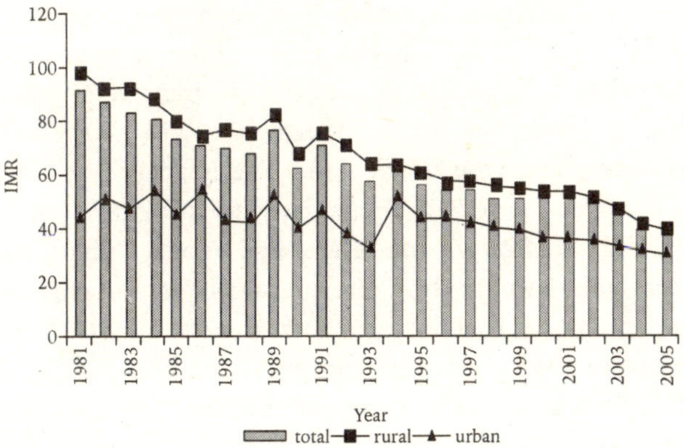

Source: Sample Registration System, Registrar General of India.

10.2.1 Health of Women and Children

The health status of women and children assume a special importance. The National Family Health Survey conducted in 2005-06 provides select important information on the health status of women and children. Generally indicators of stunting, wasting and underweight are well-accepted anthropometric measures for children's health. Table 10.1 presents the percentage of stunted, wasted and underweight children (below 3 years) in West Bengal. The state registered a significant rural-urban difference in terms of anthropometric measures and prevalence of anaemia among the children. As far as prevalence of anaemia is concerned, the urban areas (excluding Kolkata) shows better picture than Kolkata. There has been a huge rural-urban gap in the percentage of underweight women and indeed, the gap between Kolkata and other urban areas is significant.

TABLE 10.1

Select Indicators of Health Status of Women and Children in West Bengal

Indicators	*Urban*	*Rural*	*Kolkata*	*Total*
Children under 3 years who stunted (%)	22.7	35.4	21.0	33.0
Children under 3 years who are wasted (%)	14.2	20.2	12.8	19.0
Children under 3 years who are underweight (%)	30.0	46.7	24.9	43.5
Children age 6-35 months who are anaemic (%)	58.2	71.9	64.0	69.4
Women whose body mass index is below normal (%)	19.9	44.9	12.0	37.7
Ever married women age 15-49 who are anaemic (%)	59.0	65.6	56.1	63.8

Source: National Family Health Survey 3 (Fact Sheets accessed from the NFHS website).

10.2.2 Reported Incidence of Disease

National Sample Survey Organisation has collected data on self-reported incidence of illnesses or diseases. The data from NSSO's health round (60th Round: 2004) shows that in West Bengal, the average number of people reporting illness per 1000 population is 114 in the rural areas and 157 in the urban areas. The incidence of illness was lower in West Bengal compared to many other states in India. Although the state has made substantial improvement in tackling the prevalence of tuberculosis and leprosy, HIV infection cases are on the rise. Data from voluntary counselling and testing centres (VCTC) in West Bengal reveals that the number of new HIV infection cases has increased from 304 in 1996 to 3610 in 2006. The latest HIV sentinel surveillance shows that the cumulative figure of people infected with HIV in West Bengal since 1986 has crossed 9000. Besides, the state had at least 4900 people living with AIDS. According to West Bengal AIDS Prevention and Control Society (WBAP&CS), the epidemic has spread to the general population and is no longer restricted to most at-risk population.[1]

10.2.3 Disability

The disable population needs different kind of medical and mental health care, and a good health care system needs to be sensitive to both the medical as well as emotional/psychological need of the disable population. According to Census 2001, the percentage of disabled population is 2.3 per cent in West Bengal, which is marginally higher than the national average (2.13). Disability in seeing is the most prominent form of disability (48.6 per cent of the total disabled population), followed by disability in movement (22.3 per cent), mentally disable (14.8 per cent), disability in speech (9.2 per cent) and disability in hearing (7.1 per cent). Percentage of disable population is higher in the rural areas compared to urban areas. Darjeeling shows the highest percentage of disabled population (3.5 per cent).

10.2.4 Mental Health

Mental diseases are classified into the following categories: (i) organic including symptomatic; (ii) due to psychoactive; (iii) schizophrenia; (iv) mood disorder; (v) neurotic, stress-related; (vi) behavioural syndromes; (vii) disorder of adult personality; (vii) mental retardation; (viii) disorder of psychological; (ix) disorder occurring in childhood; and (x) unspecified mental disorder. The distribution of new outdoor cases (provisional figure for 2003) by disease categories show that in West Bengal, the most frequently treated cases are neurotic, stress-related (52 per cent), followed by mood disorder (32 per cent) and schizophrenia (11 per cent). The share of female in new outdoor cases is little higher (54 per cent) than the halfway mark. For mental ailments such as 'neurotic, stress-related' and 'mood disorder', the share of female patients is higher than that of males.

As far as data on treated patients at child guidance clinic is concerned, mental retardation is the most frequently reported case (46 per cent) followed by organic including symptomatic (17 per cent), unspecified mental

1. See the official website of WBSAP&CS (*www.wbhealth.gov.in/wbsapcs*)

disorder (18 per cent), neurotic, stress-related (9 per cent), due to psychoactive substance (7 per cent). Data on indoor (new and old) patients of mental disorder admitted in specialised mental hospitals for the year 2004 shows that schizophrenia and mood disorder are the main two mental diseases accounting for 83 per cent of total indoor cases.

TABLE 10.2

Incidence of Mental Retardation in West Bengal: 2003

	Conflicts and Tensions	*Feeling Sad, Low or Depressed*	*Worry and Anxiety*
Sex			
Male	44.0	58.4	66.6
Female	57.5	67.7	71.9
Residence			
Rural	52.0	66.0	71.1
Urban	45.5	49.5	61.0
Education in years			
0	61.1	71.3	74.8
1-5	57.1	70.9	79.1
6-10	34.2	49.7	58.8
11+	36.1	45.3	51.7
Income quintile			
Q1	55.6	69.5	77.7
Q2	60.7	69.3	71.4
Q3	43.3	60.4	69.7
Q4	46.1	55.6	59.3
Q5	36.9	49.7	58.3
Total	50.8	63.1	69.3

Source: World Health Organization (2006).

The World Health Survey has collected a rich set of information on various dimensions of the mental health (Table 10.2). The table shows that the percentage of people, who found difficulty in dealing with conflicts and tensions is 50.8 (44.0 for the male and 57.5 for the female). Similarly, the percentage of people who felt sad, low or depressed in 30 days preceding the survey is 73.1 (58.4 for the male and 67.7 for the female). Percentage of people who found difficulty to cope up with worry or anxiety is 69.3 per cent (66.6 for male and 71.9 for female). If we consider these figures as crude indicators of mental health of the population, then it is clear from the table that the burden is more on the female and on rural population than their male and urban counterparts respectively. It is also observed that mental health of the population (captured by these indicators) improves with increase in income and education level.

10.3 Access to Health Care, Water Supply and Sanitation

As far as access to safe drinking water is concerned, Census 2001 shows that in West Bengal 88.5 per cent of the households have access to water sources, which can roughly be considered as safe for drinking.[2] There is no great difference between rural and urban areas in this regard. In the rural areas, 86.9 per cent and in the urban areas 92.3 per cent of the households have access to safe drinking water. Estimates from NSS 60th Round data shows that only 7.7 per cent of the households purify water before drinking (3.5 per cent in the rural areas and 18.8 per cent in the urban areas). Further, excessive arsenic and fluoride in groundwater are two other problems that a number of blocks are facing in West Bengal.[3]

Census 2001 also gives an unimpressive picture of access to sanitary facilities in West Bengal. As high as 56.3 per cent of the households do not have access to sanitary facility. The picture is dismal in the rural areas where percentage of households not having toilet facility goes up to as high as 73.1. The situation is far better in the urban areas. In the urban areas, only 15.2 per cent of the households do not have any sanitary facility.[4] However, in recent years some districts (such as Medinipur) have made remarkable achievement in this regard.

The poor health status observed among the women and children in terms of anthropometric measures and higher prevalence of anaemia may not be the feature of women and children alone. Such a poor nutritional status may be a feature of the whole population, although we do not have comparable data from large surveys. Data on nutritional intake collected by World Health Survey seems to corroborate this apprehension. The World Health Survey for West Bengal has found that 94.7 per cent of

2. Census 2001 has divided all sources of drinking water into the following types: (i) tap; (ii) handpump; (iii) tubewell; (iv) tank, pond, lake; (v) river, canal; (vi) spring; and (vii) any other. Among them water from tap, handpump and tubewell can roughly be considered as safe for drinking.

3. As per latest observation, groundwater in 79 blocks (out of 341 blocks in West Bengal) in the district of Malda, Murshidabad, Nadia, North 24 Parganas, South 24 Parganas, Howrah, Hooghly and Bardhaman are affected by arsenic contamination. According to 2001 Census, population of these blocks is 166.49 lakh out of state's rural population of 577.35 lakh. Detection of fluoride contamination is a recent phenomenon in West Bengal. Excess fluoride in drinking water was first detected in the year 1996 in Nalhati-I Block of Birbhum District. According to the Habitation Survey 2003, excess fluoride was detected in 665 habitations in West Bengal spread of 45 blocks in 9 districts. (*http://www.wbphed.gov.in/Bharat_Nirman_Web.html*)

4. For Tamil Nadu, the corresponding figures are 85.6 per cent in the rural areas and 35.7 per cent in the urban areas. For Kerala, the corresponding figures are 18.7 per cent in the rural areas and 8 per cent in the urban areas.

the people do not eat sufficient vegetables and fruits. However, insufficient intake of vegetable cannot always be attributed to lack of purchasing power or poverty alone. Sometimes, it is closely related to culture and food habit of different section of the population.

As far as health care infrastructure is concerned, one needs to consider the physical infrastructure as well as manpower in the health sector. Health care facilities in West Bengal are displayed in Table 10.3.

TABLE 10.3

Health Care Facilities in West Bengal

Year	*Hospital*		*Health Centre*		*Sub Centre*	*Total Health Units*	
	No.	*Beds*	*No.*	*Beds*	*No.*	*No.*	*Beds*
1994-95	397	55090	1263	12486	8126	9786	67576
1995-96	402	56199	1263	12587	8126	9791	68786
1996-97	404	56608	1263	12592	8126	9793	69200
1997-98	405	56664	1263	12592	8126	9794	69256
1998-99	406	57303	1262	12498	8126	9794	69801
1999-00	415	58075	1268	12323	8126	9809	70398
2000-01	416	58285	1269	12329	8126	9811	70614
2001-02	429	58721	1266	12353	8126	9821	71074
2002-03	434	59110	1268	12218	8126	9828	71328
2003-04	434	59110	1268	12218	10356	12058	71328
2004-05	433	58312	1268	12207	10356	12057	70519
2005-06	2016*	78951	1268	13364	10356	13640	92315
2006-07	2081*	82160	1269	13921	10356	13706	96081

Note: * includes private hospitals.

Source: Government of West Bengal, *Economic Review*. 2007-08.

Human resources in terms of medical and para-medical manpower are as important as the physical infrastructure. Recent data from Health Information of India (Government of India, 2006) shows that the average population served per government allopathic doctor is 14064 in West Bengal compared to 9095 in Kerala and 7718 in Tamil Nadu.[5] The average population served per government dental surgeon is 233320 in West Bengal as compared to 415288 in Kerala and 343904 in Tamil Nadu.[6] In West Bengal, the average number of doctor per lakh population increased from 46 in 1983 to 51 in 2005. Like government hospital beds, strong urban bias is also observed in the concentration of doctors. More than 85 per cent of the doctors are concentrated in the urban areas. Although there is no denial of the fact that the average number of doctors and nurses per lakh population has increased over the time,[7] anecdotal evidence suggests that the existing strength of medical and para-medical manpower and its growth in West Bengal is far lower than what is needed for its growing population with increasing disease burden. A cursory look at the figures on total number of seats available for MBBS, postgraduate and nursing courses in medical and nursing colleges suggest that the state needs to expand the intake capacity gradually to meet the increasing demand for doctors, nurses and other paramedical staff.[8]

It is interesting to observe that in spite of having not so high intake capacities in its diploma and degree courses in pharmacy, West Bengal has large number of pharmacist (registered with Pharmacy Council of India). As on June 2003, West Bengal is having third largest number of registered pharmacists (89,630), after 101,240 in Tamil Nadu and 99,614 in Maharashtra. However, admission capacity to offer diploma and degree in Pharmacy does not show an impressive picture for West Bengal. With regard to diploma in pharmacy, west Bengal has 430 approved seats in 9 institutes as against 1130 in Kerala and 2900 in Tamil Nadu. Similarly, with regard to degree in Pharmacy, there are 120 seats in West Bengal as against 90 in Kerala and 2180 in Tamil Nadu.

Recent data from Health Information of India (Government of India, 2006) shows that in terms of average number of general nursing midwives, auxiliary nursing midwives and health visitor and health supervisor West Bengal lags behind Kerala and Tamil Nadu. The average number of general nursing midwives per lakh population is 54 in West Bengal compared to 219 in Kerala and 242 in Tamil Nadu. The average number of auxiliary nursing midwives per lakh population is 68 in West Bengal compared to 84 in Kerala and 80 in Tamil Nadu. The average number of health visitor and health supervisor per lakh population is 14 in West Bengal compared to 24 in Kerala and 17 in Tamil Nadu.[9]

5. For Tamil Nadu, the figures include doctor/dentists in State Government Allopathic Medical Institutions except Medical Colleges.
6. The figures on allopathic doctors and dental surgeons are pertaining to the date 1st January 2005.
7. In the rural areas, doctor per lakh population increased from 19 in 1983 to 22 in 2005. In the urban areas, it increased from 124 in 1983 to 128 in 2005. The average number of nurse per lakh population increased from 44 in 1983 to 60 in 2005 (Government of West Bengal, 2006; Census 1981, 1991 and 2001).
8. Total number of seats for MBBS in all medical colleges in West Bengal is around 1105 and total seat for Postgraduate courses is around 264 (Government of West Bengal, 2006).
9. Data for Kerala and Tamil Nadu are pertaining to year 2004, while that for West Bengal is for the year 2002. The figures for Tamil Nadu include Tamil Nadu, Andaman and Nicobar Islands and Pondicherry, while that for West Bengal include West Bengal and Sikkim. We have considered the projected population for the state or group of states to calculate the average figures.

Homeopathic seems to be the second most frequently utilised system of medicine after allopathic (National Sample Survey Organisation, 1992). Official data shows that in West Bengal there are good numbers of dispensaries manned by sufficient number of homeopathic doctors. As on 31st March 2006 total number of registered homeopathic practitioners in West Bengal is 38,898. There are total 545 state homoeopathic dispensaries[10] and 975 *Gram Panchayat* dispensaries in West Bengal (Government of West Bengal, 2006).

10.4 Utilisation of Health Care Services

Any discussion of utilisation of health care services must make a distinction between utilisation of outpatient care and utilisation of inpatient care (i.e., hospitalised care). Generally utilisation of inpatient care involves substantial monetary cost on the part of the patient in comparison to outpatient care. Moreover, health care facilities, which provide inpatient care services, are not as plenty in supply as outpatient service providers. As a result people's choice of inpatient care is often restricted by high expected cost of treatment and long distance to the health facility.

FIGURE 10.3

Utilisation of Outpatient Care Per 1000 Population by MPCE Quintiles in West Bengal

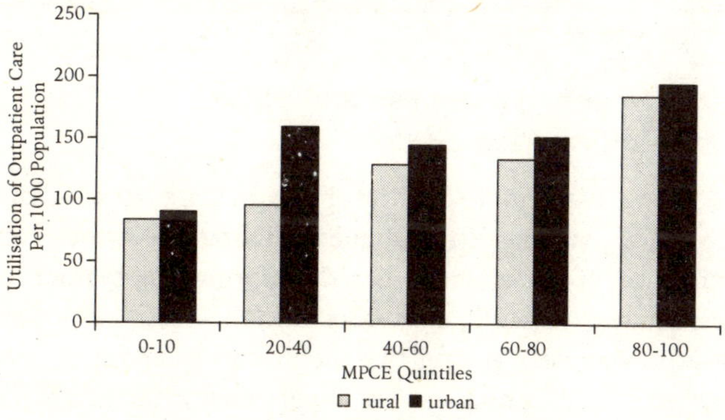

Source: Estimated from NSS 60th Round unit-record data.

NSS 60th Round data on outpatient care utilisation shows that in West Bengal, 80 per cent of the reported illness in the rural areas and 83 per cent of the reported illness in the urban areas received treatment. Figure 10.3 presents the utilisation of outpatient care per 1000 population by monthly per capita consumption expenditure (MPCE) quintiles in West Bengal. If MPCE is considered as a proxy for income or economic status, the figure shows that as one moves from poorer to richer class, utilisation of outpatient care (per 1000 population) also goes up. The figure also shows that for each level of income or economic status, the rate of utilisation is higher for the urban people compared to the rural people. In West Bengal only 19 per cent of the outpatient care in the rural areas and 20 per cent of the outpatient care in the urban areas are from government facilities.

Estimates from NSS 60th Round data show that in West Bengal hospitalisation per 1000 population is 23 in the rural areas and 35 in the urban areas. An analysis of the 'reasons for non-utilisation of government facilities for outpatient care' based on NSS 60th Round data suggests that bad treatment (as perceived by the patients), poor accessibility and long waiting time are the major reasons in West Bengal. As high as 33.2 per cent (31.9 per cent in the rural areas and 35.7 in the urban areas) of the people did not utilise government facilities as they anticipated that they would not be satisfied with the treatment. Further, 32.6 per cent of the rural people did not visit government facilities due to long distance/poor accessibility and 21.4 per cent of the people (12.9 in the rural areas and 37.8 per cent in the urban areas) did not go to the government facilities anticipating long waiting time. Furthermore, a significant portion of the population in rural West Bengal depends on unqualified medical practitioner (Soman, 2002; Kanjilal, Samanta and Mondal, 2007).

Unlike outpatient care, in West Bengal people mostly depend on government hospitals for inpatient care. Estimates from 60th Round NSS data shows that 78.6 per cent people in the rural areas and 65.4 per cent people in the urban areas depend on government hospitals.[11] Figure 10.4 shows percentage share of inpatient care from government hospitals by MPCE quintiles. Although percentage of inpatient care from government hospitals decreases as we move from poorest MPCE quintile to richest MPCE quintile, still a very high percentage of rich people utilise government hospitals.[12] There is some evidence that seems to explain why such large number of rich people still use government hospitals.

10. Number of homeopathic dispensaries: Sub Divisional Hospital – 305; Block Primary Health Centre – 105; Primary Health Centre – 135 (Government of West Bengal, 2006).

11. A comparison between NSS 52nd and 60th Rounds shows that people's dependence on government hospitals for inpatient care has come down over the years (from 82.2 per cent to 78.6 per cent in the rural areas and from 72.1 per cent to 65.4 per cent in the urban areas).

12. Mukherjee (2006) and Mukherjee and Levesque (2007) have found that economic status-related inequalities in the utilisation of inpatient care in general and inpatient care from government hospitals in particular have come down in West Bengal between two NSS rounds (52nd Round: 1995-1996 and 60th Round: 2004).

Figure 10.5 presents percentage of hospitalised cases which could avail free wards at government hospitals by MPCE quintiles. The figure shows that there is not significant difference between rich and poor population in terms of availing of free hospital wards. Availing of a free hospital ward definitely reduces one's cost of treatment at government hospitals when it is compared with private hospitals and that could possibly be one of the reasons why a large proportion of non-poor people prefer government hospitals. There is a need to have a fair exemption policy so that non-poor (especially the rich) population do not enjoy undue share of the government subsidy on health care (especially hospitalised care).

FIGURE 10.4

Percentage of Inpatient Care from Government Facilities in West Bengal

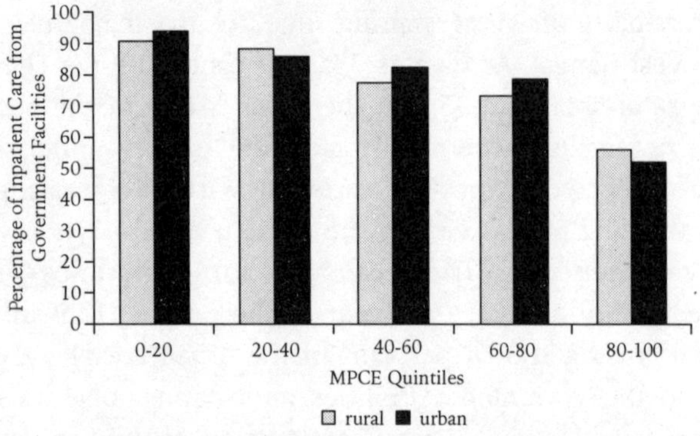

Source: Estimated from NSS 60th Round unit-record data.

FIGURE 10.5

Free Ward Availed by Different MPCE Classes in Government Hospitals in West Bengal

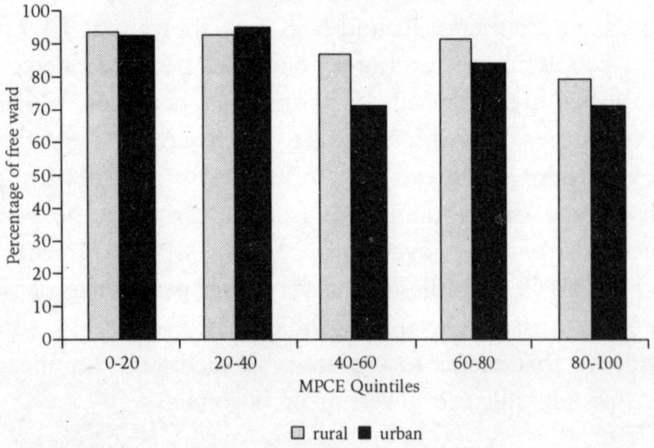

Source: Estimated from NSS 60th Round unit-record data.

The role of the government in providing necessary childbirth related health services and childcare to needy population is considered important also from a public health point of view. Therefore, one needs to examine the utilisation of health care by pregnant women, mothers and children separately from general preventive and curative health care. In West Bengal, 62.4 per cent of the mothers had 3 or more antenatal care visits for their last birth, the figure was impressive as compared to some other states, particularly Kerala and Tamil Nadu (Table 10.4). In West Bengal, percentage of institutional birth is 43.1 compared to 90.4 in Tamil Nadu and 99.5 per cent in Kerala. The percentage of fully immunised children (12-23 months) is 64.3 in West Bengal, 80.8 in Tamil Nadu and 75.3 in Kerala. In West Bengal, the huge rural-urban gap observed in the case of antenatal care and institutional birth is of moderate level for immunisation.

TABLE 10.4

Utilisation of Child and Mother Care

Indicators	*Urban*	*Rural*	*Kolkata*	*Total*	*Tamil Nadu*	*Kerala*
Mothers who had at least 3 antenatal care visits for their last birth (%)	87.3	55.8	87.7	62.4	96.5	93.9
Births assisted by a doctor/nurse/LHV/ANM/ other health personnel (%)*	80.2	36.8	88.3	45.7	93.2	99.7
Institutional birth	79.2	33.8	87.7	43.1	90.4	99.5
Children 12-23 months fully immunised (BCG, measles and 3 doses each of polio/DPT) (%)	70.3	62.8	67.6	64.3	80.8	75.3

Note: * based on last 2 births in the 3 years before the survey.

Source: *National Family Health Survey 3* (fact sheets accessed from the website).

10.5 Health Awareness and Health Information System

Along with good quality of health care at affordable cost, adequate health awareness among the people and existence of an efficient health information system are prerequisite to build up a good health system. Adequate health awareness among the people can promote hygienic practices, and consciousness about nutritional intake can help them avoid preventable illnesses. All these factors significantly contribute towards promoting health status of the population and reducing its disease burden. A good health information system allows the technocrats (doctor-administrators) and policy makers to constantly monitor different aspects of the health system and help them figure out easily the areas of concern, which need short-term, medium-term and long-term intervention. An easily accessible and good health information system is also of great help to the researchers. However, there are some preliminary observations to suggest that West Bengal needs to do more to improve health awareness among the people and strengthen its health information system.

10.5.1 Health Awareness and Community Health Care Management Initiative

It is well known that many of the determining factors of health outcome are beyond the purview of health department or health sector interventions. For example, it is observed that crude birth rate, infant mortality rate and maternal mortality rate come down when there is an increase in female literacy or/and increase in average age of marriage. Availability of safe drinking water and use of sanitary latrine with hygienic practices brings down incidences of diarrhoeal outbreaks. Use of mosquito nets and practice of keeping homes and immediate environment free from stagnant water can substantially reduce the incidence of malaria, dengue and other communicable diseases. Another pressing concern in the area of reproductive health is under-age marriage. Despite government law and intensive campaign against it, under-age marriage is still rampant in West Bengal. Since many of the contributory factors of low health awareness are beyond the scope of the health department, they can effectively be influenced only through other departments of the government and by changing people's nutrition and health-related behaviour and practices. Towards reaching this objective, the government of West Bengal has initiated a principle of community-based convergence owned by local government, known as community heath care management initiative (CHCMI). CHCMI seems to be an excellent initiative to sensitise the community, government functionaries and elected representatives of the local governments about the health issues of the community. Despite its recent origin and limited success, it can be said that capacity building has to be strengthened at local levels for making CHCMI a great success (Chakraborty, Mukherjee and Das, 2007).

10.5.2 Awareness about HIV/AIDS

Despite its intensive and innovative campaigning, it seems that AIDS awareness campaign has not achieved its desirable result in the rural areas and among the women. Data from National Behavioural Surveillance Survey, 2001 shows that in urban West Bengal for the age group 15-19 years, 78.1 per cent of the males and 66.4 per cent of the females knew about the sexual route of HIV transmission. The corresponding figures for rural West Bengal are 56.6 per cent for the male and 32.3 per cent for the female. Similar male-female and rural-urban difference in awareness about HIV/AIDS was observed in recently conducted NFHS 3 survey.

TABLE 10.5

Indicators of Awareness about HIV/AIDS among Men and Women in West Bengal

	Urban	*Rural*	*Kolkata*	*Total*
Percentage of people who have heard of HIV/AIDS				
Women	78.4	39.0	89.7	50.2
Men	91.9	65.8	95.9	73.5
Percentage of people who know that consistent condom use can reduce the chances of getting HIV/AIDS				
Women	52.5	20.0	62.6	29.3
Men	79.5	46.1	85.9	56.9

Source: National Family Health Survey 3.

Table 10.5 presents two indicators of awareness about HIV/AIDS among men and women in West Bengal. The table shows that only 50.2 per cent of the women (ever-married women of age group 15-49) in West Bengal have heard of HIV/AIDS. Similarly, only 29.3 per cent of the women know that consistent condom use can reduce chances of getting HIV/AIDS. As far as knowledge of HIV/AIDS is concerned, the men-women difference is substantial in the rural areas compared to urban areas in West Bengal. However, with regards to the knowledge that consistent use of condom can reduce the chances of getting HIV/AIDS, significant man-women difference is found everywhere (rural, urban or Kolkata) in West Bengal. This calls for strengthening and intensifying the HIV/AIDS awareness campaign in the rural areas and among the women (especially among the rural women).

10.6 Health of Workers and Changing Labour Market Conditions

The factory workers have definite economic status and entitlements to health status—the social security system known as the Employees' State Insurance (ESI) Scheme by an Act of 1948—which in many ways are different from others in the same income group. Also, their health service use and financing are distinctly different.

The ESI Scheme is unique, it being contributory in nature. All the employees in the factories or establishments to which the Act of 1948 applies are insured in a manner provided by the Act. The contribution payable to the ESI Corporation—the apex body of this scheme—in respect of an employee comprises of employer as well as employee's contribution at a specified rate.

At a time when WHO as well as the Government of India by the Health Policy have called for a reduction in health disparities by improving the health of the disadvantaged, an efficient as well as rational health service system i.e., the ESI Scheme is in a mess because of the changing labour market conditions. Three changes in the Indian labour market are particularly noticeable since the mid-1980s. First, the real wage in the (organised) Indian factories remained almost constant, while the labour productivity increased at a steady rate widening the wage-productivity gap. Second, the daily real wage in the organised manufacturing gradually approached to and ultimately nose-dived below 'one-dollar-a-day', i.e., the 'extreme' international poverty line towards the end of the previous century. Third, casualisation in the Indian factories is growing.

There is a comprehensive set of labour laws protecting employment, wage, work conditions inside the factories, and against arbitrary dismissals, yet there is so much idiosyncratic volatility in the labour markets. As a result, although the Citizens Charter of the social security scheme for the workers—contributory, of course—is there, intact, yet so many fissures have developed in the system threatening the health security of the insured workers, and creating more numbers of invisible patients.

ESI Scheme being contributory in nature, all the employees in the factories or establishments to which the Act applies, are insured in a manner provided by the Act. The contribution payable to the Corporation in respect of an employee comprises of employer as well as employee's contribution at specified rates.

The medical infrastructure of ESIC, in 2003, consisted of 141 ESI hospitals, 43 ESI annexes, 337 diagnostic centres, 1452 ESI dispensaries, 3000 panel clinics, 23500 number of beds in ESI hospitals, 3800 number of beds reserved in other hospitals, 14000 doctors/specialists, etc., and 45000 paramedical staff, etc.

10.6.1 Comparative Achievements of the ESI Scheme

The NSSO reports (based on the survey during 1995-1996 and 2006) reveal a positive association between MPCE and the proportion of ailing persons (PAP, i.e., number of persons per 1,000 reporting ailment),[13] in both rural and urban areas.[14] If MPCE is considered to be a proxy for level of living of the households, data do show that the level of morbidity tends to rise with the level of living. This implies either (a) the poor are less prone to sickness than the rich, or (b) reporting of morbidity improves with the improvement in the level of living, however, the second one seems to be more likely, when compared with ESI data. Reporting of morbidity depends on the spatial spread of the report receiving or diagnostic centres. At a relatively high level of MPCE, people could afford to travel a long distance to report ailment.

In the present context, we will be concentrating on the general health status in urban India as revealed in the NSSO Reports since our focus is the factory workers who are concentrated in the urban areas; not only the factories are mostly located in urban areas but also, the ESI implemented areas are urban. It is also to be noted that the health status (non-hospitalised cases) as reflected in NSSO Reports is based on self-assessment, while a physical examination constitutes the basis of ESI data. So, the latter turns out to be a more reliable database for health status, which policy makers often ignore.

Consecutive NSSO Reports show the prevalence rate[15] (15 days) of morbidity in urban India—taking male and females together—was 55 in 1,000 persons in 1995-96 as compared to 42 in 1973-74.[16] The proportion of persons reporting ailment (15 days) was 54 per 1,000 persons during 1995-96. This was rather higher than the comparable estimates either in 1986-87, or in 1973-74 (ibid). In 2004, PAP was 54.[17]

So far as health inequality in the urban areas is concerned, the untreated ailing persons varied between 20 per cent in the lowest expenditure group to 9 per cent in the top expenditure group.[18] While 'ailment not serious' constituted 81 per cent of the cases of untreated ailments in 1986-87, it declined to 60 per cent in 1995-96 but still remained substantial. On the other hand, the reason of 'financial problem', which accounted for only 10 per cent of the untreated ailments in 1986-87, has more than doubled (i.e., 21 per cent) in 1995-96.[19] Thus, a larger proportion of ailments in 1995-96 went untreated because the cost of treatment was higher than that the households could afford.

13. PAP gives the estimated proportion of persons reporting ailment suffered at any time during the reference period and is not strictly the prevalence rate.
14. NSSO (1998); NSSO (2006).
15. Prevalence is the ratio between the number of spells of ailment suffered at any time during the reference period and the population exposed to the risk.
16. NSSO (1998: Table 4.6).
17. NSSO (2006).
18. NSSO (1998)
19. NSSO (1998: Table 4.9)

TABLE 10.6

Ailments in Urban—Short and Long-Duration: NSSO and ESIC

	NSSO, 1995-96 (per 1,000 persons)(1)		ESI Scheme (Per 1,000 Ips)	
	Short-Duration(2)	Long-Duration(3)	Short-Duration	Long-Duration
1995-96	29	14		
1996-97			741	550
1997-98			740	598
1998-99			1156	815
1999-2000			778	589
2000-01			713	591
2001-02			669	585
2002-03			527	467
2003-04	37	6	575	470

Note: (1) Incidence rate of ailment during the last 15 days of the Survey (2) and (3). The diseases (in the ESIC data) have been classified as 'short-duration' and 'long-duration' following the classification made in NSSO (1998).

There are huge discrepancies in the reporting of ailments in the two different information entry points, i.e., ESIC and NSSO (Table 10.6). This is partly explained by the fact that in the NSSO, the enquiry on morbidity was conducted with a reference period of 15 days. All spells of ailment suffered by each member of the sample household during the 15 days preceding the date of enquiry, whether or not the patient was hospitalised for treatment, were covered in the survey.[20]

According to NSSO, the ratio of short-duration to long-duration ailments was 2.1:1 in 1995-96, whereas the same was 1.4:1 in ESIC in 1996-97. Thereafter, in 2003-2004 the ratio was 1.2:1 in ESIC, whereas it was 6.2:1 in NSSO (Table 10.6). In other words, if we are to follow NSSO, the urban population in India suffers more from short-duration than long-duration ailments. In every 3 cases of ailments in the urban areas at least 2 were short-duration in nature, in the mid-1990s. The policy suggestion perhaps then would be that an extensive network of primary and preventive health care is likely to produce a better health status in urban India.

On the other hand, the ESIC data tell us that there should be an appropriate balance between hospital and non-hospital systems for improving the health status. The frequency of short-duration ailments is greater than that of the long-duration ailments, yet the gap is not significant (Table 10.6). Following NSSO, privatisation at the lower ends may be a relatively easier option for the government to divest its role in the health care system. By contrast, ESI data tell us that hospital care—at specialised and district hospitals—at a cheaper price, along with health centres and clinics, that is, a rather comprehensive health care system than a piece-meal arrangement is needed to improving the urban health status. Hospitals do absorb the bulk—40 to 80 per cent—of public spending on health in developing countries[21] but there is still no viable and acceptable alternative, as private investments in expanding hospital facilities would only mitigate a small part of the problem.

The burden of 10 major diseases in 1995-96, as reported in NSSO (1998) are "fevers of short duration", "cough and acute bronchitis", "diarrhoea and gastroenteritis dysentery, including cholera", and so on (Table 10.7). That is, mostly those that could be taken care of at the primary health centres, dispensaries and by public action in preventive measures. There have been not many changes in the picture in the next 10 years.[22]

The burden of 10 major diseases in the ESI scheme, on the other hand, gives us a different picture. Apart from such diseases as bronchitis, acute nasopharyngitis, acute pharyngitis and tonsillitis, diseases of the teeth, anaemia, asthma and allergic disorders, avitaminosis and other deficiency states and diseases of eye constitute the list of major ailments (Table 10.8). In all these cases of ailments, the family is more affected than the employee. In fact, if we include the age group of 0-14 years in ESI data, the differences between the two data sources become even more noticeable as is evident from the incidence of morbidity among the families of the ESI IPs (Table 10.8). However, it is comfortable to find that during 1996-97 to 2003-04, the frequency of all the major diseases declined among the employees covered under the ESI scheme. PAP of short-duration diseases declined gradually from 741 per 1,000 IPs in 1996-97 to 575 in 2003-04, PAP of long-duration diseases too declined from the peak of 815 in 1998-99 to 470 in 2003-04 (Table 10.8). It is quite likely that because of a better network of health infrastructure, insurance, and of course least access inequality, the reporting of morbidity is comparatively higher in the ESI Scheme.

What is uncomfortable is the increasing incidence of tuberculosis among the workers. In the case of pulmonary tuberculosis, according to NSSO, there is less than one

20. For hospitalised treatment, however, information was collected for every event of hospitalisation of a member, whether living or deceased at the time of survey, during the 365 days preceding the date of enquiry.

21. *World Development Report, 1993.*

22. NSSO (2006).

case-to be precise, only 0.63 incidence—per 1,000 persons in urban India in 1995-96. (In 2004, 1.7 per cent cases of tuberculosis, as a whole, among all the persons hospitalised in the urban areas.)[23]

TABLE 10.7

Burden of 10 Major Diseases (Including Undiagnosed) by Age of Incidence, in 1995-96 in Urban India (Prevalence of Ailment Per 100,000 Persons)

	1995-96					*2004*
	Age Group (years)					
Diseases	*0-14*	*15-39*	*40-59*	*60 & above*	*All*	*All*
Cough and acute bronchitis	378	147	245	439	255	
Diabetes	2	20	374	1362	145	27
Diarrhoea & gastro-entritis dysentry (incl. cholera)	331	163	194	306	230	310
Diseases of the heart	17	30	236	821	102	29
Fevers of short-duration	2204	1200	1162	1414	1531	1349
Gastritis/hyper-acidity/gastric/peptic/duodendal ulcer	2	57	173	218	68	103
High/low blood pressure	4	48	447	1873	195	
Pain in the joints	7	59	247	1574	152	
Pulmonary tuber-culosis	10	54	137	235	63	5
Undiagnosed long-duration diseases	61	148	398	1210	218	

Note: NSSO data are based on self-reporting of ailments to the specific questions asked on disease. For example: During tile reference period did the member feel anything wrong relating to skin, head, eyes, ears, nose, throat, arms, hands, stomach, liver, kidney, legs, feet or any other organ of tile body?

Source: NSSO, 1998, Report No. 441, Table 3; and NSSO, 2006, Report No. 507, Table 39.

10.7 Summary Findings

There is a large rural-urban gap in IMR and the gap has not come down since the mid-60s. Low health status among the women and children in terms of anthropometric measures and prevalence of anaemia is an area of concern not only for West Bengal but also for many states. Like many other states in West Bengal the added concern is large rural-urban difference in the health status of women and children.

TABLE 10.8

ESIC, India: Burden of 10 Major Diseases (Number of New Cases Per 1,000 IPs)

	Insured Persons		*Families*
Disease	*1996-97*	*2003-04*	*2003-04*
Acute nasopharyngitis	139.9	114.07	126.23
Accidents, poisoning and violence	87.5	70.02	67.65
Acute pharyngitis and tonsilitis	46.9	42.95	59.29
Anaemia	52.6	39.7	49.62
Asthma & allergic disorders	67.8	53.57	64.95
Bronchitis	70.3	50.84	56.47
Dysentry, all forms	61.2	40.95	44.53
Diseases of eye	58.7	48.1	56.28
Avitaminosis and other deficiency states	45.8	35.76	46.4
Diseases of the teeth, and other diseases of digestive system	65.2	52.06	64.73

Source: ESIC, *Annual Report*, various issues.

Health awareness campaigning has to be strengthened. Along with other issues, practice of water purification before drinking, low awareness about HIV/AIDS among rural people and women need serious attention. The community health care management initiative (CHCMI) can be strengthened to address more issues related to community's health awareness.

In spite of the fact that the average number of doctors and nurses per lakh population has increased over the time, the existing strength of medical and para-medical manpower and its growth in West Bengal seems to be lower than what is needed for its growing population with increasing disease burden.

An analysis of the 'reasons for non-utilisation of government facilities for outpatient care' based on NSS 60th Round data suggests that bad treatment (as perceived by the patients), poor accessibility and long waiting time are the major reasons in West Bengal. In fact, high opportunity cost of time due to long distance and/or long waiting time seems to be the major reason for non-utilisation of government facilities by people belonging to labour and self-employed households.

23. NSSO 2006, Report No. 507, Statement 23.

Reference

Arrow, K J (1963). "Uncertainty and the Welfare Economics of Medical Care", *The American Economic Review* 52(5): 941-73.

Bagchi, A.K. (2007). "Governing the Market in Health Care: the Social and Political Requirements", in D. McIntyre and G. Mooney (eds.), *The Economics of Health Equity*. Cambridge University Press.

Census of India (2001). *Primary Census Abstract* (CDs containing data for West Bengal, Kerala and Tamil Nadu). New Delhi: Office of the Registrar General of India.

Chakraborty, A., S. Mukherjee and B.K. Das (2007). *An Evaluation Study on Advocacy of Safe Motherhood under CHCMI*. (Report prepared for Department of Panchayats and Rural Development, Government of West Bengal). Kolkata: Institute of Development Studies.

———. (2006). *Health Information of India 2005*. New Delhi: Central Bureau of Health Intelligence, Directorate General of Health Services, Ministry of Health and Family Welfare, Government of India.

Government of India (2003). *Health Information of India 2000 and 2001*. New Delhi: Central Bureau of Health Intelligence, Directorate General of Health Services, Ministry of Health and Family Welfare.

Government of West Bengal (2004). *West Bengal Human Development Report*. Development and Planning Department.

———. (2006). *Health on the March 2005-06*. State Bureau of Health Intelligence, Directorate of Health Services.

International Institute of Population Sciences (2000). *National Family Health Survey 2, 1998-99 West Bengal*. Mumbai: IIPS.

Kanjilal, B., T. Samanta and S.K. Mondal (2007). "What to do with them? Rural Medical Practitioner in West Bengal's Health Care System" *FHS Consortium Research Brief Series*. Jaipur: Institute of Health Management Research.

Mukherjee, S. and J-F Levesque (2007). *Inequality in Utilisation of Health Care in Indian States 1995-2004*. Paper presented in a seminar at Centre for Development Studies, Thiruvananthapuram, Kerala.

National Sample Survey Organisation (2006). *Morbidity, Health Care and the Condition of the Aged, NSS 60th Round (January–June 2004)*, Report No. 507, NSSO, Government of India.

———. (1998). *Morbidity and Treatment of Ailments, NSS 52nd Round: July 1995-June 1996*, Report No. 441. Government of India.

Soman, K. (2002). "Rural Health Care in West Bengal", *Economic and Political Weekly* 37(26): 2562-64.

World Health Organization (2006). *Health System Performance Assessment: World Health Survey, 2003 West Bengal*. International Institute of Population Sciences, WHO-India-WR Office.

Chapter 11

Education

11.1 Introduction

Education is both a constituent and instrumental component of human development. It has a significant effect on life expectancy, infant mortality, nutritional status and environmental awareness. This chapter looks at the recent developments in education in West Bengal. As West Bengal is the most densely populated state in the country because of various historical, sociological and economic reasons, provision of elementary education and also of primary health care has been a very challenging task.

A considerable variation in educational attainments and educational infrastructure has been observed across different regions in India. The literacy rate for the population aged seven years and above in West Bengal is higher than the national average.[1] But the rate of growth of literacy in the state was lower than that at the all-India level during the 50th and 55th NSS Rounds. But, West Bengal registered relatively better progress in female literacy compared to the national level. Moreover, the literacy rate improved at a higher rate in rural than in urban areas during the same period.

11.2 School Education

The West Bengal Education Act, 1973, empowers the West Bengal Board of Primary Education (WBBPE) to control and to develop the entire primary education in West Bengal. To meet the requirements of all the districts in the state, 19 District Primary School Councils (DPSC) in the district level are working for primary education under the aegis of the Board. The Directorate of School Education has been implementing the policy of the government.

The Government of West Bengal has implemented the District Primary Education Programme (DPEP) since 1997 and it has carried out Sarva Shiksha Abhiyan (SSA) to universalise elementary education (UEE) since 2001-02 in all the districts of the state. Initially, the SSA was being funded with 75 per cent contribution by the Government of India and 25 per cent by the Government of West Bengal. But the share of the Central government has been reducing over time. At present, the union government bears 65 per cent and the rest is the burden of the Government of West Bengal. SSA is a time bound programme of the Government of India to set up school buildings for inhabitations with no schooling facilities and also to improve the existing school infrastructure through provision of additional class rooms, toilets, drinking water, maintenance grant and school improvement grants.

In West Bengal, under the scheme of SSA, 1801 new school building and 42640 additional classrooms have been constructed. In addition, 500 Circle Resource Centres (CLRC) with new building facility have also been constructed at the sub-division level. To ensure health and hygiene of the learners, 9285 units of drinking water and 9539 units of toilet facility have been provided to primary and upper primary schools in different districts in the state.[2]

Table 11.1 displays the number of Shishu Shiksha Kendras during the period 2000-2005, and Table 11.2 presents the number of schools at primary, middle and secondary/higher secondary levels during 2004-05 across the districts in West Bengal. Although the number of Shishu Siksha Kendras increased significantly during the beginning of the present decade in almost every district in the state, it declined thereafter in many districts in West

1. Census, 2001; and NSSO (1999-2000) Report No. 473.

2. Data are taken from *Economic Review*, 2007, Government of West Bengal.

Bengal, mainly because primary schools became better geared to look after elementary education.

TABLE 11.1

Number of Shishu Shiksha Kendras by District

Years/Districts	2000-01	2001-02	2002-03	2003-04	2004-05	2005-06
Cooch Behar	564	693	900	887	703	696
Jalpaiguri	735	935	1121	1287	1109	1094
Darjeeling	200	630	807	1010	979	861
Uttar Dinajpur	417	409	592	1021	953	922
Dakshin Dinajpur	175	469	459	558	540	533
Malda	260	396	494	587	587	612
Murshidabad	1029	1030	1540	1426	1583	1585
Birbhum	322	495	581	627	649	647
Purulia	97	118	220	321	298	408
Bankura	200	221	404	431	449	449
Bardhaman	602	836	976	1091	1083	1067
Medinipur	1439	2145	3249	4233	3951	3921
Howrah	262	258	285	322	300	303
Hooghly	209	228	263	293	292	279
Nadia	374	459	561	485	555	557
24 Parganas (North)	361	599	868	943	978	961
24 Parganas (South)	685	1156	1379	1328	1394	1222
West Bengal	7931	11077	14699	16850	16403	16117

Source: Bureau of Applied Economics and Statistics, Government of West Bengal.

A study conducted by the National Council of Educational Research and Training (NCERT, 2005) observed that the number of primary school grew by 3.5 per cent, while the number of upper primary school declined by 28.1 per cent, that of secondary schools grew by 11.3 per cent and the number of higher secondary schools grew most spectacularly by 151.4 per cent in rural areas in West Bengal during 1993-2002. But in urban West Bengal, the number of primary schools declined by 1.4 per cent during the same period.

One of the major indicators of quality of education in schools is the net enrolment rate. Table 11.3 displays net enrolment rate by districts in West Bengal in 2007. The SSA programme provides special focus on girl's education and children with special needs. A significant performance on girl's education has been noticed in terms of their increasing enrolment rate that reduces gender disparity in primary education (Table 11.3). The National Programme of Education for Girls at Elementary Level (NPEGEL) has been introduced in 58 selected educationally backward blocks in 11 districts in West Bengal to reduce the gender gap.

TABLE 11.2

Number of Schools in West Bengal by District: 2004-05

Districts	Number of Schools		
	Primary	Middle	Secondary/ H. Secondary
Bankura	3465	117	338
Birbhum	2373	74	327
Bardhaman	3974	102	762
Kolkata	1445	68	638
Cooch Behar	1825	71	207
Darjeeling	775	63	65
Dakshin Dinajpur	1182	17	144
Howrah	2216	75	472
Hooghly	3019	102	550
Jalpaiguri	2049	67	232
Malda	1901	63	260
Medinipur Paschim	4687	214	530
Medinipur Purva	3275	191	475
Murshidabad	3166	109	388
Nadia	2644	97	358
North 24 Parganas	3905	100	463
Purulia	2974	92	242
South 24 Parganas	3670	188	582
Uttar Dinajpur	1453	73	119
West Bengal	50397	1929	7581

Source: Ministry of Human Resource Development, Government of India.

TABLE 11.3

Net Enrolment Rate by Districts in West Bengal: 2007

District	Primary Level		Upper Primary Level		Elementary Level	
	Boys	Girls	Boys	Girls	Boys	Girls
Bankura	98.9	98.9	95.3	94.3	97.3	97.0
Bardhaman	99.4	99.4	80.8	80.4	83.3	83.2
Birbhum	98.7	98.7	72.2	72.3	93.7	93.7
DGHC	98.1	95.9	126.3	65.9	99.6	94.3
Dk. Dinajpur	96.4	96.4	74.9	75.0	90.2	90.1
Howrah	96.9	96.9	69.2	69.2	94.2	94.3
Hooghly	99.5	99.5	89.2	89.6	91.8	91.7
Jalpaiguri	99.1	99.1	70.4	70.4	82.5	82.3
Cooch Behar	97.2	97.2	72.6	74.0	83.0	82.6
Kolkata	99.6	99.6	96.5	96.5	91.0	91.1
Malda	98.3	98.3	66.5	66.2	84.2	84.6
Murshidabad	98.4	98.4	61.4	61.4	3.5	-31.1
Nadia	99.7	99.7	90.5	90.7	94.7	94.7
North 24 Parganas	98.9	98.9	95.1	95.1	87.7	87.4
Medinipur (W)	97.9	97.9	68.9	66.5	61.2	60.8
Medinipur (E)	99.0	99.0	94.9	94.9	95.7	95.7
Purulia	98.8	98.8	66.2	65.7	90.5	91.2
Siliguri	98.7	98.7	96.7	96.7	99.4	99.5
South 24 Parganas	97.6	97.6	62.5	62.5	31.0	29.6
Uttar Dinajpur	96.8	96.8	42.1	42.5	84.9	82.7
Total	98.5	98.5	78.1	77.0	88.5	88.0

Source: DISE 2007-08 and District Report.

TABLE 11.4

Percentage Change in Enrolment, during 1993 to 2002

		Rural		Urban	
		West Bengal	India	West Bengal	India
I-V	Total	28.2	27.8	0.6	21.3
	Girls	38.6	42.3	4	22.2
VI-VIII	Total	62.8	42.2	22.2	29.5
	Girls	89.1	66.2	29.1	33.5
IX-X	Total	64.2	48.8	32.3	36.2
	Girls	97.7	79.6	41	46.6
(XI-XII)	Total	133.2	98	106.3	67.3
	Girls	168.4	156.7	140	84.5
(I-XII)	Total	38.4	33.8	15.4	28.9
	Girls	51.3	51	20.1	32.4

Note: * does not include enrolment in classes XI and XII attached to degree colleges.

Source: NCERT, 2005.

As compared to all-India, the enrolment rates of children, especially of girls in rural West Bengal, have increased in all the stages of school education, during 1993-2002 (Table 11.4). A school closer home is the most critical input in spreading education at the elementary level. As it was in the year 2002, the number of habitations having primary stage schooling facility within 1 km as a percentage of the total number of habitations, in West Bengal, was 92.3, while the same for all-India was 87.0.[3] In 1993, the ratio in this state was 87.7 per cent. This is certainly an achievement to reckon with that so many primary schools had been brought nearer to habitations in 9 years.

The pupil-teacher ratio is another important indicator of the quality of education. It measures the number of students per teacher or the number of students that are being taught by a single teacher on an average. The higher the ratio, the lower will be the effectiveness of education. Table 11.5 shows this ratio in primary, middle and secondary/higher secondary schools across the districts in West Bengal in 2002-03.

One of the major emphases of SSA has been the effective child tracking, particularly in elementary education. After implementing SSA and DPEP, the out of school children has declined sharply. Table 11.6 provides the number of boys and girls out of school by districts in West Bengal in 2007. While the mid-day meal programme has increased the enrolment rate at the primary stage, it is perhaps the expansion of school network especially for the girls increases the enrolment ratio at the upper primary and later stages of school education.

3. NCERT (2005). *Seventh All India School Education Survey*. New Delhi.

TABLE 11.5

Pupil-Teacher Ratio in West Bengal by District: 2002-03

Districts	*Primary*	*Middle*	*Secondary/H. Sec.*
Bankura	35	42	48
Bardhaman	44	44	49
Birbhum	47	45	53
Cooch Behar	55	79	71
Dakshin Dinajpur	46	37	55
Darjeeling	41	37	41
Howrah	51	44	50
Hooghly	46	47	48
Jalpaiguri	66	73	64
Kolkata	41	35	33
Malda	62	49	55
Medinipur (East)	48	49	57
Medinipur (West)	40	45	50
Murshidabad	70	65	68
Nadia	59	61	65
North 24 Parganas	58	49	50
Purulia	48	40	47
South 24 Parganas	74	52	63
Uttar Dinajpur	85	54	61
West Bengal	53	50	52

Source: As in Table 11.2.

TABLE 11.6

Out of School Children (5+ to 13+ Age Group) by District in West Bengal: 2007

District	*Out of School Children (Nos)*	
	Boys	*Girls*
Bankura	7997	8226
Bardhaman	9524	8777
Birbhum	11263	10528
DGHC	2691	2629
Dk. Dinajpur	9107	7999
Howrah	16073	14837
Hooghly	5947	5500
Jalpaiguri	7621	7148
Cooch Behar	6996	6653
Kolkata	7693	6369
Malda	13754	13175
Murshidabad	19550	18582
Nadia	2350	1597
North 24 Parganas	14707	14123
Medinipur (W)	20288	18647
Medinipur (E)	7264	6893
Purulia	18880	16708
Siliguri	2410	2264
South 24 Parganas	25357	24227
Uttar Dinajpur	26313	25548
Total	235787	220428

Source: As in Table 11.3.

During the period 1993 to 2002, there was a mere 0.5 per cent increase in the number of full-time teachers (including para-teachers) in the rural primary schools in West Bengal, while the same declined by 20 per cent in the urban primary schools.[4] Still, the rural-urban disparity in the pupil-teacher ratio in the primary schools is acute: the ratio is 56 in the rural as against 43 in the urban. While the accepted norm is to have a ratio of 40, the situation in the state, particularly in the rural is certainly going to affect the quality of education at the elementary level and, in turn, at the higher stage of school education.

In 2002, there were about 219 rural primary schools that did not have a single teacher (including para-teacher but excluding part-time teacher). In addition, there were 3,372 single-teacher rural primary schools. It is also important to recognise that, in 2002, of the 41,845 rural primary schools in the state, 617 were what is called 'open space', 96 are running in tents and 3,076 are *kuchcha* school buildings. Nowhere in India, except in Assam, there is such a huge numbers of *kuchcha*, tents, and open-space rural primary schools as one finds in West Bengal.

A general complaint made by teachers of primary schools was that the infrastructure itself is the biggest hindrance to teaching and learning. Six per cent of the schools visited have no classroom, 66 per cent of them have only 2 classrooms to conduct 4 classes. Only 28 per cent have more than two classrooms. In those schools in particular, where the enrolment is much higher, classrooms become overcrowded and noisy, where the teachers cannot teach, and the students cannot follow the teaching. The situation in the SSKs is much worse. Only 24 per cent of them have got small, single-room buildings. The rest conduct classes in cowsheds, verandahs and in community rooms.

The Pratichi Education Report 2002: 32

In the secondary schools the pupil-teacher ratio[5] seems to be much more adverse when compared to that at the all-India, which in West Bengal rural areas was 61 as against 31 for all-India, and in the state's urban areas was 41 as against 29 in all-India, in the year 2002 (NCERT, 2005). The situation was roughly similar for the higher secondary schools in the state; the pupil-teacher ratio was 58 in the rural as against 36 in all-India and 42 in the urban as against 34 in India as a whole.

This is another area of complaint, mainly from teachers, but some of the parents have also pointed out this problem. While the average pupil-teacher ratio in tile visited schools was 50: 1, in some schools this becomes ridiculously higher. In some schools, tile number of pupils equals tile number of teachers multiplied by hundred.

The Pratichi Education Report 2002: 32-33

11.3 Financial Commitment to School Education

The budgetary allocation on education as a proportion of SDP in the state had been consistently higher than that allocated by the Central government as a proportion of GDP in the 1980s and also in the 1990s. However, West Bengal seems to be losing that distinction over the last couple of years (Table 11.7).

TABLE 11.7

Percentage of Total Budget of Education and Training (Revenue Account) to NSDP of West Bengal and, to GOP of India

Year	*West Bengal*	*India*
1982-83	3.88	3.47
1993-94	4	3.6
1997-98	3.89	3.77
2001-02	3.96	3.74
2003-04	2.75	3.72

Source: GoI, Ministry of HRD, Department of Secondary and Higher Education.

The budgeted expenditure on education and training (in revenue account) as such in West Bengal has declined proportionately over time (Table 11.8). Although it is higher than the Central government figures, many of the states such as Assam, Bihar, Chhattisgarh, Kerala, Maharashtra, Rajasthan, Tripura, Uttarakhand and Uttar Pradesh have allocated, out of the state budget, a higher proportion on education and training in revenue account than in West Bengal.

The level of financial commitment to elementary education has been quite significant in the state. In fact, in the later years in the decade of the seventies, the highest amount of expenditure out of total expenditure on education (revenue account) used to be incurred on

4. NCERT (2005).

5. Based on full-time teachers and including the para-teachers.

elementary education. However, gradually, secondary education replaced elementary education in terms of budgetary allocation, from the early 1980s. Since 1988-89, the allocation for secondary education has increased steadily at a comparatively higher rate.

TABLE 11.8

Percentage of Education and Training Budget to Total Revenue Budget, West Bengal and India

Year	*West Bengal*	*India*
1982-83	26.4	11.1
1993-94	25.1	12.7
1997-98	24.7	13.8
2001-02	24.3	12.5
2003-04	18.5	13.1
2005-06	18.9	19.6
Plan	16.3	16.9
Non-Plan	19.3	20.1

Source: GoI, Ministry of HRD.

The budgetary allocation in the state remains critically important in human capital formation so long as the government's role in the entire education system continues to be overwhelming. In many of the otherwise developed states in India, the role of the government is not as critical as is evident from the distribution of students over different types of educational institution in West Bengal (Table 11.9). Many of the states including Kerala and Maharashtra have privatised education to a great extent and thus, minimised the budgetary liabilities of the government. Whether it is socially desirable or not, it is an issue which we are not going to assess here.

Nevertheless, increased budgetary expenditure as such is no solution to improving the quality of education. Perhaps more important at this moment is the question of efficient utilisation as well as rationalisation that crops up mainly when one finds inter-school differences in outcome indicators.

A study examined the impact, for instance, of the short-duration in-service training programme under DPEP for teachers on the primary education in five districts of West Bengal, *viz.*, Bankura, Birbhum, Cooch Behar, Murshidabad and South 24 Parganas, where DPEP was launched in 1997-98.[6] It was found that most of the teachers are emphatic on the importance of training. The training programmes seem to have contributed a great deal in orienting the teachers to modern pedagogy. However, many of them were sceptical about the applicability of some of the methods when the classroom situation is not favourable. If training has maximum impact when other conditions are favourable, it may further increase learning gaps between well-endowed and poorly endowed schools. While the physical infrastructure of schools has visibly improved under DPEP, the distribution of teachers across schools is far from optimum.

TABLE 11.9

Per 1,000 Distribution of Persons of Age 5-29 Years who were Currently Attending an Educational Institution, by Type of Institution, 2004-05

State	*Type of Institution*				
	Government	*Local Body*	*Private Aided*	*Private Unaided*	*Not Known*
Tripura	975	1	10	3	2
Orissa	926	2	46	22	3
Bihar	910	4	11	63	3
Madhya Pradesh	870	3	29	91	5
West Bengal	866	18	90	23	2
Gujarat	849	21	110	15	5
Karnataka	834	3	102	61	1
Assam	783	12	170	24	6
Uttarakhand	765	2	19	211	0
Tamil Nadu	737	47	123	94	0
Punjab	685	8	60	234	13
Uttar Pradesh	550	51	125	262	6
Andhra Pradesh	540	233	42	179	6
Kerala	497	6	278	218	1
Maharashtra	236	351	377	32	4
All-India	697	59	106	130	4

Source: NSSO, *Status of Education and Vocational Training in India*, 2004-05, Report No. 517.

Although, by and large, the training programmes have been successful in sensitising the teachers about the need for learning modern pedagogical tools, they have not been effective in orienting the teachers towards the need for closing inter-group disparities and weakening the close association between the student's innate social characteristics and her learning achievement. Teachers need to be sensitised as to how they can integrate concerns for group equity with the core pedagogy modules.

The infrastructure for primary education in West Bengal appears to be inadequate, despite there being DPEP and Sarva Shiksha Abhiyan for the last eight years. We select a set of indicators to compare 20 Indian states

6. Chakraborty, A., B. Bagchi, K. Das, D. Bandyopadhyay and S. Upadhyay (2005). *An Assessment of In-Service Teachers' Training Programme in Five Districts of West Bengal* (Sponsored by the State Project Office, West Bengal District Primary Education Programme). Kolkata: Institute of Development Studies.

based on the data available.[7] The indicators include the percentage of female teachers in primary schools as it is well recognised that parents generally would like their girl children to be taught by women, and girls find their role model in the female teacher. A shortage of female teachers can inhibit school attendance. It is important to recognise that in 1956-57, 41 per cent of the school teachers in Kerala were women. The number steadily increased thereafter, and now the percentage of women teachers stands at 73. This can be contrasted with West Bengal where the percentage is below 25.

Following Borda's method of rank-order scoring, first we ranked all the states on the basis of the numbers in col. (1) and took the rank values. We repeat the procedure for the rest of the indicators. We then add the rank values and finally rank the states according to the total rank value of each state.

Among the 20 states in India, the position of West Bengal turns out to be 18th (Table 11.10); a poor performance school education infrastructure despite best effort made in providing more than one teacher per school over the years, with huge recurring expenditure (plan and non-plan). The percentage of single-teacher school in West Bengal has come down to 8.25 per cent which is much lower compared to many other states those otherwise scored better marks in aggregate. Following the latter, it is time to put emphasis on capital expenditure, and a bit rationalisation.

11.3.1 Education Index by Districts in West Bengal

UNDP has developed Education Index by using adult literacy rate and gross enrolment ratio.[8] As data for these two parameters are not available, the total literacy rate and attendance of the children of age '6-14 years' are considered for calculating the Total Literacy Index and Gross Enrolment Index for the districts using UNDP dimension index.

Assigning two-third weight to the Total Literacy Index and one-third weight to Gross Enrolment Index we construct the Education Index (Table 11.11). Kolkata tops the Index while Dinajpur (North) is at the bottom of the table. However, the 'distance theory'—i.e., more distant

TABLE 11.10

Borda Ranking of States according to Indicators of Infrastructure for Primary Education, in 2004

State	*Ratio of 'Primary' to Upper Primary & above' Schools*	*% of Single Classroom Schools*	*Student Per Classroom*	*% of Single Teacher School*	*% of Female Teachers*	*Pupil to Teacher Ratio*	*Borda Rank*
Kerala	1.84	1.16	29.28	0.08	73	27.04	1
Himachal Pradesh	2.94	6.43	18.2	13.59	42.24	21.07	2
Gujarat	1.51	14.73	34.27	9.99	48.23	30.76	3
Tamil Nadu	2.88	12.42	31.73	10.85	69.49	36.96	4
Uttarakhand	3.3	2.91	27.15	23.1	55.03	27.73	5
Punjab	2.45	2.83	31.3	21.81	64.09	42.36	6
Karnataka	1.98	24.25	27.34	20.09	44.59	25.67	7
Tripura	2.96	18.33	29.57	12.04	18.9	24.18	8
Haryana	2.54	10.62	50.33	10.82	46.69	47.59	9
Madhya Pradesh	2.33	8.95	42.43	13.42	29.09	35.56	10
Andhra Pradesh	3.1	34.25	41.69	15.71	40.48	32.4	11
Maharashtra	3.6	19.01	35.15	16.45	45.22	33.42	12
Orissa	3.46	10.19	34.89	19.1	31.53	39.65	13
Rajasthan	3.07	4.36	35.96	38.6	24.63	38.11	14
Assam	3.25	62.72	55.5	15.72	34.04	27.8	15
Chhattisgarh	3.32	7.1	36.99	20.74	25.49	40.24	16
Uttar Pradesh	4.12	2.2	62.41	16.08	30.67	69.34	17
West Bengal	5.33	20.94	61.94	8.25	24.33	52.48	18
Jharkhand	4.51	7.52	51.51	33.34	22.09	58.09	19
Bihar	4.52	15.54	84.91	15.74	18.29	71.43	20

7. The method is, first, to assign points equal to the rank value of each state for each of tile variables. Then, add each state's scores to obtain its aggregate score, and then ranking states on the basis of their aggregate scores (called Borda scores).

8. UNDP. *Human Development Report (2001)*.

the district is from Kolkata greater is the divergence—is not strictly valid. The performance of Kolkata is followed by the districts of North 24 Parganas (but not South 24 Parganas), Howrah (but not Hooghly) and Medinipur (but not Nadia). Further, the striking feature of the development is the wide gap between Kolkata and the below-average districts such as Dinajpur (North and South), Maida, Purulia and Birbhum so far as the Education Index is concerned.

TABLE 11.11

West Bengal, District-wise Education Index

District	*Education Index*	*Rank*
Kolkata	1	1
North 24 Parganas	0.824	2
Howrah	0.814	3
Medinipur	0.797	4
Hooghly	0.786	5
Darjeeling	0.696	6
Bardhaman	0.665	7
South 24 Parganas	0.561	8
Nadia	0.507	9
Bankura	0.472	10
Jalpaiguri	0.461	11
Cooch Behar	0.452	12
Birbhum	0.361	13
Dakshin Dinajpur	0.338	14
Purulia	0.247	15
Murshidabad	0.148	16
Malda	0.042	17
Uttar Dinajpur	0.015	18

Source: Author's calculation.

11.4 Higher Education

There are primarily two kinds of roles that the higher education is expected to play: (a) as citizenship education; and (b) as human capital formation for economic activities, be it for modern industries, agriculture, the services economy like in the IT sector, and even to shape the reproduction of human capital.

In the mid-1950s, West Bengal's share in the all-India outputs of Bachelor of Engineering (BE) and BSc (Engineering) was 8.7 per cent, of BTech and BSc (Tech.) was 24.6 and of MBBS and equivalent examinations was 21.9 per cent. West Bengal then was closely following Maharashtra (including Gujarat), Tamil Nadu and Madhya Pradesh. In fact, in terms of the numbers of BTech and BSc (Tech) human-power West Bengal was one of the leading states next to Madhya Pradesh.

In the general stream (i.e., matriculation and equivalent, intermediate, BA/BSc, MA/MSc, BCom/MCom) West Bengal had a share of 11.7 per cent to the pass outs in India as a whole, while Maharashtra shared 14.7, Punjab 11.6 and Uttar Pradesh 18.6 per cent, among the states those had a share greater than 10 per cent, in the mid-1950s.

In 1981-82, West Bengal's share in the country's aggregate enrolment in technical/industrial/art and craft schools came down to 3.2 per cent as against 7.6 per cent in Andhra Pradesh, 8.6 in Gujarat, 28.7 in Maharashtra, 6.2 in Punjab and 10.4 per cent in Uttar Pradesh (data for Tamil Nadu was not available).

In the case of enrolment in BE/Architecture (BE/BSc), in 1981-82, West Bengal's share was 6.8 per cent, while Tamil Nadu had a share of 12.4, Andhra Pradesh 8.2, Gujarat 9.1, Karnataka 11.8, Maharashtra 8.7, Madhya Pradesh 7.6 and Kerala had a share of 5.8 per cent.

In other words, the states those have experienced a higher than average rate of industrial growth in the following decades also are the states with a higher initial 'stock' of technical human-power than the average state in India.

By the mid-1990s, West Bengal was still to come out of the inertia, while her counterparts were making a rapid progress in reproducing technical human power. Of the India's aggregate enrolment (boys and girls) in polytechnic institutes/technical, industrial, art and craft schools, West Bengal's share was 4.1 per cent as against 9.9 of Andhra Pradesh, 6.4 of Karnataka, 7.5 of Kerala, 11.2 of Tamil Nadu, 9.6 of Uttar Pradesh and a stupendous 24.8 per cent share of Maharashtra.

Perhaps there was no demand deficiency in the state for technical education. It was rather the supply side problem. While many other states have increased their intake capacities, West Bengal lagged behind (Table 11.12). Of course, initially it was a matter of political decision whether the private engineering colleges would be allowed in the state.

As it stands, in 2006-07, the enrolment capacity per one lakh population was 24 at the degree and 11 at the diploma level technical education, which is of course lower compared to many other states, and also the national average, that is 68 for the degree-level and 31 for the diploma-level (Table 11.13).

The situation is also not very comfortable for the IT sector: Less than 3 per cent of the student intake capacity

TABLE 11.12

State-wise Student Intake in Degree Engineering Programme Approved by AICTE

State	*% of All-India*						
	1999-2000	*2000-01*	*2001-02*	*2002-03*	*2003-04*	*2004-05*	*2005-06*
Andhra Pradesh	13.7	13.5	15.8	17.9	17.4	18.5	19.6
Tamil Nadu	17.2	17.9	22.4	22	19.2	17.1	18.6
Maharashtra	19.3	18.2	14.7	13.1	12.4	11.6	10.4
Karnataka	14.2	13.3	12.4	11.2	10.2	9.8	9
Uttar Pradesh	6.9	7.5	6.2	6.3	8	7.9	8.2
Madhya Pradesh	4.2	4.6	3.4	3.6	4.5	4.9	5.1
Kerala	2.9	3	3.6	5	4.3	4.8	4.6
Rajasthan	1.6	2.3	2	2.2	2.8	3.2	3.3
Gujarat	3.2	3.3	3.2	2.7	2.8	3.1	3.2
Punjab	2.2	2.1	1.8	2.5	2.9	3.5	3.2
Haryana	3.3	3.3	2.8	2.6	2.6	2.8	2.9
West Bengal	2.7	3.2	2.9	3	3.3	3.3	2.6
Orissa	3.4	3.1	2.9	2.6	2.9	3	2.2
India	100	100	100	100	100	100	100

Source: Lok Sabha Unstarred Question No. 4589 dated 22.4.2003; and Unstarred Question No. 1813, dated 8.8.2006

in the country is in West Bengal, while states like Andhra Pradesh, Maharashtra and Tamil Nadu far excelled the state in this respect (Table 11.14). The IT sector in West Bengal perhaps has reached a point whereby its further expansion would depend too heavily on migrant 'knowledge workers'.

TABLE 11.13

Selected State-wise Enrolment Capacity at the Degree and Diploma Level Technical Education in India, and the Number Per One lakh (Projected) Population, 2006-07

State	*Enrolment Capacity Per One Lakh Population*	
	Diploma Level Technical Education (a)	*Degree Level Technical Education (b)*
Bihar	4	3
Assam	6	4
West Bengal	11	24
Uttar Pradesh	7	36
Rajasthan	6	38
Gujarat		39
Himachal Pradesh	13	26
Andhra Pradesh	31	
Madhya Pradesh	19	
Orissa	26	55

Note: (a) Engg.+Pharm.+HMCT+Fine Arts+Arch. (excluding MBA/PGDBM); and (b) includes MBA/PGDBM, as well.

Source: Rajya Sabha Unstarred Question No. 2736, dated 18.12.2006.

The comparative statistics at least show that there exists large scale opportunities to expand the education network, and thereby that part of the services economy which would have steady and guaranteed 'returns' in the long-run. The rapid rise in global demand for 'knowledge workers' has opened up immense possibilities for the developing economies—in particular, because of the demographic changes that has seriously impaired the supply of workforce in the developed West—to gather comparative strength in certain sub-sectors of the services economy. In India, Kerala perhaps is the most prominent example of how to take advantage of the emerging path of development in the 'post-industrial' with the active role of the government. The lower capital-output ratio in the creation of 'knowledge worker' and its utilisation than that in the technology-intensive industries has rendered government participation easier and more fruitful.

The relatively high growth of the services sector, and the displacement of the industrial economy—in terms of share in SDP—by the services sector in such states as Maharashtra, Karnataka, Tamil Nadu and Kerala owe much to the processes of human capital formation that these states have experienced in the last two decades. It is important to recognise in this context that, in the 1960s, West Bengal had the largest relative size of the services economy among the major states in India. Thereafter, the rate of growth in the sector in West Bengal has been lower than in any of the major states which have subsequently improved their endowment of technical human capital.

TABLE 11.14

Selected State-wise (having a share of more than 1%) Number of AICTE Approved Students in Computer-related Courses in India, 2003

	No. of AICTE Approved Students' Intake				*% of All-India*			
States/UTs	*I.T.*	*C.S.E.*	*E.C.E.*	*Total*	*I.T.*	*C.S.E.*	*E.C.E.*	*Total*
Andhra Pradesh	9,225	14,490	21,685	45,400	19.5	19.5	19.8	19.7
Delhi	450	740	1,070	2,260	0.9	1	1	1
Gujarat	1,260	1,575	1,473	4,308	2.7	2.1	1.3	1.9
Haryana	1,200	2,410	3,225	6,835	2.5	3.2	3	3
Karnataka	2,244	6,695	9,115	18,054	4.7	9	8.3	7.8
Kerala	1,630	2,870	4,350	8,850	3.4	3.9	4	3.8
Madhya Pradesh	1,800	2,730	2,790	7,320	3.8	3.7	2.6	3.2
Maharashtra	6,405	9,345	13,230	28,980	13.5	12.6	12.1	12.6
Orissa	1,515	2,165	2,580	6,260	3.2	2.9	2.4	2.7
Punjab	700	2,080	3,030	5,810	1.5	2.8	2.8	2.5
Rajasthan	1,090	1,814	2,764	5,668	2.3	2.4	2.5	2.5
Tamil Nadu	13,145	16,430	28,880	58,455	27.7	22.1	26.4	25.3
Uttar Pradesh	2,955	5,450	7,989	16,394	6.2	7.3	7.3	7.1
West Bengal	1,810	2,320	2,390	6,520	3.8	3.1	2.2	2.8
India	47,394	74,229	109,246	230,869	100	100	100	100

Note: I.T.: Information Technology; C.S.E: Computer Science and Engineering; E.C.E.: Electronics and Communication Engineering; and AICTE: All-India Council for Technical Education.

Source: Lok Sabha Unstarred Question No. 5498, dated 29.4.2003.

However, while technical human-power formation has lagged behind many other states, the spread of 'citizenship education' in West Bengal as compared to other major states should not be glossed over as a less important factor in state development. The general features that come out from the NSSO Survey, 2004-05, are, first, a

TABLE 11.15

Per 1,000 Distribution of (Rural Plus Urban) Persons of 15 Years and above by General Educational Level, 2004-05

	General Educational Level					
	Not Literate	*Literate & up to Secondary*	*Higher Secondary*	*Diploma Certificate*	*Graduate & Above*	*Higher Secondary & Above*
Uttarakhand	333	478	92	17	79	188
Kerala	94	727	63	58	58	179
Maharashtra	271	557	69	29	73	171
Punjab	315	514	87	19	65	171
Haryana	351	485	78	15	71	164
Tamil Nadu	293	555	68	18	66	152
Gujarat	318	542	63	16	61	140
Karnataka	382	495	58	11	55	124
Madhya Pradesh	456	428	55	8	54	117
Uttar Pradesh	478	404	61	4	52	117
West Bengal	325	565	49	3	58	110
Andhra Pradesh	491	401	45	13	48	106
Rajasthan	524	379	47	5	44	96
Assam	252	663	51	2	31	84
Orissa	412	504	35	5	43	83
Bihar	516	408	40	2	33	75
All-India	382	490	558	12	57	127

Source: NSSO. *Status of Education and Vocational Training in India, 2004-05*. Report No. 517.

very significant proportion of students leave education after the secondary level, in West Bengal. Out of 1,000 persons of age 15 years and above, 565 were literate and educated up to the secondary level in the state (Table 11.15). This is, of course, a ratio which is at the upper side when compared to the all-India average, yet comparable to Kerala and Assam which had in the same age group 727 and 663 persons per thousand, respectively, in 2004-05. Either, higher education is no longer in the priority list of most of the students; they opt for jobs immediately after passing out secondary examination. Alternatively, there might be supply side bottlenecks which require immediate attention in order to minimise the dropout ratio.

A pilot survey was conducted in the degree-colleges (general education) affiliated to any of the universities in West Bengal. There are about 108 colleges who offer all the undergraduate honours courses in physics, chemistry, mathematics and economics. The colleges are classified according to their locations within the jurisdiction of KMDA and outside of it.[9]

First, the number of seats available, in all the selected subjects, has increased during 1996-2006. Many more seats are now available, especially in colleges in the non-KMDA area, than 10 years ago (Table 11.16).

TABLE 11.16

Percentage Increase in the Number of Seats Available in the Degree Colleges in West Bengal: 1996-2006

College	*Percentage Increase in No. of Seats in*			
	Physics	*Chemistry*	*Mathematics*	*Economics*
Located in KMDA	55	40	38	36
Located outside KMDA	82	90	65	49

Source: Government of West Bengal, Department of Higher Education.

During 1996 to 2006, there has been an increase of about 142 per cent in the number of students who passed Higher Secondary examination (of the WB Council of HS education) with the combination of physics, chemistry, mathematics and biology as the subjects and secured first division. In 2006, 20,690 students secured first division. In addition, the number of students securing second division in this stream of HS examination although remained almost constant is quite large, i.e., around 16,000 per year. The minimum marks required to get admission to any of the honours courses—in physics, chemistry, mathematics and economics—is often 50-55 per cent in many colleges. In other words, a large percentage of students who secured less than 60 per cent in the HS examination (science combination) are also expected to constitute part of the total number demanding seats in honours courses in the colleges in West Bengal.

However, a considerable number of the available seats in the colleges are not filled up, no matter whether the colleges are in the KMDA or outside of it. The problem is more acute in the urban colleges (Table 11.17). In areas outside the KMD area, economics (honours) undergraduate course is increasingly losing its attraction to students as compared to the colleges in the KMDA. The percentages of available seats filled-up in other subjects are higher. Of course alternative opportunities in higher education (including private engineering colleges) in the state are now much wider than it was couple of years ago. Yet, the mismatch between the number of seats available and the numbers admitted in the science subjects is noteworthy.

11.5 Concluding Observations

Though considerable gains in literacy and education have been achieved since Independence, yet we still have a long way to go as far as achieving the goal of universal elementary education. In order to increase the responsiveness of children to education, particularly among the children from the underprivileged sections of the society, Government of West Bengal has implemented mid-day meals programme. Participation in preventative health measures is another viable option to reduce the incidence of out of school children. Poor health is known to limit school participation so launching mass medical treatment drives in the schools at properly spaced out intervals is another alternative scheme for increasing the enrolment in the primary schools.

9. 26 colleges have so far responded.

TABLE 11.17

Degree Colleges in West Bengal: Percentage of Available Seats Filled Up, 1996-2006

Year	*Percentage of Available Seats Filled in Honours Courses*							
	Colleges in KMDA				*Colleges outside KMDA*			
	Physics	*Chemistry*	*Mathematics*	*Economics*	*Physics*	*Chemistry*	*Mathematics*	*Economics*
1996	101.5	105.3	89.8	83.6	95.2	106.2	94.4	44.6
1997	100	100.9	88	83.1	92.1	81.9	76.6	45.2
1998	99.5	107.4	89.8	75.4	97.5	87.3	86.5	43.2
1999	103	101.7	87.1	87	99.2	104.5	96.4	48.3
2000	97.3	94.6	97.5	80	109.3	101.9	101.1	52.1
2001	96.9	98.8	89.4	65.9	99.7	98.1	97.2	49.4
2002	92.7	90.6	93.7	78.6	93.5	98.7	99.5	44.9
2003	83.8	98	88.6	73.6	99.2	99	94.5	34.2
2004	82.6	91.7	83.3	61.1	95.3	102	96.9	26.9
2005	78.7	93.7	91	63	96.2	100	95.4	27.2
2006	88.7	93.3	99.7	69.1	101.9	103.5	102.2	23.3

Source: Government of West Bengal, Department of Higher Education.

Chapter 12

Environment

12.1 Introduction

The state of West Bengal ranks as the fourth most populous state in the Republic of India, covering an area of 88,752 sq. km., representing 2.2 per cent of geographical area of the country. The state is located in the eastern part bordering three countries, Bangladesh, Nepal and Bhutan and five Indian states *viz.*, Orissa, Jharkhand, Bihar, Sikkim and Assam. The population of the state (7.8 per cent of Indian population) is distributed over 19 districts, 40,782 villages and 375 urban units grew and by more than 18 per cent during 1991-2001.

The physiographic zones of the state starting from the Himalayan Mountain flank in the north, through the riverine alluvial plains down to the marine delta provided unique features to the state well known for rich natural resources, biological and cultural diversity. Climatologically, the maximum temperature varies between 300°C and 450°C, and the annual average minimum temperature ranges between 20°C and 130°C. In recent years, specially during 2005, an abnormal heat wave during summer extending to early part of monsoon season led to loss of life and crop. Mean annual range of temperature i.e., temperature between the mean temperature of the warmest months and the coldest month varies between 100° to 140°C as one moves from lower Bengal to the western and northern parts. The gradual sequence has a striking conformity with humidity and precipitation. So instead of considering the entire state under humid zone Misra (1992) offered a new framework for climatic regions of the state dividing it into 12 different climatic types. Rainfall pattern in the state also varies significantly between 1234 mm for Birbhum district in the west to 4136 mm for Jalpaiguri district in the north. A trend of declining rainfall has been observed in recent years especially in southern Bengal.

The trend of population growth in the state shows a declining percentage in decadal changes 23.17 (1971-1981), 24.73 (1981-1991) and 17.77 (1991-2001). Density of population per sq. km., increased from 615 to 767 and then to 903 during the same period; this is the highest among 14 major states of India. The birth rate declined from 33.2 in 1981 to 20.3 in 2001, i.e., 13 per cent as against national average of 8 per cent. Infant mortality rate per 1000 still remains high in rural West Bengal (52). Death rate per 1000 shows a declining trend achieving a 50 per cent reduction during 20 years, ranking second next to Kerala. Land use changes indicate a decline in the number of cultivators—from 37 per cent to 25 per cent in 10 years (1991-2001).

Integrating environment concern with development goals is now a universal slogan for achieving 'sustainable development'. Environmental status can be determined best taking into account the environmental resources and then assessing the impacts of development, followed by current management strategy, institution support and the role of civil society. In the following sections some key issues have been focused.

12.2 Land, Soil and Land Use

12.2.1 Land and Land Use

The land area of West Bengal is recorded as 88,752 sq. km., or 88,75,2000 hectares. Land use in the state shows that 61.6 per cent is occupied by agriculture, keeping 4.4 per cent under current fallow, totalling 66 per cent of land being used for agricultural purposes. Forest occupy 13.8

Author, Dr. Ashis Ghosh, is a Director of ENDEV.

per cent of land area, leaving 18.8 per cent of land for urban centres, rural settlements, industrial sectors, roads and sundry other uses; only 1.4 per cent land remains uncultivated excluding current fallow.

The impacts of more than three decades of Green Revolution with high yielding varieties (HYV) of seeds, chemical pesticides, inorganic fertilisers and canal irrigation have been assessed by the scientists with regard to sustainability. The negative major impacts identified so far, include loss of indigenous varieties of seeds of food crops and vegetables, water pollution, groundwater contamination, pest resistance and erosion of biodiversity, besides natural cycle of soil nutrition. The tendency for homogenisation of agriculture led to continuous decline in the area of pulses, which in turn is affecting the soil fertility. The state, therefore, needs a proper strategy for agricultural sustainability with regard to seed selection, water economy, organic farming and multi-cropping. This strategy will have direct effect on the sustainability of soil. It may be noted that conservation and promotion of agro-biodiversity has become a major thrust area of action focused by the International Secretariat for Convention on Biological Diversity, in 2008.

TABLE 12.1

Classification of Land Area in West Bengal

(in thousand hectares)

	1995-96		*2003-04*	
	Area	*Percentage*	*Area*	*Percentage*
Net sown area	5462	62.8	5522	63.5
Current fallows	220	2.5	290	3.3
Forests	1196	13.8	1184	13.6
Areas not available for cultivation	1642	18.9	1573	18.1
Other uncultivated land excluding current fallow	175	2.0	126	1.5
Total reported area	8695	100.0	8695	100.0

Source: Statistical Handbook, West Bengal, 2004.

While conversion of forest land for non-forest purposes is governed by a control Act, conversion of agricultural land or wetlands is still to be regulated by a unified law. The unplanned rural land use in the past has led to significant expanse of wasteland, especially in the old coal mining and other area; the loss of nutrient due to overexploitation has also led to unquantified amount of wasteland area in the state. The total wasteland area has been divided into barren and uncultivable land, fallow land other than current fallow and cultivated wasteland. While the total wasteland area was 501,000 ha., in 1984-1985, through a process of reclamation it declined to 144000 ha., by 1994-95; unfortunately the changes in last 10 years is not available. However, data of degraded land in on-forest area of the state (West Bengal Human Development Report, 2004) shows that 28.77 per cent is considered degraded. The districts of 24 Parganas (South and North) together are reported to have 69.2 per cent degraded land followed by Medinipur East, 65.9 per cent, Howrah 63.2 per cent and Darjeeling 35.3 per cent. The lowest land degradation is recorded at Dinajpur (North and South) at 4.36 per cent and Malda at 7.53 per cent. Of the 18 districts of West Bengal (excluding Kolkata), it appears that the northern districts have less land degradation ranking between 1 to 7 except for Darjeeling, which ranks 13 in order of degradation. The land degradation in Darjeeling district calls for special attention in view of its geomorphological structure and vulnerability.

The urban land use pattern also illustrates the limitations of planning process. The current legal framework of Town and Country Planning Act, 1979 accepted in 1982, has so far been able to cover designated 'Development Areas' administered by specially constituted Development Authority *viz.*, Kolkata Metropolitan Development Authority (KMDA), Asansol Durgapur Development Authority (ADDA), Shiliguri Jalpaiguri Development Authority (SJDA), Haldia Development Authority (HAD), Digha Sankarpur Development Authority (DSDA). Such authorities are expected to prepare land use plan and maps to control the process of development. These are called Land Use & Development Control Plan (LUDCP). But for majority of 126 urban local bodies, such planning process is yet to take off. Each urban local body has now been provided with an urban planner to initiate action.

12.2.2 Soil

The soil has been classified on the basis of six agro-ecological subregions of the state *viz.*, warm humid subregion, warm to hot humid subregion, hot humid subregion, hot moist sub-humid subregion, moist sub-humid subregion, hot dry sub-humid subregion. The soils of West Bengal has also been studied with regard to major problem areas which range from limitation of depth, drainage, erosion, salinity, texture, water logging and flooding (Table 12.2).

TABLE 12.2

Rank of Problem Area by Area

Sl. No.	Variables	Area ('000 ha)	Percentage of Area Affected
i)	Drainage limitation	4439.0	4.67
ii)	Soil texture limitation	2052.8	19.57
iii)	Surface flooding problem	1950.4	18.30
iv)	Water erosion problem	1360.5	12.77
v)	Soil depth limitation	474.3	4.44
vi)	Soil salinity problem	377.7	3.55
	Total	11654.7	63.30

Source: NBSSLUP (1992). *Soils of West Bengal for Optimising Land Use.*

10.2.3 Landslides

The history of landslides in Darjeeling since 1899 shows a distinct increase in the frequency of such events. The northern hill region of Darjeeling district has been a major problem area for landslides especially during monsoon rains. The increasing vehicular traffic, deforestation of hill slopes, rampant violation of land use planning process are largely identified for causing landslides. Breach of communication, disruption of essential supplies, loss of lives, properties and tourist revenue are resultant effects of landslides in the hills. The population of Darjeeling town was 16,924 in 1901. The 2001 census data shows a population of 10,85,023; this population pressure on the entire ecosystem, especially due to unregulated urban growth perhaps played the most vital role. To stabilise hill slopes, by planned afforestation was setback by felling even the soft wood trees like *Crytomeria japonica,* locally called Dhupi. Felling of Dhupi trees is consistently followed by slope failure.

10.2.4 River Erosion

The mighty Ganga and Padma are said to be life line of largest basin area in the subcontinent. The Ganga and Padma have over the years and centuries inexorably nurtured and sustained human civilisation. The rivers are gnawing away land used for growing food and human habitation in two of the 19 districts of the state of West Bengal. In the district of Malda, till 2004, a report says it has taken away nearly 20,000 ha; during 1994-2004 and as many as 22 villages have disappeared. In the adjoining district of Murshidabad, it has taken away 359 sq. km of land belonging to Jalangi Ghosh Para Gram Panchayat, located in 14 mouzas. If an embankment gives away, the Bhagirathi (Ganga) could well merge with the Padma near Behrampore town.

Experts opine that a massive volume of water, 2.6 million cusecs, flows through these channels. It all started with human intervention in the natural course of the river. A circuit embankment was constructed at 'Bhutni Diara' island, 60 km upstream of Farraka which led to straying of river between Manikchak and Panchnandapur—a 15 km stretch (in Malda district). Near Farraka enormous pressure is being exerted at 109 bays which forces the water through a 2 km long channel, causing left bank to strain (Kalyan Rudra, River Expert, Pers. Communication). In the Murshidabad district, the river now has a linear stretch of 106 km.; no one, however, could point out to the exact cause of the depredation of Padma.

Three expert commissions, between 1980 and 2005 suggested variable solutions. None unfortunately has given any reprieve. The Pritam Singh Panel in 1980 suggested use of spurs at Manikchak to force the river flow straight between Rajmahal and Farraka which was supported by Keskar Committee but never really materialised. The latest one, Varhirht Commission (2003) stressed on the need for dredging to deepen the channel—a project estimated to cost Rs. 1200 crores. Whatever may be the cause, the crisis demand safety of Farakka Barrage Project. An allocation of Rs. 50 crore has been made for embankment protection, which, however, may not solve the problem until upstream silt load is significantly controlled.

While the government commissions, barrage authorities and river experts debate, people continue to face untold miseries. Boulders in the form of bedbars are washed away. As many as 58,000 people are reportedly putting up in the newly emerged chars or riverine islands. As *The Times of India* (July 31, 2005) report states "they are caught between vagaries of the river and vicissitudes of being isolated". These chars are in Bihar now Jharkhand but they depend entirely on Malda in West Bengal. However, basic amenities like school, hospital, police station are all a far cry.

Besides the problems of northern districts like Malda and Murshidabad, river erosion has also been reported from Bardhaman. In several blocks of the district, erosion and flooding is being evident. Worst affected areas in Bardhaman district are: Char gobindapur, Naihati, Nastachar, Noachar, Jamaipara, Gobindapur, Nastakhola, Charghoshhat, Sitahati and Kalitala.

It is reported that both the Ajoy river and Bhagirathi river are encroaching the villages rendering hundreds homeless. Worst affected areas include Purbasthali I and II, Ketugram I and II, Katwa and Jaluidanga village. Irrigation department is blamed for not completing the barrage on the Bhagirathi. Expert committee recommended reconstruction of river banks using geo-textile binding process and district administration sought Rs. 5.0 crore based on a draft plan.

The problem of river erosion is directly hitting upon the scarce land resources on one side, and evicting the people from their homestead land making them a new group of environmental refugees. While the government departments remain busy on compiling reports of expert committees, hordes of people are driven out of their home. People in the inter-state area between Jharkhand and Malda districts of North Bengal can tell stories of woes. There are 58,000 people putting up in the chars or islands that have resurfaced caught between vagaries of the river and the vicissitudes of being stateless. Right now river erosion problem spreads over the vast area from Sundarbans (like the disappearance of Ghoramara Island) in the south to Malda in the north (Ghosh, 2008).

12.3 Physiography and Water Resources

The state could be subdivided into four climate zone—humid north montane, super humid terai, semi-humid north and south and sub-humid east and west. The riverine system of West Bengal, dominated by the Ganga and Brahmaputra besides the smaller Subarnarekha provide major surface water resources. The river Gaiyal has a catchment area of 74,720 sq. km. and spread over 15 of the 19 districts of the state, providing 46.3 per cent surface water; while the Brahmaputra sub-basin in the north, contribute 39.17 per cent, the Subarnarekha basin spread over western part, contributes 2.74 per cent of the surface flow. As such, these three riverine systems can together contribute nearly 90 per cent of freshwater surface flow in the state.

The groundwater resource has been calculated at nearly 2.8 million hams, highest being in the southern districts of Paschim Medinipur and Burdhaman while one of the lowest one being in Darjeeling. Stage of groundwater development now stands at 41.30 per cent (Sikdar, 2008). The demand for freshwater, a finite natural resource, can be analysed from the Table 12.3.

TABLE 12.3

Requirement of Water in West Bengal up to 2025 AD

Sector	*Quantity (in mham)*
Agriculture	5.38
Domestic	0.26
Industry	0.26
Power generation (thermal)	0.31
Inland navigation	3.63
Forestry	0.01
Ecology environment and others	1.00
Total	10.85

Source: Ghosh, A.K. (ed.) (2008). *Status of Environment in West Bengal* ENDEV.

The major demand can be categorised into economic functions (agriculture, power, industries and urbanisation) or to meet survival needs. Agricultural demand dominates the current and futuristic projection. If one compares currently available surface and groundwater and utilisable amount, the water crisis scenario will sharply emerge (Table 12.4).

The population of West Bengal increased from 680.75 lakh in 1991 to 801.75 lakh in 2001 (Census Report). The increase in population on one side and changing land use pattern (for urbanisation and industrialisation) on the other, along with emphasis for higher agricultural production led to increased demand of freshwater. The farmers are withdrawing huge amount of groundwater for high yielding cultivation, without a proper planning process. Such agricultural practices also involve extensive use of chemical pesticides and inorganic fertilisers; run off from the agricultural field often contaminate neighbouring water bodies and streams and rivers. The chemical contamination of surface water in north Bengal is largely attributed to the tea plantations in Darjeeling Hills, Dooars and Terai region. Water requirement for multiple cropping is taken universally as 1 metre per hectare per year. The requirement of water based on these considerations has been estimated to be 5.38 mham by 2025 AD (GoWB, 1999).

TABLE 12.4

Availability of Water in West Bengal

Surface & Ground Water	*Quantity (in mham)*
Surface Water	
Gross	13.29
Utilisable	5.31
Groundwater	
Gross	1.46
Utilisable	1.46
Total	Gross 14.77 mham Utilised 6.77 mham

Source:. As in Table 12.3.

12.3.1 Urban Water Demand

Rapid urbanisation has a consequential effect on water requirement. The status of water requirement in 1991 in non-CMA municipal areas when compared with the requirement after 20 years (2011 AD) or 30 years (2021 AD) with 2 per cent growth rate of population, reveal a projected demand level varying between 30 per cent and 40 per cent. While only 13 of the 77 identified municipal areas in non-CMA municipalities are recorded to be wholly or partly dependent on surface water, the impact on groundwater is likely to be substantially higher. But in terms of wastewater, the entire quantum is only to go back to the surface flow. The data on wastewater discharge in these 77 non-CMA principal areas is sadly lacking. The demand of water in the urban centres outside the CMA, in 16 districts, is given in Table 12.5.

Of the 37 municipal bodies (35 municipalities and 2 corporations) in Calcutta metropolitan area, 21 municipal bodies are significantly dependent on abstraction of groundwater and 16 are utilising surface as also groundwater. The estimated requirement in 2011 and 2021 AD would be 1039 and 1210 mham, respectively. The data on quantum of wastewater presently generated or to be generated in future is again sadly lacking except for the Calcutta Municipal Area and the Howrah Municipal Area. However, as a thumb rule, 80 per cent of the water used can be taken as possible quantum of wastewater.

TABLE 12.5

Water Demand (m/d) in Non-CMA Municipalities of West Bengal

Town in Districts	*Year (Base)*	*Projected Water*	*Demand*
	1991	*2011*	*2021*
Darjeeling	51.59	75.15	86.07
Cooch Behar	14.83	22.74	29.37
North Dinajpur	32.68	45.72	52.26
South Dinajpur	17.97	25.2	28.8
Jalpaiguri	13.46	25.92	36.06
Malda	22.02	30.87	35.82
Murshidabad	43.85	61.35	70.08
Nadia	72.41	104.61	122.64
North 24 Parganas	64.34	92.16	111.48
South 24 Parganas	6.06	8.4	9.6
Hooghly	8.12	11.4	12.96
Bardhaman	220.16	311.97	371.06
Bankura	26.93	37.71	43.08
Birbhum	24.87	34.92	39.8
Medinipur	88.32	125.18	134.74
Purulia	14.39	25.62	25.5
Total	722	1038.92	1209.68

Source: "Urban West Bengal", ILGUS, 1994-95.

The importance of assessment of wastewater arises from the fact that it can be treated and recycled. In the event of facing unmitigated shortfall between demand and availability of water, the need for recycling would emerge inevitably. The technology is expensive but may be affordable in the urban areas. It is difficult to envisage any application of this technology for the rural areas, because it will be difficult to collect wastewater in the absence of drainage system in the rural areas. Even in the urban areas, 100 per cent treatment of wastewater is a farfetched goal. So far, no wastewater treatment plant contributes towards municipal water supply system in West Bengal; till 1999-2000, only 28 of the 125 urban local bodies are reported to operate treatment plants for supply of drinking water and only 9 urban local bodies had sewage treatment plants. ("Urban West Bengal", ILGUS, 2000-02).

12.3.2 Water Use in Power Sector

The use of water in power sector is mostly non-consumptive in nature. About 90-95 per cent of water, withdrawn for power generation, returns back to the surface water system. However, the total installed capacity of the power stations has increased significantly from 7330 MW in 2003-04 to 8034 MW (upto November 2007). It is to be noted that most of the power stations in the state (except Teesta Canal Fall Hydel Power Station, Rammam Hydel Power Station, Jaldhaka Hydel Power Station and currently constructed Purulia Pumped Storage Project), are run by thermal power.

12.3.2.1 Water Quality

Environmental concerns for surface water resource can be related to both quantity of utilisable water and the quality of the water available. Currently, major rivers of India are being brought under a centrally sponsored National River Conservation Programme; this is a sequence to Ganga Action Plan launched in the mid-1980s. In the state of West Bengal, the results of the water quality monitoring provides a differential profile in terms of some basic parameters, largely indicating that the Dissolved Oxygen (DO) level remain mostly higher than the permissible limit, as also the coliform bacteria count. Under such water quality scenario, preventive action at source becomes compulsive but the want of infrastructure for waste water treatment facilities continue to pose a major problem.

12.3.3 River Hooghly

The water quality of river Hooghly is being monitored from Behrampore (upstream) to the end point, Diamond Harbour (downstream). The other six locations are Palta, Srirampur, Dakshineswar, Howrah (Shibpur), Garden Reach and Uluberia. The water quality monitoring data for four prime parameters, namely BOD, DO, TC and FC (in the year 2006-07), showed that the average concentrations of BOD at most of the locations in the river were found to be approximately below the maximum permissible limit of 3 mg/l and the level of DO was always found to be above the permissible limit of 4 mg/l. This indicates that the quality of the river water is suitable for aquatic life.

However, the coliform density was found to be high in almost the entire stretch of the river in West Bengal. In other words, the water quality in terms of the bacteriological parameters is unsafe for human consumption. (WBPCB, 2006-07)

12.3.4 River Damodar, Rupnarayan and Barakar

In the year 2006-07, the average concentrations of BOD monitored in the rivers Damodar, Rupnarayan and Barakar was noted to be below the maximum permissible limit of 3 mg/l and the level of DO was found to be above the permissible limit of 4 mg/l. The total coliform and faecal coliform count, however, was much higher than the permissible limits. (WBPCB, 2006-07)

12.3.4.1 Groundwater: Current Concerns

The groundwater resource of the state, as has been mentioned earlier is fast undergoing a stressful condition. Groundwater resource of the city of Kolkata is being developed on a large scale since the late 50s. The extent of groundwater development can be understood by the following data of groundwater withdrawal from Kolkata Municipal Corporation owned tubewells (Banerjee and Roy, 1992; Sikdar, 1999):

1956 – 55 million litres per day

1989 – 182 million litres per day

1992 – 219 million litres per day

1994 – 227 million litres per day

As a result of this development, there has been a noticeable change in the hydrological regime. Obviously the situation must have changed further over last more than a decade. The over-abstraction of groundwater may not only cause serious concern for the future, but Kolkata being located in delta, the city can also face the problem of subsidence.

Arsenic pollution of groundwater in some parts of West Bengal was first reported in 1978. During the 1980s, a sizeable population of these areas was suspected to be suffering from arsenic-related diseases. The first diagnosis of arsenocosis was made in 1984 in a village in North 24 Parganas district. Arsenic at concentration above 0.05 mg/l in tubewell waters has been reported in parts of 79 blocks, 11 municipalities and 18 non-municipal urban areas of 8 districts of West Bengal (PHED, 2004). The 8 districts are Malda (7 blocks), Murshidabad (19 blocks), Nadia (17 blocks and 3 municipalities), Bardhaman (5 blocks), Hooghly (1), Howrah (2 blocks and 1 municipality), North 24 Parganas (19 blocks and 7 municipalities) and South 24 Parganas (9 blocks). Very recently arsenic has also been reported from some locations in Kolkata city along the course of the Adi Ganga River and in an isolated pocket in Behala region. The arsenic affected areas lie on a NNE- SSW tract of approximately 470 km extending from Malda in the north to South 24 Parganas in the south. Along this linear tract arsenic-contaminated groundwater has been found almost to the east of the Bhagirathi-Hooghly river system.

During the 1980s, a sizeable population of these areas was suspected to be suffering from arsenic-related diseases. At present the population at risk in the eight districts is about 16.7 million out of a total population of 45.6 million, affecting some of them dermatologically. In addition to the rural sector, about 12 million people (out of a total urban population of 22.5 million) are also at risk. Thus, the population at risk in the state is about 28.7 million (about 35.8 per cent), out of a total state population of 80.2 million (Sikdar, *op. cit.*).

Besides arsenic, high fluoride content in groundwater was first reported in 1997 around Nasipur village in Nalhati-I block of Birbhum district. Here the fluoride concentration has been reported to be as high as 10-16 mg/l causing deformity in bones, fluorosis, dental caries, etc. The contaminated water was reported from tubewells tapping groundwater from basaltic rocks at around 90 m depth. Concentration of fluoride above 1.0 mg/l has been reported from 14 of 19 districts of West Bengal. The population exposed to fluoride contamination is about 6.34 million people spreading over 1073 villages of 131 blocks and 1 municipality of which about 4 million people are at risk residing in 643 villages of 63 blocks (PHED, 2004). Hydrogeologically, the areas underlain by basalt, granite and older alluvium have possibilities of high fluoride in groundwater.

Groundwater in Kolkata and Howrah cities show metal toxicity. In some areas concentration of metals such as cadmium, chromium, copper, nickel and arsenic is high (Sikdar and Dasgupta, 1997). Besides Kolkata and Howrah, groundwater samples collected around Tamla *nalah* in the Durgapur Industrial Belt in Bardhaman district have been found to contain high concentration of zinc and manganese. The groundwater in this area also contains high concentration of chloride, sulphate and nitrate. Another important type of groundwater pollution, which is generally overlooked, is bacteriological pollution. Analytical results of groundwater samples for bacteriological quality are meager.

The status of groundwater resource has been analysed about a decade back in 1997 by the Groundwater Estimation Committee. A total 231 blocks of the state were put under 'safe' category, 37 were considered semi-critical and one block as critical. Obviously, the situation is likely to have changed over last 10 years.

12.3.4.2 Wetlands

Besides the surface water in the river and the streams, wetlands play a vital role in providing impounded water resource. West Bengal has 3,44,527 hectares of wetland area including 54 natural and 9 man-made wetlands of more than 100 hectares. Wetlands in West Bengal are classified into four categories *viz.*,

- Wetlands of Gangetic Alluvial Plains
- Coastal Wetlands
- Wetlands of Semi-arid Regions
- Wetlands of North Bengal

Of the four categories mentioned above, the coastal wetlands are mostly saline in nature and are largely used for brackish water fisheries and shrimp culture. All freshwater wetlands provide vital goods and services contributing towards freshwater fisheries, valuable wetland plants, bathing and irrigation. Wetland also acts as receptacle for rainwater during monsoon.

Wetlands are currently facing conversion to meet the demand of urbanisation and industrial expansion. A report shows that in Kolkata Municipal Corporation Area as many as 3000 wetlands have been converted during 2000-2005 (Saha, 2008). Conversion of wetlands measuring 5 kathas and above which have potential for pisci culture or currently be used for the same purpose is recognised as a cognizable offence under West Bengal Inland Fisheries (Amendment) Act. Till 2005, more than 400 FIRs have been lodged in various police stations against illegal filling of wetlands.

Of the urban wetlands, east Kolkata wetland area has been declared a Ramsar Site to protect it from illegal land use changes and prevent encroachment. Other urban wetlands like Subhas Sarovar in the north east of Kolkata, and Rabindra Sarovar in the south of Kolkata as also the Mirik lake in Darjeeling Hill district have attracted national attention due to lack of appropriate management in the past.

12.4 Forests and Wildlife

The forest cover in West Bengal occupies 12,413 sq. km. area of the state (FSI, 2005) distributed over four important regions *viz.*,

Northern hill and Sub-montane tract.

Southern mangrove forests in the Gangetic delta.

Sal Coppice forest in the laterite soil in the south west.

Freshwater swamps in Malda and West Dinajpur.

Forests and trees cover 14,682 sq. km., representing 16.55 per cent of the land area of the state. However, very dense forests in the state accounts for only 2,302 sq. km., followed by moderately dense forest of 3,777 sq. km. and open forests area of 6,334 sq. km. (FSI, 2005). Adding up the forest and tree cover, the state has little over 0.02 ha. of per capita forest and tree cover. A time series analysis based on FSI data shows that the forest cover (not tree cover) has gained by 73 sq. km. between 1995 and 1997 and it has significantly increased between 1997-2001 from 8,349 sq. km to 10,693 sq. km. i.e., 2,344 sq. km.; this figure further increased between 2001-2003 by 1,650 sq. km. However, most recent State of Forest Report (2005) shows that forest cover has increased only by 24 sq. km. between 2003-2005, showing a critical, declining trend in progressive afforestation and almost a static scenario.

12.4.1 Threats to Forests and JFM

Major threats to forest are reported from north Bengal and parts of Sundarbans. Organised illegal tree felling for timber has been reported from various parts of the state along with illegal poaching of wildlife. While overall increase in net forest cover may be praiseworthy, the losses of prime forest cover in these two vital areas have caused serious concern. However, management of forests in the state has been largely directed towards Joint Forest Management (JFM) since the 1990s. This is a programme which originated in the state of West Bengal and has now been taken up as a global model for participatory forest management.

The total number of Forest Protection Committee (FPC) have reached 3614 with a membership of 4,15,200 looking after 5,29,945 hectare of forest i.e., per capita responsibility is 1.28 ha. In addition 87 Eco Development Committees (EDC) have been working in the protected areas (till December 2001) covering an area of 77,462 ha., under Wildlife Division I (24 committees), Wildlife Division II (9 EDCs), Buxa Tiger Reserve East (14 EDCs), Buxa Tiger Reserve West (6 EDCs), Sundarbans Tiger Reserve (14 EDCs) and Cooch Behar (20 EDCs).

The implementation of JFM has shown positive results in many states. A decline in the incidents of wood theft is an important consequence. After years of protection by villagers, the coppice forests of West Bengal regenerated, from what was a degraded scrubland, to its multi-tier structure. Canopy cover and crop height have improved to a considerable extent. Biodiversity also improved with the age of protection (Malhotra and Deb, 1992). The success of JFM through involvement of villagers may be measured by the increased flow of NTFP—the very motive of villagers to protect the forest. A survey in West Medinipur district estimated that NTFP accounted for about 20 per cent of the total annual household income (Malhotra *et al.*, 1992).

In summery, according to the available data, forest cover has increased, timber production has increased, conflict between foresters and communities has decreased and the yield of NTFPs has increased in West Bengal (Joshi, 1996). According to satellite surveys, the forests cover in West Bengal increased by 4.5 per cent between 1988 and 1991. Of this increase in forest cover, 67 per cent has occurred in south West Bengal, the region that contains the largest number of FPCs, although it has only 37 per cent of forest land. The number of forest personnel assaulted is another broad indicator—this has decreased from a high of 60 in 1982-83 to 18 in 1994-95. Similarly, the number of forest offences (cases of illegal extraction) of timber has decreased. (Deb, 2008).

12.4.1.1 Wildlife

The state is the home of many endangered and threatened species listed under Indian Wildlife Protection Act of 1972, amended till date. Census of Wildlife largely is conducted on some of these selected species of mammals.

The threatened and endangered species is not limited only to 13 species for which Census figures are available. At least 46 species of mammals, 20 species of birds, 9 species of reptilian and one species of amphibian listed in the schedule of Indian Wildlife (Protection) Act, 1972, amended till date, inhabit the state. For many of these species, no regular population monitoring system has been adopted in the country or in the state. The status is largely decided on the frequent records from random surveys. However, targeted programmes, as a part of National Wildlife Strategy, has been undertaken to protect tiger (Project Tiger), elephants (Project Elephant) and crocodiles.

Wildlife Census Data of Selected Species

1.	Tiger	350
2.	Leopard	331
3.	Rhino	96
4.	Elephant	330 to 350
5.	Hog Deer	2500 to 3000
6.	Barking Deer	3500 to 4000
7.	Spotted Deer	32,000 to 35,000
8.	Sambar	900 to 1000
9.	Gaur	1200 to 1400
10.	Wild Boar	15,000 to 17,000
11.	Goral	400 to 450
12.	Tahr	70 to 90

Source: Glimpses of Wildlife Statistics—2002-03. Forest Dept., GoWB.

12.4.2 Threats to Wildlife

The poaching of wildlife has been a major concern in the state. The Government of West Bengal has decided to pay incentives to informers on any planned poaching activities. The Forest Department provides an account (GoWB, 2002-03; 2005-06) of poaching of Schedule I animals between 1999 and 2005-06. It shows that 37 elephants, 17 leopards, 4 tigers and 3 each of rhinoceros and bison have been killed during the period. However, the recent report of Tiger Task Force (August 2005) identified West Bengal as holding 3rd rank in tiger poaching in the country.

A total of 74 km of railway line in the prime forest area of north Bengal has caused serious concern for protection of wildlife; as many as 28 elephants have been killed due to train accident between 195 threats to wildlife. The expansion of National Highway through prime wildlife area in north Bengal has also become a focused issue. In a most recent study report prepared by Expert Team from the Ministry of Environment and Forests, Government of India, it is mentioned that proposed alignment for East-West Corridor, if built, would cut through some of the finest forests in north Bengal and pose a threat to its wildlife. The highway to be built by National Highway Authority of India (NHAI) is to connect north Bengal to Assam. The expert team after seeking the view of local community, forest department and other stakeholders, an alternate route, passing alongside the state highway is proposed through Fulbari near Shiliguri, Jalpaiguri, Dhupguri, Manegarm Falakata, Pundibari and Tufanganj. The team has submitted the report to the National Wildlife Board.

Fragmentation of continuous, rich biodiversity areas in north Bengal is also creating controversy between development demand and national conservation policy. One such growing menace is the Sankosh Hydro Project near the Jaldapara Wildlife Sanctuary in Jalpaiguri district. Sankosh project canals are designed to dissect the core area of Buxa Tiger Reserve to carry water to Farakka Barrage. Incidentally, the Sankosh project was earlier rejected by an expert team constituted by the Ministry of Environment and Forests in the 1990s. The new proposal is proposed at a time when population of endangered one horned rhino has more than doubled in the Teesta valley over a period of 12 years (now numbering 80 in Jaldapara and 24 in Gorumara).

In the western part of West Bengal, the migration of elephants from Dalma Hills in Jharkhand to the neighbouring districts of Bankura and Purulia has become a serious problem in the state. Often the elephant herds tend to stay in the area and feed on paddy, sugarcane and vegetables. The number of elephants may reach 60, being increased from a mere 5 in 1983; local villagers have become desperate and allege that state forest department did not provide either a solution or arrange for adequate compensation for damage to the crop. While crops per *bigha* are estimated at Rs. 5000.00, the forest department offers only Rs. 150.00. The compensation paid for elephant killing has recently been increased from Rs.10,000.00 to Rs. 25,000.00. Elephant depredation in the villages around Ajoydha hills has also become almost an annual event. Between November 2003 and April 2005, as many as 9 cases of elephants straying into village areas of Bankura and Purulia have been reported; the number of elephants totaled nearly 200, individual straying group consisting of 2 to 54.

The Forest Department of Jharkhand had proposed to build fences around boundary of Jharkhand, Orissa and West Bengal to prevent elephant migration from Dalma hills. A corridor with 10 km width was also proposed in September 2003. Apparently the plan has never materialised and people in West Bengal continue to confront the problem without any solution in the foreseeable future.

In the southern part of the state, the main area of concern centres around the Sundarbans. The hazards of Sundarbans include death due to snakebites (poisonous snakes include protected species like common cobra, common krait, russell's viper, king cobra and banded Krait), with an average number of fatal bites in Gosaba, Basanti, Canning I, Canning II blocks at 50.86 per year [Das, 2005. Ph.D thesis, unpublished, *Environmental Studies of Hazards Induced by Vertebrates in Sundarbans, West Bengal*, Vidyasagar University]; highest number of deaths occur between June to October; the high percentage of mortality is ascribed to dependence on *Ojhas* and quacks, poor transport facilities, irregular and inadequate supply of anti-venom serum.

The straying of tigers pose another conflicting areas between conservation policy and safety of human society. Most of the tiger straying (1986-1999) numbering 107, occurred during monsoon; of the 107 cases, 102 can be related to 16 villages in Bagna and Sajnekhali ranges of Sundarbans Tiger Reserve; in most of the cases tiger resorted to cattle lifting or poultry feeding. People always become alarmed, sometimes thousands of people gather to kill or drive away the straying tiger. Tigers may be poisoned by the villagers—as many as 09 tigers have been killed between 1990 and 2001. Tiger attacks on human beings have been highest in Gosaba (300), followed by Hingalganj (73), Basanti (48), Hasnabad (19), Canning II (14) and other areas (38), between 1985 and 2000. In recent years (2007-08), the forest department has been able to rescue 3 tigers which strayed into human habitation.

Fishermen are the worst sufferers from tiger attacks followed by honey collectors, wood cutters and staff of the Forest Department. During 1985-2000 as many as 341 fishermen were killed by the tigers; a total of 822 persons were killed during the period. Recently (2007-08) further killing by tigers have been reported from Kultali Block, while the local people were engaged in fishing or crab collection.

The conflicts between conservation need of endangered species and livelihood need of local population is yet to be resolved. Millions of people can never be taken out of this fragile ecosystem; neither need for conservation can be denied. One of the answers is to introduce extensive eco-development project and offer alternative livelihood to the most vulnerable groups. Both the mechanism of eco-development and joint forest management, if properly implemented may help to resolve the conflict.

12.4.3 Wildlife Conservation

Wildlife conservation within designated forests and freshwater and marine ecosystem is a National Programme. The Wildlife Conservation Programme in the state has been aimed at *in-situ* conservation strategy with a chain of protected area (PA) designated as biosphere reserve (1), national parks (5), wildlife sanctuaries (15), tiger reserves (2) and elephant reserves (2) but many PA's have overlapping areas like Sundarbans; total protected area comes to 4064 sq. km., representing 34 per cent of the total forest area.

These conservation areas apart, most of which are in the forest areas (except Narendrapur Wildlife Sanctuary near Kolkata and Jorepukhri Wildlife Sanctuary in Darjeeling), several areas have been identified as of potential wildlife values. A list of such areas is given in the Table A-12.1.

The major *ex-situ* conservation sites in the state are Alipore Zoological garden at Calcutta established in the 1880s and the Himalayan Zoological Park at Darjeeling, the latter being specially known for captive breeding of endangered species *viz.*, red panda and snow leopard. Private menageries and zoos have now been restricted by the rules laid down by Central Zoo Authorities.

Ex-situ floristic conservation is best served by the Botanical Garden on the west bank of river Hooghly at

Shibpur near Kolkata in 1787. It remains a living repository of 15,000 trees and shrubs belonging to 2350 species together with several thousands herbaceous plants. The garden was used for introduction of number of exotics by the colonial rulers. Besides the Botanical gardens, the Agri-Horticultural Garden at Alipore, Calcutta and Lloyds Botanical Garden at Darjeeling deserve special mention in this regard. It may be mentioned that the Agri-Horticultural Society succeeded Agricultural Society of India with William Carey as the President (1824-1826). The society encouraged collection of seed and experimentation in the garden and had branches at four districts in undivided Bengal, besides its branches elsewhere. Introduction of better varieties of exotics has still now remained as a major objective. The Lloyd's Botanical garden at Darjeeling was set up for plants of temperate conditions and continues to function till date.

The Forest Conservation Act, 1980 and the National Policy on Conservation of Natural Resources has led to a series of plantation programme with local floral species in recent times. The number of nurseries at the district level, largely initiated by State Forest Department, supported by non-government organisations and village *panchayats* have contributed towards the process of *ex-situ* conservation of many Bengal plants such as *sirish, kadam, kamranga, neem, kanchan, simul, palas,* sandal, *chalta, gaub, anshphal, bot, dumur, Kurchi, aam, bakul, karanj, putranjiva, tentul,* etc., which were otherwise getting replaced by exotics. Such plantations are welcome ventures in the conservation of flora (Ghosh, 2008).

Besides these *ex-situ* conservation efforts, collection of agricultural crops, specially rice, was first initiated in West Bengal by Chinsura farm. *Ex-situ* conservation of flora, both wild and cultivated, as such has a long history in the state. The threatened species of wildlife in West Bengal are given protection in these identified protected areas and *ex-situ* conservation areas of the state.

Special mention should be made to two recent efforts for wildlife conservation in peri-urban areas. One relates to Narendrapur Wildlife Sanctuary, a heaven for more than 100 species of birds which faced the danger of de-notification (notified in 1982) and converted into a housing estate. The bird heaven also have civets, mongoose, jungle cat, snakes and amphibian; bird life include resident (crested serpent eagle, oriole, cuckoo thrush, minivet, drongo) and migratory species (sealy thrush, tickell's thrush, verditec flycatcher, tickell's blue flycatcher etc.)

The second area under protection is Santragachi *Jheel*, a property of South-eastern Railway near Howrah. A host of amphibian, reptiles, resident and migratory birds use the *Jheel* as preferred habitat. Winter migrants attract many visitors. West Bengal Forest Department has recently taken step to protect this wetland. Public awareness campaign and management plan is being implemented. (Ghosh, 2008)

Besides, Santragachi *Jheel*, water bodies in Santiniketan (Ballavpur Sanctuary), Purulia (Sahebbandh), Bardhaman (Purbasthali) and several others are considered valuable habitat for protected resident and migratory bird species. The Sundarbans in south Bengal, being one of the major brackishwater habitats has multiple statuses of biosphere reserve, national park and bird sanctuary etc., and remain one of the most important protected areas for diverse wildlife on land and in water, ranging from Royal Bengal Tiger to host of birds, marine turtles, crocodiles and marine mammals.

12.5 Biodiversity

India is a signatory to the 'Convention on Biological Diversity' (CBD) adopted at the UN Conference on Environment and Development, Rio de Janeiro, Brazil in June 1992. Since then, the Government of India has prepared a 'Status Report on Biodiversity' (1998), a 'National Biodiversity Strategy and Action Plan' (NBSAP) in 2002 (Draft) and enacted 'Biological Diversity Act' in 2002 followed by Rules in 2004. West Bengal in Eastern India is known to have a rich biological diversity both in the wild and in agriculture and animal husbandry. Biological diversity is assessed at ecosystem, species and genetic level.

12.5.1 Ecosystem Diversity

The State of West Bengal occupies 2.2 per cent of the geographical area of India and exhibits all major ecosystem diversity *viz.*, mountain ecosystem (Darjeeling district), forest ecosystem (hill forest, forest of Dooars—Terai, forests in Gangetic plains, mangrove forests in Sundarbans), freshwater ecosystem (both lentic and lotic systems prevalent in riverine area, natural and man-made wetlands and lakes), coastal and marine ecosystem (220 km of coast line in Medinipur and South and North 24 Parganas), semi-arid ecosystem (Purulia, Bankura and Birbhum districts of red laterite zone), island ecosystem (Islands of Sundarbans in the Hugli-Malta estuarine region).

12.5.2 Species Diversity

The state of West Bengal has almost all major groups of fauna from protozoa to mammals, recorded from India.

This includes 117 species of mammals, 219 species of birds and 517 species of fishes; the total number of faunal species originally estimated at 7553 in 1999 has now increased to 8708 species, representing more than 10 per cent of the species recorded in India in 2.2 per cent of geographical area occupied by the state. A total of 3580 species of flora belonging to seven groups has been recorded from the state out of 47,000 species known from India but these represent largely the Angiosperm or Flowering plants (17,000 species in India).

Lack of details of floristic diversity is hindering the current state of knowledge. However, for some ecosystem *viz.*, mangrove forests of Sundarbans, a complete account is available; it is composed of 70 species of which 35 species are true mangroves, 28 species are associates and 7 species are obligate associate. Population of some of the mangrove flora like Sundari (*Heriteria fomes)* is becoming rare and endangered. Darjeeling Himalaya has been identified as one of the major centre for endemic species (originally described and largely restricted in the region) in the state.

12.5.3 Genetic Diversity

The studies on genetic diversity are largely restricted to agricultural crops and livestock. Ghosh (2004) has provided number of varietals diversity recorded in cereals and grains and also in non-cereal crops; breeds of livestock, each being genetically different have also been estimated to a limited extent. The West Bengal University of Animal and Fishery Sciences have recently recorded two additional indigenous breeds of livestock, in poultry and piggery.

TABLE 12.6

Varietals Diversity of Non-Cereal Crops

		Number			Number
Vegetable	Potato	2+	Spices	Chili	12
	Brinjal	25		Ginger	2+
	Cabbage	18			
				Coconut	5
	Cauliflower	22	Plantation Crop	Areca nut	3
	Tomato	17	Fibre Crop	Jute	2
	Lady's Finger	15		Mesta	10
	Cucumber	11	**Flower**		Numerous varieties
Fruit Crop	Mango	150+	**Medicinal** Plants		750 (75 commercially collected)
	Banana	25			
	Guava	8			
	Pineapple	6			
	Litchi	7			

Source: Ghosh, A.K. (2004). *Conservation Measures for Biodiversity with Special Reference to Important Crops in West Bengal*. Govt. of West Bengal.

12.5.4 Threat to Biodiversity

The major threat to biodiversity can be identified as fragmentation of habitat, loss of dense forests, conversion of wetland and over exploitation of resources; the impact of atmospheric pollution load is yet to be fully appreciated but water pollution has been responsible for loss of aquatic species and diminishing size of population of some species. In a recent report of Zoological Survey of India entitled "Biodiversity: Present Status and Past Exploitation", it is stated that seven species of mammals, 14 species of birds, 13 species of fishes have disappeared from West Bengal during 1985-2005. The report also points out to the declining population of Gangetic dolphin, fishing cat, vultures and large whistling teals etc.

TABLE 12.7

West Bengal: Varietals Diversity of Cereals and Grains

Rice	± 400 (5556 Pre-Green Revolution Period)
Finger Millet	Several
Wheat	2

Source: As in Table 12.6.

TABLE 12.8

West Bengal: Breeds of Livestock

Cattle	One : Siri fum (Darjeeling)
Goat	Three : Black (24 Parganas), Brown (Malda), White (Dinajpur)
Sheep	One : Garol (South 24 Parganas)
Poultry	One : Assel (Bankura, Birbhum, Purulia)

Source: As in Table 12.6.

12.5.5 Biodiversity Conservation

The Government of West Bengal has formed a State Biodiversity Board (SBB) in September 2004 following the stipulation of Biological Diversity Act, 2002. The West Bengal Biological Diversity Rules, 2005 came into effect after January 2006. Biodiversity Management Committees (BMC), which are to be formed at the local level have been constituted in seven of the *Panchayat Samiti*/ Municipality Area in the district of Darjeeling, Jalpaiguri, Hooghly, Bankura, West Medinipur and South 24 Parganas. The BMCs are to prepare People's Biodiversity Register (PBR) with participation of the local community; these PBR are to document information on local biological resources and traditional knowledge. BMCs will oversee the sustainable use of bio-resources and are empowered to charge cess for commercial exploitations. Currently, the board has initiated PBR activities in five districts of the state covering 15 *gram panchayats* with a future plan to extent the activities to all the 19 districts (Annual Report, WBSBB, 2006-07).

12.6 Industrial Pollution

Industrial pollution can be traced back to the sources i.e., untreated wastewater, uncontrolled emission and unplanned disposal of solid/hazardous waste. For each of these, specific Acts are available suggesting appropriate punitive measures. But, evidences of violation of extant laws are increasing. A report dated December 2000 states that the Supreme Court of India had listed 68 categories of polluting industries in India. Out of which 54 were found in West Bengal. In response to a Public Interest Litigation case, Supreme Court directed the Calcutta High Court to deal with the matter. The West Bengal State Pollution Control Board had submitted three reports to the High Court on the action taken and current status. It stated that out of 54 categories identified in 1996, 12 categories are still operating in the state. The High Court then stated that no more time should be given to these 'obsolete, unclean technology'. All the polluting industries were to be served notice by WBPCB warning that appropriate control technology is to be adopted or face closure. These include small industrial units also—like ceramic, pigments and dye, stone crushing, comb manufacturing and others besides hospitality industries.

A list of grossly polluting industries still features in the Annual Report of WBPCB (2006-07), numbering 334 which includes besides the ferro-alloy and sponge iron industries, foundry, secondary lead smelting, textile, ceramic, chemicals, paper and pulp, cement, asbestos and power units. It is interesting to note that 13 Thermal Power Plants (Garden Reach, Kashipur, Titagarh all of CESC, NTPC plant at Farakka, W.B. Govts., Bakreshwar TPP and DVC's 3 units Power Supply, as also W.B. Govts., Durgapur plant) prominently feature in the list. In 2003-04, the number of grossly polluting industries was 294, indicating that within four years more than 12 per cent increase in number of such units. The soft drink industry now monopolised by multinational companies (Pepsi at Fartabad, P.S. Sonarpur), Hindustan Coca Cola, Raniapur, Jalpaiguri also prominently feature in the list. The large public sector undertaking like Indian Oil Refinery, Haldia, Haldia Petrochemical, Durgapur Projects Ltd, Chittaranjan Locomotive Works, Dankuni Coal Complex have been identified under grossly polluting industries in the state, along with units of large industrial houses of ITC and ICI.

12.6.1 Sponge Iron and Ferro Alloy Factories: A New Threat

West Bengal has now 50 sponge iron plants according to the President of the Sponge Iron and Ferro Alloy Association. Factories were mostly located in the peri-urban areas but fast extended into the *panchayat* zone. Sponge iron and ferro alloy factories belong to "Red Category" industries, due to hazardous nature, following CPCB guidelines. The manufacturing process involves reducing iron ore with crushed coal at 850-1050°C, releasing smoke with oxide of sulphur and carbon, unburned carbon particles and silica.

In a report released in April 2005, a special environmental impact assessment committee appointed by the West Bengal Pollution Control Appellate Authority made revealing observations. The Committee observed that the "plants regularly shut down their Electrostatic Precipitators (ESP) (a mandatory requirement for such operation) after sun down to save electricity costs and speed up production process" (*Down to Earth*, June 15, 2005). Estimated cost of running ESP comes to 0.6 million rupees in a month. More alarming is the observation that despite repeated warnings and fines running into lakhs of rupees, the plants continue to violate WBPCB regulation.

This was further confirmed by a team from Centre for Science and Environment, New Delhi, which visited eight such plants and Bardhaman and Bankura district and found seven are operating with their ESP's turned off. The EIA Committee also recorded that dust collected from ESP's isn't converted to slurry but simply dumped outside the plants in dry form, causing severe air pollution. A factory typically produces 20-40 tonnes of coal dust per day, which is also dumped near human habitation. EIA Committee reaffirmed NGO team's observation on the damage caused by such units in village and forest areas especially to agricultural crop yield, cattle health, forest plantation and occupational health hazards of the workers and neighbouring residential areas. The violation of government rules in the absence of any system of providing protective gadgets like helmet, masks, gloves and gumboots was too obvious. According to State Labour Department, "the effect on health is chronic in nature and doesn't have any cure at present. Occupational health specialist listed gas poisoning, blood cancer, pneumoconiosis, silicosis, loss of hearing as possible hazards from the uncontrolled operation of such units."

Recently, the West Bengal Government has announced that no further permission for setting up sponge iron and ferro alloy factories will be given but the pollution from the existing units continue to create problem.

12.6.2 Mining and Quarrying

Mining is considered as one of the most damaging activity for environment but become compulsive to meet development need. Mining and quarrying often lead to significant changes in the air quality, water quality and noise level besides loss of groundwater resources. Water pollution in mining area has created public health hazard. The affected districts include Bardhaman, Bankura, Purulia, Purba and Paschim Medinipur, Jalpaiguri, Malda and Cooch Behar. The impact of stone quarry and crushing operation on public health has also been pointed out earlier in 1999 (Status of Environment Report, Government of West Bengal). EIA notifications of 1994/2006 also stipulated a policy of compulsory resettlement and rehabilitation of project affected families. Often, evicted people do not get appropriate rehabilitation. Reclamation of mined area has been made compulsory as also creation of green belt.

While environmental cost of mining and quarrying has never been seriously investigated, expansion of old mining project and opening up of new mines either under public, joint or private sector, continued unabated; prior permission of WBPCB may act as an initial control, but lack of monitoring mechanism may continue the problem. Although, the new Mineral Policy of the State (2002) has listed many of sectors in a selective manner, but Index number of Industrial Production taking 1980 as the base year, shows a gradual decline of production in the Mining and quarrying sector.

12.7 Air Quality

The quality of air that we breathe is one of the vital life support system. When natural air quality changes and affects human health and the surrounding, it is considered polluted. The major air pollutants include Suspended Particulate Matter (Total and Respirable), sulphur dioxide (SO_2), hydrocarbons (HC), nitrogen oxides (NOx), carbon monoxide (CO), photochemical oxidants (Smog), sulphates and lead (Pb).

Kolkata's average Suspended Particulate Matter (SPM) and Respirable Particulate Matter (RPM) counts recorded last winter (2007) showed that "SPM was 343, RPM stood at 181, which should ideally have been 140 and 60 respectively". A Report by the Asian Development Bank (ADB), on annual average concentration of RPM in Kolkata also shows that it is nearly 100 mg per cubic metre as compared to the annual national ambient air quality standard of 60 mg per cubic metre. Other parameters such as carbon monoxide, benzene-soluble organic matter, heavy metals and poly-nuclear aromatic hydrocarbon, benzene-toluene-xylene, organolead, inhalable particulate matter (IPM) and acidity of moisture are not being recorded in the city. In general, sources of air pollution can be grouped under industrial sources, automobile sources, indoor air pollution and other sources (Ghosh, Saha and Sen, 2008).

12.7.1 Industrial Sources of Air Pollution

In West Bengal, there are 8,887 registered factories operating (*Statistical Handbook*, West Bengal, 2004). These include coal fired thermal power plants, integrated iron and steel plants, pharmaceutical industries, fertilisers, paper and pulp industries, cement, distillery, brewery, chemical, etc. Besides these large and medium scale industries, about 3,20,309 small-scale registered industrial units are operating within the jurisdiction of the state. Out of these 17 types of critically polluting industries are identified by West Bengal Pollution Control Board (WBPCB).

Special emphasis can be given on the coal fired thermal power plants (TPP) for the air pollution potential. In our state, 15 coal-fired thermal power stations are functioning with their significant role in the state's air pollution scenario; the pollutants from TPP include CO, CO_2, SPM, SO_2, NOx, heavy metals and others.

12.7.2 Automobile Sources

Besides industrial sources, exhaust emission from automobiles is also contributing towards air pollution to a large extent. Following reasons may be considered for increased auto-emission leading to air pollution:

- Use of old vehicles.
- Decreasing road space for each vehicle.
- Bad road condition.
- Absence of maintenance system.

The number of vehicles is increasing day by day in all major cities and towns of West Bengal worsening the air pollution scenario. In 1991, the total number of vehicles on road was 918,768 which reached a figure of 2,547,962 by 31st March 2004 (nearly 3 times in 13 years); with new vehicles being manufactured in larger numbers and in more brands, the upward trend is continuing at a faster pace.

12.7.3 Indoor Air Pollution

The major sources of indoor air pollution can be attributed to burning biomass based fuels for cooking, smoking, using carpets, use of pets, keeping plants inside the room etc., with high population density and high percentage of slum dwellers, the use of biomass-based fuels like kerosene, coal etc., are considerably high in the state specially in the city of Kolkata. The pollutants generated during burning get trapped inside the house with improper ventilation. Changing trends is, however, noticed among the lower middle class families as they are shifting towards LPG for cooking. But people below poverty line are worse affected due to continuing use of fossil fuels, specially the women of the family. Indoor air pollution can cause serious bronchial diseases, lung cancer, child asthma and allergic reactions.

12.7.4 Other Sources

Other sources of air pollution include burning of dry leaves and branches, re-suspension of road dust, construction activities, dumping of garbage etc. These sources vary from place to place and not quantified till date.

12.7.5 Impacts of Air Pollutants

The air pollution is adversely affecting the human population along with other animal life, plants and materials. The short and long-term health impacts of various air pollutants are given in Table A-12.2. According to a study, initiated by Department of Environment (DoE), Government of West Bengal (GoWB) and conducted by scientists of Chittaranjan National Cancer Institute, Kolkata and University of Calcutta during 1998-2001, population of Kolkata city are more susceptible to respiratory disorders than rural population. The study revealed that alveolar macrophage count is nearly seven times higher in population of Kolkata, especially in the street hawkers, garage workers, traffic police and other people who are exposed to higher air pollution due to their occupation, than their rural counterpart. This particular group of people also is suffering from severe lung impairment. Study conducted on smoking population also show a higher macrophage count than non-smoking population. Women having more alveolar macrophage count than non-smoking male population, both in urban and rural groups may be attributed to the indoor air pollution from domestic cooking. The study shows that prevalence of respiratory problems is much more in winter season than during summer and monsoon seasons in the city.

Another study on effect of ambient lead on children group of Kolkata was carried out by Regional Occupational Health Centre, Eastern Region and supported by DoE, GoWB. This two year long study with medical examination of 471 school children revealed that average lead concentration in the blood of city children was about 1.5 times higher as compared to the rural school children. In addition, it was also found that 56 per cent of surveyed children's blood samples contain less than 10µg/dl of lead. The situation of rural children is much better (98 per cent) than city children.

10.7.6 Impact of Automobile Emission

The automobile population in the state has increased significantly during last 10 years period with the introduction of new brands of vehicles. While such new brands have more fuel-efficient technology, the old vehicles continue to ply even with the higher road tax structure. The use of old vehicles have, therefore, created major problem and there is demand for replacement of the same.

So the level of auto emission continues to pollute the city air, while the capital city Delhi successfully endorsed conversion of all public vehicles into CNG fuel, the situation in West Bengal continues to be critical due to repeated failure in keeping the deadlines. Recently, Government of West Bengal declared that instead of changing fuel type from diesel to LPG, thousands of three wheelers will be given support to change from two stroke engines to four stroke engines.

12.7.7 Actions Taken

WBPCB has taken various actions to control the air pollution in the state. Regulatory measures are taken for controlling industrial air pollution including the following:

- Declaring air pollution control area.
- Stricter policy for locating new industries.
- Ensuring regulatory compliance by grossly polluting industries.
- Regulatory orders for non-complying industries.
- Introducing stricter emission standard for boilers, ceramic kilns and foundries operating within the city of Kolkata.
- Making mandatory the use of cleaner fuels for small boilers, ceramic kilns etc., of Kolkata.
- Environmental compliance to be achieved by the cluster of small industries.
- Giving financial assistance to the small industries for installing pollution control measures by the WBPCB and the state government.
- Encouraging industries to adopt cleaner production practices.

Actions are also taken to control the automobile emission like:

- India 2000 mass emission norms for new private vehicles within Kolkata Metropolitan Area (KMA) and for all new vehicles in the state.
- Bharat Stage II mass emission norms for all new four-wheeled passenger cars in KMA.
- Unleaded petrol available throughout the state.
- Reduced benzene content of petrol.
- Introduced cleaner automotive fuel.
- In association with State Department of Transport, Facilitating setting up of 148 computerised and upgraded Emission Testing Centres (AETCs) and Pollution-under-Check (PUCs) centres in West Bengal. For petrol/LPG/CNG engines, four or five gases analysers with facility for testing exhaust gases like CO, CO_2, O_2 and HC are being installed at the AETC premises. (*Source:* Green Governance, August-September 2005, WBPCB).

Other actions like construction of flyovers, banning rubber burning and open *chullah* burning at pavement etc., are taken to reduce the air pollution and improve the air quality of the state.

12.8 Noise Pollution

Noise pollution, by definition is unwanted sound. It covers all sound, which can result in hearing impairment or be harmful to health or otherwise dangerous. In scientific parlance, noise is a pressure oscillation in air, water or any medium, which radiates away from the source. Pollution from legal point of view is the wrongful contamination of the environment, which causes material injury to the right of an individual. Noise pollution can be divided into two categories, natural and man-made. Natural causes of noise pollution are volcanoes, seas, rivers, exchanging and voices of living organs including man-made noises. Some of the chief causes of man-made noises which can cause pollution are machines and modern equipment of various types of automobiles, trains, aeroplanes, use of explosives, bursting of firecrackers and other activities leading to rising noise level. Noise is an inescapable byproduct of industrial environment, which is increasing very fast with the advancement in industrialisation and urbanisation.

The unit of measuring noise is decibel denoted as dB. Experts believe that continuous noise level in excess of 90 dB can cause loss of hearing and irreversible changes in nervous system. World Health Organization (WHO) has fixed 45 dB as safe noise level for a city. If the sound level is more than 90 dB (A) then the effects are: hearing loss (auditory effect) and non-auditory effects which include, interference with speech, interference with communication, interference with sleep, annoyance, fatigue, low work efficiency, blood pressure increases, cardiac problem, nervousness and headache (Ghosh, 2008).

12.8.1 Ambient Noise Standards

Ambient noise is the culmination of both noise at close proximity and noise at a distance from the source. National Standards have been prescribed for daytime and nighttime for four types of zone due to environmental impact of noise on human health and other biota (specially fauna). Norms have been prescribed for human-related settlements as well as for protected areas.

TABLE 12.9

National Ambient Noise Standards

Area Class	*Day Time (dB)*	*Night Time(dB)*
Residential	55	45
Commercial	65	55
Industrial	75	70
Silent zone	50	40

Note: *Daytime* = 6.00 AM - 9.00 PM (15 hours), *Nighttime* = 9.00 PM - 6.00 AM (9 hours).

Source: Ministry of Environment and Forest, 1981.

Competent authorities have declared silent zones as areas upto 100 metres around certain premises like hospitals, educational institutions and courts. Honking of vehicle horns, blaring of loud speakers, bursting of crackers and hawkers noise should be banned in these zones.

12.8.2 Laws and Standards

The Environment Protection Act, 1986 (3rd Amendment, 1989 Schedule III), is a major law for regulatory control of noise level. Indian Standards (IS: 3028) prescribed vehicular noise levels for different categories of vehicles. In addition, abatement of noise pollution has been made mandatory in Municipal Corporation Act, Motor Vehicles Act, Police Act and Noise Pollution (Regulation and Control) Rules, 2000. West Bengal Pollution Control Board (WBPCB) and the State Police Department are empowered to enforce regulatory measures.

While conducting Environment Impact Assessment for obtaining environmental clearance for any development project, it is mandatory at both state and Central level to monitor the noise level by the individual project proponent. The trend of noise pollution in the residential localities, traffic intersections and other areas of monitoring clearly indicate a declining process. However, no data is available on the noise pollution in different industrial sectors which is directly related to occupational health hazards. It is essential that selected industries should be regularly monitored both for daytime and nighttime noise level to ensure safety of the workers from the noise pollution. In many of the industries with proven higher noise level, use of ear muff or ear plugs have never been imposed by the controlling authority. Only in those industrial areas where ISO 14000 certification for Environmental Management has been adopted, adequate steps have been taken to control the noise pollution either by changing of technology or by strictly enforcing the use of protective devices (Ghosh, 2008).

12.8.2.1 Waste Management

The solid waste generated in any human habitation is now being classified into five categories, *viz.*, municipal solid waste (MSW), bio-medical waste, hazardous waste, e-waste and plastic waste.

Municipal Solid Waste (MSW)

With rising urbanisation and change in lifestyle and food habits, the amount of municipal solid waste has been increasing rapidly and its composition is changing. Traditional methods of waste disposal under the purview of municipal and civic bodies have largely limited themselves to the "collect and dispose" mode, which are becoming inadequate to cope with its increasing quantity and changing nature. Studies show that with every Rs.1000 increase in income, the generation of solid waste goes up by a kilogram per month. The Kolkata Metropolitan Area (KMA) is one of the largest and most densely populated areas in India. There has been about 140 per cent increase in the municipal population in KMA during the last decade. The municipal area of West Bengal comprises of 125 municipal bodies including six Municipal Corporations. Kolkata Municipal Corporation is the largest municipal body having area 187.33 sq. km. with a population strength of 45,80,544 (as per the 2001 Census) whereas Tarakeswar Municipality in Hooghly district represents the smallest member of the family, in 1.5 sq. km. area. The city of Kolkata generates a total of 2500 MT of waste per day. District-wise waste generation in the municipal area is given in Table A-12.3.

12.8.3 Current Initiatives in West Bengal

Under the provisions of MSW Rules, 2000, the Department of Urban Development, Government of West Bengal and the District Magistrates of the concerned districts has the overall responsibility of the management of municipal solid waste in the state. The West Bengal Pollution Control Board oversees the implementation of solid waste management by the municipalities and the district authorities in order to comply with the provisions of the Rules.

12.8.4 The Solid Waste Management Mission, 2005

- The state government has developed a systematic approach called the West Bengal Solid Waste Management Mission to provide "the best combination of safe, clean, and efficient disposal". On May 4, 2005, the State Department of Municipal Affairs constituted the Mission, a registered society for systematic management of solid waste. The 21-member governing body of the Mission is headed by the Chief Secretary and comprises of the Secretaries of the relevant departments of the government, representatives from the Union Ministry of Municipal Affairs, Union Ministry of Environment and Forests, Kolkata Metropolitan Development Authority (KMDA), three NGOs, three experts of the field, three representatives of urban local bodies as well as the Member Secretary of the West Bengal Pollution Control Board (WBPCB).

The Mission aims to set up common facilities under a public-private partnership (PPP) framework, for development and management of landfill site, compost facility, waste recovery and recycling, management of the transfer stations, management of waste transportation and arrangement of primary collection through NGOs particularly in new areas.

12.8.4.1 Biomedical Waste

Bio-medical waste is considered potentially hazardous; disposal of untreated bio-medical waste poses both environmental and public health hazards. Considering the seriousness of the problem, Government of India notified the 'Bio-Medical Waste (Management and Handling) Rules in 1998 which has been amended in 2003. These rules are applicable to hospitals, nursing homes, pathological laboratories and clinics, blood banks, etc. An analysis showed that during 1998-2007, out of 125 urban local bodies in 19 districts of West Bengal, only 4 areas, *viz.* Howrah, Kalyani, Haldia and Asansol have been covered by the common bio-medical waste treatment and disposal facilities by private operators. A summary of status of treatment of biomedical waste in urban centres of West Bengal is given in Table A-12.4.

12.8.4.2 Hazardous Waste

Earlier, management of solid waste was identified as a

single issue. But during the 1980s, Ministry of Environment and Forests (MoEF) has recognised different categories of wastes calling for appropriate disposal. Those wastes which cause hazard to human health and also to the ecology are categorised as hazardous wastes. As a result, MoEF has issued a legal notification under the Environment Protection Act, 1986, called the Hazardous Waste (Management and Handling) Rules, 1989. The producers of hazardous wastes have to abide by the rules, which states that the authorised person can collect, treat, transport, store or dispose of hazardous wastes in accordance with the guidelines to be issued by the competent authority from time to time.

The state government has the responsibility to identify the site and compile and publish periodically an inventory of disposal sites within the state for the disposal of hazardous wastes. The occupier who intends to get his hazardous waste treated by the operator of facility should provide him with proper information about the hazardous waste as may be specified by the State Pollution Control Board. Before hazardous waste is delivered at the hazardous waste site, the occupier or the operator of facility should ensure that the waste is packaged in a manner suitable for storage, transport and labelling and packaging should be readily visible and be able to withstand physical conditions and climate factors. The occupier generating hazardous waste should maintain records of such wastes and if any accident occurs during transportation of hazardous wastes, the occupier should report immediately to the SPCB.

Total number of hazardous waste generating units identified in West Bengal now stands at 705; out of these 609 are operating units and rest have been reportedly closed down. In 2003, a joint venture company named M/s, West Bengal Waste Management Limited has been started to develop and operate integrated waste management complex for treating industrial hazardous waste of the entire state. Currently, a Common Hazardous Waste Storage Treatment & Disposal Facility (CHWSTDF) is being developed near Haldia.

12.8.4.3 e-Waste

The Information Technology (IT) revolution has been one of the mainstay in the present system of governance. West Bengal has fast forwarded the process in last eight years. Desk Top Personal Computers (PC's) are now being used at every major institution. IT industry is considered a Greenfield industry and remains outside the purview of State Pollution Control Board.

A look at the components of desk top computers (DTC) can reveal that each glass cathode ray tubes (CRT's) found in computers' display monitor contains an average of 2 kg of lead; US Environmental Protection Agency declared that CRT failing toxicity criteria, is to be considered as hazardous waste. Circuit boards and batteries also contain plenty of lead and smaller amount of mercury and hexavalent chromium. Plastics used in electronic equipments often contain polyvinyl chloride which produces dioxin (a carcinogen) when burnt. Other component may include brominated flame retardants (BFR's), several of which can cause disruption of hormone system and can accumulate in animal and fish tissue.

Environmental impacts of e-waste are yet to emerge fully. However, a list of 13 components used in PC's (Table A-12.5) clearly shows the potential danger posed to human health.

Based on a household sample survey and selected institutional sample survey, reveal that at least 33 per cent households go for changing or upgradation of computer peripherals within 2-3 years and more than 50 per cent complaints are related to hard discs which are largely replaced. The results from institution and corporate sector survey, 1 out of 8 computers are disposed of every 2 years. Computers condemned are sold off to vendors as scraps.

Of the e-waste, hard plastics of the casings find their way to plastic recycling factories in Topsia-Tangra-Tiljala area in east Calcutta to be turned into plastic crystals to be reused again. Huge amount of plastic dust is generated in the process. The printed circuit board containing, lead and toxic heavy metals are burnt in selected alleys of central Calcutta to retrieve metals in a crude manner. Small printed circuit boards of smaller electronic goods like calculator or 'remote control' are simply dumped by the street side to be taken away to Municipal Dumping Ground. However, no estimate has ever been made on electronic waste dumped in the Dhapa Dumping Ground. CRT's are sold to traders to be transported to Delhi.

No e-Waste management system has so far been implemented in West Bengal or in the capital city of Kolkata. e-Waste could be separated out at specific facility point (Switzerland for instance runs e-waste recycling industries in a highly mechanised form with only 12-16 persons). In India and in Kolkata, the entire process of e-waste recycling is carried out without any technical back up and the people engaged in this informal sector remains vulnerable to the hazards of handling of components. Adequate training for handlings, a minimum standard for such recycling units, introduction of proper recycling procedure to minimise environmental and health hazard is urgently called for (Ghosh, 2008).

12.8.4.4 Plastic Waste

This all-pervasive use of plastics stems from the benefits it has to offer—lightness, flexibility, durability and water-resistance—to name a few. Of the wide range of plastic polymers, thermoplastics and thermosetting plastics are the most popular. The largely used thermoplastics are polyethylene (PE), polypropylene (PP), polyvinyl chloride (PVC), polystyrene (PS), nylon, polyethylene tetra-phthalate (PET) while thermosetting plastics include polyurethane (PU), phenol formaldehyde resins, amino resins, epoxy resins etc. Several industrial sectors are highly dependent on plastics, namely, packaging, pipes, cables, electronic, automobile and aviation, medical including population control systems, agriculture and water management, appliances and household products, and many others.

Discarded plastics, in general, pose a threat to human health and environment. Being non-biodegradable by nature, plastics remain intact for hundreds of years without rotting or transforming into compost. Waste plastics find their way into various surface water bodies, hindering the natural reaeration process. Plastics choke municipal sewer lines and storm water drains and clogs the bar-screens of sewage treatment plants. Spread on the ground, they interfere with various agricultural operations and also prevent natural recharge of underground water. Plastic-filled litter in public places contributes to visual pollution. Consuming food, which has been wrapped in coloured plastic, has lethal effects on health. These coloured bags contain harmful toxic metals like chromium and copper that cause allergies. Confusing them with real food, animals consume plastics that cause internal injury, intestinal blockage and starvation. Municipalities routinely report the death of cows and other animals from ingesting plastic bags.

In India, plastics account to four per cent volume of the total of solid waste generated everyday. Thus, in terms of quantity, the safe plastic disposal is a highly important matter. The municipal authorities presently have two options of plastic disposal, incineration and landfill, neither of which is wholly satisfactory. Plastics remain fairly inert in the landfills or large open pits in which they are dumped. Besides, the large volume to mass ratio of plastics aggravates the already-receding landfill space. On the other hand, open and uncontrolled burning has possibly even graver consequences as it produces environmental hazards far beyond the burning site. The hazard comes in the form of unintended by-products, the persistent organic pollutants, commonly called the POPs. Incineration of plastics especially, chlorinated ones like PVC and PU releases harmful dioxin, which is a potent human carcinogen. However, various studies reveal that controlled incineration is effective as it recovers maximum energy from fuel and ensures complete breakdown of the toxic substances. The most common plastic waste includes plastic bags, PET Bottles, as well as some plastic items from biomedical waste like used plastic syringes, and medical appliances like catheters, blood bags, etc.

12.9 Environmental Education

Environmental Education (EE) has been incorporated in all level of school education. The state has 67107 primary and junior basic schools, 2985 junior high schools and 8640 high and higher secondary schools. At each level, *"Poribesh Shiksha"* (= Environmental Education) has become a part of curriculum. However, since the marks obtained in high and higher secondary final examinations are not added to determine the ranking, there is positive dearth in the level of interests both on the part of students and teachers. However, in some front ranking schools, the students have shown keen interest in running "Nature Club" participating against "Noise Pollution" or for conservation-related movement. A total of 4750 Eco-Clubs are reported to be running from school system in West Bengal under the National Green Corps (NGC) Programme initiated by the Ministry of Environment and Forests, Government of India. It is interesting to note that in some the districts more than 300 Eco-Clubs are working (540 Eco-Clubs in North 24 Parganas, 413 in Bardhaman, 330 in South 24 Parganas, 319 in Paschim Medinipur); in the capital city of Kolkata the number of Eco-Clubs stands at 364. (Annual Report, WBPCB, 2006-07)

Selected schools are also participating in the "Global Learning and Observation of Benefit the Environment" (GLOBE). Many educational institutions participate in the yearly "National Environmental Awareness Campaign" (NEAC) sponsored by MoEF, Government of India, either directly or in collaboration with environmental NGO's.

West Bengal is perhaps the second state after Karnataka, where school and collage students have started participating in documenting local level biodiversity and related traditional knowledge to prepare "Peoples' Biodiversity Register" (PBR). Such PBR's have been prepared in 12 villages in the districts of South 24 Parganas, Nadia and Hooghly and 15 more PBR's are under process of preparations. In all the PBR exercises, students get first hand experience of working with expert teachers and scientists. PBR is now mandatory for each *Panchayat Samiti* or Community Block level under Biological diversity Act, 2002 and Rules, 2004.

Besides Eco-Clubs (under National Green Corps Programme of MoEF), "GLOBE" and "NEAC" programmes, students also participate in significant number in WWF-I sponsored "Nature Club". A total of 150 nature clubs are now functioning in West Bengal. WBPCB has also launched an effective environmental campaign divided into two categories, awareness and field action. During 2006-2007, a total of 29 programmes were conducted by WBPCB in collaboration with educational institutions and NGO's.

At college level, following up the directive of Supreme Court, all undergraduate students are to study "Environment", for which 50 marks have been allocated. In-service college teachers are required to undergo Refresher and Orientation Courses at the Academic Staff Colleges, where environment education has become a part of curriculum.

At Post Graduate level, all seven major Universities offer Master Degree Course in Environmental Sciences; 'Environmental Engineering' is being offered by the Jadavpur University as a Post Graduate Diploma. 'Environment Management' as a full fledged 2 years Post Graduate Course is offered in 'Indian Institute of Social Welfare and Business Management' (IISWBM), the first Business School of India, located in the city of Kolkata. M. Phil degree in Environmental Sciences is being offered at the Jadavpur University and Kalyani University, West Bengal.

12.10 Environmental Governance

The Government of West Bengal may be credited for establishing the Department of Environment in 1982, two years after Government of India's setting up the department in 1980. Since then, DoEn has been put under a cabinet minister and has been playing a significant role in the system of environmental governance, in collaboration with West Bengal Pollution Control Board (WBPCB). While DoEn has been confined with its administrative headquarters in Kolkata, WBPCB has its HQ in Kolkata with a network of 9 regional office located in strategic location, 1 Sub-regional office and 3 offices, each under Senior Environment Engineer. Till the end March 2007, WBPCB had 135 meetings to discuss the key issues faced by the state at periodic intervals. WBPCB organised Public Hearing for Environment Impact Assessment Studies conducted for Development Projects and also attended to the Public Complaints. The analysis shows that in a given year more than 95 per cent of the complaints are attended and disposed off; the number of the complaints received between 1999 and 2007 varied between 1750 to nearly 3000 per year. WBPCB has appointed a Public Information Officer to attend to the cases related to Right to Information Act, 2005; during 2006-07, as many as 35 applications were received from different districts, of which 33 were disposed off.

The WBPCB has also declared an Industrial Siting Policy, denoting the possible location of Special Red category industries, Ordinary Red category industries, Orange category industries and Green category industries. (Annual Report, WBPCB, 2006-07). The Department of Environment with limited manpower and budgetary support, mainly looks after administrative issues. DoEn published the First "Status of Environment" Report in 1999 and has subsequently been engaged in bringing out sectoral report, one such being on Air Quality in West Bengal.

But, most of the activities related to environment, it appears, are being carried out by WBPCB; it may be due to the autonomous status of WBPCB and better infrastructural support system. DoEn is largely discharging the responsibility of issuing certificate for environmental clearance (the State Level Environment Appraisal Committee [SEAC] being constituted by DoEn).

The state has 12 state acts, which along with 22 major central acts/notifications provide the main legal support for environmental governance. During last 25 years, the public awareness about environment has positively witnessed a change. Members of the civil society have become aware about their environmental rights and duties. The Calcutta High Court has a green bench, now comprised of the Hon'ble Chief Justice and two other members; a series of Public Interest Litigation Cases (PIL) during last 20 years show that collective action can help in better governance. [Ghosh (ed.), 2008]

12.11 Climate Change and West Bengal

The environmental scenario of West Bengal is likely to have serious impacts of the phenomenon of climate change and global warming. No state specific study is available but on the basis of available research data, some comments may be made. With global warming and climate change, the Himalayan Glaciers are reportedly melting at an all time faster pace. The result of such melting may result in flooding on one side and declining river flow at other time. The major water sources of the state, Ganga system, provides water for irrigation, power plants, industries and drinking water to the capital city. The changing hydrology is apt to impact these vital sectors of development.

West Bengal depends, like many other parts of India, heavily on the good monsoon. Current studies predict an abrupt change in monsoon which in turn will hit food security. The Gangetic plains of West Bengal can face a crisis of agricultural production with changing rainfall and hydrological changes.

Flood in north Bengal, largely attributed to big dams and barrages, may increase in intensity and with heavy rainfall even in pre-monsoon can enforce release of water from reservoirs of multipurpose river valley projects in West Bengal and neighbouring states of Bihar and Jharkhand; this has been witnessed in 2008. West Bengal is known as an epicentre of water-borne disease and water related vector-borne diseases *viz.*, malaria, dengue and unidentified viral fever; with climate change, the possible impact on public health due to water-borne or water-related vector-borne disease, need also a critical evaluation. With increasing temperature, the vectors are likely to breed faster and cause more widespread diseases.

With rain and cyclonic weather becoming unpredictable, the vulnerability will increase in coastal areas of Medinipur and South 24 Parganas and the areas within proven pathway of tidal influx, including city of Kolkata. The sea level rise in the Sundarbans has already been recorded by School of Oceanography, Jadavpur University. Out of 102 islands, three have already disappeared in the Sundarbans creating a serious problem of environmental refugees. In 2007-08, two high velocity cyclones, namely 'Cider' and 'Nargis' barely spared the Sundarbans and Kolkata, but inflicted serious damage on Bangladesh and Myanmar, leading to numerous death and loss of livelihood. Historical records show that a severe cyclone and strong surge took a toll of 300,000 people in Kolkata in September 1737.

Above all, the lives and livelihood of the people of the state, especially poor, may face rather unpredictable crisis of survival. Adaptation to climate change is urgently called for as also steps to be undertaken for mitigation. Efforts in the increasing use of renewable energy (biomass, solar, microhydel, wind, tidal) are noted in the state. The greening of West Bengal outside forest area is perhaps the single most successful venture of the civil society and the state. Green and Clean Technology are being advocated in some sectors but on the other hand, some of the new industrial ventures (*viz.*, sponge iron and ferro alloy) are causing adverse serious impact in the efforts of carbon reduction.

The proximity to the Bay of Bengal and climate changes of the last 100 years and more, has made Kolkata the most vulnerable of all megacities in the world; this has been projected in the Fourth IPCC Report, released in November 2007. The capital city has all the power plants by the side of the river, a major riverine port; rail and road links to rest of India, especially south-east and north-east. Major industries are located by the side of the river Hooghly *viz.*, petrochemicals, refinery, fertiliser, jute, foundries; as also vast population of poor and marginalised citizens live by the river side. The process of sensitisation and adaptation along with mitigation measures to cope with the climate change should be priority area for the state government. The World Bank is reportedly launching a study on 'Kolkata and Climate Change'—as a case study, under 'Climate change and variability impact assessment and adaptation to coastal cities of Asia' project. These case studies have over reaching objectives, to

- Identify most vulnerable urban infrastructure and populations in Kolkata.
- Assess the magnitude to physical and economic damage.
- Especially measures and costs needed to respond to climate change.
- Set priorities for decision makers for responding to the threat.

The changing climate may have serious impacts on water-resources, agriculture, industry, transport and health sectors in the state. The state, as a geopolitical entity, has to draw a strategic action plan to combat the effects of the climate change.

References

Banerjee, I. and Sinha Roy, S.P. (1992). "Management of Groundwater resources in Calcutta Metropolitan District Area", *Proc. Sem. Calcutta Water Supply-Techno-Economic Options*.

Bhunia, A. K. (1993). "Status of Municipal Water supply: Calcutta Metropolitan District I and Non-CMD Municipalities of West Bengal II". In *Proc. Workshop on Water Resource Development of West Bengal*. (eds. A. B. Goswami and P. Bose), School of Water Resources Engineering, Jadavpur University, Calcutta.

CGWB (1988). Hydrogeological Atlas of West Bengal, Central Ground Water Board, Eastern Region.

Deb, Debal (2008). "Agriculture": Chapter 7, in *Status of Environment in West Bengal: A Citizen's Report*, (ed. A.K. Ghosh) ENDEV, Society for *Environment and Development*, Kolkata.

FSI (2008). "State of Forest Report, 2005". Forest Survey of India, Dehradun.

Ghosh A.K. (2004). "Conservation Measures for Biodiversity with Special Reference to Important Crops in West Bengal", p.15-22 in *Biodiversity Conservation, Proceedings of the Round Table Discussion*, Department of Environment, Govt. of West Bengal and West Bengal Pollution Control Board.

———. (2004). "Avian Diversity in East Calcutta Wetlands", *Environ* IX (I): 8-13

———. (2008). *Status of Environment in West Bengal: A Citizen's Report*, ENDEV. Kolkata: Society for Environment and Development.

———. (ed) (2008). *Status of Environment in West Bengal: A Citizen's Report*, ENDEV. Kolkata: Society for Environment and Development.

Ghosh, A.K., Saha, Soma and Sen, Piku (2008). "Air Quality": Chapter 12, in *Status of Environment in West Bengal: A Citizen's Report*, (ed. A.K. Ghosh) ENDEV. Kolkata: Society for Environment and Development.

Ghosh, Gargi (2008). "Noise Pollution", Chapter 13, in *Status of Environment in West Bengal: A Citizen's Report*, (ed. A.K. Ghosh) ENDEV. Kolkata: Society for Environment and Development.

Govt. of W.B. (2004-2005). *Economic Review*. Bureau of Applied Economics and Statistics

———. (2007-08). *Economic Review*. Bureau of Applied Economics and Statistics.

———. (2002-03). Glimpse of Wildlife Statistics, Forest Directorate, Government of West Bengal.

———. (2005-06). Annual Report, *Wildlife Wing*, Forest Directorate, Government of West Bengal.

———. (1999). *Status of Environment Report*, Department of Environment, Government of West Bengal.

———. (2004). *Statistical Handbook*, West Bengal, Bureau of Applied Economics and Statistics. Government of West Bengal.

———. (2004). *West Bengal Human Development Report*, Development and Planning Department, Government of West Bengal.

GSI (1995). Detailed Study of Geofactors in selected hazard prone stretches along surface communication routes in parts of Darjeeling and Sikkim Himalayas *ENV/ER/WSA/1993/008*. (C.K. Sengupta and S.K. Das)

ILGUS (2000-02). "Urban West Bengal", Institute of Local Government and Urban Studies.

Joshi, Anuradha (1996). *Progressive Bureaucracy: an Oxymoron? The Case of Joint Forest Management in India*. Rural Development and Forestry Network Working Paper 24a. London. Overseas Development Institute.

Kalyan Rudra, River Expert, *Pers. Communication.*

Kester, C. (2005). "Diesel *versus* Hybrids", *World Watch* 18 (4): 19-21

Malhotra, K.C., Debal Deb, M. Dutta, T. Vasulu, M. Adhikari and G. Yadav (1992). *The Role of Non-Timber Forest Products in Village Economy*. IBRAD: Calcutta.

Misra, Swadesh (1992). "Climatic Regions of West Bengal". *Ind. J. Landscape Syst. Ecol. Studies* 5 (1): 924.

Nagarik Mancha (2005). "Industrial Pollution in Durgapur", February, Kolkata.

PHED (2004). *A Note on Fluoride Contamination of Ground Water in West Bengal*. Public Health Engineering Department, Government of West Bengal.

Saha, Soma (2008). "Wetlands": Chapter 6, in *Status of Environment in West Bengal: A Citizen's Report*, (ed. A.K. Ghosh) ENDEV. Kolkata: Society for Environment and Development.

Sikdar, P.K. (1997). "Bacteriological Contamination of Groundwater of Calcutta and Howrah Cities", *Man and Environment*, Annual Volume No. 8: 39-41 Sikdar, 2003

———. (1999). "Development Dynamics and Management of Groundwater In and Around Calcutta, India", *Indian Journal of Geology* 71(3): 173–186

———. (2008). "Ground Water Resources": Chapter 5, in *Status of Environment in West Bengal: A Citizen's Report*, (ed. A.K. Ghosh) ENDEV. Kolkata: Society for Environment and Development.

Sikdar, P.K., Biswas, A.B. and Saha, A.K. (1996). "A Study on the Possible Land Subsidence in Calcutta and Howrah Cities due to Groundwater Overdraft", *Indian Journal of Geology* 68(3): 193-200.

Sikdar, P.K. and Dasgupta, S.P. (1997). "Pollution—Risk Analysis of Ground Water of Calcutta and Howrah City", *Indian Minerals* 50(4): 397-402.

Sikdar, P.K. and Banerjee, S. (2003). "Genesis of Arsenic in Groundwater of Ganga Delta—an Anthropogenic Model", *Journal of Human Settlements*, April 2003, p.10-24.

TERI (2006). "Environmental Hazards to Human Health: Focus on West Bengal: Background Note". West Bengal State Seminar, 22nd August, Kolkata, EU – India Economic Cross Cultural Programme.

WBPCB (2005). Green Governance, August-September, West Bengal Pollution Control Board.

WBPCB (2006-07). *Annual Report*, West Bengal Pollution Control Board. Government of West Bengal.

Appendix

TABLE A-12.1

List of Sites Outside Forest Area of Wildlife Value

No.	Name	District	Dominant Species
1.	Ahiran Beel	Murshidabad	Manikjore Stork
2.	Baneswar	Cooch Behar	Kachuga Turtle
3.	Farakka	Murshidabad	Large Whistling Teal
4.	Kulik	Balurghat	Largest open bill Stork nesting area in Asia
5.	Mayapur	Nadia	Gangetic Dolphin
6.	Papuria	Birbhum	White Ibis
7.	Purbasthali	Bardhaman	Spoonbills
8.	Rasulpur	Medinipur	Irrawady Dolphin
9.	Rasik Beel	Cooch Behar	Birds
10.	Shyampur and Panchala	Howrah	Fishing cat
11.	Tilpara Barrage	Birbhum	Siberian Graylag and Bareheaded Goose
12.	Santragachi Jeel	Howrah	Many bird species

Source: Ghosh, A.K. (ed.) (2008). *Status of Environment in West Bengal*. ENDEV.

TABLE A-12.2

Short- and Long-Term Health Impacts of Various Air Pollutants

Pollutant	Impact on Human Health	
	Short-term	Long-term
SPM	Sneezing, deposition of trachea, etc.	Susceptibility to respiratory problems, death from respiratory causes and carcinogenic effects
RPM	Exacerbation of airways disease	Heart attack, stroke and malfunctioning of liver
NO_2	Lung edema, eye and nasal irritation	Respiratory infection, damage to lung tissues
SO_2	Increased asthma attacks, irritation of respiratory tracts	Reduced lung function
CO	Reduced supply of oxygen to body tissues	Impairment of time discrimination abilities, adverse effect on central nervous system
Pb	Adverse effect on blood hemoglobin and central nervous system	Affects renal and reproductive system adversely

Source: West Bengal Human Development Report, 2004.

TABLE A-12.3

District-wise Total Municipal Bodies and Waste Generation

Sl. No	District	Total Municipal Bodies	Total Population in Municipal Areas (Census 2001)	Total Municipal Areas (in sq. km.)	Total Waste Generated/Day (in MT)	Per Capita Waste Generation (gms/day)
1.	24 Parganas (N)	27	4610019	429.89	2106.24	456.88
2.	24 Parganas (S)	7	940453	141.69	192.29	204.47
3.	Bankura	3	218102	52.67	77.65	356.03
4.	Bardhaman	11	2021971	568.56	746.00	368.95
5.	Birbhum	6	284120	68.15	203.62	716.67
6.	Cooch Behar	6	175521	32.92	114.60	652.91
7.	Darjeeling	5	670031	72.22	254.31	379.55
8.	Hooghly	12	1354163	152.88	510.80	377.21
9.	Howrah	3	1472374	97.00	1015.00	689.36
10.	Jalpaiguri	4	234469	44.33	73.66	314.16
11.	Kolkata	1	4580544	187.33	2500.00	545.79
12.	Malda	2	224392	22.83	337.95	1506.07
13.	Medinipur (E)	5	369276	183.92	169.69	459.52
14.	Medinipur (W)	8	529965	129.34	214.31	404.39
15.	Murshidabad	7	467366	92.00	305.95	654.63
16.	Nadia	10	749443	139.60	208.10	277.67
17.	North Dinajpur	4	279518	55.00	106.31	380.33
18.	Purulia	3	153448	30.00	188.19	1226.41
19.	South Dinajpur	2	189064	20.00	55.00	290.91
	Total	126	19524239	2520.33	9379.67	

Source: ILGUS.

TABLE A-12.4

Status of Biomedical Waste Treatment in West Bengal during 2006-2007

Sl. No.	Health Care Facilities	Total no. of Health Care Facilities	Total no. of Beds	Total Amount of Biomedical Waste Generated (kg per day)	Total Amount of Biomedical Waste Treated (kg per day)	Total no. of Units that have Obtained Authorisation
A.	Health care units in towns with population of 30 lakhs or above	368	25575	6383	6383	362
B.	Health care units in towns with population below 30 lakhs					
i.	With 500 beds and above	17	10909	2727.25	1709	16
ii.	With 200 beds and above but less than 500 beds	51	13922	3480	1028.75	45
iii.	With 50 beds and above but less than 200 beds	167	13114	3448.5	820.5	108
iv.	With less than 50 beds	2975	30607	7651.75	1420.75	1075
C.	Health care units generating biomedical waste not included in A and B	Inside KMA= 495 Outside KMA 2363				27** 38**

Note: ** These are non-bedded health care units like pathology, diagnostic centre, clinic etc.

TABLE A-12.5

Materials of Health Concern in a Typical Desktop Computer

Name	*Use/Location*	*Health Effects*
Plastics	Includes organics and oxides (other than silica)	PBDE—endocrine disruption and effects on fetal development; PBBs-increased risk of cancers of the digestive and lymph systems
Lead	Metal joining, radiation shield/CRT, PWB (printed wiring board)	Damage to central and peripheral nervous system, circulatory system and kidneys; effects on endocrine system, serious adverse effects on brain development
Aluminum	Structural, conductivity/housing, CRT, PWB, connectors	Skin rashes, skeletal problems, and respiratory problems including asthma; linked to Alzheimer's disease
Gallium	Semi-conductor/PWB	Clear evidence of carcinogenesis in experimental animals
Nickel	Structural magnetivity/(steel) housing, CRT, PWB	Allergic reactions, asthma, chronic bronchitis, impaired lung function; reasonably anticipated to be a human carcinogen
Vanadium	Red phosphor emitter/CRT	Lung and throat irritation
Beryllium	Thermal conductivity/PWB, connectors	Lung damage, allergic reactions, chronic beryllium disease; reasonably anticipated to be a human carcinogen
Chromium	Decorative, hardener/(steel) housing	Ulcers, convulsions, liver and kidney damage, strong allergic reactions, asthmatic bronchitis, may cause DNA damage; a known human carcinogen
Cadmium	Battery, blue-green phosphor emitter/ housing, PWB, CRT	Pulmonary damage, kidney disease, bone fragility; reasonably anticipated to be a human carcinogen
Mercury	Batteries, switches/housing, PWB	Chronic brain, kidney, lung and fetal damage; increases in blood pressure and heart rate, allergic reactions, effects on brain function and memory; a possible human carcinogen
Arsenic	Doping agents in transistors/PWB	Allergic reactions, nausea, vomiting, decreased red and white blood cell production, abnormal heart rhythm; inorganic arsenic is a known human carcinogen
Silica	Glass, solid state devices/CRT, PWB	Respirable-size crystalline silica can cause silicosis, emphysema, obstructive airway disease, and lymph node fibrosis; a known human carcinogen

Source: Ghosh, A.K. (ed.) (2008). *Status of Environment in West Bengal.* ENDEV.

Environmental Laws (Selective List)

01. THE WATER (PREVENTION AND CONTROL OF POLLUTION) ACT, 1974
02. THE WATER (PREVENTION AND CONTROL OF POLLUTION) CESS ACT, 1977
03. THE AIR (PREVENTION AND CONTROL OF POLLUTION) ACT, 1981
04. THE ENVIRONMENT (PROTECTION) ACT, 1986
05. THE ENVIRONMENT (PROTECTION) RULES, 1986
06. HAZARDOUS WASTES (MANAGEMENT AND HANDLING) RULES, 1989
07. THE MANUFACTURE, STORAGE AND IMPORT OF HAZARDOUS CHEMICALS RULES, 1989
08. THE BIOCHEMICAL WASTE (MANAGEMENT AND HANDLING) RULES, 1998
09. THE PLASTIC MANUFACTURE, SALE AND USAGE RULES, 1999
10. THE NOISE POLLUTION (REGULATION AND CONTROL) RULES, 2000
11. THE MUNICIPAL SOLID WASTES (MANAGEMENT AND HANDLING) RULES, 2000
12. THE BATTERIES (MANAGEMENT AND HANDLING) RULES, 2000
13. CHEMICAL ACCIDENTS (EMERGENCY PLANNING, PREPAREDNESS AND RESPONSE) RULES, 1996
14. ENVIRONMENTAL IMPACT ASSESSMENT NOTIFICATION, 2006
15. NOTIFICATION ON SITING OF INDUSTRIAL PROJECT, 1999
16. NOTIFICATION ON FLY ASH, 1999
17. THE PUBLIC LIABILITY INSURANCE ACT, 1991
18. THE INDIAN EXPLOSIVE ACT, 1994
19. THE EXPLOSIVE SUBSTANSES ACT, 1908
20. THE FACTORIES ACT, 1948
21. INDIAN PENAL CODE, 1860
22. THE POLICE ACT, 1861

State Acts

23. BENGAL SMOKE NUISANCE ACT, 1905
24. THE WEST BENGAL MUNICIPAL ACT, 1993
25. WEST BENGAL GOVERNMENT TOWNSHIPS (EXTENSION OF CIVIC AMENITIES) ACT, 1975
26. WEST BENGAL TOWN AND COUNTRY (PLANNING & DEVELOPMENT) ACT, 1979
27. THE WEST BENGAL PANCHAYAT ACT, 1973
28. THE CALCUTTA MUNICIPAL CORPORATION ACT, 1980
29. CALCUTTA METROPOLITAN WATER AND SANITATION AUTHORITY ACT, 1966
30. CALCUTTA METROPOLITAN PLANNING AREA (USE AND DEVELOPMENT OF LAND CONTROL ACT, 1965
31. THE HOWRAH MUNICIPAL CORPORATION ACT, 1980
32. HOWRAH IMPROVEMENT ACT, 1956
33. THE CALCUTTA POLICE ACT, 1861
34. THE CALCUTTA SUBURBAN POLICE ACT, 1866

Chapter 13

State Finance

13.1 Introduction

The fiscal structure of the Indian economy suffers from serious imbalances—both vertical and horizontal. The responsibilities assigned to the states of providing a wide range of social and economic services, creating necessary infrastructure, delivering administrative services including maintenance of law and order and provision of justice etc., are grossly incompatible with the resources the states can raise on their own. In order to redress the mismatch of resources as against the responsibilities of the states, the Constitution of India provided for a Finance Commission (FC) mandated to be set up at an interval of five years for the transfer and allocation of resources from the Centre to the states. Article 280 of the Constitution, as amended by the 73rd and 74th Amendments of 1992, directs the FC to make recommendations regarding the distribution of net proceeds of divisible taxes as between the Union and the State governments and also for transfer of resources to be made by the state governments to the local bodies of governance in rural and urban areas.

Apart from assigning the responsibility of adjudicating the allocation of resources between the Union and the States, the Constitution in terms of its Seventh Schedule and Articles 245, 246, 268 and 272 has clearly defined and earmarked the jurisdictions over which the respective governments can exercise their powers of raising resources through taxes. In spite of all these provisions of safeguard, the mismatch between the endowments and responsibilities of the states continued unabated. The trend towards the flow and control of resources being concentrated in the hands of the Union government has been obvious since the inception of planning in our country. As the Committee headed by Prof. Amita Kumar Bagchi has noted in its Report (2002): "The Planning Commission was set up by the Union Government to oversee planned development. Through its agency, the role of the Union has extended into areas such as agriculture, fisheries, soil and water conservation, rural reconstruction, housing etc., which lie within the exclusive State field. The Constitution envisages that fiscal resources would be transferred to the States on the recommendations of the Finance Commission. But in practice, the role of the Finance Commission has come to be limited to channelling of revenue transfers (including a very small capital component) only. The capital resources (including a revenue component) for planned development are now transferred on the recommendation of the Planning Commission" (Bagchi Committee Report, 2002).

The Planning Commission apart, the Union Ministries and Departments have also been playing a big role in subverting the autonomy of the states. A significant proportion of the plan transfers is increasingly being accounted for by Centrally Sponsored Schemes (CSS) or by Central Plan Schemes (CPS). During the Eighth Five Year Plan, 40 per cent of total amount of plan transfers made to the states were controlled by various Central Ministries under CSS or CPS. Such lateral channels of flow of resources from the Centre to the states not only erodes the autonomy and encroaches upon the jurisdiction of the states, but also upsets the priorities of planned development of the state governments. The mode of allocation of funds adopted by the Planning Commission has been instrumental in pushing the states in debt trap. Seventy per cent of Central plan assistance comes to the state as loans and therefore, as the states undertake larger volume of expenditure on plan and non-plan accounts the debt burden of the states accumulates.

Author, Jayanta Acharya, is a former Principal of S.A. Jaipuria College, Kolkata.

The Constitution of India provides for transfer of resources from the Centre to the states through the mediation of the Finance Commission mandated to be set up at an interval of five years with a view to correcting the imbalance between endowments and responsibilities of the states and also to smooth out the inequalities in respect of capabilities and incomes among the states. However, in spite of the efforts and interventions made by various Finance Commissions to address the issues of imbalances, the problems of State finances loom large on fiscal landscape of the Indian economy. All states—poor or rich across the board encounter severe fiscal stress arising out of these inherent imbalances. West Bengal, though considered to be a good performer in respect of growth of output is no exception.

13.2 Overview of State Finances

13.2.1 Growing Imbalance: Deficit Indicators

West Bengal is one of the states worst hit by chronically growing imbalances between its revenues and expenditures. Major indicators of the imbalances in the state finances are revenue deficit (RD), gross fiscal deficit (GFD) and primary deficit (PD). The concepts of these various kinds of deficits need be clarified at the outset before our analysis begins. Gross fiscal deficit (GFD) is the difference between aggregate expenditure net of debt repayments and aggregate revenue receipts and non-debt capital receipts. Revenue deficit (RD) is the difference between total revenue expenditure and total revenue receipts. Primary deficit (PD) is the gross fiscal deficit (GFD) less interest payments. Analysis of the state's finances reveals that the fiscal stress deepened during the later part of the 1990s (Figure 13.1).

FIGURE 13.1

Major Deficit Indicators: West Bengal

(in Rs. Crore)

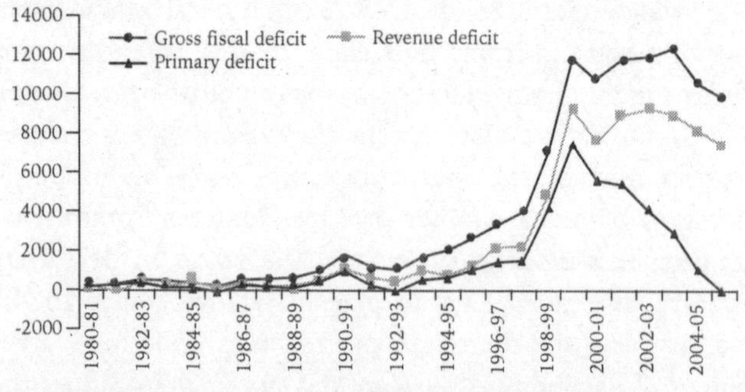

Source: RBI (Various Issues). *State Finances: A Study of Budgets.*

Till 1995-96, the RD of the Government of West Bengal was 1.7 per cent of the gross domestic product (GSDP) and accounted for 46.2 per cent of GFD. The situation thereafter worsened and in 1999-2000 GFD stood at 9.2 per cent of the GSDP and from then on RD accounted 70 per cent or more of the gross fiscal deficit of the state (Table 13.1).

Figure 13.1 shows the movement of major deficit indicators of the state since 1992-93 i.e., the time when the impact of liberalised economic reforms pursued by the Central government began to be felt on the state economy. It is evident that the fiscal imbalance began to deteriorate since 1996-97 and aggravated most since 1999-2000 onwards. RD accounted for more then 60 per cent of GFD in 1996-97 and from 1999-2000 onwards more than 70 per cent of GFD was contributed by RD.

TABLE 13.1

West Bengal: GFD and RD as Percentage to GSDP and RD as Percentage to GFD

Year	*GFD as % of GSDP*	*RD as % of GSDP*	*RD as % of GFD*	*RR-RE Ratio %*
1992-93	2.2	0.9	43.1	92.0
1993-94	3.1	1.8	58.9	85.0
1994-95	3.2	1.2	39.0	89.0
1995-96	3.7	1.7	46.4	85.5
1996-97	4.1	2.6	62.9	79.3
1997-98	4.1	2.3	57.2	79.7
1998-99	6.2	4.2	68.3	65.4
1999-2000	9.2	7.3	79.6	52.3
2000-01	7.8	5.4	69.4	65.7
2001-02	7.5	5.6	75.0	62.7
2002-03	6.3	5.1	81.0	62.7
2003-04	6.8	4.8	71.0	64.4
2004-05	5.1	3.9	77.0	70.7
2005-06	4.1	3.1	77.0	76.2

Source: RBI. *State Finances—A Study of Budgets*, various issues.

The ratio of revenue receipts (RR) to revenue expenditure (RE) is also another crucial indicator of the health of the state's public finance. In 1992-93, the ratio of RR to RE was 92.0 (Table 13.1), meaning thereby that revenue receipts of the state covered 92 per cent of revenue expenditure undertaken by the state government As we move on into the decade of the 90s, we find that less and less proportion of revenue expenditure was being met out of state's revenue receipts. The obvious outcome of this trend was that the state had to rely more and more on borrowing for financing its revenue expenditure, i.e, to fulfil its commitment to spend on interest payment on previously contracted loans, salaries and pensions, social development and provision of economic services. This has inevitably led to escalation in GFD and RD by 10 and 20 times respectively over a period of about 10 years (Figure 13.1 and Table 13.1).

It is noticeable, however, that the state's effort for improving fiscal health have started yielding results. Both the GFD and RD in relation to the GSDP have been on a downward trend since 2002-03. It may further be noted that the primary deficit started declining from 2001-02 onwards, even though the RD continued to rise. Thus, the major reason for the upward climb of the RD was surely the burden of interest payments (IP).

The most reasons behind the development of such a severe imbalance in state's finances, and with the latter getting embroiled in a critical debt crisis are listed below.

1. When the Central government accepted the recommendations of the Fifth Pay Commission and hiked the pay of its employees from January 1996, the state government also had to give effect to the recommendations for pay hike of state government employees. Moreover in West Bengal, the state government has committed itself to pay salaries, allowances and other benefits to teachers and staff of the aided non-government. educational institutions and employees of local bodies as well. The state government in order to provide social security has always extended the benefits of enhanced allowances to superannuated government employees, teachers and the like. As a result, the annual expenditure of the state government on account of payment of salaries, pension and other retirement benefits has shot up from Rs.6177 crore in 1997-98 to a staggering figure of Rs.12239 crore in 2002-03—a two-fold increase at that. The full impact of the pay revision on the lines of Central government's decision began to fall heavily on the finances of the state government during the period 1998-99 to 2001-02 causing a quantum jump in all the deficit indicators.

2. The deepening of fiscal imbalance in the state coincided with the award period of the Eleventh Finance Commission (EFC) (2000-2005). The awards recommended by the EFC in the nature of debt relief, tax devolution and grants aggravated the crisis even more. The EFC devised a fiscal reforms programme aimed at reduction of the revenue deficit of the states and grants to the states to cover the assessed deficit in their non-plan revenue account were linked to progress in implementing the reforms programme. As a result, the Net Devolution and Transfer (NDT) in relation to GSDP, aggregate expenditure (AE) and aggregate receipts (AR) registered a decline during the award period of the EFC over that of the previous Commissions (Table 13.2).

TABLE 13.2

India: Net Devolution and Transfers: Annual Average

Period	*NDT (Rs. Crore)*	*NDT/GDP (per cent)*	*NDT/AE (per cent)*	*NDT/AR (per cent)*
Ninth FC (1990-1995)	39,798	5.2	32.8	32.5
Tenth FC (1995-2000)	62,965	4.1	27.6	27.8
Eleventh FC (2000-2005)	84,515	3.3	19.4	19.3
Twelfth FC (2005-2010)	2,04,058	4.9	30.1	29.8

Source: RBI, *State Finances A Study of Budgets 2007-08.*

3. The resource gap of the state is increasingly getting widened because of the huge debt burden. The debt profile and its various aspects will be dealt with subsequently (section 13.2.2) of this Report. But as we have discussed earlier, the plan assistance from the Centre mediated through the Planning Commission constitutes important source of indebtedness for the states. But apart from plan loans, states have to take resort to borrowing for meeting revenue expenditure for development of social sector and economic services as well. As past debts accumulate interest payment obligations continue to mount. The indebtedness of the state governments have a unique feature in that the states owe a large proportions of the loans to the Centre and all the Central loans are very high cost loans. More than 60 per cent of the present debt burden is on account of loans extended by the Centre with interest rate of 12 per cent. The other components of loans incurred by the states, their movement over time and the interest liabilities thereupon will be taken up later in Section 13.2.2. But if we focus on the period between 1999-2000 to 2004-05, we find that the net interest payment liabilities of the West Bengal Government consumed 40 to 55 per cent of its revenue receipts during the period. Thus, huge interest payment liability is one of the principal reasons for such fiscal stress.

4. During this period the collections of taxes by the Centre as well as the state suffered decline due to recessionary conditions of the economy. This is also an outcome of the policy of liberalisation and opening up of the economy pursued by the Centre. Due to indiscriminate reduction in import duty by

the Centre, the competition among the states to promote new enterprises through tax relief and exemption, a significant distortion in the overall tax structure was created and because of slowdown in the economic activities of the country during the period caused by recession, the state suffered a loss of its own revenues to the tune of Rs. 600 crore in 2001-02. There was a short fall of Rs. 10,000 crore in the divisible pool of Central taxes collections in 2001-02 and West Bengal in consequence suffered a shortfall of Rs. 736 crore in its entitlements.

TABLE 13.3

Share in Central Taxes: West Bengal

Year	*Amount Recommended by the 11th Finance Commission (Rs. in crores)*	*Actual Amount Received by the States (Rs. in crores)*	*Col (3) as Percentage of Col (2)*
2000-01	54,059	50,734	93.85
2001-02	63,026	52,215	82.85
2002-03	73,493	56,655	77.09
2003-04	85,724	67,079	78.25
2004-05	1,00,013	78,551	78.54
Total	3,76,315	3,05,234	81.11

Source: RBI. *Handbook of Statistics on Indian Economy, 2005-06* and Finance Commission. *Report of the 11th Finance Commission*, June 2000.

The unprecedented flood and consequent extensive damage in West Bengal in 2000-01 and the failure of the Central government to provide grant (only a meager amount of Rs.103 crore was granted) for such a big calamity had forced the state government to take resort to a loan of Rs.1173 crore raised at a high interest rate from Hudco for provision of relief measures and reconstruction works in the flood affected districts.

All these general and special factors combined to create such a fiscal catastrophy for all states in general and for West Bengal in particular. The policies pursued by the Central government over which the states had little control were responsible for inequalities and imbalances to persist with ever growing severity. The successive Finance Commissions—the Ninth (1990-1995), the Tenth (1995-2000) and the Eleventh (2000-2005) have presided over the show of increasing centralisation of monetary and fiscal powers in the hands of the Centre on the one hand and gradual divestment of resources of the states on the other.

13.2.2 Debt Burden of the State

The outstanding liabilities of West Bengal has crossed the mark of Rs. 1,00,000 crore in 2005-06. In the early years of the decade of 1990s, the debt stock was a little over Rs. 10,000 crore. The enormity of debt burden can be better understood in relation to the GSDP (Table 13.4).

TABLE 13.4

Total Outstanding Liabilities: West Bengal (as at end March)

Year	*Total Outstanding Liabilities (Rs. Crores)*	*As percentage to GSDP*
1992	10,135	23.3
1993	11,281	24.2
1994	12,926	24.2
1995	15,128	24.4
1996	17,716	24.0
1997	21,114	25.7
1998	25,173	25.7
1999	32,192	27.9
2000	44,042	34.7
2001	54,929	39.3
2002	66,396	43.2
2003	78,325	47.3
2004	89,472	48.0
2005	97,342	47.1
2006	1,14,419	49.4
2007 (RE)	1,22,895	47.2

Source: As in Table 13.2.

Such a high level of debt in relation to the GSDP (in case of the Central government, the Debt-GDP ratio is more than 50 per cent) has raised anew the issue of sustainability of debt or for that matter, the wisdom of debt financed expenditure whether on revenue or capital account. The Twelfth Finance Commission has, in particular put all emphasis on reduction of GFD and RD for all states and also formulated an outline of a new regime of borrowing for the state governments. The Finance Commission has recommended that from 2005-2006, all plan assistance in the shape of Central loans would be dispensed with. If we look at the composition of outstanding liabilities of the states, we find that the loans from the Centre had been the principal source of borrowing for the state governments till 1998-99 (Table 13.5), when such loans used to finance more than 60 per cent of the GFD in case of West Bengal. From 1999-2000, phasing out of Central loans had begun and the states had to rely on market borrowings and loans against securities issued to national small savings fund (NSSF).

TABLE 13.5

Total Outstanding Liabilities as Percentage to GFD of West Bengal

Year	*Loans from the Centre (net)*	*Market Borrowing (net)*	*Others*
1992-93	59.2	58.3	-17.5
1993-94	52.9	16.7	30.4
1994-95	79.0	20.2	0.8
1995-96	63.0	16.6	20.4
1996-97	61.3	14.5	24.3
1997-98	79.6	13.5	6.8
1998-99	69.0	8.6	22.4
1999-00	7.6	5.7	86.7
2000-01	5.8	7.5	86.7
2001-02	5.2	8.7	86.0
2002-03	8.9	22.8	-12.9 (81.2)
2003-04	6.2	42.1	35.9 (15.8)
2004-05	9.2	37.7	-36.1 (90.7)
2005-06	-2.5	13.2	12.5 (72.3)
2006-07	-0.8	18.2	-5.5 (73.2)

Note: 'Others' include loans from Financial Institutions, Provident Fund, Reserve Fund, Deposits and Advances and NSSF Loans.

Source: As in Table 13.1.

There has been a sharp decline in the component 'Loans from Centre' since 1999-2000 with a concomitant rise in another component, namely, loans taken against net small savings collections in the NSSF. Both the plan loans from the Centre and NSSF loans are high cost loans compared to market borrowings, the average interest rate on which had been declining continuously since the closing years of the last century. The interest rate on market loans was 14 per cent in 1995-96, and declined to 11 per cent in 2000-01. It went down further to a range of 6.7 and 8.0 per cent. Compared to this, Plan and NSSF loans carried an interest rate between 11 to 12 per cent. After restructuring of outstanding debt of the states as announced in the Union Budget for 2007-08, the share of the states in the NSSF collections would be limited to 80 per cent. Furthermore, the interest rate on loans from NSSF from 1999-2000 to 2002-03 had been reset at 10.5 per cent effective April 2007.

Presently, securities issued to NSSF have emerged as the dominant source constituting more than two-third of GFD financing (Table 13.5). But one should remember that it is a compulsory route available to the state governments. The NSSF is an autonomous source of funds as the state governments cannot determine either the quantum or the cost of these borrowings (RBI, November 2007). In the environment of free and competitive market, the state governments cannot access the open market borrowings freely.

The public finance expert and development economists have joined the debate on sustainability of financing GFD and RD through heavy borrowing and critically examined the issue. A large cutback in government expenditure for compressing the deficits, may prove to be counterproductive (Bagchi, 2005). In the presence of deficiencies in demand and bottlenecks on the supply side of the economy, "such conventional mode of tackling the structural (long term) deficit would lower the trend growth [of national income] further and aggravate fiscal imbalances" (Rakshit, 2005). It has been strongly argued that the state government expenditures, both on revenue and capital accounts would unleash a process with multiplier effect on enhancement of literacy level, reduction in incidence of poverty, development of soft skill, promoting well-being, nutrition, research and innovation, technical skill, knowledge-based activities and such as all those which government expenditures cater to. Cogent arguments have been advanced to show that as fall-out of expenditures by the state governments, the fiscal balance may as well be restored to some extent through creation of flows of income.

13.2.3 State's Revenue Profile

13.2.3.1 Own Tax Revenue (OTR)

In spite of the difficulties in coping with severe fiscal stress, the government of West Bengal has stepped up efforts in raising own tax revenues. As Figure 14.2 shows, the volume of Own Tax Revenue of West Bengal Government has doubled during the years between 1999-2000 and 2005-06 when fiscal crisis was at its height. OTR cover at present is about 35 per cent of revenue expenditure of the state. However, during the period 1985-1995, the OTR used to cover between 45 to 49 per cent of state's RE.

The annual growth rate of the state's own taxes during the period 1980-81 to 1993-94 was 13.8 per cent, the rate declined to 9.8 per cent during the next period. The overall growth rate for the entire period from 1980-81 to 2005-06 was 11.7 per cent (Table 13.6). The resource base of the state is very limited as 88 per cent of the tax resources is raised through indirect taxes. The ratio of tax revenues to GSDP in the state has remained stable at around 5 per cent with some minor fluctuations (Appendix II). The state government has taken steps to increase its revenue collection through various measures. In 2006-07 Electricity Duty alone has recorded a growth rate of 38 per cent. The state government has also enhanced stamp duty, land revenue rates and rationalise other rates to broaden its own tax base.

FIGURE 13.2

Own Tax Revenue: West Bengal

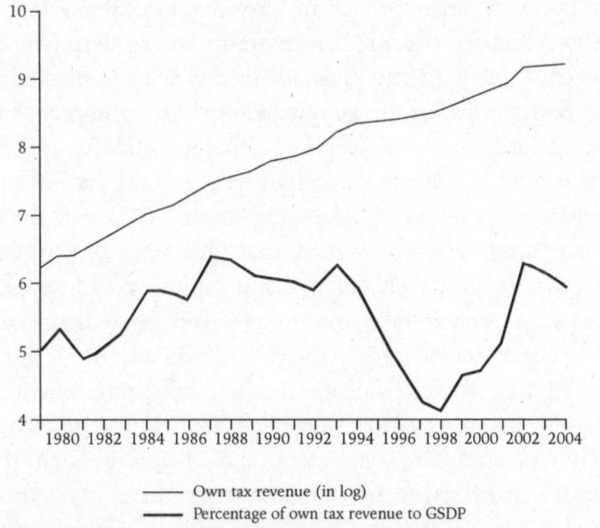

Source: RBI (Various Issues). *State Finances: A Study of Budgets.*

TABLE 13.6

Trend Growth Rate: OTR in West Bengal

Period	*Trend Growth Rate*
1980-81 to 1993-94	13.8
1994-95 to 2005-06	9.8
1980-81 to 2005-06	11.7

Note: Trend growth rate has been obtained by fitting log linear trends to the data on state's own tax revenue.

Source: RBI. *Hand Book of Statistics on State Government Finances (2004), State Finance*, various years.

13.2.4 Value Added Tax

Value added tax (VAT) has been in force in the state since 1st April 2005. Unlike sales tax, VAT is a multi-point tax imposed during different phases of value addition. We may look at how tax revenues of the state have changed since the imposition of VAT (Table 13.7)

The major sources of state's own tax revenues are VAT in lieu of sales tax, land revenue, stamp and registration, state excise duties, taxes on vehicle, cess on petrol, diesel and ATF and sales tax still continuing for some items like motor spirit etc. The land revenue yields in the state have been declining over the years, though from 2000-01 there is an upturn in land revenue collections through enhancement of rates of various taxes.

TABLE 13.7

Collection of Revenue from VAT, West Bengal

(Rs. Crore)

Year	*VAT*	*% increase*	*Total Tax Revenue*	*% increase*
2005-06	4661.51	-	7253.73	-
2006-07	4957.70	6.0	8284.54	13.0

Source: Government of WB. *Administrative Report of Directorate of Commercial Taxes, 2007-08.*

13.2.5 Non-Tax Revenues

Non-tax revenues of the state comprise interest receipts, receipts from general service like lotteries, fees received from providing various social and economic services etc. But the rates and fees charged for such services are insignificantly low. But the growth in mobilising non-tax revenues in the states is very commendable as it exhibits about 10-fold increase during 1990-91 to 2002-2003 (Figure 13.3)

FIGURE 13.3

Own Non-Tax Revenue: West Bengal (Rs. Crore)

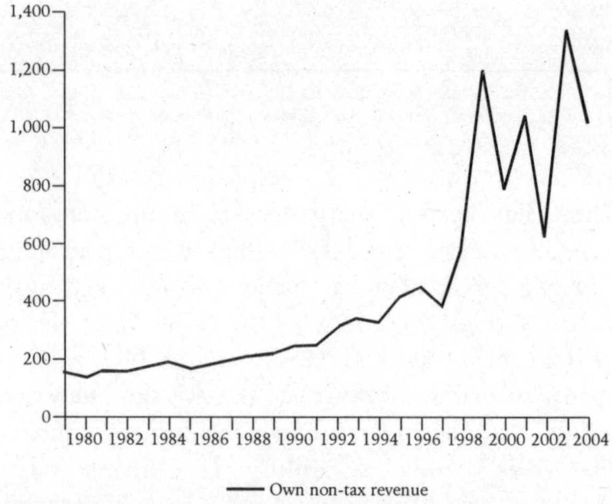

Source: RBI (Various Issues). *State Finances: A Study of Budgets.*

In spite of this marked increase in the absolute level of collection of non-tax revenues, it has remained static at less than 1 per cent of GSDP. The state government during the 10-year period from 1995-96 to 2005-06 has surely enhanced its own revenue mobilisation by more than 200 per cent but as its revenue expenditure have gone up simultaneously, its capacity to finance revenue expenditure out of own revenue receipts has declined by more than 16 per cent (Appendix A-13.2) during the same period. The buoyancy of revenue collections would remain heavily constrained as the state governments have no constitutional power to levy tax on services though the service sector (tertiary) contributes the largest share to GSDP (about 55 per cent).

13.2.6 *Share in Central Taxes (SCT) and Grants-in-Aid (GIA)*

The proportion of gross Central tax revenues shared with the states and grants-in-aid are two important resource bases for the states. These are also strategic instruments which have been used by successive Finance Commissions to close the vertical as well as horizontal gaps in the resource endowments of the states as the commitments and responsibilities of the states increased over the years. The share in central taxes (SCT) and grants-in-aid (GIA) for West Bengal government for different years are shown in Figure 13.4.

TABLE 13.8

Devolution of Taxes and Grants—Annual Average All States

Period	*SCT/GDT*	*GID/GDT*	*GDT/GDP*	*GDT/AD*
Ninth FC (1990-1995)	38.0	33.4	6.8	42.6
Tenth FC (1995-2000)	42.6	27.7	5.7	38.4
Eleventh FC (2000-2005)	46.2	35.2	5.2	30.4
Twelfth FC (2005-2010)	51.3	43.9	5.5	33.4

Note: GDT: Gross Devolution and Transfer; AD: Aggregate Disbursements of States.

Source: RBI. *State Finances A study of Budgets of 2007-08.*

SCT and GIA together constituted 71 per cent (1990-1995), 70 per cent (1995-2000), 82 per cent (2000-2005) and 95 per cent (2005-2008) of GDT from the Centre. Another component of GDT i.e., loan from Centre has been declining since 2000-01 when phasing out of Central Plan Loans began. The Twelfth FC has recommended discontinuation of Plan Loans from 2005 onwards. But by then the earlier practice of availing Plan Loans at high cost have left a blazing trail of interest payment burdens for them. Table 13.8 shows that although GDT for all the states as recommended by the Twelfth FC (2005-2010) has increased to 5.5 per cent of GDP, the GDT was lower in relation to GDP compared to the periods of 1990-1995 and 1995-2000. Again, our earlier analysis shows that the period of worst crisis was the period from 1999-2000 to 2002-03 which coincided very much with the award period of the EFC. The GDT awarded by the EFC was the lowest precisely during this period (2000-2005). It should be further noted that the GDT over the years was not capable of covering more than 42 per cent of aggregate expenditure of the states. However, ratio GDT to aggregate disbursements (AD) has been declining over different periods of FCs, forcing the state governments to look for borrowings to meet their commitments to social, economic developmental goals and compulsory obligations like interest, pension and salary payments.

FIGURE 13.4

Grants from the Centre and Share in Central Taxes West Bengal

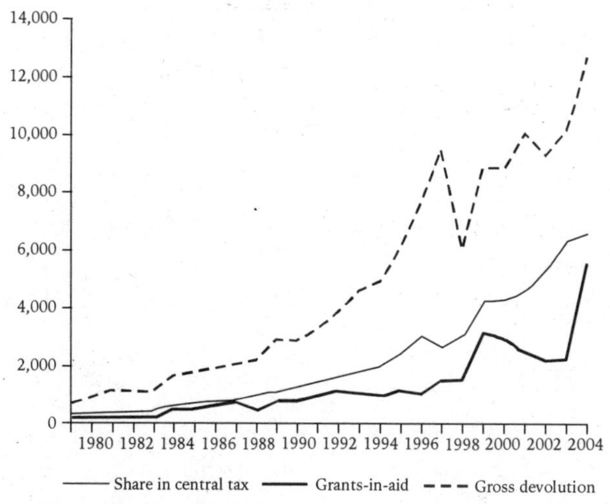

Source: RBI (Various Issues). *State Finances: A Study of Budgets.*

13.3 Expenditure Pattern

13.3.1 *Revenue Expenditure*

Keeping in mind the polemics on debt-financed expenditure, we now turn to examining the time profile of revenue expenditure (RE) of the state (Figure 13.3), as this particular component of state government expenditure is alleged to be the piece of villain responsible for escalation in GFD. Between 1990-91 and 2000-01, revenue expenditure has exhibited an increase of more than 300 per cent.

13.3.2 *Development Expenditure*

The major component of both revenue and capital expenditure of the state is development expenditure. Development expenditure is undertaken by the state government to provide social as well as economic services. Social services include education, sports, art, culture, public health, family welfare, water supply sanitation, housing, urban development, welfare of backward classes, social security, so on and so forth. Economic services provided through undertaking revenue expenditure cover agriculture and allied activities, rural development irrigation and flood control, energy, industry including village and small industry, transport communications, science, technology and environment, etc. The services provided through revenue expenditure give one the impression of the wide range of social and economic activities the state government has to engage itself in. It is needless to argue about the necessity of state initiative and action for providing these services as huge externalities are associated with such social and economic services. State expenditure for provision of social and economic services also creates necessary social and physical infrastructure that contribute immensely to both economic and human development. During the period from 1990-91 to 1999-2000, development expenditure (on revenue and capital account taken together) in the state has grown by more than 230 per cent (Figure 13.6).

FIGURE 13.5

Revenue Expenditure Profile (in Rs. Crores)

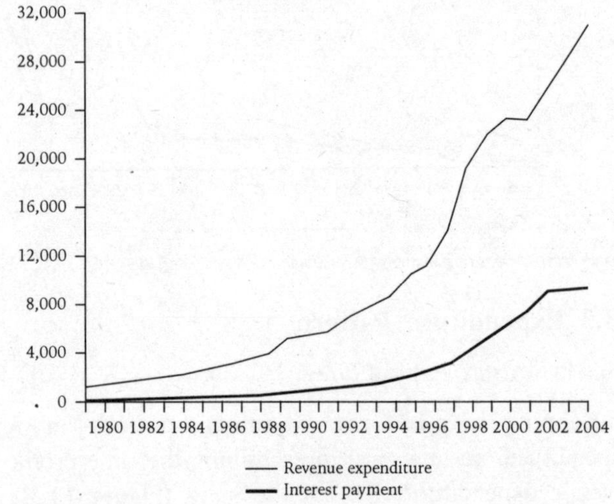

Source: RBI (Various Issues). *State Finances: A Study of Budgets.*

The annual growth rate of development expenditure in the state estimated is based on a log linear trend is found to be 12.53 per cent for the period 1985-86 to 1994-95 and 9.27 per cent for the next 10-year period (Table 13.9).

TABLE 13.9

Growth Rates of Development Expenditure

Year	*Growth Rate (In per cent)*
1985-86 to 1994-95	12.53
1995-96 to 2004-05	9.27

Note: Growth rates estimated by fitting log-linear trends to the state development expenditure data.

Source: 1. RBI. *Handbook of Statistics on State Government Finances, 2004.*
2. EPW. *Special Statistics-37 Finances of State Governments, 2004.*

13.3.3 Expenditure on Social Sector (SSE)

Development economics while judging the quality and structure of governmentt expenditure would focus on the component of social sector expenditure and its proportion to total expenditure. Within developmental expenditure, social sector expenditure (SSE) of a state government comprises expenditure on social services, rural development and food storage and warehousing on revenue account and capital outlay, loans and advances on the same items (RBI, 2007-08). There are 12 subheads under expenditure on social services like education, sports, public health, family welfare, water supply and sanitation , housing, urban development, etc., and these constitute the major component of SSE followed by rural development and food storage and warehousing, all having positive externalities and impact on quality of life people live. The overall ratio of SSE to total expenditure has been declining across the states, particularly during the latter years of the 1990s. But West Bengal government has maintained the ratio at 30 to 33 per cent till 2006-07 (Table 13.10).

FIGURE 13.6

Profile of Development Expenditure (in Rs. Crore): West Bengal

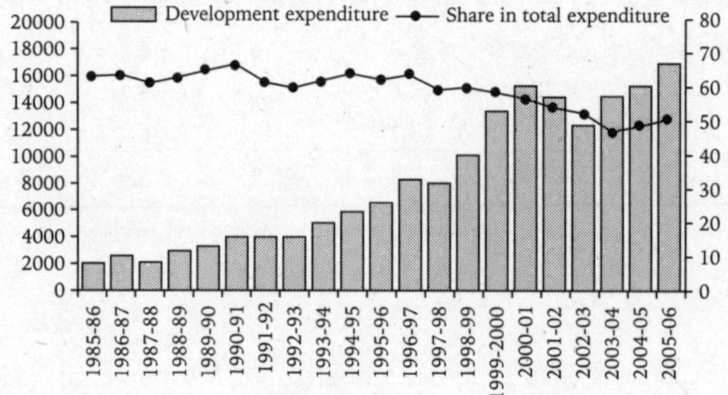

Source: RBI (Various Issues). *State Finances: A Study of Budgets.*

TABLE 13.10

Social Sector Expenditure: West Bengal

Period	*Total SSE (Rs. in Crore)*	*SSE as % to Total Exp*
1994-95	3827	41.2
1995-96	4097	39.0
1996-97	4991	38.3
1997-98	5180	38.2
1998-99	6626	38.6
1999-00	9338	31.2
2000-01	9623	36.0
2001-02	9581	34.1
2002-03	8463	30.5
2003-04	9008	23.4
2004-05	9732	29.1
2005-06	11445	28.2
2006-07	14470	33.5

Source: As in Table 13.9.

13.3.4 Plan Expenditure

Though many public finance experts have argued against continuance of the distinction between plan and non-plan expenditure, in the Indian context, the classification seems to have some relevance. Items of plan expenditure in the State budget add up to size of the plan for the given year and the State has to sit with the Planning Commission (PC) and satisfy it about the feasibility of the plan size. This process gives the PC a leverage in the matter of dispensation of Central funds on a large scale. As Dr. Amaresh Bagchi has argued (Bagchi, 2003), such dispensation of funds by the PC, has cast a centralising influence on the federal nature of Indian fiscal system. "Expenditure policies of the States came to be influenced heavily by the Centre as the States are required to draw up their plans to subserve the objective of the Central plan and have their 5-year and annual plans approved" (Bagchi *op. cit.*). But the major part of the funds transferred by the Centre to the states in the name of plan grants comes as loans. Indeed, 70 per cent of plan assistance is provided as loans. The Twelfth Finance Commission, amongst its major recommendations, has proposed that the system of imposing a 70: 30 ratio between loans and grants for extending plan assistance should be done away with. Instead, the Centre should focus on extending plan grants to the states and leave the decision-making about quantum and source of borrowing to the states altogether.

TABLE 13.11

Plan Expenditure (in Rs. Crore): West Bengal

Year	*Plan Expenditure*	*% of NSDP*
1992-93	1087.47	2.4
1993-94	1613.49	3.3
1994-95	1983.54	3.5
1995-96	2466.82	3.7
1996-97	2725.03	3.7
1997-98	2962.47	3.3
1998-99	3860.70	3.6
1999-2000	3918.84	3.4
2000-01	5647.99	4.4
2001-02	4639.74	3.3
2002-03	2711.14	1.8
2003-04	2529.47	1.5
2004-05	3753.54	2.0
2005-06	5989.78	-

Source: EPW. *Special Statistics—37 Finances of State Governments, 2004.*

The data on plan expenditure (Table 13.11) of the state for the period 1980-81 to 1989-90 exhibit an annual rate of growth of 12.3 per cent. The annual rate of growth for the next 10-year period is estimated to be 19.1 per cent. Considering the severe fiscal stress, the state is experiencing the efforts to keep the volume of plan expenditure growing at an annual compound rate 12 to 19 per cent is remarkable. It is more so as in the difficult years of 1999-2000 to 2002-03, there was deceleration in the growth rate in development expenditure for all States (RBI, 2002-03), and within development expenditure the growth in expenditure on social and economic services was also found to decelerate. In the backdrop of such decelerating trend for all states, the rising trend in development and plan expenditure in West Bengal speaks highly of efficient fiscal management and commitment of the state government to providing economic and social services on a wider scale.

TABLE 13.12

Growth Rate of Plan Expenditure

Period	*Growth Rate*
1990-91 to 1999-2000	16.54
2000-01 to 2005-06	6.40

Note: Growth rates estimated by fitting log-linear trends to the State Plan expenditure data.

Source: As in Table 13.11.

13.3.5 Non-Developmental Expenditure

It is true that non-developmental expenditure also has grown from 20.4 per cent of total expenditure in 1985-86 to 38.5 per cent in 2001-02. But a major part of non-developmental expenditure is accounted for by interest payment and for West Bengal, the net interest payments represent 55 per cent of total non-developmental expenditure. It would be evident from the profile growth of non-developmental expenditure over the years (Table 13.11) that there was a steep rise since 1998-99, when Pay Commission recommendations for revision of pay and allowances for state—government employees and also for those working in the state aided institutions were being given effect to. Pension outgo another committed expenditure for the state government is also an ever increasing part of non-developmental expenditure.

13.3.5 Plan Outlay

Plan outlay (Table 13.14) is the size of the state plan approved by the planning commission in consultation with the state government. To satisfy various prudential norms imposed by the centre in regard to fiscal management, the state governments have to, more often than not, prune the size of the state plan.

In West Bengal, the plan size has been kept intact at the approved level and expenditure on education and health has been raised over the years. This has occurred in the face of declining central transfers, limited buoyancy of state's own resources and the legacy of awesome debt liabilities. The efficient governance and management of fiscal affairs is reflected in the performance of the state in achieving such growth of output and employment as would include all sections of population of the state and reduce significantly the incidence of poverty and underemployment.

TABLE 13.13

Non-Development Expenditure

Year	*Non-Development Expenditure (in Rs. Crore)*	*Percentage of Total Expenditure*
1985-86	654.7	21.9
1986-87	780.6	22.2
1987-88	920.5	23.2
1988-89	1075.7	24.9
1989-90	1239.6	25.4
1990-91	1558.2	25.9
1991-92	1798.0	28.6
1992-93	2021.8	30.4
1993-94	2417.5	30.3
1994-95	2728.7	29.4
1995-96	3280.1	31.2
1996-97	3953.6	30.3
1997-98	4713.5	34.8
1998-99	5934.0	34.6
1999-2000	8138.1	35.9
2000-01	9759.9	36.5
2001-02	11,243	
2002-03	12,625.2	
2003-04	14,437	
2004-05	15,737	
2005-06	16,377	

Source: As in Table 13.11.

TABLE 13.14

Plan Outlay (in Rs. Cr)

Year	*Plan Outlays*	*As Percentage to GSDP*
1990-91	1150	3.1
1991-92	907	2.1
1992-93	882	1.9
1993-94	1217	2.3
1994-95	1484	2.4
1995-96	2141	2.9
1996-97	2427	3.0
1997-98	2840	2.9
1998-99 (Approved)	4595	4.0
1999-2000 (Approved)	5787	4.6
2000-01 (Approved)	5685	4.0
2001-02 (Approved)	7186	4.6
2002-03 (Approved)	6307	

Source: As in Table 13.11.

TABLE 13.15

Growth Rate of Plan Outlay: West Bengal

Period	*Growth rate*
1990-91 to 1994-95	8.37
1995-96 to 1999-2000	30.4
2000-01 to 2002-03	5.58

Note: Growth rates estimated by fitting log-linear trends to the Plan outlay data.

Source: As in Table 13.11

Public investment through plan outlay however, meagre has been supplemented by private investment done by corporate sector or households and thus, has made the story of this commendable growth of income and output possible in West Bengal. The state government is to be credited for its efforts in directing the resources towards providing social and economic services especially education, health, power, irrigation, rural infrastructure and welfare of poorer sections of the people which shows huge externalities in stimulating growth.

13.4 Finances of Local Bodies

Following the 73rd and 74th amendments to the Constitution in 1992, a third-tier of Government—the Local Self Governments (LSG) was created with Panchayati Raj Institutions (PRI) in the rural areas and the municipalities and corporations in the urban areas. With a view to endowing the local bodies with adequate finance to discharge their responsibilities regarding development activities and administration of local affairs, the Constitution envisaged that each state should constitute a State Finance Commission (SFC). The SFC would determine the principles of transfer and sharing of net tax resources of the State and the LSGs. The First State Finance Commission was accordingly constituted in 1994 and it's award period covered the years 1996-97 to 2000-01. The recommendations of the First and the Second SFC on devolution of fiscal powers, responsibilities and entitlements to the lSGs have been submitted. The Third SFC is at work on the issue at present.

The recommendations of the SFCs include transfer of a part of (16 per cent) state's revenues to LSGs as untied fund for which Plans would be drawn and implemented by the LSGs to meet their felt needs; transfer of entertainment tax in full to the local bodies; transfer of the share of the Central government and the proportionate share of the State government under Centrally Sponsored Schemes (CSS) to the LSGs as grant and a substantial part of Plan expenditure for the districts to be allocated to the local bodies in the form of untied funds.

TABLE 13.16

Transfer and Grants to Local Bodies and PRIs (in Rs. Crore)

Year	*Plan*	*Non-Plan*	*Total*
1994-95	0.04	205.34	205.38
1995-96	76.5	108.03	184.53
1996-97	91.14	87.44	178.58
1997-98	86.69	116.94	203.63
1998-99	92.21	113.02	205.23
1999-2000	242.79	-	242.79
2000-01	18.45	202.05	220.5
2001-02	5.05	256.13	261.18
2002-03	2.51	229.21	231.72
2003-04	1.0	256.59	257.59
2004-05	2.0	250.2	252.2
2005-06	5.98	328.14	334.12

Source: RBI. *State Finances: A Study of Budgets,* various years.

The State government in its annual budgets has provided for transfer of funds to local bodies and PRIs under the head of revenue expenditure with plan and non-plan allocations thereunder. In fact, the government of West Bengal in line with it's firm commitment to fiscal and administrative decentralisation has been providing funds to lSGS long before the First SFC report or for that matter the 73rd and the 74th Constitutional amendment. The three-tier local governments have been in place in West Bengal since 1978. The devolution of funds in the form of grants-in-aid to local bodies in the State is shown in Table 13.16.

It would appear from Table 13.16, the transfer to LSGs from the state has been far too less than recommended by the SFCs. However, the state government had submitted to the SFCs that 50 per cent of plan allocations for the districts were being spent through the *Zilla Parishads*. The provisions made in the state budget for various departmental schemes for the districts flow through the line departments and at the district level these provisions are made use of in collaboration with the ZPs. The expertise, technical know-how and the manpower necessary for preparation and execution of such economic and planning activities are not available to the desired extent at the levels of LSGs.

References

A.K. Bagchi Committee Report (2002).

Bagchi, Amaresh (2003). *Fifty Years of Fiscal Federation in India: An Appraisal, Working Paper* No.2. New Delhi: NIPFP.

———. (2005). "Symposium on Report of Twelfth Finance Commossion", *EPW,* July, 30.

Chelliah, R.J. (2005). "Malady of Continuing Fiscal Imbalances", *EPW,* July, 30

Rakshit, M. (2005). "Some Analytics and Empirics of Fiscal Restructuring in India", July 30.

APPENDIX A-13.1

West Bengal: Major Deficit Indicators

(in Rs. Crore)

Year	*Gross Fiscal Deficit*	*Revenue Deficit*	*Primary Deficit*
1980-81	289.2	23	180.3
1981-82	380.1	87.8	263.1
1982-83	497.8	242.4	328
1983-84	413.9	206.2	229.6
1984-85	339.7	371.9	95.5
1985-86	259	-82.9	-15.9
1986-87	587	188	253.5
1987-88	551	115	156.9
1988-89	579	137.2	130.2
1989-90	1,055.00	477	525.1
1990-91	1,633.70	1,018.90	1,006.80
1991-92	1,143.70	646.1	316.7
1992-93	1,012.50	436.6	46.3
1993-94	1,671.90	984.3	503
1994-95	1,965.30	767.1	637.9
1995-96	2,696.30	1,250.20	1,080.10
1996-97	3,396.90	2,135.20	1,456.60
1997-98	4,007.70	2,294.10	1,597.70
1998-99	7,109.10	4,856.20	4,159.20
1999-2000	11,666.40	9,287.30	7,497.30
2000-01	10,920.20	7,581.30	5,670.60
2001-02	11,804.10	8,856.10	5,428.70
2002-03	11,990.50	9,301.10	4,082.20
2003-04	12,383.00	9,052.40	2,957.70
2004-05	10653	8228	1030
2005-06	9801	7391	48

Source: RBI. *Hand Book of State Finances, 2004, State Finances: A Study of Budgets,* different issues.

APPENDIX A-13.2

West Bengal: Own Tax Revenue

(Rs. Crore)

	States' Own Tax Revenue	*GSDP*	*OTR as Percentage of*
1980-81	514.1	1034525	5.0
1981-82	616.1	1157532	5.3
1982-83	637.8	1304936	4.9
1983-84	768.7	1530222	5.0
1984-85	937	1767643	5.3
1985-86	1,124	1903297	5.9
1986-87	1,219	2080328	5.9
1987-88	1448.6	2507783	5.8
1988-89	1735.1	2710698	6.4
1989-90	1938.2	3062308	6.3
1990-91	2133.7	3479710	6.1
1991-92	2449.8	4038037	6.1
1992-93	2608.8	4329039	6.0
1993-94	2,913	4953414	5.9
1994-95	3,730	5965671	6.3
1995-96	4,133	6937698	6.0
1996-97	4,259	7939369	5.4
1997-98	4,517	9476554.9	4.8
1998-99	4,775	11174221	4.3
1999-2000	5,101	12375358	4.1
2000-01	5,918	12852484	4.6
2001-02	6,505	13797519	4.7
2002-03	7,344	14318977	5.1
2003-04	9,532	15142198	6.3
2004-05	9,942	16148017	6.2
2005-06	10,387	17460337	5.9

Source: As in Appendix A-13.1.

APPENDIX A-13.3

West Bengal: Non-Tax Revenue (Rs. Crore)

Year	*Own Non-Tax Revenue*
1980-81	155.8
1981-82	139.5
1982-83	164.7
1983-84	158
1984-85	172.7
1985-86	186.8
1986-87	165.1
1987-88	181.9
1988-89	189.7
1989-90	213.2
1990-91	219.2
1991-92	242.4
1992-93	247.8
1993-94	308.5
1994-95	341.9
1995-96	327.6
1996-97	417.5
1997-98	449.5
1998-99	384.5
1999-2000	587.2
2000-01	1,214.50
2001-02	775.9
2002-03	1,055.90
2003-04	606.00
2004-05	1,346
2005-06	1,019.00

Source: As in Appendix A-13.1.

APPENDIX A-13.4

West Bengal: Grants from the Centre and Share in Central Taxes

Year	*Share in Central Tax*	*Grants-in-Aid*	*Gross Devolution*	*% of Share in Central Taxes to Gross Devolution*
1980-81	309.9	112.4	686	45.17
1981-82	348.1	120.1	854.1	40.76
1982-83	379.3	197.5	1,127.40	33.64
1983-84	433.9	172.5	1,099.10	39.48
1984-85	472.4	196.5	1,103.10	42.82
1985-86	623.5	409.3	1,643.00	37.95
1986-87	678.3	447.2	1,753.70	38.68
1987-88	728.7	553.3	1,924.50	37.86
1988-89	754.1	657.7	2,115.10	35.65
1989-90	961.5	381.4	2,208.90	43.53
1990-91	1,044.00	712.3	2,883.10	36.21
1991-92	1,235.40	750	2,917.30	42.35
1992-93	1,473.80	896.7	3,307.40	44.56
1993-94	1,609.50	1,090.40	3,896.60	41.31
1994-95	1,798.20	993.1	4,631.20	38.83
1995-96	2,017.30	898.4	4,934.40	40.88
1996-97	2,420.20	1,130.60	6,039.90	40.07
1997-98	3,047.80	1,013.80	7,668.60	39.74
1998-99	2,692.10	1,535.60	9,630.50	27.95
1999-2000	2,984.40	1,538.60	5,993.00	49.80
2000-01	4,235.60	3,154.50	8,928.90	47.44
2001-02	4,318.72	2938.7	8929.3	48.37
2002-03	4,586.4	2498.1	1,0212.4	44.91
2003-04	5342	2152	9,322.4	57.30
2004-05	6385	2264	10288	62.06
2005-06	6669	5650	12903	51.69

Source: As in Appendix A-13.1.

APPENDIX A-13.5

West Bengal: Revenue Expenditure Profile

(Rs. in Crore)

Year	Revenue Expenditure	Interest Payment	Interest Payment as Percentage of Revenue Expenditure
1980-81	1,115.20	108.9	9.8
1981-82	1,311.60	117	8.9
1982-83	1,621.70	169.8	10.5
1983-84	1,739.30	184.3	10.6
1984-85	2,150.50	244.2	11.4
1985-86	2,260.30	274.9	12.2
1986-87	2,697.50	333.5	12.4
1987-88	3,027.50	394.1	13.0
1988-89	3,474.60	448.9	12.9
1989-90	3,971.30	529.9	13.3
1990-91	5,128.10	626.9	12.2
1991-92	5,323.70	827	15.5
1992-93	5,663.70	966.2	17.1
1993-94	6,905.60	1,168.90	16.9
1994-95	7,630.70	1,327.40	17.4
1995-96	8,626.30	1,616.20	18.7
1996-97	10,362.40	1,940.30	18.7
1997-98	11,321.90	2,410.00	21.3
1998-99	14,242.90	2,949.90	20.7
1999-2000	19,498.40	4,169.00	21.4
2000-01	22,103.50	5,249.50	23.7
2001-02	23,394.5	6,252.5	26.7
2002-03	23,160.78	7,563.7	32.7
2003-04	25,754.4	9100	35.3
2004-05	28,146.12	9034	32.1
2005-06	31,116.8	9375	30.1

Source: As in Table A-13.1.

APPENDIX A-13.6

West Bengal: Profile of Development Expenditure (in Rs. Crore)

Year	Development Expenditure	Share in Total Expenditure in Per cent
1985-86	1932.1	64.6
1986-87	2288.5	65.0
1987-88	2486.0	62.8
1988-89	2773.7	64.3
1989-90	3246.4	66.5
1990-91	4085.6	67.9
1991-92	3938.9	62.6
1992-93	4070.0	61.2
1993-94	5025.6	63.0
1994-95	6016.9	64.8
1995-96	6708.6	63.8
1996-97	8473.2	65.0
1997-98	8178.5	60.3
1998-99	10396.0	60.6
1999-2000	13533.8	59.7
2000-01	15555.2	58.2
2001-02	14530.32	55.4
2002-03	12451.0	53.5
2003-04	14875.0	48.41
2004-05	15329.0	50.14
2005-06	17247.0	51.75

Note: 1. Development Expenditure includes expenditure on revenue and capital account and loans and advances extended by State government.

2. Growth rates estimated by fitting log-linear trends to the state development expenditure data.

Source: 1. RBI. *Handbook of Statistics on State Government Finances, 2004.*

2. EPW. *Special Statistics-37 Finances of State Governments, 2004.*